WILDERNESS IN NATIONAL PARKS

WILDERNESS
IN NATIONAL PARKS

PLAYGROUND OR PRESERVE

JOHN C. MILES

UNIVERSITY OF WASHINGTON PRESS

SEATTLE AND LONDON

THIS BOOK IS PUBLISHED IN MEMORY OF MARSHA L. LANDOLT (1948–2004),
DEAN OF THE GRADUATE SCHOOL AND VICE PROVOST, UNIVERSITY OF WASHINGTON,
WITH THE SUPPORT OF THE UNIVERSITY OF WASHINGTON PRESS ENDOWMENT.

© 2009 by the University of Washington Press
Printed in the United States of America
Designed by Pamela Canell
14 13 12 11 10 09   5 4 3 2 1

University of Washington Press
PO Box 50096, Seattle, WA 98145
www.washington.edu/uwpress

Library of Congress Cataloging-in-Publication Data
Miles, John C., 1944–
Wilderness in national parks : playground or preserve / John C. Miles.
p. cm.
Includes bibliographical references.
ISBN 978-0-295-98874-0 (hardback : alk. paper)
ISBN 978-0-295-98875-7 (pbk. : alk. paper)
1. Wilderness areas—United States.   2. National parks and reserves—United States.
3. Nature conservation—United States.   I. Title.
QH76.M53 2009   333.78′2160973—dc22   2008037838

The paper used in this publication is acid-free and 90 percent recycled from at least 50
percent post-consumer waste. It meets the minimum requirements of American National
Standard for Information Sciences—Permanence of Paper for Printed Library Materials,
ANSI Z39.48–1984.♾ ♲

TO ROTHA, WHO DEFINES LOVE AND COURAGE FOR ME

CONTENTS

ACKNOWLEDGMENTS

The idea for this book emerged from a study of the National Parks and Conservation Association, where I became aware of the role that Robert Sterling Yard had played in both national park and wilderness history. Why, I wondered, did Yard shift his primary allegiance late in his career from national parks, where he long headed the National Parks Association, to The Wilderness Society, of which he was the initial president? Digging into this question, I unearthed a host of additional questions about how the wilderness idea had influenced the course of national park history. I must extend thanks to all who helped with that NPCA project, especially Paul Pritchard, Anne Miller, Bruce Craig, Sue Dodge, Gil Stucker, and Don Field, all of whom helped me complete the NPCA work and develop ideas for this next project.

Financial support was granted for this work by Western Washington University through its Bureau for Faculty Research and professional leave program. I received generous support to work in the Denver Public Library's Conservation History College through a Hilliard Fellowship in Environmental History there. Additional financial help came from the International Symposium on Society and Natural Resources, where Rabel Burdge and Don Field were solid supporters of this effort.

Michael McCauley, Sean Cosgrove, and Alison Isenberg were students who provided much legwork, encouragement, and insightful criticism. Western Washington University colleagues Ken Hoover, Scott Brennan, and Michael

Frome raised thoughtful questions and gave solid advice and encouragement over the long process of this study. Bill Paleck and Tim Manns of the North Cascades National Park, which lies virtually in my back yard, were helpful in many ways, reading portions of the manuscript and offering their perspectives on the National Park Service. Other Park Service professionals past and present, including Ed Zahniser, John Jarvis, Wes Henry, Ted Swem, Steve Ulvi, Jim Walter, and Tina Copeland, read portions of the manuscript and straightened me out on critical issues. I must especially thank John Reynolds, who read the entire manuscript over several years as it evolved, providing invaluable critiques, suggestions for improvements, and advice on who I should consult on particular issues.

Two central sources of documents for this study have been the National Park Service History Collection at the NPS Harpers Ferry Center and the Conservation History Collection at the Denver Public Library. David Nathanson, Nancy Flanagan, and Diann McCoy helped me navigate the collections in Harpers Ferry and Wade Myers was invaluable in locating photographs in their vast archive. Barbara Walton, Colleen Nunn, Coi Drummond-Gehrig, Tom Wilson, Bruce Hanson, and Jim Kroll were of great help in Denver. The staff at the National Archives at College Park, Maryland, was also instrumental in tracking down documents from the history of the National Park Service.

Others too numerous to mention at individual parks, libraries, and archives responded to my inquiries about photographs and specific documents or puzzling elements of the story I was piecing together. Special thanks are due to Brad Tuininga and Susan Morgan for assisting in the final stages of the project and to my wife, Rotha, without whose patience and forbearance none of this would have been possible.

WILDERNESS IN NATIONAL PARKS

A t the beginning of the park wilderness story—in the late nineteenth century—no sharp distinction was made between "national park" and "wilderness." One definition of wilderness is "wasteland," and as historian Alfred Runte has argued, politicians often agree to designate portions of the public domain as parks because they do not think them of much use for anything else.[1] Early national parks were remote, high, rocky, snowy, icy—in general not useful for growing corn or usually even good timber. They were hard to reach, unsettled, and therefore "wild." These places were not, of course, "wastelands"—politicians who thought of them that way had never visited them, and advocates were happy to let them think little was at stake in removing them from entry by settlers. Many qualities of these parks had not been appreciated or even yet discovered. When tourists set out to visit Yellowstone or Yosemite, they spoke of going to the "wilderness," even though they might view the wilds from the window of a stagecoach or a fine hotel. In most people's minds national parks and wilderness were synonymous.

National parks were created as cultural landscape units because they were somehow special. Their scenery was sublime or beautiful, their geology unique, their wild condition a romantic fragment of the past. When a park boundary was drawn it meant that most land-changing activities were forbidden inside the line. Logging, mining, homesteading, farming, grazing, and speculation on real estate were not permitted. The parks were set aside for the people. The apocryphal story of the Yellowstone campfire where a group of upstanding citizens pledged to sacrifice personal opportunity for the common good by advocating a people's park confirmed that parks were for the human community. They were not for elk or bears, swans or eagles, but for the American public. If they helped these creatures, all the better, and sometimes the creatures were the attraction, so the parks were their saviors. The bottom line, though, was that parks were, as the Yellowstone legislation said, "pleasuring-ground for the enjoyment and benefit of the people."[2] Initially an American gentry could, in relative comfort, visit protected remnants of the wild frontier and, for a time, live out their Wild West fantasies.

A national park is an American institution, a product of the idealistic impulse in a largely individualistic society to offer something for the common good. That good in the case of national parks is heritage. Early in the national park movement the heritage being preserved was an endowment of exceptional natural features that inspired, puzzled, and entertained. Later the mission of preservation was extended to the historical legacies of native and historical Americans. At the earliest stages of the park movement there was much wilderness. Pioneering was still under way, a frontier remained, and "wildness" was still a quality of place that was abundant and even, in some places, an obstacle to civilization. Late in the nineteenth century the opinion about wilderness began to change, and the seeds of another idealistic American notion began to grow in the mature idea of wilderness as land use. "Wilderness" became another American institution that ultimately became a public land system—the National Wilderness Preservation System. This system was conceived and, for the most part, created separately from the national park system. Wilderness, unlike a national park, came to be defined by a single quality—the absence of extensive and permanent modification of the natural landscape. Wilderness was a piece of geography where humans were not in control, where nature was "natural" and following whatever course it was destined to follow without any human intervention. The fact that little land was then or is now unaffected by human activity was lost on early wilderness advocates who believed there was a pristine, primitive, wild nature that was rapidly disappearing. The goal became to preserve remnants of such nature for various reasons, and that goal spawned a cadre of activists who worked for wilderness preservation.

When these activists defined a place that should be a national park or an area that possessed wilderness quality they thought should be preserved, they usually were advocating an allocation of public land to these purposes. That land might be in a national park, a national forest, or elsewhere in the public domain. Conservationists had to work with government to achieve their goal, and this brought Congress and federal land management agencies like the National Park Service into the process. Congress, over time, established a national park system and a national wilderness preservation system. The consequence is that today Americans are endowed with both systems, conceived separately but overlapping. This overlap is confusing and seems redundant to many Americans who assume that a national park is (or should be) by definition a wilderness. When visitors go to a big natural national park—a Yellowstone, a Yosemite, a Grand Canyon—they go to the "wilderness," even though they might barely get out of their car or beyond the campground during their visit.

This book aims to explain how this situation of national park wilderness came to be. It traces how the national park system began and what role the idea of wilderness played in that early stage. It follows development of the idea of the national park and seeks to explain how, in the early stages, the ideas of park and wilderness were separate and then converged, at least in the minds of some park advocates. After World War I and the creation of the National Park Service in 1916, a turf battle commenced between that agency and the Forest Service. Among the issues were which lands should be national parks and which should remain national forest, and who could better preserve wilderness. Wilderness became a bone tossed around in this struggle and, while both agencies milked public relations value from their proclamations about wilderness, neither knew quite how to deal with it. As they argued over it, wilderness advocacy grew and became sufficiently powerful in the post–World War II period to force the issue and ultimately pass legislation giving both agencies responsibility for wilderness protection (along with the Fish and Wildlife Service and later the Bureau of Land Management). The interagency conflict over wilderness was a stimulant to evolution of the idea of wilderness, and the Park Service role in this process is followed here over the decades that the two agencies faced off in their bureaucratic competition. The wilderness story most thoroughly studied has been that of national forest wilderness. The aim here is to fill out the story by examining how national park wilderness slowly came to be.

The Wilderness Act of 1964 was a milestone in many ways. The National Park Service opposed the idea that Congress would be given the role of deciding what parts of national parks should be dedicated to wilderness and thus for a time stood adamantly against legislation that would make this happen. It already had the authority from its 1916 Organic Act, it argued, to manage and protect wilderness in the parks. Furthermore, it had been doing so. The Wilderness Act, in its view, would simply inject more politics into park management decisions that should be made by trained and experienced professionals. Wilderness advocates wanted a voice in decisions about what parts of national parks should be kept wild. They did not trust the Park Service to protect as much wilderness as they thought it should, especially in the post–World War II period of rapidly increasing visitation to the parks. With visitation came pressure to develop, and many doubted the Park Service could resist this pressure.

A political window of opportunity opened in the early 1960s and Congress, after long and tortuous political maneuvering and deliberation, approved the Wilderness Act of 1964. This legislation, among other provisions, mandated that the National Park Service review its wild lands and recommend to Congress what should be designated as part of the National Wilderness Preservation System. The act defined wilderness and set broad management guidelines. It forced a reluctant Park Service to define wilderness boundaries, to "zone" the parks, something it had resisted for decades. The core of this history examines why the Park Service resisted zoning and designated wilderness in national parks; how it frustrated conservationists with the slowness of its park wilderness reviews; why its reviews were so slow and, in the views of conservationists, often inadequate; and how ultimately wilderness came to be designated in many national parks. The issues are not resolved to this day, with some major parks such as Yellowstone, Glacier, and Grand Canyon still without congressionally designated wilderness. The Park Service still struggles to fit the wilderness idea into its stewardship of its extensive system.

The national park system contains many types of units—national parks, monuments, seashores, historic sites, battlefields—in more than twenty administrative categories. The history of wilderness involves primarily (but not exclusively) national parks and monuments, large areas where the quality of "wild" survived. The history told here reveals that the Park Service had preserved the majority of its large natural areas "unimpaired" as directed by the Organic Act. It consequently faced a big job when it had to review all of its parks with qualifying wilderness, which, in the decade after the Wilderness Act, numbered fifty-four. The job was made more difficult by its persistent, creative, but ultimately futile attempts to use various ploys to retain as much of its administrative control over what became wilderness as it could. It completed its review as mandated in 1974.

After passage of the Wilderness Act and its required ten-year review period, attention turned to Alaska, where the Native Claims Settlement Act demanded another review of public lands for potential additions to the nation's conservation area system. The potential for new parks and wilderness there was vast. The scale of the landscapes at issue was huge. Indigenous people practiced a subsistence lifestyle across the "wild" lands, forcing a rethinking of concepts of national park and wilderness. People could not, as in many earlier parks, simply be excluded from land they had used for millennia. Would visitors accept wilderness where people lived and worked? Did this not challenge the very definition of wilderness in the Wilderness Act? As to park wilderness, should Congress establish national park and wilderness simultaneously or require Park Service review of wilderness suitability as it had in the Lower 48? It did both in the end, because Alaska presented challenges for which no one was adequately prepared. The history of park wilderness in Alaska is worthy of a lengthy study in itself, which is beyond the scope of this book. Still it must be summarized, for knowledge of the Alaska episode, late in the chronology of national park wilderness history, is essential to understanding the current condition of national park wilderness in Alaska and throughout the national park system.

The history of national park wilderness follows changing ideas about the purposes of parks and wilderness. It involves constantly shifting attitudes and ideas about nature and public land in the American mind. It is a story of changing outdoor recreation values and practices, and evolving conceptions of natural resources and how they should be managed and stewarded. At the conclusion of this history the Park Service is still struggling to figure out how it can and should manage the nearly 44 million acres of designated wilderness in its domain and additional millions not yet designated on which it works to retain wilderness values until the designation question is resolved. New issues regularly arise, driven by science and new values derived from the changing natural and cultural contexts of national parks. The history told here may be of help to contemporary park and wilderness stewards, users, and policy makers as they wrestle with current issues. It may help to understand why some national parks contain designated wilderness and some do not, why park wilderness boundaries are drawn where they are, and why the task of stewarding park wilderness remains today a challenging and frustrating task.

National parks are and must be both playgrounds and preserves. Every history of the national parks in the United States yet written reveals the tension between the goals of providing pleasuring grounds for the American people and leaving them "unimpaired" for future generations of park users. Absolute adherence to both goals is impossible. The National Park Service must balance these goals, serving many varied and changing constituencies. It must facilitate recreation while protecting from degradation the resources that define the parks. One of these resources in many parks is wilderness, and this is the story of how the National Park Service has worked to define and implement policies and practices to protect the remaining wilderness in those pieces of American geography under its management.

1 WILDERNESS AND THE ORIGINS OF NATIONAL PARKS

Historians have identified many motives for the designation of early national parks. Yellowstone became the first truly national park in 1872 (Congress had designated a Yosemite Park in 1864 and ceded it to the state of California, but since in 1872 the Yellowstone area was in a territory rather than a state, it became a national park by default). The origins of the idea for Yellowstone National Park were for many years attributed to a September 1870 campfire discussion in the soon-to-be park in which a group of idealists pledged to protect the unusual landscape they were exploring. The story was that after visiting the Yellowstone country, members of the Washburn-Langford-Doane Expedition speculated about how they could profit from tourism in the area but then rejected that selfish idea in favor of the land's preservation as a public park. They then took the idea to the world, and soon the world's first national park came to be. While this is an inspiring story of altruism, there is much more to the origin of the national park idea than the story suggests.[1]

According to Roderick Nash and other historians, there is no evidence that the initial advocates of Yellowstone National Park, whatever their motivations, were primarily interested in preserving wilderness.[2] Not that the idea of wilderness preservation was absent in American society in 1870. Voices had been raised for fifty years, among them the artist George Catlin, who had written in 1833 of the Great Plains that these regions "might in future be seen (by some great protecting policy of government) preserved in their pristine beauty and wildness, in a magnificent park."[3] Henry David Thoreau wrote famously of the value of wildness in *Walden*, arguing, "We need the tonic of wildness. . . . At the same time that we are earnest to explore and learn all things, we require that all things be mysterious and unexplorable. . . . We need to witness our own limits transgressed, and some life pasturing freely where we never wander."[4] Thoreau in 1858 asked, "Why should not we . . . have our national preserves . . . in which the bear and the panther, and some even of the hunter race, may still exist, and not be 'civilized off the face of the earth.' . . . Or shall we, like the villains, grub them all up poaching on our own national domain?"[5] Catlin and Thoreau linked wilderness and the idea of park and preserve, but protecting wilderness, of which there was much in 1872, was not prominent among the motives of Yellowstone advocates.

One public-spirited motive for protecting the unique features of the headwaters of the Yellowstone River was to prevent private exploitation of this unique area.[6] Truly remarkable natural features like Niagara Falls had, some thought, been damaged and the experience of them cheapened by the exploitation of private entrepreneurs. Six years earlier Yosemite Valley had been given a measure of protection because of fear that it would fall into private hands and that its natural features would be defaced or destroyed by exploitation.[7] A measure of high-minded concern for the common good was present in the establishment of Yosemite Park and in the Yellowstone movement as well.[8] Other motives at work in creating Yellowstone were profit, as in the mind of Jay Cooke of the Northern Pacific Railroad, and even a search for national identity. Americans found in places like Yosemite and Yellowstone an architecture of landscape that they thought equal to European monuments and sought to promote these landscapes as cultural icons.[9] Historian Robert Utley summarizes the motivations of early national park founders, observing that "altruism and materialism warred in the Yellowstone proposal, have warred in virtually every park proposal since, and war more or less regularly in most existing parks."[10]

The debate among scholars about what led to the Yosemite and Yellowstone parks reveals the ideas and forces at work in the 1860s and 1870s that brought about emergence of the national park idea. Thoreau's notions about the value of wilderness were present in the discourse of the time, but in the West there was still so much wilderness that preserving it seems not to have occurred to those thinking about Yosemite and Yellowstone. Initially there was little or no linkage between the ideas of national park and wilderness preservation. Soon, however, an articulate transplanted Scot would make the connection.

John Muir arrived in the Sierra Nevada of California in 1869. After herding sheep during his first summer there, he returned in 1869 to become a year-round mountain dweller, living mostly in Yosemite Valley until 1873. As he explored, climbed, botanized, and studied the geology of the landscape around him, he reflected long on the qualities of the place and his experience of them. As he tramped the high country, traversed canyons, and climbed mountains, he was increasingly impressed by the wild grandeur he encountered and he fervently embraced the wildness of California's lofty granite mountains.

During his early years in the Sierra—what might be called his "bohemian period"—Muir searched for his personal identity and concluded that he was a mountain man and would devote himself to wilderness. He wrote to his friend Jean Carr in 1874, when he realized that his days of year-round seclusion in Yosemite were coming to an end, that "I am hopelessly and forever a mountaineer . . . and I care to live only to entice people to look at Nature's loveliness."[11] He decided to interpret and advocate for wilderness, to preach a gospel of nature. After years of self-absorbed exploration of nature and mountains, he would take what he had learned to the world. He would work to protect what wilderness remained. Muir was not leaving Yosemite and wild places for good, though he would spend long periods away from them. A journal entry expresses the insight gained in this phase of his life, now ending, that he was by nature a man of the wilds: "Some plants readily take on the forms and habits of society, but generally speaking soon return to primitive simplicity, and I, too, like a weed of cultivation feel a constant tendency to return to primitive wildness."[12] He might leave the wilderness, but he knew he would return.

Muir married, managed his father-in-law's fruit ranch in California, started a family, and for seven years (1881–88) did not visit the wilderness. Restlessness grew in him, and at the end of this period of self-imposed exile he visited the Cascades of Washington and Mount Shasta in northern California. On this trip he found much wild nature, but he also found that the destruction of wildness he had observed years before in Yosemite was progressing rapidly in many places. He had written essays in the 1870s that won a national audience. At this moment of return to his beloved wilderness, Robert Underwood Johnson, associate editor of the prominent Century magazine, came into Muir's life. Johnson shared his concern about destruction of wild lands, knew the power of Muir's pen, and thought he would be the ideal spokesman for an effort to protect wild nature in places like the Sierra. He sought Muir out and the two made a trip to Yosemite, where they found, as they expected, the valley's "garden wilderness" still under siege. They agreed that an effort to stem the degradation of the place was necessary, and Johnson suggested they begin with a campaign to preserve the federal land around Yosemite Valley. Why not, he proposed, model a reserve here on Yellowstone National Park? They agreed on a plan. If Muir would write two essays for Century about Yosemite and the idea of reserving land around the valley, Johnson would lend editorial support and push the necessary political campaign in Washington, DC, for Yosemite National Park.[13]

Muir took up his pen, and in "The Treasures of the Yosemite" he made the case for what he called "the range of light."

> And after ten years in the midst of it, rejoicing and wondering, seeing the glorious floods of light that fill it . . . it still seems to me a range of light. But no terrestrial beauty may endure forever. The glory of wildness has already departed from the great central plain. Its bloom is shed, and so in part is the bloom of the mountains. In Yosemite, even under the protection of the Government all that is perishable is vanishing apace.[14]

He published "Treasures" in Century in August 1890 and followed it with "Features of the Proposed Yosemite National Park" in September. The essays extolled especially the waters of Yosemite, arguing that "all the fountain regions above Yosemite . . . should be included in the park to make it a harmonious unit instead of a fragment, great though the fragment be."[15] He described his adventures in this wild and holy place and made it clear that part of what must be saved was wildness, the opportunity to experience raw, powerful, even dangerous nature. Muir biographer Michael Cohen writes of Muir's "Features" essay that "in showing his reader how he discovered himself as a part of the power of the wilderness, Muir presented the strongest possible argument for national parks as wild places where each man could seek, according to his ability, direct, unmediated intercourse with the elemental forces of nature."[16]

In "Features" Muir wrote more descriptively of what precisely he thought the boundaries of the proposed park should include. He described a 250-square-mile reservation that was mostly wilderness, beginning this description with the Big Tuolumne Meadows in the northern drainage. This was the more "improved" and accessible part of the proposed park. The second part of the essay described Hetch Hetchy Valley, which, unlike Yosemite Valley, remained wild. Cohen and others have argued that Muir was thinking strategically here: "Thus Muir hoped to save Hetch Hetchy by making it a wild and inaccessible hinterland of a larger, improved park."[17] Yosemite Valley would not be part of the proposed national park (at least in this round of preservation politics; Muir and others would later seek recession of the valley to the federal government and would achieve their goal in 1905 when the valley became part of the national park). The tourist seeking easy access to the improved temple of nature could go to Yosemite Valley. Someone seeking to know the wild would work harder and find it in Hetch Hetchy. Cohen goes on to say that "while he [Muir] realized that there was no such thing as large-scale recreational use and wilderness in the same place, he was willing to sacrifice Yosemite Valley if he could preserve Hetch Hetchy."[18]

While Muir was writing, Johnson was carrying out his end of the agreement by organizing the lobbying effort for the park in Washington, DC. He did his work well, and by the time Muir's essays appeared in *Century*, a bill for Yosemite National Park was well on its way to an October 1 approval. The Yosemite bill was preceded on September 25 by approval of a Sequoia National Park, which, along with a General Grant Park included in the Yosemite legislation, protected magnificent stands of giant sequoia from the axes of loggers. The concept of national park established by the Yellowstone precedent had borne abundant fruit in 1890, and part of the rationale for the new Yosemite National Park was protection of its wildness. John Muir had made wilderness protection a central national park value.

Muir's advocacy of wilderness preservation was not finished with this Yosemite work; he was only beginning. He next argued, unsuccessfully, for a Kings Canyon National Park. He founded the Sierra Club and devoted much of the twenty-four years remaining to him to park and wilderness preservation. Muir came to be called, perhaps unfairly in the eyes of his many allies like Robert Underwood Johnson, the "father" of the national park system. He did not argue only for national parks, also arguing for forest reservations in the 1890s, and he did not advocate any separate designation of wild places as would others later. As Michael Cohen has noted, in the 1890s the distinctions among national park, forest, monument, and wilderness had not been established. In Cohen's words, "These artificial distinctions would be made only as a result of the increasing power and complexity of the bureaucracies which would administer federal funds."[19] In Muir's thinking national parks, and even for a time forest reservations, were the means to protect wilderness.

Muir published *Our National Parks* in 1901 and in it gave his readers a tour of Yellowstone, Sequoia, General Grant, and, of course, Yosemite national parks. The opening chapter is titled "The Wild Parks and Forest Reservations of the West," and it begins:

> The tendency nowadays to wander in wilderness is delightful to see. Thousands of tired, nerve-shaken, over-civilized people are beginning to find out that going to the mountains is going home; that wildness is a necessity; and that mountain parks and reservations are useful not only as fountains of timber and irrigating rivers, but as fountains of life.[20]

Later in the book Muir celebrates the wildness of Yosemite, writing that "the Yosemite Park region has escaped the millmen. . . . it is still in the main a pure wilderness."[21] In 1912, as he approached the end of his life (he was seventy-four that year), Muir wrote to Howard Palmer, secretary of the American Alpine Club, regarding a conference on national parks called in Yosemite by the secretary of the interior. Muir had attended and told Palmer that the principal topic of discussion had been whether automobiles (which he called "blunt-nosed mechanical beetles") should be allowed into the park. He wrote sarcastically that "a prodigious lot of gaseous commercial eloquence was spent" on this topic. Among all such eloquence, wrote Muir, some spoke "on the highest value of wild parks and places of recreation, Nature's cathedrals, where all may gain inspiration and strength and get nearer to God."[22] The ideal park, in Muir's view, must contain wilderness, and the range of "mechanical beetles" must be strictly limited.

John Muir was a prolific writer who, in his long life, filled sixty journals with his reflections and wrote hundreds of letters, eleven books, and many articles. Sprinkled through forty-six years of writings are hundreds of allusions to the "wild" in nature and the experience of it and to "wilderness." All Muir biographers document his dedication to wilderness preservation and his linkage of such preservation with national parks. His ideas and example inspired other park advocates. His work was widely read, and he became a national figure in the emergent "conservation" movement. A part of that movement aimed to preserve wild and beautiful places.

THE EVOLVING WILDERNESS IDEA

Roderick Frazier Nash, in his classic *Wilderness and the American Mind*, has traced how, as Muir traveled the Sierra finding himself and developing his ideas about wilderness, other events were contributing to the idea of national park wilderness. Noting that Congress was not thinking of wilderness preservation when it established Yellowstone National Park, he observes that "gradually later Congresses realized that Yellowstone National Park was not just a collection of natural curiosities but, in fact, a wilderness preserve."[23] A Northern Pacific Railroad proposal to build a branch line into the park in the 1880s was defeated in Congress and the decision was, in Nash's view, a milestone. "Never before had wilderness values withstood such a direct confrontation with civilization."[24]

Legislators in the state of New York, convinced that preservation of forests in the Adirondacks was necessary for the long-term welfare of the growing New York community, created a "Forest Reserve" in 1885 and in 1892 made this part of a 3-million-acre state park. A state constitutional convention and public vote stipulated in 1894 that public forests in this park would be kept "forever wild," and, as Nash notes, while watershed protection for utilitarian purposes was the most powerful motive for this action, nonutilitarian arguments were also important. "The rationale for wilderness preservation was gradually catching up with the ideology of appreciation."[25] This action in New York boosted the conceptual linkage in the minds of preservationists between "park" and "wilderness." Ed Zahniser recently made the point that New Yorkers were the first to inject into the nature preservation movement the notion that what was needed was to preserve not just forest but "wild forest lands" and not just for a while but "forever."[26]

Thus the idea of wilderness preservation was strengthened and given protective power, and the goal of protecting wilderness in perpetuity was added to park making. Not even Muir had argued for the level and nature of wilderness achieved in New York. He perhaps assumed that designation of a national park meant such protection, at least for such wild places as Yosemite's Hetch Hetchy Valley. Even as the Adirondack campaign was unfolding, Muir was advocating that presidents use the new power granted them by Congress in the Forest Reserve Act of 1891 to proclaim forest reserves in the West, believing that this action would protect wilderness. He soon saw the error of this notion as Congress opened the reserves to commercial activity in 1897. Then, in 1914, congressional approval of a dam in Hetch Hetchy demonstrated how wrong Muir had been about the level of wilderness protection national park designation might provide. In the Adirondacks, precedent had been set for a stronger government commitment to wilderness preservation.

Part of the park wilderness story at this stage involves wilderness rhetoric. When a politician like Congressman William McAdoo, in debate over the railroad proposal for Yellowstone National Park, spoke of "sublime solitude" and "virgin regions," or when John Muir wrote of the "wild" and "wilderness," were they thinking of wilderness in the modern sense of an area unmodified by human activity? They were indeed thinking of landscapes that they assumed had not been changed by human activity, settings in which people could know a place as God or nature made it. McAdoo spoke of a park like Yellowstone as a place where people could achieve "closer communion with omniscience."[27] Muir used religious references throughout his arguments for wilderness. They perceived wild land, in the West at least, as entirely unmodified by human activity, generally ignoring the quite obvious fact that Native Americans had been or were present in such landscapes. At Yellowstone and Yosemite (and presumably other national parks to come), the nature-changing ways of "civilization" could be excluded, and people could experience "sublime" nature. The absence of human-induced change defined, for these men, the wilderness ideal.[28]

There is no doubt that the dominant force driving Americans in the West at this time was conquest. The goal was to conquer and use nature, and this involved changing it—killing the wildlife, mining the mountains, and "taming" the land by making it accessible with roads, railroads, and other developments. But this taming usually changed the landscape so much that the experience of the sublime or the "omniscient" was prevented. A person using the rhetoric of "wild" and "wilderness" in the late nineteenth century was indeed thinking of qualities like those of modern wilderness preservationists who still aim to keep loggers, miners, road builders, and other change agents out of the as yet "natural" and wild places.

On the other hand, many who used the term "wilderness" in the nineteenth century were thinking less of untouched places than of scenery and a genteel experience of a more natural setting than that of their daily lives. American travelers might go in search of "divine rapture and terror" found in such places as Yellowstone and Yosemite, but many of them hoped for "the accouterments of tourist travel [that] would allow them to view Yellowstone's spectacular features without trepidation; its sublimity known more than feared."[29] These travelers might speak of the wilderness as they gazed from the windows of a railroad car or a luxury hotel, referring to a "wild" place and their experience of it in a very different sense than would a solitary John Muir wrapped in his blanket in the far reaches of the Sierra. Use of identical words conveyed quite different interpretations of the meaning of "wild" and "wilderness."

This rhetorical situation is important because, as one looks for evidence that wilderness preservation was on the minds of late-nineteenth-century national park advocates, there is no denying that they often used "wilderness" to describe the goal of their efforts. Attraction to a mythical untouched and sublime nature brought the wilderness traveler like Muir and the more genteel tourist to Yosemite, Yellowstone, and later Mount Rainier, Glacier, Rocky Mountain, and other "nature" parks. All of these visitors embraced an idea of wilderness, but all did not have the same idea. Still, in search of evidence that wilderness was part of the motivation of early national park advocates, one finds that an idea of wilderness protected in national parks was widespread. It was not the only idea, or even the foremost rationale for park making; but, as historian Theodore Catton has noted, it "is misleading to look for a single value at the core of the national park idea" because that core is "more aptly construed as a shifting constellation of value."[30] One value in the constellation was wilderness in its many meanings.

THE DRIVE FOR MORE NATIONAL PARKS

The success of campaigns for national parks in the Sierra inspired similar efforts in other places, with this wilderness rhetoric present in crusades for all of them. The case of Enos Mills in Colorado is an example of how Muir's ideas influenced national park advocacy and how wilderness rhetoric continued to be important. The campaign for Rocky Mountain National Park began in 1908. The area around Estes Park and Longs Peak had, since the early 1890s, become increasingly popular with tourists who came to escape the hot and humid summers of the Midwest and East. Resorts and hotels and private summer cabins appeared. One resident was Enos Mills, an energetic, articulate, and entrepreneurial fellow who had come to Estes Park as a teenager and stayed to become a mountain guide, innkeeper, and ultimately a leading proponent of Rocky Mountain National Park. For many years Mills made his living as a miner each winter and as a guide for tourists in the summer. His mountain travels exposed him to many adventures and misadventures, and he became a storyteller, weaving his tales of wilderness wanderings into lectures and books. His writings (eventually sixteen books and dozens of articles) brought him to prominence. In 1907 he was appointed "Government Lecturer on Forestry," a job that took him across America lecturing about the wisdom of government management of forests as it was emerging in the new national forest system under the Forest Service.

As he lectured, Mills became increasingly disenchanted with forest reserves that, in 1906, became national forests. He realized, as had other preservationists, John Muir foremost among them, that the forest reserves/national forests would not offer the protection necessary for preservation of natural landscapes. Mills proposed a national park in 1908 for the Rocky Mountains around Estes Park, and the battle to carve a national park out of forest reserves began. The Rocky Mountain Park, like proposed parks before it at Mount Rainier and Crater Lake, was opposed by people who wanted unfettered development of the natural resources of proposed parklands. These opponents found an ally in the Forest Service. Formed in 1905, this agency had already asserted itself across America's public domain forests, regulating stockmen and timber harvest, building trails and ranger stations, and generally asserting its "gospel of efficiency" and "wise use" philosophy of land management.[31] While the Forest Service under its first chief, Gifford Pinchot, had not embraced recreation as one of the multiple uses it focused on in its first years, it would soon do so.[32] Pinchot and his Forest Service colleagues thought national parks unnecessary, arguing that they could do a much better job of managing areas of "park" quality as parts of the national forests. There was no national park bureau and no consistent management policy for national parks at this time. Underlying Forest Service opposition was the prospect that a Rocky Mountain National Park would mean a loss of territory for them, because the park would be carved out of national forests. It would go back under the jurisdiction of the Department of the Interior from which it had only recently been transferred when Pinchot and Theodore Roosevelt had succeeded in bringing forest reserves to the Department of Agriculture and placing them under the management of the newly created Forest Service.

To Enos Mills and other park advocates, the Forest Service priorities were wrong. Park advocates sought more protection and less development, or at least a different sort of development, than was likely under Forest Service management. The campaign for Rocky Mountain National Park grew, eliciting support regionally and nationally. The first park bill was introduced into Congress in 1910. Five years of debate, discussion, and compromise followed until, in January 1915, President Wilson signed the bill establishing the park. Enos Mills was disappointed that only one-third of his original park proposal had made it into the park, but he was satisfied, confident that he could add the missing portions later.[33]

Wilderness preservation was one among many motives cited by Rocky

Mountain National Park advocates. Mills knew John Muir and his work, and he embraced Muir's wilderness philosophy. He told the Denver Chamber of Commerce in a 1905 speech that "people are feeling the call of the wild. People want the wild, wild world beautiful. They want the temples of the Gods, bits of the forest primeval, the pure and fern-fringed brooks."[34] There is little doubt that wilderness preservation was a cause close to Mills's heart and one of the goals of his park advocacy. Yet, as his biographer Alexander Drummond notes, Mills's wilderness advocacy was "ambiguous." He wrote books about wilderness, extolling its virtues. Yet he advocated development in national parks while calling them "wilderness empires . . . snatched from leveling forces of development." And, writes Drummond, Mills "could advocate mass visitation, yet assure his readers that parks would remain 'forever wild, forever mysterious and primeval.'"[35]

Can this ambiguity be reconciled? Could one both love wilderness, advocate for its preservation in national parks, yet at the same time support development of them? Mills and others at this time did just that, believing that national parks could and must serve both people and wilderness preservation. Wild land would be better protected in national parks than in national forests, in their view, yet parks would need to be accessible. The American people must benefit from them in order to support the parks. Some advocates were not purists and believed that people and wilderness could coexist as long as development did not degrade the values on which the park was founded. They were not troubled by what today might seem contradictory goals. Most were anthropocentric in their thinking. John Muir expressed his conviction that nature had intrinsic value, and even rights, but he did not argue for preservation on these grounds. As Roderick Nash notes, "Muir knew very well that to go before Congress and the public arguing for national parks as places where snakes, redwood trees, beavers, and rocks could exercise their natural rights to life and liberty would be to invite ridicule and weaken the cause he wished to advance."[36] National park advocates like Mills and Muir might extol the virtues of pristine wilderness, but they knew, at this stage of the wilderness idea, that Congress would not set aside any part of the public domain if it remained so wild that people could not gain access to it.

Wilderness was one in an array of park values that fueled the drive for new national parks in the two decades before the National Park Service was created. Wilderness preservation was one among several goals of park preservation, as John Muir made clear in his advocacy. The lands included in early parks were, for the most part, wild and primitive and primeval, unchanged by the hand of "civilized" man. Wildness was in the eye of the beholder, and advocates for wilderness preservation did not notice, or did not think significant, the changes in the land caused by aboriginal people. Nor did they consider diminished wildlife or effects of grazing to have reduced the "primeval" nature of the places they fought to protect. Wild parks would be places where people could find nature as God made it, where the works of loggers and miners and other nature changers would be prohibited. For some they were places where the unique experience of nature unchanged could be realized. For others parks were protected scenery to be enjoyed, economic opportunity to be reaped, objects of scientific interest and curiosity to be preserved. The campaigns for early nature parks were often long and involved many people, ideas, and objectives. Always present in some form, explicit or implicit, was "wilderness," an idea that meant different things to different people. In this early stage of the national park movement, the idea of wilderness became part of the conception of "national park" and was embedded in the consciousness of the American people.

LINKING NATIONAL PARK AND PRESERVATION

Other forces were at work on the idea of park wilderness during this period. One of them was the forest conservation movement. Since the 1870s, people had tried to protect forests for various reasons. One was that the public's forests were often being stolen. Another was the growing recognition that forests were important to water quality and quantity, which was a key concern for the people of New York in preserving "forever wild" the Adirondack Park. There was uneasiness at the prospect of a "timber famine." The campaign to conserve forests reached a milestone with the Forest Reserve Act of 1891, which allowed presidents to proclaim forest reserves. Presidents Harrison and Cleveland exercised this new power and set aside over 38 million acres of reserves in the West. Between 1891 and 1897 these reserves were closed to all entry and commercial activity, which infuriated Western business interests and their representatives in Congress. They tried to open the reserves to logging, grazing, and other commercial activities, but Cleveland blocked them. William McKinley, Cleveland's successor as president, supported legislation to suspend forest reserves for a year while commercial interests pursued claims they believed the reserve designation had denied them. When the year was up, the reserves were reinstated but with a difference — resource development and commercial activity were allowed. This change convinced John Muir, and later Enos Mills, that national parks were the vehicle for protecting wild nature.

Gifford Pinchot was all for opening the forest reserves to "wise use," as he later called the management program his Forest Service implemented on these forest lands. In his view the decision to open forest reserves to management (rather than simply reserve them from entry under land laws on the books) "was and still is the most important Federal Forest legislation ever enacted."[37] Pinchot worked for years to define what this management should be, ultimately setting forest policy and management direction as the first chief of the Forest Service. The importance of this forest conservation story to the history of national park wilderness is that it helped differentiate the national park idea from other "conservation" initiatives. Though it took time for the definitions of national park and forest reserve to become clear, the different roles forest reserves (which became national forests in 1907) and national parks would play in conservation emerged from and were clarified by Pinchot's efforts. Pinchot campaigned for national parks to be returned to Forest Service supervision and to assert his management philosophy in national parks should they remain outside the national forests. The Hetch Hetchy case, in which Pinchot supported a dam on the Tuolumne River in Yosemite National Park, is the most famous case of the latter. During the first fifteen years of the twentieth century, it gradually became clear to those trying to protect naturalness and wildness on public lands that national parks offered a better prospect to achieve these goals than did national forests.

A conception of preservation emerged at this stage of wilderness history that associated national parks with the maximum level of resource protection. Carsten Lien, in his history of timber politics in the Olympic Mountains of Washington State, credits Pinchot with being "the father of the National Park Service." Pinchot's attacks on national parks, Lien argues, built support for them. People wanted wilderness protected and saw Pinchot's efforts to weaken national parks as a threat to the last bastion of preservation. His support of a dam in Hetch Hetchy Valley brought this threat to national attention. Pinchot inadvertently, according to Lien, "succeeded in creating the political constituency that would create a National Park Service. That constituency would take lands away from the Forest Service continually . . . and preserve them."[38] When Hetch Hetchy became an issue, the meaning of "national park" was not yet clear. If a dam could be built in such a place, then protection of wilderness there was not likely. Conservationists rallied to protect a wild Hetch Hetchy and lost, which served to strengthen their resolve to find a way to bring national park and wilderness preservation together.

All of this contributed to the definition of "national park" early in the twentieth century, and that definition involved a strong association with preservation of naturalness and wildness as well as beauty and uniqueness. The emerging distinction between national park and national forest in the years from 1897 to 1916 is of critical importance to the story of national park wilderness. When the National Park Service appeared, the association of national park with preservation was clear and taken for granted by many people. As statements by park advocates like Muir and Mills make clear, the goals were to preserve scenery, unique natural features, recreational opportunity, and the wild and primeval character of parks. Eventually the objects of preservation broadened significantly, but at this stage natural features and qualities were principally what were to be protected.

Landscape architect Frederick Law Olmsted Jr. was a central figure in the drive to create a national park bureau. Writing in 1916 as part of the campaign for this legislation, Olmsted summarized the distinction that had evolved between national park and national forest. He asked why, if both could be used for recreation, there should be separate administrations for each of them.

The National Forests are set apart for economic ends, and their use for recreation is a by-product properly to be secured only in so far as it does not interfere with the economic efficiency of the forest management. The National Parks are set apart primarily in order to preserve to the people for all time the opportunity of a peculiar kind of enjoyment and recreation, not measurable in economic terms and to be obtained only from the remarkable scenery which they contain—scenery of those primeval types which are in most parts of the world vanishing for all eternity before the increased thoroughness of the economic use of the land.[39]

Olmsted went on to say that whatever economic returns parks might provide were of marginal importance and that the principal goal of a national park was always "preserving essential esthetic qualities of their scenery unimpaired as a heritage to the infinite numbers of the generations to come."[40] He emphasized aesthetics in this but was clear that park scenery was "primeval" and best when "unimpaired." This quality was an important part of its aesthetic value. The case for a separate administration for national parks was that a different point of view was essential to administer areas in which economic values were secondary to aesthetic values. Scenery defaced by logging, mining, or other economic activity, as seemed likely under Forest Service management, was scenery lost. Landscape preservation was necessary, and a park bureau would be dedicated to that goal. Olmsted was, as his article was published, working on the wording of legislation to create the park bureau. A few months after his article appeared, Congress passed legislation establishing the National Park Service. Olmsted's word "unimpaired" was a core value stated in the service's mandate.

There is irony in the fact that Pinchot's pursuit of his utilitarian goals of forest management may ultimately, as Lien argues, have boosted the national park movement and the later wilderness preservation movement that involved national forests. As wilderness preservation would develop, Pinchot in some ways enabled it as much as did John Muir. While Muir offered eloquent rationales for preserving wilderness values, Pinchot successfully campaigned to allocate public land for forest reserves, portions of which would eventually become national forest (and national park) wilderness. By his aggressive anti–national park (and by association anti-preservation) stance, Pinchot strengthened the resolve of park advocates. He did not intend this, of course, but such was the result. All of this suggests that during the nearly two decades between the Civil Sundry Act of 1897, which opened the forest reserves to use and management, and the National Park Service Act of 1916, the preservationist nature of "national park" became more clear in the minds of the American people. In virtually all discussions of national parks, as in that by Olmsted above, a quality of the place to be protected involved its primeval and wild character. Preservation of this character became an integral part of the mission of those advocating and caring for national parks.

THE DRIVE FOR A NATIONAL PARK BUREAU

From the moment Gifford Pinchot arrived at the Department of Agriculture to head the Division of Forestry, one of his goals was to transfer the public forests (including the national parks) to his bureau. President Roosevelt and his interior secretary supported this ambition, but conservationists interested in preserving the "primeval" character of parks gradually understood that Pinchot meant to manage all forests for development. They sought a separate bureau that would have a preservation mandate.[41] Representative John Lacy introduced legislation as early as 1900 to create a bureau to manage national parks. Similar legislation was introduced in 1902 and 1905 but went nowhere, largely because of Pinchot's opposition.[42] Lacy, in turn, from his power position as chair of the House Public Lands Committee, thwarted Pinchot's efforts to transfer national parks to his domain in 1906 and 1907.

National park supporters campaigned for a park bureau to block Pinchot's ambitions, but they also did so because national parks needed more attention and consistent management. No full-time staff attended to park affairs in Washington. There was little funding for any of the parks. The U.S. Army administered some of them, and others were overseen by people with various backgrounds and agendas. The aggressive forest lobby led by Pinchot accused park advocates like Muir and J. Horace McFarland, leader of the influential American Civic Association, of peddling "sentimental nonsense" in the advocacy of scenic and wilderness preservation.[43] With the advent of the Forest Service and the polarization of the conservation movement by the Hetch Hetchy controversy into the "wise-use" versus "nature-loving" factions, the drive for a park bureau intensified.

McFarland led the campaign and garnered powerful support for the park bureau proposal after Roosevelt left office and Pinchot was fired by his successor, William Howard Taft. Both the Taft administration and its successor, the Wilson administration, supported the park bureau idea, and Wilson's interior secretary, Franklin Lane, appointed Adolph Miller to oversee national park administration. Miller, a Californian like Lane, brought a young assistant named Horace Albright with him, and in 1915 Stephen Mather was recruited and replaced Miller. With Albright's help, Mather stepped up the campaign to promote the parks and create a national parks bureau. Legislation creating the National Park Service was passed in 1916.

Three national park conferences were convened during the campaign for a park bureau: one in 1911, another in 1912, and a third in 1915. The thrust of these meetings, which convened many national park stakeholders, was to define what the proposed park bureau should do. The first conference, at Yellowstone, focused on parks as tourist destinations and the development that would be necessary to attract tourists to them. While railroad interests dominated the Yellowstone conference, the 1912 meeting convened at Yosemite was a forum to discuss the prospect of the automobile in the national parks. Should it be let in? The head ranger at Sequoia, Walter Fry, commented that "the American people, in my opinion, have outgrown the stagecoach habit, and the automobile is a factor that will have to be recognized. . . . I strongly advise that its admission be encouraged."[44] The Sierra Club representative, William Colby, stated that "we think the automobile adds a great zest to travel and we are principally interested in the increase of travel to these parks."[45] The arrival of the automobile in national parks seemed inevitable, and those present at Yosemite saw both challenge and opportunity.

Mather called the third conference, which he hosted in Berkeley, California. He wanted to learn as much as possible about the problems with park administration as part of his campaign for a park bureau. He saw from the start what would be necessary to improve administration of the parks, and that was money. This would come only with park visitation. According to Albright, Mather "believed that Congress had the cart before the horse, that it wouldn't appropriate money until proof was furnished that the parks were being used. Yet with no roads, trails, or other facilities, the parks couldn't be used. The only way to get ahead was to show that people were actually using the parks."[46] All of these conferences concluded that national parks, whatever their values, needed better management and more access. The principal charges to a new park bureau would be to address these challenges.

Preserving wilderness was not on the agenda at these meetings. The problem was, in the thinking of most in attendance, that the national parks were too wild in the sense that the facilities necessary for the American people to access and enjoy their parks were inadequate. Perhaps reflecting this reality, the language of the legislation creating the National Park Service did not explicitly mention wilderness. Reflecting on this in one of his memoirs, Horace Albright mentions the absence of any overt policy statement about wilderness in the National Park Service Act (which he calls the "Organic Act"). He writes that "we didn't specifically state policy about wilderness at this time because we concluded it was understood. Every previous act demanded that the parks be preserved in their natural state. Their natural state was wilderness."[47] Though Albright may have been reacting in hindsight in the 1980s, when the Park Service had become a major player in wilderness management, to questions raised about lack of specific wilderness preservation language in the act, there is no reason to doubt his account. Even wilderness advocates like Muir and Colby said little about wilderness in their speeches and writings in the park bureau campaign, perhaps assuming (as Muir had earlier in his support of forest reserves) that the presence of wilderness as a park value would be protected. The goal was a government bureau to help preserve the parks in the face of attacks on them by utilitarian conservationists like Pinchot and his followers. The goal was also to build public support for the parks, and that support would depend on the ability of people to visit them. Paradoxically, this would require development, and everyone, even the hardcore preservationists, recognized this.

Albright wrote that conservationists like McFarland, Colby, Mather, and himself lived in a time when the general philosophy toward resources was "use." "No use of resources, no change in the general state of national park areas," he wrote. The automobile was changing the nature of travel and would affect the future of national parks and wilderness. If a park bureau was to be of any significance it would need public support, and that support would depend upon visitation. If roads were necessary for visitation, then roads would be built. According to Albright, roads were accepted as essential to help people "enjoy the outstanding, easy-to-visit features of a park while leaving most areas in wilderness."[48] Wilderness was an assumed national park value that would not be served by adherence to a pure doctrine of preservation.

Historians have argued about when wilderness preservation entered into thinking about national parks. The record indicates that this goal became primary when John Muir began his national park advocacy. Looking back from the twenty-first century when the category "wilderness" is a defined public land unit and the concept "wilderness" is an idea honed by a century of debate and experience, one sees that the wilderness concept was not as clear back in the days of Muir, Pinchot, the Adirondack Park, and the early clash of ideologies between national forest and national park advocates. Nonetheless, there is evidence to support the claim that the idea of wilderness and the goal of its preservation were foundational elements of the national park movement. As forest conservation developed power as a political movement, driven by strongly utilitarian ideas about wise use and long-term resource development, the conviction grew in the minds of Muir, Mills, and others that national parks would provide the greatest protection of wild, primeval nature. Since many of the resources to be preserved in national parks—scenery, unique natural features, opportunity for adventure and recreation—depended upon maintaining this primeval and wild character of landscapes, the park and wilderness preservation goals came together. Thus in the mid-1910s, when the National Park Service Act was drafted, its architects tried to incorporate the reality that parks must be used with the goal that wilderness values must be protected.

2 WILDERNESS AND THE NEW AGENCY

The national park movement was an effort to protect parts of America's heritage. To this point in the story the movement had focused its attention almost exclusively on landscapes of the American West, and the heritage to be protected consisted primarily of the unique scenery and natural wonders of that remote part of the country. The protection provided by national park status was protection from forms of development that would damage scenery or restrict access to important features. Logging threatened the giant sequoias of the Sierra. Grazing threatened to destroy the meadows of wildflowers at Mount Rainier and Crater Lake. Careless and uncontrolled tourist activity created a wildfire threat everywhere. The intent of park advocates was to protect the values and qualities of special landscapes from the dramatic change that often accompanied development.

Many motives led Congress to authorize the National Park Service in 1916. Administration of national parks was inconsistent and needed to be strengthened. Better administration would result in better resource protection. A strong pro-park constituency needed to be built and, as was being demonstrated by a young and vigorous Forest Service, a well-led federal agency overseeing park resources would increase the likelihood of this being achieved. In the case of the parks this constituency building required better access, more park visitation, more national parks, and eventually a national park system of significant scale. All national parks, of course, meant business opportunities for local communities and transportation interests. They also meant protection of more wilderness. All of these and more were motives that drove national park bureau advocates.

Several processes in American society boosted the movement for a park bureau. One was the rise of utilitarian conservation that, as noted earlier, enjoyed the leadership of the progressive, aggressive, and effective Gifford Pinchot. Pinchot's conviction that land should be allocated to its highest use meant that it should be developed, not protected. Conservation, by Pinchot's definition, equated with development.[1] If national parks and potential parks were to be protected from dams, grazing, logging, and other threats to scenery and wilderness, a politically forceful agency was needed to fight off developers of various stripes, including the Forest Service.

The automobile was emerging in American society and changing the world, including tourism. Muir's "mechanical beetles" posed both threat and opportunity for the national parks. Uncontrolled building of roads for autos would certainly change and likely degrade park resources just as any other development, yet autos could also increase and broaden visitation that park supporters knew was necessary. If people could visit and enjoy their parks, they would support protection and campaigns for more of them. The challenge of dealing with roads and all of their effects would become a major preoccupation of the new park bureau.

A third process boosting the park bureau movement was the growth of the park system itself. While "nature parks" dominated the earliest stages of national park history, the Antiquities Act of 1906 authorized the president to proclaim and reserve as national monuments "historic landmarks, historic and prehistoric structures, and other objects of historic and scientific interest" on lands owned or controlled by the United States.[2] By 1916, when the National Park Service was authorized, twenty national monuments had been proclaimed. No funds had been appropriated to manage these units, and many were hardly managed at all. Presidents might proclaim monuments and set boundaries, but with little management, the protection of the resources that defined them was minimal. A government agency accountable for their protection was essential.[3] While the monuments were not initially of great interest to "national park men," their importance grew gradually, especially when an area like Grand Canyon National Monument was made a national park and transferred from the Forest Service to the Park Service.[4] National monuments increased the national park system quickly, making the need for unified management under a federal agency all the more urgent.

All three of these processes were threats to wilderness as a core value of national parks. Utilitarian conservation did not recognize wilderness preservation as a goal of public land management. If the ideology of Pinchot were to prevail, then the dam in Hetch Hetchy was simply the precursor to many similar projects to come. Irrigators already had designs on Yellowstone National Park to water their Idaho potatoes. If all the desires of auto tourists were accommodated, roads would permeate all corners of the national parks and wildness would succumb to gas stations, hotels, restaurants, and all the other facilities necessary to serve motor tourists. Finally, the proliferation of national monuments might make the national park system into something other than a system of parks intended to preserve natural values. Some park advocates saw this as a threat. Even as the National Park Service Act was being debated, congressmen perceived the political hay they could make out of national parks in their districts. Almost from the day of its organization the Park Service faced the problem of park standards, which raised the underlying issue of national park purpose. Soon, in the 1920s, this issue would heat up. Wilderness would become part of the discussion.[5]

THE NATIONAL PARK SERVICE IS ESTABLISHED

The leader of the effort to create the national park bureau was J. Horace McFarland, president of the American Civic Association. On behalf of the association, McFarland advocated parks of all kinds. The goal was to protect beauty wherever it might be found on the American landscape. McFarland was a national figure, representing the parks movement at Theodore Roosevelt's 1908 Conservation Conference of Governors (John Muir was not invited). He launched a campaign for a park bureau in 1910 by drafting language that he thought should go into a bill creating the new agency. He asked Frederick Law Olmsted Jr. to assist him, and Olmsted agreed to help. The bill should, in Olmsted and McFarland's view, emphasize recreation and protection of natural scenery as the mission of the park bureau. Its mandate should be clearly different from that of the Forest Service.

McFarland garnered support for the legislation from President Taft and three secretaries of the interior, but little progress could be made in Congress. One reason for the difficulty was Forest Service opposition, but in 1916 McFarland convinced Forest Service chief Henry Graves to write a statement in support of the bill. This was not the end of conflict with the Forest Service, but it may have tipped the delicate political balance. President Wilson signed the legislation on August 25, 1916.

The idea that the mission of the new park bureau was to preserve wilderness was not prominent in the campaign for the legislation or in the language of the Organic Act itself. As noted earlier, Horace Albright's reflection about this was that a policy regarding wilderness was not stated because it was assumed. As substantiation of Albright's point, the word "wilderness" continued to appear in discussions of national parks, such as in the National Parks Portfolio, a book funded by Stephen Mather and written by publicist Robert Sterling Yard (whose salary was provided by Mather) in 1916 promoting the national park idea. The first paragraph of the section introducing Yellowstone National Park, the lead park profiled in the book, begins, "The Yellowstone National Park is the largest and most widely celebrated of our national parks. It is a wooded wilderness of over thirty three hundred square miles."[6] Here is wilderness as a prime quality of this park. Later, in reference to Yellowstone, appears the statement, "Were there no geysers, the Yellowstone watershed alone, with its glowing canyon, would be worth the national park. Were there also no canyon, the scenic wilderness and its incomparable wealth of wild-animal life would be worth the national park."[7] Geysers, canyons, scenery, wildlife, and wilderness all are touted as park values. At this point, as earlier, the wilderness value of the national parks is present but is wrapped in with many others.

In drafting language for the park bureau bill, Olmsted was concerned that the legislation establishing the various national parks had not been consistent and had been vague in stating the purpose of parks. He aimed to be as specific as possible about the purpose of the park system in drafting the park bureau bill. He insisted over the long campaign that "scenery" be included in any statement of purpose. Olmsted is credited with drafting the language that was finally approved by Congress. The key passage reads:

> The service thus established shall promote and regulate the use of the Federal areas known as national parks, monuments and reservations, which purpose is to conserve the scenery and the natural and historic objects and the wild life therein and to provide for the enjoyment of the same in such manner and by such means as will leave them unimpaired for the enjoyment of future generations.[8]

These much-analyzed words in Section One of the National Park Service Act gave the new agency its mandate; while it may have seemed a clearer statement of purpose than collectively present in earlier legislation establishing national parks, it was still very ambiguous, as the Park Service has found to its chagrin ever since. The language set up a tension between use and preservation. It would make it especially difficult for the Park Service to respond to the soon-to-emerge call for explicit management for wilderness, the ultimate "unimpaired" state of the land.

The National Park Service Act reflected what was politically possible at the time of its passage. While it was not strictly preservationist and contained the conflict between preservation and use, it did make "conserve" central to the purpose of the national parks. Richard Sellars has noted that the act used this word, while most early national park enabling acts had called for "preservation." Was this a

2.1 Frederick Law Olmsted Jr. influenced the course of national park wilderness debate for decades. National Park Service Historic Photographic Collection, Harpers Ferry Center

lessening of commitment to preservation? Sellars thinks it was "an accord between the aesthetic and utilitarian branches of the late-nineteenth and early-twentieth century conservation movement."[9] He suggests that the act recognized that "wise use of scenic lands in the national parks to foster tourism and public enjoyment" was an important element of conservation. This was a response to growing public interest in outdoor recreation.

Conservation of park resources, wilderness among them, was established as a paramount goal, though not the only one. The act specified that recreation was the other, which was indicated by the words "provide for the enjoyment." With this language the drafters handed a difficult charge to the new agency, but one they must have thought reasonable. The 1864 Yosemite Act had referred to "public use, resort, and recreation" as purposes of the park, and the 1872 Yellowstone legislation called that park a "pleasuring ground." People had, by the time the park bureau campaign was engaged, come to expect to enjoy visits to parks, with some amenities provided to make this possible. Drafters of the park bureau legislation were simply recognizing this. Also, as people began visiting national forests for similar enjoyment and the issue of whether the Forest Service should administer all outdoor recreation appeared, park advocates needed to establish the clear goal of providing for recreation in national parks. They argued that national parks offered more protection for outdoor recreation resources than national forests, even though many forests were as wild (or in some cases more so) than national parks. Foresters ultimately had other plans for their forests. Designation of national parks meant that recreation and preservation would be priorities, which they would not ultimately be in national forests. All of this thinking was reflected in the language of the National Park Service Act.

Mather and Albright set about building the National Park Service. The pressures of doing so resulted in Mather suffering a nervous collapse early in 1917, and the twenty-seven-year-old Albright took over for him. This exceptional young man presided over the initial task of organizing the new agency. According to his memoirs, Albright asked himself what Mather would want done and proceeded accordingly, consulting Mather whenever he could.[10] Mather's aim since coming to Washington had been to promote the national parks and gain public and congressional interest and support for them. With a bureau established, the promotional effort needed to continue in order to build support for an agency budget, to expand the system, and to develop infrastructure necessary for people to enjoy their parks. Albright faced the problem of developing the parks without impairing them, though there is little evidence he worried much about the problem at this point. Albright's view was that most parts of the parks were wild and the early stages of development would do little harm to that quality.[11]

Among the first tasks was to develop access and resources to meet people's basic needs once they were in the parks. The access problem was driven by the automobile, which was increasingly coming into parks over terrible roads built for stagecoaches. Mather had aggressively promoted the parks to auto clubs, and his success meant demand for better roads. Another task was the development of a professional staff to run the agency and the parks. Mather began the process of identifying good candidates before he was taken ill. The ranger force was originally funded and entered the field in the summer of 1918. It consisted of a chief ranger, four assistant chiefs, and twenty-five rangers. These men needed to be equally at home in the wilderness backcountry and the crowded confines of campgrounds and hotels where most visitors gathered.

Another job for Albright was incorporating appropriate expertise into the agency and establishing a managerial tradition for the Park Service. While the superintendents and rangers carried on the daily operations out in the parks, other professionals, mostly engineers and landscape architects, began to direct development of them. Engineers were necessary to build roads and construct such facilities as administrative offices and water and sewer systems. Landscape architects would fit these developments into the landscape. To McFarland and Olmsted, national parks were principally scenery, and they believed strongly that aesthetic considerations should lie at the center of decisions regarding park development. This was the province of landscape architects. Thus, as Albright built the agency administration and did the political work, engineers addressed the development necessary for the American people to enjoy their parks, while landscape architects worked to assure that such development was done in a manner that would leave the scenic landscape as "unimpaired" as possible.

THE IMPACT OF THE AUTOMOBILE

Paul Sutter has argued that in the early twentieth century American culture shifted "away from an ethos that stressed the virtues of work, savings and delayed gratification, and toward a more therapeutic worldview that sanctioned consumption and self-realization." This shift included a changed perception of nature from "raw material" to "a place of relaxation, therapeutic recreation, and moral regeneration."[12] This shift was central to the emergence of outdoor recreation and nature tourism. Outdoor recreation and tourism (especially "nature tourism") became a consumer activity as people traveled to a nature "separate, distant and exotic" and a natural world "marked and collapsed into a manageable canon of sites to which tourists can travel."[13] The canon included national parks, and auto camping and motor touring were increasingly the means by which people were able to realize their dreams of visiting such places as the Grand Canyon and Yellowstone. These activities required roads, and thus the auto became a major driver of national park development and, as Sutter explains, of wilderness preservation.

Transportation to the national parks in the nineteenth century was overwhelmingly by railroad. By the time the National Park Service appeared on the scene, the automobile had changed this. At first the auto was accessible only to the rich. Dr. H. Nelson Jackson made the first transcontinental auto crossing with his chauffeur in 1903 and reported that "the trip cost him $8000, took nine weeks, and in the course of the journey he lost twenty pounds."[14] Soon, however, autos became more affordable and their use increased. In 1910 there were 458,000 automobiles registered nationwide, which rose to 8 million by 1920 and 23 million by 1930.[15] This growth led to agitation for road construction as early as 1905, which grew year by year as more people took to the mostly poor roads.

By 1912 the automobile invasion of the national parks was underway. They had driven into Mount Rainier in 1908, General Grant in 1910, Crater Lake in 1911, Glacier in 1912, Yosemite and Sequoia in 1913, and finally Yellowstone in 1915. The automobile slowly changed the very nature of tourism and the place of national parks in American society, as Hal Rothman has argued.

> The rise of automobile travel played a crucial role in the transformation of western tourism. As automobiles became common possessions of the middle-class families . . . the cultural dimensions of tourism shifted from the tastes of the elite, the sometimes cumbersome intellectualizing of places such as the Grand Canyon, and toward the more common tastes of ordinary people, often oriented toward recreation.[16]

When most visitors came by train, they were transported from railroad station to park destination by stagecoach, and activity was concentrated around specific destinations and accommodations. Many auto tourists followed a similar pattern, but others could use the freedom of the auto to follow their own itinerary. According to Rothman, "Recreational tourism embodied a more personal set of values instead of the broad and community-defined ones of the earlier era when tourism functioned as part of a national affirmation."[17] Even as the Park Service was organizing, the experience of the parks it managed was changing because of the automobile.

Each year the director of the Park Service prepared a report for the secretary of the interior, and from the start these reports emphasized the growth in "motor travel" and the challenges that posed to the Park Service. Visitation grew annually: from 198,606 in 1910 to just over 900,000 in 1920 and over 1.7 million in 1925. Private autos entering the parks were first counted in 1918 and numbered nearly 54,000. By 1925 the count was 368,000.[18] Year after year the director described the auto-related needs of the park system. In 1921, for instance, there was need for a "definite and comprehensive program for road construction . . . proportionate to similar programs for Federal road construction throughout the states." There was need for "public automobile camps" and "enlargement of existing hotel, camp, and transportation facilities in some of the parks to meet the tremendous demands caused by large travel."[19] Only a few years earlier, national park advocates could not have imagined the automobile and the demands for road building it would generate. The auto was adding new dimensions to the problem of leaving park resources "unimpaired."

In the face of this, Albright did not worry about wilderness. He later observed, "As for the natural features of the parks, I stated that only the outstanding ones, which were the prime reasons for creation of a park, would be considered for development. The remainder, usually seventy-five percent or more of the total, were to be preserved as wilderness areas."[20] In Yellowstone, Albright thought a proposal to extend the Grand Loop Road unacceptable "for the simple reason that enough roads had been built and that the remaining regions of the park should remain 'untouched wilderness.'"[21] Stephen Mather declared that he did not want the parks "gridironed" with roads, though there is no doubt he supported road construction where he thought it necessary.[22] Roads invaded wilderness in parts of the system, but this was not considered an impairment of park values as long as it was limited to the most coveted scenic or natural features of a park. The people wanted to get to the attractions and the Park Service could not ignore this desire.

Leaders of the early Park Service do not seem to have considered wilderness a "land use" to which portions of the landscape should be dedicated. This idea was about to appear in the thinking of Forest Service officers Arthur Carhart and Aldo Leopold, who believed that the quality of wildness would be the defining feature of the land to be designated and protected as wilderness. Early Park Service leaders seemed to think that the national parks were wilderness except where they were developed of necessity. This idea that all that is not developed in a national park is (must be) wilderness would persist for decades and block efforts of those seeking to actively identify and zone sections of parks as "wilderness." It would figure prominently in later park wilderness history. In the Mather era the principal concern of the new agency was to enable people to visit the mostly wild and inaccessible parks, and this seemed to require that roads be built to and within them.

Landscape historian Ethan Carr has extended the debate about the role of automobiles in national park history, arguing persuasively that mass production of them was a critical factor in the expansion of the national park movement itself. Up until the appearance of the automobile, as Rothman has also noted, national parks were semiprivate resorts used primarily by the well-to-do. Auto tourists were a different sort of "public," and this implied that the cost of services they needed to experience the parks was a government responsibility. Carr writes:

2.2 Camping facilities, tents, and automobiles at the Paradise Public Campground, Mount Rainier National Park, WA, ca 1925. University of Washington Libraries, Special Collection, RNP44

> The picturesque alchemy that shifted wild lands into valued landscapes—still the principal mechanism of scenic preservation in the 20th century—occurred through shared public experiences of landscape beauty. The expansion of this phenomenon on a national scale depended on large numbers of people being able to reach national parks affordably.[23]

Carr here makes the critically important point that wild lands per se could not at this point be defended against those who sought to derive value from public land in the form of logs, grass, or minerals. Wild lands needed to be transformed by some "alchemy" into objects of value, and that value at this stage was principally scenery.

Carr also points out that Congress passed both the National Park Service and Federal Aid to Highways legislation in 1916. Thus "the fate of the national park system was linked, for better or worse, to the construction of a national system of federally financed, modern roads."[24] Mather understood this and targeted automobile clubs for park promotions, even touting a Park to Park Highway. He wanted to position the national parks and the Park Service at the center of the emerging auto-driven tourism. New parks, his agency's budget, development of parks, a supportive constituency, and survival in the struggle with the Forest Service might depend on this positioning. Carr notes:

> To successfully compete (in other words to fulfill the Park Service's preservation mandate) Mather knew the national parks must be made accessible and convenient to the swelling ranks of automotive tourists who were ready to make the cause of the national parks their own. The limited construction of roads, more than any other aspect of park development, would strengthen and validate the goal Mather described as the "complete conservation" of national park areas.[25]

This idea might seem anathema to modern wilderness preservationists for whom roads are one of the worst threats to wilderness, but Carr makes a good point: for parks to "conserve" scenery and other park values (this being the operative word in the National Park Act), a constituency would be necessary, and that could come only with access. So the engineers began to lay out the roads, and the landscape architects came along and did their best to fit them into the park landscapes. At the cost of loss of the wild in some portion of the parks, the wild in the rest would be protected.

THE FOREST SERVICE EMBRACES RECREATION AND WILDERNESS

The Forest Service had opposed creation of a national parks bureau from the inception of the idea. If there were to be national parks, and if the Forest Service could not manage them, it would seek to minimize the damage to national forests that would be inflicted by the national parks movement. Many in the Forest Service thought that removal of forested land, or any land, from national forests so as to create a national park was a loss to the Forest Service and to the nation. Utilitarian conservationists believed to their core that the highest use of public land was to meet multiple needs of people. More benefit would come from multiple-use management of land than from single-purpose management, which is how they perceived national parks. National parks, in their view, were strictly reserves for recreation. The clash of these views had received national attention in the struggle over Hetch Hetchy.

Harold Steen has noted that Pinchot and his early Forest Service colleagues had big issues to deal with in setting up the agency and assuring its survival. They left what they perceived as lesser issues, like outdoor recreation in the forests, to take care of themselves.[26] When Pinchot was fired by President Taft in 1910, Henry Graves became chief. His view of recreation was different than Pinchot's.[27] One reason may have been that a campaign was under way for legislation that would authorize national forests in the East, and preservationists and outdoor recreationists were allies of the Forest Service in this effort. Also, as Graves assumed his office, the campaign for a park bureau was gaining momentum, and Graves's boss at Agriculture and even President Taft seemed to favor the idea. At the time, national forests were beginning to feel the effects of growing outdoor recreation and tourism. The Forest Service might not yet have developed any recreation policy, but it was being pushed toward doing so by these growing pressures. In 1915 Congress authorized more diversified use of national forests, and one use was recreation. The Forest Service could grant permits for construction of summer homes, hotels, and other structures needed for recreation. Further, Congress appropriated $33 million for road building in the national forests between 1916 and 1921. The roads provided access for increasing numbers of visitors. In 1917 the Forest Service estimated that 3 million visitors came to the forests for recreation.

One irony of the rising recreation pressure on the Forest Service was that building roads for timber production, its principal mission, contributed to recreation use of the national forests. Foresters hoped to log their mature forests as fast as possible to avoid waste and increase the efficient production of wood from public lands, but they were somewhat frustrated in this. During its first decade, the Forest Service had not been able to meet congressional expectations that it be self-supporting, and its harvest plans had been frustrated by the private sector. Owners of private timberlands feared that public timber would flood the market, lower timber prices, and thus lower their profits.[28] In the face of this, the Forest Service could only plan and prepare for the time when its timber would be in demand. This meant building roads and trails for access and fire protection, one effect of which was to open the forests to recreation. People increasingly got into their cars and headed up forest roads.

Increasing pressure from recreating visitors and passage of the National Park Service Act prompted Forest Service leaders to attend to policy issues raised by outdoor recreation and tourism. They wrestled with the question of whether they should have a plan for recreation and whether they should build recreation facilities or depend on private initiatives to do so, as had been the practice to this point. Steen observes that it may be more than coincidental that, the year following authorization of the Park Service, Frank Waugh completed a report for the Forest Service on recreation uses and potentials of national forests. Donald Swain, Albright's biographer, concluded that the appearance of the Park Service definitely had the effect of nudging the Forest Service into action on the recreation front. He writes that "Mather and Albright deserve credit for goading the Forest Service into recognizing the concept of preserving natural beauty, once described by Pinchot as 'sentimental nonsense.'"[29] Waugh concluded his report with the observation that "on the principal areas of the National Forests recreation is an incidental use; on some it is a paramount use; on a few it becomes the exclusive use."[30] Waugh suggested that while recreation was still a minor part of Forest Service work, parts of the forests should be dedicated to recreation as the primary or even "exclusive" use. As it would turn out in a few years, "exclusive" use for recreation in national forests would mean wilderness recreation.

In response to all this, and to continued struggles between the Forest Service and Park Service over areas to include in the national park system, Chief Graves issued a policy letter in January 1919.[31] He rejected the idea that foresters were not interested in and supportive of national parks and articulated what he called the "National Park Principle." He still believed that the Forest Service was capable of administering national parks but acknowledged that the public lacked confidence in its ability to do so. Graves expressed regret that the Forest Service had come to be seen as opposed to preservation. Its earlier stances emphasizing use and development had been necessary in the campaigns for forest reserves in order to counter opposition to them. He even admitted that the public outcry over Pinchot's stand on Hetch Hetchy had been unfortunate. Some areas should be preserved and, if those areas were to become national parks, so be it. He thought many years would pass before "the national parks would be drawn upon for raw materials" unless too much productive land went into the parks. The multiplication of national parks would, in his view, be unwise. Only areas of the highest standard (principally as scenery) should become national parks.

Graves was being supportive but minimalist in his statement about national parks. He was diplomatic, encouraging his colleagues in the Forest Service to get on with their recreation policy development, one intent of which was to minimize the damage to the national forest system from the national park movement. As noted earlier, out in Colorado Enos Mills had celebrated Rocky Mountain National Park, the extent of which was far less than he had hoped because of Forest Service opposition. He was sure he could get the park enlarged but failed as the Forest Service fought to block the addition of Mount Evans to the park and established its own recreation area there. This tactic of embracing recreation (and especially wilderness recreation) would be employed by the Forest Service across the system to blunt national park initiatives.[32]

Chief Graves's letter may have briefly calmed the turbulence of the gulf between the Forest Service and the Park Service, but it did not end their competition. Even as he was circulating his letter, thinkers in his agency were exploring the idea that the "highest use" of some parts of the national forest (Pinchot had established the policy of "highest use" for national forest allocation) might be to protect them for wilderness recreation. The national park movement thus, ironically, was one of the forces that drove the Forest Service to embrace outdoor recreation, and its use of the idea of wilderness would in turn become a driver of national park wilderness policy.

In his first public statement about the national parks after being appointed assistant to the secretary of the interior in 1915, Stephen Mather stated that Secretary Lane had asked him for a "business administration" and charged him to "develop the highest possible degree of efficiency the resources of the national parks both for the pleasure and the profit of their owners, the people."[33] Mather thought the parks were "practically lying fallow" and "only await proper development to bring them into their own." Six years later he observed that "in the administration of the parks the greatest good to the greatest number is always the most important factor determining the policy of the Service."[34] He followed this 1921 statement with a lengthy discussion of the need for roads, which he was confident would be improved and extended in Yosemite and elsewhere. Mather was a businessman, a pragmatic problem solver, and the problems at this time involved improving park access, strengthening the Park Service, and building the national park system. He was not a wilderness advocate but a national park advocate, so he seldom singled out wilderness in his speeches and writings about parks.

Yet he, Albright, and others were confident that there was plenty of wilderness and that this was a good thing. They would not "gridiron" the park system with roads but would build only what was needed. The rest of the park system—most of it—would remain wild. Wilderness was de facto a quality of most of the places they sought to include in the national park system, so this was a value to be protected where possible. The hard-driving Mather was probably unaware of the irony in his 1921 use of the classically utilitarian language so fundamental to Pinchot's philosophy and so challenging to Muir's. The national parks and the National Park Service had come into being partly as a reaction to the classic use-oriented stance of Pinchot and the Forest Service. Mather was not an ideologue like Pinchot and had not been part of the early debate over use versus preservation. He believed in the national park system and thought that the more people who could benefit from the parks the better. In this sense his fights with the Forest Service were bureaucratic rather than ideological. National park system gains would be national forest system losses, wins for his ideals in the interagency competition. For Mather, creation and use of national parks were the goals, just as "wise use" of the forests was for Pinchot. The uses were just different— or were they?

3 WILDERNESS BECOMES AN ISSUE
FOR THE PARK SERVICE

As the 1920s began, the United States entered a period of prosperity and change. The postwar economy began to heat up. Automobiles became more common, and road-building projects to accommodate them were under way all across the nation. People took to the roads as tourists and outdoor recreationists on an unprecedented scale. They sought out the national parks and, increasingly, national forests for their outings. For many Americans, these were good times. The world war with its restriction of domestic resources was past, and the economy was growing into its "roaring twenties" period of boom prosperity for many. As people's economic fortunes improved, they bought automobiles. Urbanization had been increasing rapidly for decades, and many city dwellers headed into the countryside for relief from the growing stresses of urban life. If a national park or forest was within range, they went there.

Stephen Mather had recovered from his illness and was vigorously leading the National Park Service. His 1920 *Annual Report* revealed that national park visitation was rising substantially with each year, passing 1 million in 1920.[1] He was improving the staffing and professionalism of the Park Service, but the agency's growth was not keeping up with increasing demands upon it. Even as he noted the rate of growth and the strain on staff, he called for more park promotion to sustain the increase in visitors and more development to accommodate this visitation. More roads, hotels, camps, and transportation facilities needed to be constructed. A "touring division" needed to be set up to work with the travel industry to meet increasing demand upon national parks and monuments. This 1920 report reiterated Mather's long-held goals: raise the consciousness of the American people about their national park system and its value; do so by encouraging them to visit the parks (where they would find facilities inadequate and demand better ones); translate the increasing numbers and appreciation into a rationale for a bigger national park system and a stronger National Park Service.[2]

Mather had much work to do. New parks in Alaska and Hawaii needed to be set up. No money had been appropriated for national monuments, protection of which was minimal, and archaeological treasures were quickly disappearing from monuments in the Southwest. Proposals were floating in Congress for irrigation projects in Yellowstone National Park, and the Federal Power Act of 1920 created a commission with power to authorize water development on public lands, including parks. Prospects for expanding the national park system were ripe in the Tetons and at Sequoia National Park. He had to mount park promotion, protection, and expansion schemes simultaneously.

Expansion of the national park system had in the past and would in the future come at the expense of the Forest Service, and the conflict between the two agencies continued. In his annual reports Mather seems to have been putting the Forest Service on notice that the Park Service coveted lands in the northern Rockies and Sierra that were in national forests. Chief Graves resigned and was replaced in April 1920 by forty-one-year-old William B. Greeley, a clever administrator and bureaucrat who had been with the agency since 1904. Greeley would prove to be a strong leader and crafty adversary of Mather and the Park Service as they wrestled over issues involving outdoor recreation and national park system expansion.

A national election also brought change in 1920 as the Republican Party returned to power with the administration of Warren G. Harding. Mather worried that the new administration, which held a very different view of conservation than the Wilson administration or its progressive Republican predecessors, would replace him and other Park Service leaders. At the least he expected change in policy that would be less supportive of national parks and the Park Service. Harding had no interest in conservation and believed the government should interfere in business and individual enterprise as little as possible.[3]

National park friends lobbied to keep Mather in place and to continue development of the Park Service, and they were successful. Secretary of the

Interior Albert Fall, a former senator from New Mexico with strong leanings toward resource development (as was true in general of the Harding and subsequent Coolidge administrations), was surprisingly supportive of Mather and his agenda. As Mather wryly observed, there were "certain conspicuous holes in Fall's philosophy of land use" that would cause problems for the Park Service, but the momentum of its programs was not slowed.[4] The 1920s would prove a challenging decade for conservation because of political support for unfettered private enterprise, reduced government regulation, a policy favoring states' rights and state responsibility over federal activism, and an emphasis on individual rather than government action. Yet much was accomplished as "the conservation bureaus carried on unobtrusively and, in general, effectively."[5] Mather and the Park Service flourished during this period. He was a businessman, comfortable with the realities of limited government support for expansion of the park system. Always entrepreneurial, generous with his personal fortune when it came to the parks, and successful in interesting philanthropists in his cause, he forged ahead.

A NEW CONCEPT OF WILDERNESS EMERGES

While Mather and Albright worked to get the Park Service firmly established, forester and nascent ecologist Aldo Leopold began thinking about wilderness in ways that would change the course of national park history. Leopold was, of course, with the Forest Service at this time, and one of his first assignments was to visit and report on recreation conditions at the Forest Service's Grand Canyon National Monument. He and his partner in this investigation documented many problems resulting from increasing tourist use of the monument. They recommended that growing conflict between scenic appreciation and satisfaction of visitor desires for convenience be addressed through regulation, zoning, and establishment of clear business standards. The importance of this experience for Leopold was that he came to appreciate the growing challenges posed by commercial tourism to the West's public land and to land managers like the Forest Service.[6]

The pressure to make recreation a recognized use of national forest land was growing. The Forest Service was engaged in its internal debate about how to do this while attending to its other priorities. One response to Frank Waugh's recommendation on this challenge, which was to consider some parts of the national forests as primarily useful for recreation, was to bring in a landscape architect to plan how this recreation service might be provided. Arthur Carhart was hired and one of his assignments was to lay out sites for summer homes around Trapper Lake in Colorado's White River National Forest. He was to plan a road around this lake, but Carhart was struck by the beauty of the place and concluded that the best use of the lake would be to preserve its exceptional scenery. Carhart's supervisor agreed with this recommendation.

In December 1919 Aldo Leopold met Arthur Carhart, and the two men discussed what Carhart had achieved at Trapper Lake and how a policy to preserve similar pristine places might be achieved in other national forest areas. Carhart later sent some of his ideas about preservation in the national forests to Leopold, who continued to think about recreation and preservation. Carhart soon left the Forest Service, and Leopold published an article in 1921 in the *Journal of Forestry* in which he raised a question about Gifford Pinchot's doctrine of "highest use." Had the process of development of national forests, he asked, "already gone far enough to raise the question of whether the policy of development (construed in the narrower sense of industrial development) should continue to govern in absolutely every instance" or might it "not itself demand that some portions of some forests be preserved as wilderness?"[7] Writers in sporting magazines, said Leopold, had been groping with "reconciliation between going back to nature and preserving a little nature to get back to." This conflict was, he thought, "the old conflict between preservation and use . . . just now coming to be an issue with respect to recreation."[8] Here, in Leopold's view, was the crux of the problem. Recreation was posing a threat to wild nature, to wilderness, and had become industrial development not unlike other economic uses of natural resources.

Leopold wrote mostly of national forests in this essay but did mention national parks:

It may be asked whether the National Parks from which, let us hope, industrial development will continue to be excluded, do not fill the public demand here discussed. They do, in part, but hunting is not and should not be allowed within the Parks. Moreover, the Parks are being networked with roads and trails as rapidly as possible. This is right and proper.[9]

Leopold is not criticizing national park development, but here relegated the parks to tourism and recreation of the industrial sort he saw as a threat to wilderness. He did not see national park management as directed toward preservation of wilderness and the type of recreation he thought wilderness could provide. This being so, he suggested, the Forest Service must preserve wilderness and the wilderness experience, as he defined them, if they were to be preserved at all.[10]

Leopold defined wilderness as "a continuous stretch of country preserved in its natural state, open to lawful hunting and fishing, big enough to absorb a two weeks' pack trip, and kept devoid of roads, artificial trails, cottages, or other works of man."[11] His emphasis was upon the sort of recreational experience one could have in a wild place. He extolled "primitive modes of travel and subsistence" as essential to wilderness experience.[12] This definition of wilderness might be understood and embraced by John Muir, but those using the term in the fashion of McFarland, Olmsted, Albright, and park watchdog Robert Sterling Yard might not grasp what Leopold was describing. In Leopold's opinion, wilderness could not be experienced from the window of a hotel or automobile. When a road penetrated a landscape, it was not wilderness. Fortunately the government still owned areas "scattered here and there in the poorer and rougher parts of the National Forests and National Parks, to make a very good start [in preserving wilderness]. The one thing needful is for the Government to draw a line around each one and say: 'This is wilderness, and wilderness it shall remain.'"[13]

Leopold worked for the Forest Service as he wrote these essays and was thinking principally of national forests. Still, he often mentioned national parks. The threat of roads was great in the national forests where recreation use was growing and in national parks where Mather's administration was ever striving to increase access. While many in the National Park Service believed that the directives in the National Park Service Act established a policy of wilderness preservation, Leopold seems not to have agreed. He thought wilderness needed to be identified and designated by drawing lines around it. He added that "the action needed is the permanent differentiation of a suitable system of wild areas within our national park and forest system." The forests could serve wilderness recreation needs as "public hunting grounds," while national parks could be "public wildlife sanctuaries, and both kinds [serving] as public playgrounds in which the wilderness environments and modes of travel may be preserved and enjoyed."[14]

Leopold acted on his ideas, seeking protection for one of his favorite areas in New Mexico's Gila River country. He succeeded in 1924, convincing his district forester to draw lines around what became the first wilderness area in a national forest. Soon similar lines were being drawn in other forests. Chief William B. Greeley took Leopold's ideas seriously, issuing an in-house discussion of them in 1926. He could not support a preservation approach that excluded all economic uses because, as Paul Sutter argues, "what Greeley and other foresters feared was that permanently preserved wilderness areas would become equivalent to national parks, which might work to remove them from Forest Service control." Leopold, on the other hand, "saw wilderness as a form of preservation uniquely adapted to Forest Service administration."[15] So in the mid-1920s the Forest Service and Park Service wrestled with the implications of Leopold's idea.[16]

In an unexpected twist, at the beginning of the 1920s, a new and important concept of wilderness had emerged from the agency founded by Gifford Pinchot. John Muir, dead seven years, would have been surprised and probably suspicious. He would have understood that Pinchot had nothing to do with this development and that the Forest Service was unlikely to enthusiastically embrace wilderness as he conceived of it, even if it had come from one of the Forest Service's own. He would likely have grasped immediately the significance of this new thinking for national parks. It raised at least the potential for a new standard of judging national park preservation policy. He would likely also have felt more kinship with Leopold than with Mather and Albright. The "blunt mechanical beetles" he had worried about in 1912 were not yet everywhere in the national park system, but national park policy seemed bent on accommodating them at the expense of wilderness. Muir would have approved of Leopold's call to designate wilderness, to draw lines around the parts of the public domain allocated for this protective purpose. What, Muir would have wondered, would be the Park Service response to Leopold's idea?

THE PARK SERVICE FORGES AHEAD

The Park Service did not directly respond to the challenge posed by the wilderness ideas coming from its rival agency. Still, at this early stage in its history, Mather and his staff were well aware that Park Service survival was not assured. Some lawmakers, they knew, thought the Forest Service could do a better and less expensive job of managing scenery in the national parks.[17] A 1922 meeting of national park superintendents at Yosemite drafted a resolution on overdevelopment in which they stated that park development was necessary but should be carefully limited. The resolution was a response to critics who were accusing the agency of compromising its resources by development of various sorts. The resolution stated that some development of national parks was necessary. They were the people's parks, and the people should be given access to them. This thought was not new. What was new was the admission that parks could be overdeveloped. The Park Service wished to assure its critics that it was aware of this possibility and would strive to define how much development was enough or too much.

> It is the intention to make the chief scenic features of each park accessible to the average visitor, but to set aside certain regions of each park, which will not be traversed by automobile roads, and will have only such trails or other developments as will be necessary for the protection of the area.[18]

The superintendents were sure no park had yet developed over 10 percent of its area, and they thought it a conservative estimate that 90 percent of the visitors never went far from roads. They insisted that "at present the educational and economic value of national parks to the nation is restricted by insufficient development." But they sought to reassure the public that they would not build roads all over the parks and thereby presumably threaten the wildness that lent parks some of their value. "Some portions will be fully developed," they wrote, "others partly developed, and still others will be left in their natural, wild condition." Some level of development was necessary, for "if there were no development, no roads or trails, no hotels or camps, a national park would be merely a wilderness, not serving the purpose for what it was set aside."[19] The purposes were recreation, education, and inspiration. The superintendents' resolution indicates that they were caught in a struggle between park visitors who wanted roads and those who did not. The resolution was a response to the same challenge that inspired Leopold's thinking involving issues of outdoor recreation and road building, but the superintendents were not convinced that any lines needed to be drawn around areas from which roads would be excluded. They stood "for adequate development, but against over-development."

Developing parks was not the only work the Park Service was doing at this time. It was fighting off schemes to dam Yellowstone National Park streams for irrigation. A bill to create a Federal Power Commission with authority to site power developments on federal land was moving toward congressional passage, and lobbying to exempt parklands from such siting was needed. Substandard park proposals abounded, with one coming from Secretary Fall himself. These needed to be squelched and usually were. Stephen Mather wrote in his 1920 annual report that he had agreed to be National Park Service director "to undertake in the public interest the development of the national parks into a smoothly running, well-coordinated system."[20] He brought in strong leaders, men like Roger Toll, John R. White, and Owen Tomlinson, who would shape the agency in its early years. As he developed parks he saw the need for planning and landscaping, and began hiring landscape architects to accomplish this. He supported initiation of educational programs in the parks and built a ranger force as the core of the agency in the field. He put the rangers in uniform so they would be visible and develop an esprit like that of Forest Service rangers.[21] Mather believed to his core in the importance of his work, and biographer Robert Shankland describes how much fun he had out in the parks. Field people understood how much he cared about "his" parks and the men who tended them, and there was a shared respect and affection. A Park Service "family" was the result.

Work was also ongoing to expand some of the parks and the park system. Attempts to enhance Yellowstone National Park by annexing the Tetons and Jackson Hole met strong opposition. Expansion of Sequoia National Park was also controversial, with opposition coming not only from the Forest Service but also from the city of Los Angeles, which coveted the water and power potential of the Kings River. The conflict between the Park Service and the Forest Service was heating up and now contained the ingredient of wilderness introduced by Aldo Leopold.[22] Fuel was added to the fire when Secretary of the Interior Fall drafted an executive order for President Harding's signature that would transfer the Forest Service back to the Department of the Interior. Nothing came of this but a greater uneasiness on all sides about who should be overseeing outdoor recreation on the public lands.

Fall's initiative and growing Park Service ambitions brought increasingly tense relations between the Park and Forest services. Back in 1919 Henry Graves had suggested there was a need for a national outdoor recreation policy that would address some of the issues causing the interagency competition. He had, in his policy letter, supported the national park idea, but he raised questions regarding national park standards and the respective roles of the two agencies administering to the outdoor recreation needs of the American people. No step toward formulating a national policy was taken until 1923, when Charles Sheldon, a big-game hunter, leader of the successful effort to create Mount McKinley National Park, and friend of Henry Graves, decided the time had come to tackle the outdoor recreation policy issues. In drafting a policy statement for the Boone and Crockett Club addressing public land issues, he closed as follows:

The Club believes that the President should cause to be made a complete survey of the question with a view to a definitive [policy] which will finally include a determination of the areas to be included in national parks, national monuments, and other regions with recreational possibilities. . . . Only by the establishment of such a National Recreation Policy can maximum recreational opportunities be given to the nation and the numbers of people who will then be increased.[23]

President Coolidge responded by appointing a Committee on Outdoor Recreation, which recommended that a national conference be convened to formulate policy. The president called together a conference in May 1924 and asked it to find a way to achieve better coordination between agencies engaged in providing outdoor recreation at all governmental levels. It was also charged with surveying and classifying outdoor recreation resources, especially those on federal lands. The meeting convened on May 22 with 309 delegates from 128 organizations.

THE NATIONAL CONFERENCE ON OUTDOOR RECREATION

The 1924 conference spent little time on wilderness, addressing broad outdoor recreation policy issues, but it made itself a "permanent conference" and reconvened in January 1926. This time wilderness was on the agenda. John C. Merriam, a distinguished scientist and national park advocate, compared the roles of national parks and forests, noting that for him "the parks are not merely places to rest and exercise and learn. They are regions where one looks through the veil to meet the realities of nature and of the unfathomable power behind it." He did not think that "complete conservation," which he defined as "unbroken maintenance of primitive conditions in national parks," would be achieved if the parks were viewed only as sites for recreation and even education. Only if their value to inspire and lift the spirit was recognized would their "complete conservation" be achieved.[24]

Aldo Leopold reiterated to the conference his belief that wilderness areas should be "a specialized form of land use within our existing or prospective forests and parks." He now recognized a role for national parks. Two types of wilderness areas should be provided: "one kind in the national parks devoted to the gunless type of wilderness trip, another kind in the national forests devoted to all types of wilderness trips including hunting."[25] Leopold spoke also to the movement afoot at that time to establish national parks and forests in the East, and he stated unequivocally that some parts of them should

3.1 Aldo Leopold, inspecting a pine tree near the Shack in 1946, contributed to the evolving idea of wilderness in the 1920s and 1930s. Photo courtesy of the Aldo Leopold Foundation Archives and the Robert McCabe Family Collection

be dedicated to wilderness recreation. Wilderness in those areas might not be as large or "absolute" as those in the West, but he challenged the assumption that "an area is either wild or not wild, that there is no place for intermediate degrees of wilderness."[26]

While on the subject of eastern wilderness, Leopold challenged the commonly held assumption that only mountainous lands were appropriate as wilderness. Would not "swamps, lakelands, river routes, and deserts" also provide opportunities for wilderness experience? "Surely our sons are entitled to see a few such examples of primeval America, and surely the few nickels which exploitation would put into their pockets are less important than the fundamental human experience which would be taken out of their lives."[27] In this talk Leopold was extending his thinking about wilderness and was responding to concerns being raised by the National Parks Association, Robert Sterling Yard in particular, that eastern national parks were a threat to national park ideals and standards. These skeptics were arguing that areas in the Shenandoah and Great Smoky Mountains, which were being discussed for national park status at the time, could not be as large, as "pristine," and thus as wild as the great national parks of the West. Leopold did not share their concern. There was no absolute wilderness, in his view. Types of wilderness experience could be enjoyed in diverse areas.

Here Leopold shifted from his definition of wilderness as space that would allow a two-week pack trip without encountering roads. Wilderness was still defined by the absence of roads, but the presence of human activity that did not severely degrade the wild character of a place should not prohibit that place from being considered a resource for wilderness recreation. Nor were mountains essential to having a wilderness experience. Leopold made the case for eastern national forests, parks, and wilderness, all of which were eventually to be established.

Other business of the conferences involved recreation resource inventories, and this huge job was assigned to a joint committee of the National Parks Association and the American Forestry Association. The committee issued its large and detailed report in 1928. It asserted that wilderness was a value of both national parks and forests. National parks were, in its view, mostly wild and should remain that way. The decision to create a national park had been tantamount to establishing wilderness. The Joint Committee did not resolve the controversy of which agency should administer wilderness. It recognized that national parks were mostly wild but also that scenic wild lands under Forest Service management provided an opportunity to preserve wilderness.

The committee report emphasized the threat of roads to wilderness, whether it be in national parks or forests. Wilderness areas "are disappearing rapidly, not so much by reason of economic need as by the extension of motor roads and the attendant development of tourist attractions."[28] It listed potential designated wilderness areas, all in national forests, three of which at the time were being touted for national park status—the Tetons, the High Sierra near Yosemite and Sequoia national parks, and the Olympic Mountains in the state of Washington. Finally, the report concluded with the assertion that wilderness recreation was preferred by a growing minority of users of national parks and forests. These people "have as legitimate a claim as those who desire any other forms of outdoor recreation," and any national outdoor recreation policy "which does not provide for wilderness recreation . . . would be inadequate."[29]

By 1928, only seven years after Leopold had introduced the idea in his *Journal of Forestry* essay, the wilderness idea was the subject of national discussion. This discussion focused primarily on national forests because, as indicated by the words of the committee report, most people considered designation of a national park as virtually a designation of wilderness. At the same time, some powerful voices, the National Parks Association among them, were concerned that even though most of the national parks were wild at that point, the prospect of growing automobile traffic with consequent demand for roads threatened park wilderness. The National Conference accepted the *fact* that most national park land was wild but raised doubts about National Park Service claims that it would always remain so under the Organic Act.

The Joint Committee inserted a chapter in its report, "Relation of National Parks and National Forests." The Park Service's mission in outdoor recreation was "to provide safety, comfort and facilities for observation to visitors of all kinds . . . to these superlative national spectacles; that of the Forest Service to afford visitors to national forests the completest possible freedom in enjoying the wilderness each after his own chosen fashion."[30] The distinction made between "spectacles" and "wilderness" suggests that the committee saw the recreational attractions of the two systems as being very different. Also, committee members wrote that "for the thorough protection of park areas from disturbance of natural conditions, their use by the public in ways involving possible damage is carefully directed and controlled at all times. Camping places . . . are assigned in every case." In national forests, on the other hand, "People use the forests without restriction or restraint . . . except in rare cases of emergency or fire danger."[31] Decades later, as "wilderness management" became a recognized discipline of outdoor recreation, regulating people to minimize resource damage would be a core principle of such management. The Park Service, by the late 1920s, was already practicing this approach, though it did not call it "wilderness management." Park rangers were simply managing their parks to leave them "unimpaired," and this required a level of people management the Forest Service did not feel necessary on its vast domain.

The importance of the National Conference on Outdoor Recreation lies not so much in direct results of the deliberations as in what they reveal about how people were thinking about park wilderness at the time. No resolution of the conflict between the Park and Forest services was achieved. Some overlap in mission seemed inevitable, even acceptable. Parks and forests, even in the arena of outdoor recreation, served different goals. The experience of one, the parks, was more strictly regulated than the other. The wilderness experience of parks embraced scenery, inspiration, and education. That of forests involved long outings, exercise of primitive living skills, even hunting. The Park Service was doing an acceptable job protecting its resources, but prospects of more roads and attendant development threatened that record. The issues addressed by the National Conference would continue to wax and wane until, in the late 1950s, they were addressed again by the Outdoor Recreation Resources Review Commission and deliberations about the Wilderness Act.

National park advocates in the 1920s fought hard to expand the national park system, especially in the East. Their efforts raised issues of purpose and purity, as alluded to in the National Conference by Aldo Leopold. Stephen Mather believed it critically important to bring national parks closer to the American people, and since most of the population of the United States was in the East and the Midwest, parks there were essential to his campaign to build the park system, the Park Service, and support for both. Purists objected, arguing that parks should be "pure" examples of nature, places where humans had not changed the natural world so much that students of it could not see a clear picture of nature and its purposes. Places like the Shenandoah and Great Smoky Mountains had been changed by generations of settlers (and before that by Native Americans, though the "purists" were not thinking of them). They did not qualify for national park status.

Purists were often opposed to recreation development but admitted that some outdoor activities like hiking and camping were necessary for the public to enjoy the educational and inspirational qualities of the parks. A minimal level of convenience was necessary. The argument was over how much convenience was enough. John Merriam once remarked in a talk to the National Parks Association about his experience of Yosemite that "I like to sit at my hotel and enjoy the view. There are a good many hundred other people enjoying the view also. I would like to discover some means by which human beings could be made invisible in the national parks."[32] Perhaps he said this in jest. The best park would be one in which there were no people (or effects of people). Yet how he and they could become learned and inspired in national parks without affecting them was not explained.

In the argument over national park standards—over what qualified for national park status—purists like Robert Sterling Yard and John Merriam constantly used words like "primitive" and "primeval" in explaining why one area should be a park and another not. The qualities of the primitive and primeval were an essential qualification for national park status. If they were absent, park status for an area was questionable. Mather and his Park Service colleagues disagreed, believing that natural park values could be protected by using techniques of landscape planning and architecture and careful engineering of park development. The fact that 90 percent of the parks remained wild in the opinion of the National Conference experts seemed to confirm that the Park Service approach had been successful. Furthermore, this level of protection was being achieved without any lines being drawn to designate wilderness.

In 1928 Horace Albright, then National Park Service director, with the help of a freelance writer named Frank Taylor, published an article in the *Saturday Evening Post* in which he responded directly to "anxious inquirers who want to know if we propose to checkerboard the last wilderness with highways." One inquirer had written, "Let us not destroy the few remaining bits of wilderness in the national parks by building paved highways through every one of them." Albright's response was that "this is a sentiment which the National Park Service endorses without a single reservation."[33] He described at length and with abundant statistics precisely where the roads were, where any new roads would be, and how both old and new roads would be blended wherever possible into the landscapes by the work of landscape architects. The Park Service was, he argued, steering a "middle course" between those "who want no roads into the parks" and the automobile tourists and business interests "whose appetites for road building are never appeased." The statistics revealed, he assured his readers, that most of the national park system remained wilderness. There were many tourists and considerable road work in parks like Yellowstone, he admitted, but "nine-tenths of Yellowstone is still—and we hope it always will be—an everlasting wilderness."[34] These reassurances did not placate the purists, but they indicate that Albright was sensitive to the criticism his agency was receiving on the wilderness issue and was confident that the wilderness preservation part of the national park mission was being accomplished.

WILDERNESS ISSUES IN THE FIELD

Even as Albright was issuing his reassurances, events in the field cast doubt on them. A long-simmering struggle over roads in Mount Rainier National Park was reaching a boil. Plans for the park, if carried out, would place more roads in Mount Rainier than had so far penetrated any park. If all of these roads were built, the concerns of those to whom Albright had addressed his article would be legitimized. Yet while those who would develop Mount Rainier pushed hard for that goal, forces were at work within the Park Service that would thwart them and advance the cause of national park wilderness.

Tourist development had begun even before Mount Rainier National Park was established in 1899. A railroad reached close to the park in 1904 and work on road access to it was well under way by then. Hiram Chittenden, who had built the Grand Loop Road in Yellowstone, proposed a scheme for a "round-the-mountain" road at Mount Rainier that would circle the glaciated peak just below its glacier line. By 1913 preliminary surveys had been done for this ambitious project. By 1915 a road had been built to Paradise at an elevation near 5,000 feet, and a major approach to the park named the National Park Highway was soon completed by the state of Washington. The Rainier National Park Company was formed and in 1916 was granted the tourist concession for the park. It opened Paradise Inn in 1917, and in 1918 6,000 cars entered the park over the new highway.

The state funded a highway project in 1916 that would reach to the park's White River entrance in its northeast corner. Mineral springs at Longmire in the park's southeast corner had been the original attraction for development there, and more hot springs were found in the Ohanopecosh River region just southeast of the park. With a road and railroad reaching toward the Carbon Glacier region of the park's northwest corner, by 1919 all four corners of the park showed potential for tourist development. Meanwhile the Mountaineers, a large and active mountaineering club in Seattle, had hiked the proposed route of the round-the-mountain highway, and in 1916 a trail had been completed roughly over the route of this proposed highway. Many members of the Mountaineers were opposed to this trail becoming a road, and concern was growing about the level of development proposed for "their" park.

In the early 1920s, Congress responded to Stephen Mather's campaign to build roads to accommodate the growing auto tourism in the parks. The Going-to-the-Sun Road was funded for Glacier, the Generals Highway for Sequoia, and the Carbon River Road for Mount Rainier. Mather and Mount Rainier superintendent Roger Toll favored connecting the four corners of the park with roads and revived Chittenden's round-the-mountain road idea. Toll's successor as superintendent drew up a budget for the project in 1921.

The Rainier National Park Company, with its investment in visitor facilities at Paradise, pushed aggressively for the roads. The Mountaineers, in response, in 1922 accused the Park Service of administering the park more for the concession than for the public. The company replied, tempers flared, and charges flew. Roger Toll, now superintendent at Rocky Mountain but an enthusiastic mountaineer himself, was brought in to calm the waters, which he did. He pointed out to Park Service critics that it was not unreasonable for the concession to wish to make some money—it had so far spent more money developing the park than had the government. Calm was restored, though preservationists among the Mountaineers were not placated. The clash between those who thought the national parks should be preserved and those who thought they should be developed for the ever-growing tide of auto tourists continued to grow throughout the national park system.

Construction of the Carbon River Road was begun and soon ran into serious difficulties. Realizing that road building was not a strong suit of the Park Service, Mather negotiated an inter-bureau agreement with the Bureau of Public Roads. They took over the park road work, increasing the concern of those who feared too many roads in the parks. The inter-bureau agreement began to change the Park Service's thinking. To this point it had been employing its own staff of engineers and landscape architects. Bureau of Public Roads engineers were not as concerned as their Park Service counterparts about the aesthetics of their projects, and as road projects in the parks progressed, landscape architects increased their influence. They began to raise questions not only about how roads should be sited and built, but whether some should be built at all.

Ethan Carr describes the intensified debate over roads in the mid-1920s.[35] He points out that by this stage in national park history, the nature of the parks and the pressures on them had changed from the days when Yellowstone's Grand Loop was conceived by Chittenden. The Grand Loop was a carriage road that could be built to less environmentally damaging and aesthetically intrusive specifications than a modern auto road. Also, parks like Yellowstone and Yosemite were on a different scale than Mount Rainier or Rocky Mountain, and loop roads would affect much more of these smaller parks than the roads in the larger parks. The potential impacts of roads on national park values were much greater in parks like Mount Rainier, as preservationists argued and landscape architects came to see.

At the 1925 superintendents' conference at Mesa Verde, Horace Albright and Arno Cammerer, Mather's assistant director, suggested that it was time to begin comprehensive planning of national parks. With the Bureau of Public Roads involved and more money flowing from Congress for park road building, a clearer picture of what parts of the parks should be developed and what parts preserved was necessary. Albright and Cammerer were thinking of zoning the parks, an idea being applied in town planning at the time. The Park Service, forced by public opinion and the discussions of the National Conference, realized that it had to be more systematic about its decisions as to what should be preserved, how it should be preserved, and what to call portions of the parks protected from development. The Mount Rainier situation brought this to a head.

At Mount Rainier, the Rainier National Park Company continued to push for more roads. It proposed yet another road, a scenic loop road around Paradise Valley. Superintendent Owen Tomlinson and the Rainier Park Advisory Board gave their approval. Once again the Mountaineers protested vehemently, comparing the likely consequences to what was happening to Yosemite Valley, where development, in their opinion, was out of control. Tomlinson, responding to the call for planning, drafted an Outline for Planning that was reviewed by Mather and by Thomas Vint, who at that time had become head of the Park Service landscape architecture division. Tomlinson and Vint agreed that any road across the north side of the mountain connecting the Carbon River region to the White River areas was not a good idea. It would be too intrusive and costly. Their decision dashed the hopes of those advocating a round-the-mountain road and unofficially allocated the northern part of the park to wilderness. At the same time, Tomlinson outlined a road-building plan for the rest of the park that was, despite loss of the round-the-mountain scheme, still the most ambitious yet proposed for any national park.

The Mountaineers responded to Tomlinson's plan with a resolution from its board in April 1928 claiming that the proposed road plan would subject three-quarters of the park to development and leave only one-quarter of it in wilderness. Tomlinson did not agree with their characterization of the plan but endorsed the Mountaineers' proposal that a portion of the park be declared a wilderness. He suggested, in a letter to Director Mather, that "such action would be in entire accordance with national park policies and ideals, and it would have the effect of assuring those concerned with the preservation of national wilderness areas that the National Park Service is guarding against over-development of the national parks."[36] Mather was away, and Cammerer and others in the Washington office were uncertain how to respond to this proposal. The precedent in the park system for a "wilderness area" was a small tract that had been set aside for scientific study in Yosemite National Park. No recreation was allowed in this Yosemite area, and this was obviously not what the Mountaineers had in mind. They were thinking of a designated road-free area where they could hike and climb— wilderness recreation of the sort described earlier by Aldo Leopold. Cammerer and his assistant Arthur Demaray suggested that the area not be called "wilderness" but instead be designated on the planning maps as "to be free from road and commercial development."[37] Tomlinson did as they advised, sending them a map that identified the area to be so designated. When Mather returned, he approved this approach, and thus did the Park Service designate its first "wilderness," though it could not bring itself to use the term. The incident did, however, initiate internal debate about what to call areas to be kept free of roads. It was also significant because for the first time (the small off-limits Yosemite area excepted) the Park Service admitted that more than general policy statements such as the Organic Act were necessary to achieve the level of protection being called for by wilderness advocates at this time. Specific designation of areas to be kept wild might need to be made. They could not take the step to officially call the north side of Mount Rainier a "wilderness," but they could identify a specific area that would "remain free of road, hotel, pay camps and all commercial development."[38]

While all of this was happening at Mount Rainier, the situation in Yosemite National Park also had bearing on the park wilderness story. The issues there did not so much involve wilderness designation and terminology as broader questions about priorities. The first stirrings of yet another view of wilderness were appearing, a view defined by concerns beyond recreation and scenery. Yosemite National Park was, in the minds of national park boosters like Mather, a great success story. People loved the park and flocked to it in ever-increasing numbers. Alfred Runte has chronicled the situation there, noting that by the late 1920s the park averaged nearly a half-million visitors each year. Runte writes that "the Park Service greeted each visitor as a measure of success, proof that the American public wanted and supported its national parks."[39] Yet these ever-increasing visitors caused new clashes between preservation and development. Runte describes how, in the 1920s, external criticism of Park Service policy at Yosemite came principally from Joseph Grinnell, a biologist and director of the Museum of Vertebrate Zoology at the University of California at Berkeley. Grinnell became increasingly critical of what he perceived as too much emphasis on recreation at the expense of Yosemite's wildlife. He thought park officials were catering to the needs and desires of visitors and concessions at the expense of other park values. Events were being staged that were simply entertainment rather than contributions to education or appreciation of the park. A growing "bear problem" exemplified, for him, the difficulty.

Wherever bears were present in the park they were an attraction, and in the 1920s visitors expected to see bears at Yosemite, Yellowstone, and other national parks. Concessionaires at Yosemite built platforms and put meat on them to attract bears on schedule so visitors could see them. Visitors fed bears and, as more bears were attracted to these sources of easy fare, incidents involving bears and visitors increased, always to the detriment of the bears.

When bears injured people, concessionaires feared bad publicity and demanded that the National Park Service control the bears. This spotlighted a "conflict of interest between profit and preservation."[40]

The Yosemite concessionaires had contributed to the bear crisis and now wanted the Park Service to control the situation. The Yosemite superintendent seemed inclined to do so. Writing to the Washington office, he commented that "while I am personally opposed to killing off bears if there is any other practical solution, conditions are fast reaching the stage where we must determine whether the Valley is being administered for the use and enjoyment of the people or for the use and enjoyment of the bears."[41] For the Park Service and concessionaires the bears seemed to be props useful for entertaining visitors, but for Grinnell and park naturalists the bears were part of the ecological system and deserving of protection. Runte explains how the issues involved in managing Yosemite Valley in the 1920s reveal the slowly emerging role in park management of biology and ecology. New interpretations of the meaning of the Organic Act's mandate to "conserve . . . unimpaired" were emerging. Manipulating parts of the landscape for visitor entertainment without careful consideration of the consequences to the ecology of the park's natural systems was not, contended the critics, good management.

In 1928 a Yosemite National Park Board of Expert Advisers was appointed, which agreed that there were problems and suggested where the Park Service should draw the line regarding development. Wilderness figured in the board's recommendations in a back-door sort of way. The line on development should be drawn, argued advisory board member Frederick Law Olmsted Jr., inside the valley, thereby protecting the heart of the park. In this recommendation he pulled the veil off the argument used by Horace Albright and others that development was acceptable in places like the valley because, after all, the rest of the park was wild. Runte writes of Olmsted's point:

> In fact there was not more room for the common brand of subterfuge, for the argument that development, because it *was* concentrated in the valley, somehow was insurance that the rest of the park would remain wild. . . . The challenge of preservation was to protect the entirety of the park, not just those parts—however large—that were previously undeveloped.[42]

Runte argues that in this way wilderness was being used as an argument against preservation. "The irony of conservation was perfectly mirrored in Yosemite Valley, where those favoring greater development already commonly

3.2 A visitor and car with a bear in the road in Yosemite National Park are symbolic of the clash of recreation and nature protection in the growing national park system. Yosemite National Park Research Library

invoked the argument that wilderness enthusiasts had the rest of the park (that is, the high country) practically all to themselves."[43] If all that conservationists were concerned about was having their own wilderness playground, which was certainly the case with some, such an argument might satisfy them. But others, like Grinnell, were concerned about the entire park as an ecological unit. The bear situation, for them, revealed the folly of thinking that the park's nature, its wilderness, could be preserved by freely manipulating nature in one area while arguing that preservation was being served by leaving other parts relatively untouched (at least for a while). Olmsted, Grinnell, and others argued for a change in thinking about park preservation that would move away from the primacy of recreation. They were not, as will be seen, successful.

Still, Yosemite National Park was, as noted earlier, the site of the first "wilderness reserve" in the national park system. The park had, in 1927, designated such a reserve of roughly seven square miles of the high country that would be used only for scientific study of the area in its "natural state." In a token way the reserve, its name later changed to "research reserve," was a response to calls from scientists for reservation of natural areas for scientific purposes. Back in 1918 the Ecological Society of America had appointed a committee to study how natural areas might be preserved for science. One conclusion of this committee was that neither national forests nor national parks qualified as scientific reserves given the potential for development of them. The Park Service responded slowly to this, mounting a research reserve program that, for various reasons, never amounted to much.[44]

The Mount Rainier and Yosemite episodes illustrate how, during the 1920s, the Park Service was being nudged to pay attention to wilderness preservation. In the case of Mount Rainier the concept of wilderness as a place for a specific type of recreation, developed by Leopold, was in play. At Yosemite, an emergent concept of national park as more than simply a place for outdoor recreation or even human education and inspiration was appearing. As Richard Sellars has amply documented, the ecological awareness that was stirring in the minds of scientists and that manifested itself in Yosemite's "research reserve" was not to become significant in park management for decades, but the seed of an ecological definition of wilderness and of its importance to national parks was planted.[45] The idea of wilderness was being thrust into policy deliberations of the National Park Service in new and important ways.

THE FOREST SERVICE RELUCTANTLY EMBRACES WILDERNESS

While the Park Service danced around the problem of its wilderness policy, the Forest Service addressed its wilderness challenge more directly. Forced by public pressure to embrace recreation as part of its mission, it struggled to decide how that use should be balanced with other forest uses. In 1925 Assistant Forester Leon F. Kneipp wrote that "the National Forests are the richest of all land areas in the United States in terms of recreation value."[46] Despite such statements it could not bring itself to say that recreation would be the exclusive or even primary resource value anywhere. A list of recreation "principles" was drawn up in 1925, and one of them advocated "the retention under National Forest management of all areas of recreation value, except where Congress considers that the value so completely transcends all others and is of such public importance as to require a separate and specialized management."[47] This suggested that should some part of a national forest be judged (by Congress, not the agency) to be of exclusively recreational value, then perhaps it should be transferred to the Park Service. The Forest Service, of course, would contest such a judgment.

Chief Greeley addressed the idea of forest wilderness, issuing a general policy statement on wilderness preservation in 1926. He called for a review of forest road development plans "to make sure they do not contemplate a needless invasion of areas adapted to wilderness forms of use."[48] He suggested that district foresters might designate wilderness areas but left it to their discretion. Each area would be considered on its own merits, and the welfare of timber-dependent communities was always to be considered. The policy was so vague that by 1928 the district forester for Colorado and Wyoming had created forty-two wilderness areas totaling 2.5 million acres, while the district forester for nearby Montana had created none. Greeley also ordered an inventory of all national forest roadless areas larger than 230,400 acres. In his 1926 and 1927 annual reports he affirmed that the Forest Service was examining the wilderness issue and would, after careful study, take steps to give some areas wilderness status.

Historians disagree about how much of Greeley's attention to wilderness was an attempt to foil Stephen Mather's national park expansion plans. There is anecdotal evidence that this was part of Greeley's motivation. James Gilligan, for instance, interviewed Greeley in 1952, and Greeley recounted how at a congressional hearing where he was testifying a veteran congressman leaned forward and shook his finger at the chief. "I know why you set up these wilderness areas, Greeley. Just to keep them out of Mather's hands." Greeley did not deny it.[49] Gilligan also observes that when the Forest Service issued regulations in 1929 regarding what it called "primitive areas," a term that for a time replaced "wilderness" in its official lexicon, it did not establish a minimum size for them. Leopold had suggested a minimum of 500,000 acres, and the inventory of roadless areas ordered by Greeley used a 230,400 acre minimum. Perhaps the flexibility on the size of primitive areas was calculated to give the Forest Service the opportunity to designate a primitive area when it was faced (as it was at the time and expected to be in the future) with national park proposals for national forest land.

A 1927 article by Greeley in *Sunset* magazine, in which he strongly supported wilderness, indicates how much the threat from the Park Service was on his mind. In a tone more strident than usual for this veteran bureaucrat, Greeley criticized the Park Service preservation policy. Recalling his trip to Yellowstone with Stephen Mather and the president's Coordinating Committee on National Parks and National Forests, which was in 1926 examining a proposal to expand the national park, Greeley wrote, "Let us add it [the Upper Yellowstone River–Two Oceans Pass area] to the national park if that is where it belongs; but curses on the man who bisects it with roads, plants it with hotels, and sends yellow buses streaking through it with sirens shrieking like souls in torment."[50] Greeley may have let his guard down here, but there seems little doubt that he was piqued at the aggressive efforts of Stephen Mather to expand his domain at the expense of the Forest Service.

The most definitive step yet by either agency toward a wilderness policy was the Forest Service's 1929 issuance of its L-20 regulations. These defined management priorities for designated primitive areas and required the drafting of a management plan for them. They created a stir because they appeared to offer more permanent protection for wilderness than was acceptable to many foresters. Leon Kneipp, who had drafted them, softened them and Chief Roy W. Stuart issued them in 1929. Primitive areas and "research reserves" would be established in national forests, but "establishment of a primitive area will not operate to withdraw timber, forage or water resources from industrial use."[51] Thus the Forest Service gave the appearance of protecting wilderness when the regulations in fact provided little prospect of permanent protection. Gilligan notes that the instructions from the forester to the field were much more liberal than the restrictions suggested by the text of the regulations, and in effect the Forest Service gained public relations benefits in its competition with the Park Service without alienating its usual clients in the West, the loggers, grazers, and miners.[52]

The Forest Service actions on the wilderness front are brought into the national park wilderness story here because the interplay between the two agencies affected development of Park Service wilderness policy. From the moment the Forest Service accepted, however reluctantly, the idea that it had some responsibility to preserve portions of its domain as wilderness, it laid a challenge before its rival. The Park Service could not claim to be the preservation agency as compared with the development-oriented Forest Service. It now had competition in the preservation realm. John Muir, Enos Mills, and others had once believed the forest preserves would protect natural landscapes, but when the reserves were opened to development and the Forest Service was formed to administer them, preservationists embraced the national park idea as their best chance of preserving natural landscapes. This group was an important original constituency of the Park Service, but when Mather and his associates began to develop some of the national parklands to serve visitors, some of them became critics. Aldo Leopold formulated his ideas about wilderness, suggesting that the "highest use" of some national forest land might be wilderness recreation. This gave foresters a tool they could use to blunt what they saw as raids by national park interests on national forests.

During the 1920s the increased Forest Service interest in wilderness pushed the idea increasingly into the consciousness of the Park Service. Biologists, preservation activists, and even some of its own field officers pressed for a sharper definition of resource preservation policy in the national parks. When Stephen Mather retired as director, the Park Service was well along toward establishing itself in the world of government bureaus. His efforts had effectively assured a future for the young agency. He had elevated the national parks in the minds of the American people, encouraged visitation to them, and made progress toward assuring that when visitors arrived they would have access and services necessary for enjoyment. To achieve these goals he had, without apology, emphasized the "provide for the enjoyment of" part of the 1916 Organic Act more than the "conserve . . . unimpaired" part. He had not ignored the latter but had prioritized the former. Mather began, by using landscape architects and comprehensive planning, to deal with the conservation mandate. The growing profile of the wilderness idea posed new challenges and opportunities to address that mandate. One challenge came from Forest Service designation of wilderness: the drawing of a line around areas allocated, if only temporarily, to wilderness preservation. Leopold had argued for the necessity of this, and the Forest Service had done it. The Park Service had not.

The Park Service began to evolve a policy that might be called the "all that is not developed is wilderness" policy. As Director Horace Albright said repeatedly, the parks were 90 percent wilderness. He did not think the Park Service faced any dearth of wilderness or that it was doing more development than was necessary. Why designate one part of a park, like the north side of Mount Rainier, as wilderness and not other undeveloped parts? What would such designation mean for the other parts? This question, of course, is what concerned the conservationists who had a clear idea of what it should mean—no roads or "commercial" development. Albright, with his growing interest in comprehensive park planning, undoubtedly believed that the Park Service and the national park system were not ready for zoning. More informed thought needed to go into a decision such as designating a wilderness at Mount Rainier, thought that involved the entire park resource and probably more experienced and mature understanding of the parks than the young Park Service had so far acquired. The Landscape Engineering Branch of the service was only just being organized under the strong leadership of Thomas Vint. The Park Service cannot be excused for not more aggressively addressing the "conserve . . . unimpaired" part of its mission, but its position can be understood by considering the factors that came into play at this time.

As the National Park Service moved into the 1930s, it faced many unresolved issues, wilderness among them. The new decade would bring many new challenges and opportunities. All of the dimensions of the wilderness issue that emerged in the 1920s—confusion about terminology, activist pressure, competition with the Forest Service, internal debate about priorities, standards for new parks—would continue into the next decade. New issues would arise as outdoor recreation continued to evolve, the Park Service mission broadened significantly, and park development progressed at an increasing pace as part of the Great Depression–driven conservation, jobs, and public works programs. Huge new parks would be proposed that contained vast tracts of wilderness but that were part of national forests. Important new players interested in wilderness would appear.

PRESERVATION OF THE PRIMEVAL

IN THE POST-MATHER ERA

Horace Albright was a gifted administrator. He had preceded Stephen Mather to Washington, served as his assistant, virtually set up the organization of the National Park Service while his boss was ill, then moved on to become the Yellowstone superintendent. When Mather suffered a stroke in 1928, Albright became Park Service director and filled that job until August 1933. He proved exceptionally adept in every job he held. Ambitious, confident to a fault, politically astute, and possessed of an enormous capacity for work, Albright continued the policies of the Mather administration and pressed initiatives he had long been nurturing. When he left the Park Service in 1933 for a more lucrative career in business, he did not abandon his deep commitment to national parks, remaining active in park affairs for thirty years.

The worst stock market crash in America's history came nine months after Albright became director, and the world slipped into the Great Depression. Despite the onset of economic crisis, visitation to the national parks stayed strong, growing slowly but steadily during the early Depression years. When he moved to the director's office, Albright found much work to do. The Park Service was studying twenty bills for new parks under congressional consideration, most of which he thought "lacked merit." With the approval in 1926 of eastern national parks at Shenandoah, Great Smoky Mountains, and Mammoth Cave, members of Congress had become very enthusiastic about new parks. The Park Service made recommendations on this plethora of proposals and, with the help of defenders of national park standards like the National Parks Association, killed most of them. Two good parks—Grand Teton and Isle Royale (which was authorized in 1931 with provisions to be met before the park would finally be established)—joined the system.

These new parks are important to the national park wilderness story because they were set up as wilderness parks. No roads, hotels, or even permanent camps were to be established in them. Ironically, the provision written into the act establishing Grand Teton as the first legally mandated wilderness park was not entirely the work of wilderness preservationists. The Senate Committee on Public Lands held hearings in Wyoming in the summer of 1928 on the bill to establish Grand Teton Park. A group of park opponents, when they realized that the support was strong and a park was likely to be approved, demanded concessions, among which were stipulations banning roads, hotels, and permanent camps. Interests pushing for the park, including Horace Albright, supported the idea, and it went into the legislation. The opponents insisted on the provision because the merchants wanted protection from competition and dude ranchers wanted to keep their monopoly providing accommodations to park visitors. Regardless of why the provision was there, this marked the first time that legislation creating a park included a specific prohibition against development and wrote de facto wilderness protection into the law.[1]

The Isle Royale story was a bit different in that it was not legislated a wilderness park but from its beginning was managed by the Park Service to sustain its wilderness character. As the largest island in the Great Lakes, twenty miles from the mainland, Isle Royale was first proposed as a national monument in 1923. The idea languished until, in 1931, a Michigan senator introduced a bill in Congress to establish Isle Royale National Park. Representative Louis Cramton of Michigan, a powerful friend of the national parks, introduced a similar bill in the House, and with little debate it was quickly approved by both chambers. As with the Appalachian parks, Isle Royale National Park was authorized but not established. When the state of Michigan acquired the lands for it and ceded them to the federal government, it would be formally dedicated a national park. This would finally happen in April 1940.

Isle Royale had been advocated for national park status because, as Horace Albright testified, "It's a type of scenery utterly distinct from anything now found in our national-park system; its primitiveness, its unusual wildlife and interesting flora, its evidence of prehistoric occupation, all com-

bine to make Isle Royale and its neighboring Islands of national-park caliber."[2] Some doubt must have lingered regarding the suitability of Isle Royale
as a national park, for the Department of the Interior in 1933 sent highly
respected wildlife biologist Adolph Murie to look the island over and report
on its suitability. Murie reported that it was indeed suitable and that its wildness was its greatest asset.

> Isle Royale is practically uninhabited and untouched. The element of pure wilder-
> ness which it contains is rare and worthy of the best care. True wilderness is more
> marvelous (and harder to retain) than the grandiose, spectacular features of our
> outstanding parks. It alone labels Isle Royale as of park calibre.[3]

He recommended that it be a wilderness park and went further to suggest
that "the administrators should be told that their success and achievements
will be measured, not by projects accomplished, but by projects sidetracked." Murie recognized a penchant for "projects" in park building that
he cautioned against if this park was to be dedicated to its highest value—
wilderness.

The National Park Service soon followed Murie's visit with one by a team
that included Harold Bryant, head of the Branch of Research and Education,
and Thomas Vint. The Bryant committee recommended that a network of
trails be built in the interior of the island but that no roads be constructed
and no machines, including airplanes and motorboats, be allowed on the
island. Some development would, they conceded, be necessary on the lakeshore, but it should be designed to minimize impact. Albright's successor
as Park Service director, Arno Cammerer, consulted further with Murie, who
argued against even building trails in the interior. Cammerer then adopted
Murie's recommendations.

Trails would appear over time on interior ridges of Isle Royale, but these
would be informally beaten there by visitors. Civilian Conservation Corps
crews worked on the islands, but the Park Service generally followed Murie's
advice and kept development to a minimum, resisting constant pressure to
improve access and visitor accommodations. Isle Royale was among the earliest parks where the Park Service followed an overt policy of managing for
wilderness. John Little, in his history of the park, points out the difficulties
the agency faced. "Advancement within the Park Service seldom came," he
writes, "from watching nature take its course. Yet this is what Murie implied
when he recommended the Isle Royale leaders be judged by a different stan-

dard."[4] Staffing a park, and ordering that staff to leave it as it is, was something new. The small park staff at Isle Royale was engaged in managing for wilderness, practicing restraint of its development-oriented tendencies as no national park staff had before.

THE PARK SYSTEM EXPANDS

Thus the Park Service, in the early days of the Albright administration, was nudged slightly in the direction of wilderness preservation. It did not actively seek new roadless parks, but if that was congressional will, so be it. Albright was every bit as ambitious for the national park system as his mentor had been, and in general he carried on the successful expansionism of Mather. When he took charge there were twenty-one national parks and thirty-three national monuments under Park Service management. Visitation had climbed every year since the agency was created, and so had budgets. Albright intended to continue this growth, and he did. By the time he left in August 1933 he had seen enlargement of nine national parks, entrance into the system of three new parks (Grand Teton, Carlsbad Caverns, and Great Smoky Mountains), and several important new national monuments, including Badlands, Arches, and Death Valley. He had also broadened the mission and scope of the National Park Service and set it up to flourish during the extensive public works era of the New Deal.

Horace Albright was, from an early stage of his Park Service career, an exceptional political operator. His performance as acting director during Mather's illness had established his ability in this regard. When he took over for Mather in 1929 he knew personally no fewer than 155 members of the House of Representatives and 51 senators. He was on excellent terms with Michigan's Louis Cramton, chair of the House Subcommittee on Interior Department Appropriations, and was friendly with President Hoover's Interior secretaries, first Roy O. West and then Ray Lyman Wilbur. He used all of these contacts to good effect. Albright had long believed the National Park Service should administer and preserve sites of historic significance. From its beginning, the agency had sought to gain control over all national monuments, and it had taken steps in this direction with transfer of the Grand Canyon National Monument in 1919 and the incorporation of Bryce Canyon National Monument into Bryce Canyon National Park in 1928. Both transfers had been from national forests, contributing to the bad blood that boiled between the two agencies. Albright believed that his bureau was still too small for its survival to be assured and for it to be strong competition for the Forest Service in the struggle over the mandate to provide outdoor recreation services. Furthermore, while some parks had been authorized in the East, the Park Service domain was largely in the West. A way must be found to interest more of Congress in National Park Service issues by including eastern areas in the system. One way would be to make the Park Service custodian of the nation's historical heritage, as well as its natural heritage, and Albright set out to accomplish that goal.[5]

Since the 1890s the War Department had been preserving historic sites such as battlefields, forts, and memorials. The Park Service coveted these sites and argued for transfer to Interior, but skeptics in the War Department and Congress questioned whether an agency primarily involved in the management of natural parks could protect and interpret historic sites better than the military.[6] Albright launched his campaign to expand into historical site management by convincing Congress to establish three new historical parks in the East. He then convinced Franklin Roosevelt's Secretary of the Interior Harold Ickes to support the idea of the transfer.

Roosevelt ordered moved to jurisdiction of the Park Service national monuments previously administered by the Forest Service and War Department as well as battlefield parks and cemeteries and the public parks in Washington, DC. This constituted a huge expansion of the national park system and realization of a Park Service ambition. Hal Rothman summarized the importance of this expansion:

> This hard-won "inheritance" made the National Park Service an entity with a national constituency and multiple responsibilities. It also made the agency not only arbiters of the natural and prehistoric heritage of the nation, but the guardian of its federally preserved history as well.[7]

This action changed the nature of the national park system, much to the chagrin of conservation groups like the National Parks Association. The association was very concerned that Albright and the Park Service were moving away from their dedication to preservation of natural areas. They were, thought Robert Sterling Yard and others, diluting their effort, and the consequences would not be good for the long-established national parks in the West, or for wilderness.

At the same time as he achieved national scope and greater significance for the park system, Albright addressed the challenge of the ongoing conflict with the Forest Service. Roosevelt's executive order transferred the Olympic National Monument from the Forest Service to the Park Service, thus improving the likelihood of achieving a wild national park in the Olympics, though this was by no means clear at the time. The agencies had long been battling for control of this area. Speaking in 1939 to a national park conference convened by the American Planning and Civic Association (of which he was president at the time), Albright spoke of his motives in pushing reorganization:

> In 1931, we had to face the problem of what the National Park Service was to be in the future, for general governmental reorganization became a burning issue. Was our small bureau to be merged with the great Forest Service as an economy measure or as a step in moving the latter bureau to the Interior Department, a sort of sacrifice on the altar of executive department reconstruction?[8]

The Forest Service might reasonably claim that it could manage outdoor recreation or even conserve wilderness as well as the Park Service, but could its mission be stretched to include historical preservation and interpretation? By moving in this new direction Albright thought he could assure a role for the Park Service that was sufficiently unique to decrease any likelihood of the two agencies' merger or of any part of the Park Service mission being transferred to the competition. With persuasion and "vigorous action" Albright saw to it that his agency's position was strengthened in this reorganization, but that was not his only strategy for building the Park Service.

Seventeen days after his inauguration, President Roosevelt sent a message to Congress urging them to pass legislation to create a civilian conservation corps to provide employment for young men in forestry, prevention of soil erosion, and other conservation work on public land. Ten days later Congress did as asked, passing the Emergency Conservation Act and giving the president authority to set up the Civilian Conservation Corps (CCC). Even before Congress acted, Albright saw the opportunity this new program provided the Park Service—an infusion of funds for projects never before possible—and he instructed his people to identify work the CCC could do in the parks. The CCC was set up with a director and an advisory council representing the Departments of Agriculture, Labor, War, and Interior. Ickes appointed Albright to represent Interior on the council. Albright was well positioned to make the most of the opportunities for the Park Service that might come from the CCC, and he did.

Also in 1933, President Roosevelt asked Harold Ickes to administer the Public Works Administration (PWA), a public works program set up by Hoover in 1931. Ickes needed good projects that were well planned and ready to be constructed. The Park Service had been developing master plans for several years and had just what Ickes needed. In its first year under Ickes, the PWA funded over 150 projects in the national parks. Almost overnight the Park Service expanded dramatically. An army of young men went into the parks and started building roads, trails, campgrounds, fire lookouts, and other facilities. Money flowed in from the PWA to fund projects park managers had only dreamed of for years. Yet Albright went even further. The CCC would work in state as well as national parks, and the Park Service would administer a state parks assistance program focused on recreation.

This expansion and diversification of the Park Service's domain affected the course of its struggle with the wilderness idea. One effect was that the tremendous infusion of money and manpower into the parks meant that development could proceed as never before. During its nine years of work, the CCC built more infrastructure in the parks than in the entire history of national parks to that time. This posed a threat to wilderness that was not lost on purists and other critics of the Park Service. Rosalie Edge, leader and prolific pamphleteer of the Emergency Conservation Committee, a small and aggressive conservation group, circulated a pamphlet critical of CCC road building. While conceding that national parks must have roads, she asked, "Can anyone suppose that a wilderness and a CCC camp can exist side by side? And can a wilderness contain a highway?" Most of the parks in 1936 were already, in her opinion, crowded and overdeveloped, but "some primitive areas . . . still exist in almost all the parks. These should be guarded as the nation's greatest treasure; and no roads should be permitted to deface their beauty."[9] Edge's view was shared by the Sierra Club, the Mountaineers, the National Parks Association, and other conservation groups.

Even some Park Service insiders recognized that accelerated development was a threat to park wilderness and the park experience. John Roberts White, the long-serving and respected superintendent of Sequoia National Park, spoke on wilderness policy to the 1936 American Planning and Civic Association national park conference. As had Leopold, Edge, and others before him, White stated that roads and associated developments were a threat to park wilderness. With increased resources the Park Service should remain vigilant in its mission of preservation.

> We have had to handle the increasing flood of motor visitors in some cases before we had funds, and while we were training personnel, to plan development and protect the wilderness values entrusted to our care. Under such pressure it is conceivable that we have made mistakes. But we have preserved the vastly greater part of our scenic and wilderness inheritance in the national parks; and we are now in many cases able to undo the mistakes of the too hurried past.[10]

White was a veteran superintendent who understood that preservation might in some places be a casualty of his agency's new riches and opportunities.

Albright left the National Park Service in 1933, and Arno Cammerer presided over the "boom" in development that Albright had engineered. In a talk to the same American Planning and Civic Association national park conference in January 1936 at which White spoke on wilderness policy, Cammerer assured his listeners that wilderness had not been a casualty of three years of CCC projects. Many good works had been achieved, he claimed, but he too admitted that there "has also been the danger of overdevelopment . . . where the wilderness is involved, and we took special precautions to avoid that." He added, "We do not want primeval areas modified. . . . A wilderness cannot be 'improved,' because its unimproved state is what we are trying to preserve."[11] He did not specify how the Park Service had avoided overdevelopment of wilderness, and some, like Edge and Yard, might challenge the veracity of his claim. The fact that he felt the need to offer these reassurances at this prestigious meeting indicates that concerns about wilderness development were being taken seriously. Superintendent White's words and works in Sequoia were even stronger testimony that at least some in the National Park Service were aware of the threats to wilderness coming from accelerated development.

Another wilderness-related concern was expressed by those who felt that the nature of the national park system had been changed by inclusion of the many new kinds of units, such as the historical sites, that Roosevelt had transferred in 1933. Foremost among the critics of this change was the National Parks Association (NPA). When Roosevelt's reorganization order went out in 1933, the NPA had little to say about it, but three years later the *National Parks Bulletin* featured a discussion of reorganization under the heading, "Losing Our Primeval System in Vast Expansion." For a decade the association had repeatedly expressed its view that there should be a single standard for selection of national parks. That standard should be that national parks would be unmodified and natural, the finest examples of scenery, of national significance, and delineated so that they could be managed for traditional national park values. The NPA's concern about standards had led it to raise many questions, from the advisability of including areas like Shenandoah in the system to a continuing fight against the substandard park proposals that had emerged in Congress in the late 1920s and early 1930s. While the Park Service was also concerned about standards, it took a more pragmatic and inclusive approach, less pure than the NPA.

The association was not opposed to moving historical areas under the jurisdiction of the Park Service but argued that if this were done, the historic areas should be designated as a system separate from national parks. It proposed that they be called national historical sites rather than parks. Parks should be natural rather than cultural areas. As the national park system expanded during the 1930s and other types of sites came into the system, the NPA continued to express its concerns. A 1936 Bulletin article stated that the main interest of the NPA "will continue to be that of the last seventeen years, namely, the development, beneficent use and protection of the great standard National Parks System as a unique expression of primeval nature in supreme beauty." The system's identity was, in the NPA's view, in danger of being lost if it were not lost already.[12]

All of this led the NPA to propose that a separate system for the "real" national parks be designated, which they proposed be called "National Primeval Parks." These would be "those national parks which, by reason of possessing primeval wilderness of conspicuous importance and supreme scenic beauty, conform to the standards originally recognized under the title of National Parks."[13] Parks such as Yellowstone, Sequoia, Mount Rainier, Glacier, Rocky Mountain, and Grand Canyon should be part of this system. The rationale for such a system was that management of primeval parks required special training, skills, and administrators "imbued with National Primeval Park ideals," according to the NPA. The way things were going, specialized management of the parts of a diverse system would be necessary, and one of the specialties would be wilderness (or as the NPA preferred, "primeval") management. The NPA would campaign into the early 1940s for this special designation, which would not, for reasons to be explained later, come to anything.[14]

The National Parks Association's concerns indicate how the issue of defining the national park system and its purpose continued from the 1920s to the 1930s and how wilderness played a role in the engagement of that issue. People inside and outside the Park Service continued to ask what the management implications of "unimpaired" should be. The development of parks, justifiably pursued by Mather when access to parks really was difficult, became a different issue in the 1930s as vast sums of money were poured into park projects. Many of these projects could not be justified in the same way as those that earlier "opened" the people's parks for access in the 1920s. A small but determined group of wilderness preservationists critiqued the Park Service for using the opportunities presented to it by the New Deal work relief programs to move in new directions. These new initiatives were, in their opinion, away from its core mission of preserving wild nature.

WILDERNESS NOT DEVELOPED IS WILDERNESS PROTECTED

Other organizational and policy changes during the Albright administration bear on the situation of wilderness and deserve mention. These include wildlife policy and planning. Horace Albright had issued assurances in a 1928 *Saturday Evening Post* article that national park wilderness was being protected. Roads and other developments at Mount Rainier and other parks cast doubt on those reassurances. As Richard Sellars explains in his detailed treatment of national park wildlife policy, in the 1930s the Park Service's own wildlife biologists, few though they were, strongly disagreed with Albright's view on protection. Albright took the position that if large parts of the parks were not penetrated by roads and associated development, the "everlasting wilderness" was protected. Scientists like Ben Thompson countered that, though roads might be absent, the wilderness was nonetheless modified. Species had been removed entirely from some parks. At Grand Canyon, feral burros ran everywhere. Yosemite National Park had lost its bighorn sheep and grizzlies and had created a black bear problem well documented by Joseph Grinnell and his students. From an ecological perspective, which scientists like E. Lowell Sumner Jr., another Park Service wildlife biologist, and Thompson were developing, the parks were not "unimpaired." Sellars summarized the contrasting views of Albright and the scientists:

> Thompson's views of park conditions were in striking contrast to Albright's depiction of the parks as "preserved forever in their natural state." Albright's ideas arose from essentially romantic perceptions of the majestic landscapes, equating the

parks' undeveloped and unoccupied lands with unimpaired conditions—a perception almost certainly shared by Park Service officials and by the public.[15]

In Sellars's words, scientists became a minority "opposition party" within the Park Service throughout the 1930s, studying wildlife and documenting loss of species in some parks and threatened species in others. They described habitat destruction and ways that natural environments had been altered by predator control, fire suppression, grazing, and recreational use. The publication in 1933 of *Fauna of the National Parks of the United States: A Preliminary Survey of Faunal Relations in National Parks* (hereafter *Fauna No. 1*) was an important step. The study, conducted by three Park Service biologists, defined "unimpaired" in essentially ecological terms and "marked a revolutionary change in the understanding of national parks by Service professionals."[16] While it offered a revolution in understanding, *Fauna No. 1* did not initiate a revolution in management. Significant impact of this ecological perspective on park management would only come decades later.

Emergence of this ecological perspective added another dimension to the wilderness idea as it appeared in discussions of national parks, which took the form of a critique of national park "wilderness" policy from within the Park Service. Awareness was growing that, while Park Service policy was protecting scenery and the conception of wilderness as a place where visitors could remove themselves from the works of human society, it was not protecting the natural state of affairs. The critique cast doubt on the idea that parks could protect nature from change, and especially on the idea that mandates for development and wilderness preservation could both be served on nearly all lands inside park boundaries. Neither Park Service managers nor their preservationist critics in organizations like the National Parks Association seem to have understood this message that the scientists were conveying. They continued to hold "romantic perceptions" of parks as places that could be "preserved forever in their natural state," as Albright expressed the goal. They did not understand, or would not accept, the perspectives that were coming from scientists at this time.

As for planning, since the mid-1920s Albright had been advocating the use of comprehensive or master planning for national parks. At the 1925 superintendent's conference at Santa Fe, he and Assistant Director Cammerer had suggested that master planning should begin. The process of master planning, increasingly in vogue with city and regional planners, should, they argued, involve building comprehensive plans for park resource development

4.1 The National Park Service Wildlife Survey Team, George M. Wright, Ben H. Thompson, and Joseph S. Dixon, at Mono Lake, California, July 24, 1929. National Park Service photo, collection of Pamela Wright Lloyd and Jerry Emory

and protection. The emphasis of such planning should be on what was to be developed, where the roads would go, and where facilities would be built. "Zoning" of parks would be involved, and in this way wilderness would figure into the process.[17] In the years that followed, associate landscape engineer Thomas Vint moved to implement this approach. As mentioned in the previous chapter, Vint became involved in a discussion of wilderness at Mount Rainer. He and superintendent Tomlinson advocated a wilderness zone at the park, which resulted in a northern portion being designated as roadless but not as wilderness. Vint supervised a master plan for Mount Rainier that was completed in 1931. This was the first such plan for a national park, and in the text of the plan the park was divided into land-use zones called "wilderness," "research," "sacred," and "developed." This terminology was controversial and carried no official imprimatur—it was very much under discussion—but was being applied in planning efforts across the national park system. "Research area" was, as at Yosemite, a part of the park that would exclude humans. It was for scientific research and was to be kept completely undisturbed. Areas in the parks that had been developed but needed total protection from further development that might mar their nature or attractiveness were the "sacred" areas. These were limited areas around major attractions like Old Faithful that were closed to construction and access. "Wilderness," then, became "the rest of the park" that was not developed or designated in the other two categories. Humans could enter the wilderness and trails would be built there, but other "nonconforming uses" such as roads for tourists were not allowed.

Ethan Carr has pointed out that since 1926 Vint and Tomlinson had been trying to designate parts of Mount Rainier National Park as wilderness in order to control road development. "The master plan strengthened this tactic; with a regional zoning plan in place that designated wilderness as a land use, road construction or other uses that constituted essentially a zoning variance could be rejected on that basis."[18] Master planning as demonstrated in the Mount Rainier plan was a way to consider the wilderness issue in each park. Carr observes that it is difficult to assess how much effect a designation like that at Mount Rainier had on everyday park management, but it did force managers to at least think more carefully about wilderness values. Reflecting in 1938 on the beginning of master planning, Vint remarked that "the subject that received the most attention was that of the wilderness area." He and his colleagues struggled to define wilderness and determine what areas should qualify to be so designated. They had so much difficulty that by 1938 Vint was thinking that the concept of *discrete* wilderness areas was not useful.

> In the long run, I feel that we shall have to give up the idea, as it was first proposed, and rather than approach the problem from the angle of setting aside wilderness areas within the national parks, we must approach it from the other direction—that is, we must restrict the limits of developed areas and apply the protection that would be given to the wilderness area to *all* of the area within the boundaries of the park that is not a developed area.[19]

This comment is significant in several ways. Despite Director Albright's reassurances, it confirms that planners had, in this first national park master planning cycle, been trying to figure out how to address concerns of wilderness preservationists that national parks were not adequately protecting wild qualities of park landscapes. Vint went to Webster's dictionary for his definition of wilderness and found the trouble in the part of the definition that describes it as "a wild; waste; hence, a pathless waste of any kind." The "pathless" quality gave him the most trouble. If that were accepted, then "the development

4.2 Tom Vint, second from left, and other Park Service landscape architects and master planners in 1934. National Park Service Historic Photographic Collection, Harpers Ferry Center

plan could be limited to the construction of an effective barrier around the boundary. The administration would not need to go beyond an adequate control to prevent trespass."[20] This was not acceptable because of the "for the benefit and enjoyment of the people" part of the Park Service mandate. What should be done? Vint's answer was to determine how many people would be allowed into the parks, ascertain what they would do there, and plan development for that. The rest of the park would be managed as wilderness, though what such management would involve, aside from not "developing," was not specified. Ethan Carr says of Vint's conclusion, "Whether this is seen as the triumph or the defeat of 'wilderness' designation within national parks, it essentially describes how the word has been used in the context of park planning since that point."[21] Master planning was about what and where development would occur in parks. It could not embrace "planning" for not doing anything, as would be the case in designating wilderness. Thus, in the 1930s, wilderness became an issue in the emerging art of national park planning, but the planners seem to have concluded that Albright was right after all: wilderness not developed was wilderness protected. No specific designation was necessary.

Vint's conclusion marks a significant milestone in the park wilderness story. The Park Service took a different path than the Forest Service, and this would be important later. The Forest Service adopted regulations that appeared to commit it to designation of protected areas. It drew boundaries around these areas. When it lagged in pursuing its avowed commitment, conservationists mounted a campaign to force the issue, which led to the Wilderness Act. At the same time, the Park Service refused to designate protected areas, claimed to be protecting everything not yet developed, and this policy stance, seen as an evasion by conservationists, added to the growing conservationist conviction that another approach to assuring wilderness protection would be necessary. Both agencies, in different ways, thus contributed to the emergence of the view that legislation for wilderness was necessary.

MORE CONFLICT WITH THE FOREST SERVICE

The Forest Service, meanwhile, continued to engage in its own internal struggle about wilderness, constantly aware that under Albright the Park Service was continuing to grow and strengthen itself. The conflict between the agencies in the 1920s over who should manage wild and beautiful lands in the West continued after Mather and Greeley left the scene. The struggle was engaged at many levels: between the strategists in the Washington offices who were always tuned in to the political fine points, between men in the field who were engaged in struggles over specific places, and even at the highest level of national politics, where a long struggle over government reorganization featured skirmishes between FDR's Interior and Agriculture secretaries. Wilderness was part of the conflict.

As the 1920s drew to a close, conservationists could compare the Park Service and Forest Service stances on wilderness. On the one hand, the Park Service could not bring itself to use the term "wilderness" and, for that matter, neither could the Forest Service. The latter had gained some ground in the interagency competition by generating enthusiasm for its primitive area idea, even though its rank and file was not supportive of it. Leon Kneipp, as an assistant to the chief, remained a strong advocate of primitive areas. At the close of the decade the Forest Service, with its designation of "primitive" areas, seemed to be winning the wilderness public relations battle.

The Park Service continued to covet portions of the national forests. The

National Conference on Outdoor Recreation recommendations had solved few problems between the two agencies, and in 1930 Chief Forester Roy Stuart wrote to Albright complaining that pending proposals for boundary changes between national parks and forests were a problem. Procedures were not adequate, citizens who might be affected by changes were not as involved as they should be, and the economic and industrial aspects of the proposals were not being given enough attention. Stuart seemed to be asking for a respite from the proposals, and Albright replied that he would respond to concerns about the standards and objectives of specific boundary changes being sought. When he finally sent Stuart his detailed response several months later, it described eleven expansion projects, all of which would come at the expense of surrounding national forests. He put Stuart on notice that the Park Service would not relent. The exchange ended in March 1932 with Stuart laying out the Forest Service's arguments against each of Albright's proposals. He had not achieved his desired respite.[22]

The Forest Service moved ahead with designating primitive areas, some of them including areas being considered for national parks or additions to national parks. Stuart continued Greeley's approach of using administrative wilderness designations in an attempt to foil national park expansion. Internally the argument among foresters over the role of outdoor recreation in Forest Service management continued, as did debate over the advisability of establishing primitive areas. In the spring of 1932 Stuart called a meeting of senior staff to discuss the primitive area issue. James Gilligan summarizes the arguments for and against primitive areas offered at this meeting: the leading argument for primitive areas was that "they act as a resistance to Park Service expansion." The leading argument against was that primitive areas "are areas which the Park Service can readily claim more suitable to their administration."[23] By 1933 sixty-three primitive areas had been approved and included nearly 8.5 million acres. However, no logging was planned in only eight of the areas, and timber harvest proposals had been drawn up for twenty-three areas. All but ten primitive areas allowed grazing. Some primitive areas were already being modified, Aldo Leopold's original Gila Wilderness among them. The Forest Service continued to try to foil Park Service expansion by appearing to protect wilderness, though scrutiny of primitive area plans raised serious doubt among conservationists about the Forest Service's commitment to protection.

Horace Albright left the Park Service in August 1933, and Chief Stuart died in October. In 1933 Bob Marshall began to exert considerable influence on the debate about wilderness. He was retained by the Forest Service to write the forest recreation chapters in the first comprehensive survey made of the forestry situation in the United States. The report, A National Plan for American Forestry, was referred to as the Copeland Report, since Senator Royal Copeland in 1932 had introduced in Congress a resolution to establish the survey.

Marshall's recommendations in the Copeland Report for a system of national forest recreation areas that included extensive protected areas received a cool reception from many in the Forest Service. The recommendations were considered extreme by many foresters, and at this point Marshall was not even in the Forest Service; he was director of the Indian Forest Service in the Department of the Interior, Harold Ickes's department. When Marshall realized that the Forest Service was bent on building roads into his proposed wilderness areas using funds provided by the Public Works Administration, of which Ickes was administrator, he asked the secretary to withhold funds for road building in primitive areas pending further study. This got the Forest Service's attention, and in 1934 Chief Forester Ferdinand Silcox suggested to regional foresters that they pay more attention to their primitive areas. He was worried that if they did not take better care of the primitive areas, Ickes and the National Park Service might get them. He wrote that "the Forest Service cannot ignore this sentiment [for primitive areas]. . . . If the Forest Service cannot fully realize the potentialities of the areas it will have little valid grounds for objection to a change in their administrative supervisor."[24] Despite Silcox's urging, the Forest Service resisted Marshall's ideas. Even Silcox wrote in 1935 that "I do not believe our present policy will satisfy the extremists, and on the other hand I do not think it is a wise policy to lock up large areas solely for primitive type recreation."[25] In May 1936 Silcox brought Marshall into the Forest Service as chief of the Division of Recreation and Lands.

Bringing him into the organization did not stop Marshall's criticism of what he saw as lack of commitment by the Forest Service to wilderness preservation. He, Yard, and others had formed The Wilderness Society in 1935, and it continually stepped up the pressure for wilderness preservation, as did the Sierra Club and other conservation groups. Marshall wrote in 1937 to William P. Wharton, president of the National Parks Association, that "personally, I have long criticized the present Forest Service standards for primitive and natural areas. They are so broad as to not be very significant."[26] In his detailed analysis of Forest Service wilderness policy, James Gilligan concluded that the tireless work of Marshall, the vocal pro-wilderness sentiment of conservation groups, and pressure from the Park Service and others driving for new national parks in national forest roadless areas (such as in the Olympics and Kings Canyon) led Forest Service leaders in the late 1930s to take wilderness preservation more seriously. Saying they would protect wilderness, while moving forward with development plans, would no longer fool anyone. Still, the agency did not move far or fast enough to satisfy Marshall, who remarked in 1939 that he was "going to resign from the Forest Service and devote his full time to promoting and organizing public support for wilderness preservation."[27] Unfortunately, Bob Marshall did not live to enjoy the fruits of his labor, dying unexpectedly in 1939.

While he had an uphill fight within the Forest Service to gain acceptance of his ideas, Marshall's work directly helped the agency in its struggles against national park system expansion. Many foresters thought "locking up" land to protect its wilderness values was a waste of essential resources, yet they understood that if the land was added to a national park or became a new park, its timber and other resources would truly be lost to production. Even if designated a primitive area, national forest land could, if necessary, be entered for production of commodities. National parkland could not. As James Gilligan observed:

> Some supervisors were as keenly aware that their particular forest contained scenery equal or superior to that in national parks as they were convinced that national forest lands would be needed in the not too distant future for their economic products. Such forest regions as the Uncompahgre Mountains in Colorado, the Mission Mountains in Montana, and the Sawtooths of Idaho (which compare very favorably to the nationally known Tetons of Wyoming) and probably many more were recommended [as primitive areas] because of their park potentiality.[28]

Ultimately the Forest Service rejected suggestions in the late 1930s that it give legal status to protection of even the most beautiful areas such as those mentioned above. It argued that demands upon the land were difficult to predict, and legally protected wilderness would interfere with the agency's efforts to meet the changing needs of the nation. Foresters genuinely believed in their utilitarian mission. Though a forester, Marshall joined the lineage of Muir and Leopold in his deep-seated belief in the critical importance of protecting remnants of wilderness on the public lands.

Despite its struggles over its wilderness policy, the Forest Service remained a worthy rival and threat to the National Park Service. The buildup of the national forest primitive area system was both a response to and a stimulus for a growing public interest in wilderness in the 1930s. Preservationists like Robert Sterling Yard had long thought that their best and perhaps only hope for wilderness protection lay with national parks. As Leopold, Leon Kneipp, and Bob Marshall pressed the Forest Service to accept preservation and wilderness recreation as the "highest use" of some national forest areas, the primitive area system grew and support from some conservationists drifted from national parks to national forests. In California, for instance, the Sierra Club was dismayed by what it saw as Park Service–inspired desecration of Yosemite Valley. It believed the Forest Service might do a better job protecting the wilderness of the Kings Canyon country than the Park Service as led by the likes of Stephen Mather and Horace Albright. Such shifts of allegiance brought pressure on the National Park Service because it could not afford to lose its base of support among conservationists. It needed them in its effort to achieve new parks and additions to existing parks. The Park Service did not think it needed to designate wilderness to achieve protection, but it was paying increasing attention to wilderness. The remarks of Director Cammerer, John R. White, and others at successive American Planning and Civic Association national park conferences in the 1930s indicate that the Park Service understood the challenge posed to it by the growing Forest Service primitive area program.

That Forest Service program was openly denounced by Cammerer at an American Planning and Civic Association conference in 1936.

The primitive and recreational areas within national forests do not exclude uses which tend to modify them and are destructive of their primeval character. That is, grazing, hunting, and mining are permitted, and logging and power developments will be permitted if and when they are economically feasible. These are the compensations which are given for maintaining certain wilderness aspects of such areas. Such practices are not permitted in parks, except in the few instances in which Congress, as the final authority, has so ruled, or in which we have not yet been able entirely to eliminate them. Those few cases stand as exceptions only. It is evident, then, that such terms as "wilderness," "primitive," and "primeval" do have an entirely different meaning as applied to parks than they have in any other form of Federal land classification.[29]

Cammerer left no doubt that in his view real protection of wilderness would be provided only in national parks, whatever the Forest Service might decide to call its "wilderness" areas.

The Park Service proclaimed itself to be the premier wilderness protector. Writing in 1938 in *Appalachia*, the journal of the Appalachian Mountain Club, Cammerer simply stated that "our national parks are wilderness preserves where true natural conditions are to be found." He concluded the article with an assurance and an exhortation:

> Because of specified duties which bring protection to all features, the National Parks are in a most favored position to provide truly primeval areas suitable for the highest scientific and educational use and such recreational use as may be consistent thereto. . . . For those who seek a primeval environment, just try the National Parks! For those who seek a maximum protection for a primeval area of natural importance, let them investigate the administration afforded such areas by the National Park Service, the Government bureau designated to "retain areas in their natural condition."[30]

Cammerer does not mention the Forest Service or national forests, but there is no doubt he is saying, "We protect the primeval [code word: wilderness] better than they do." At his political level he was feeling a need to espouse wilderness preservation as a priority of the Park Service. This undoubtedly was motivated by the pressure he was feeling to counteract the Forest Service's primitive area program. The interagency rivalry thus pushed the Park Service to be more vocal about its preservation mission and to couch that mission in terms of the wilderness preservation movement under way at the time.

The 1930s were thus a period of challenge and opportunity for the Park Service on many fronts, wilderness among them. On the recreation scene, bolstered by Civilian Conservation Corps manpower and money, the Park Service was administering an ever-growing recreation enterprise. While Secretary Ickes did not consider Cammerer an effective administrator, he continued to favor national parks, the Park Service, and wilderness. For a time, the Park Service seemed to embrace an "expand at all cost" stance—that, at least, is how the wilderness purists saw it. Cammerer told the American Planning and Civic Association in January 1938 that he thought the old national park standards emphasizing the primeval were outmoded. Albright, as president of the association, told the same conference that it was necessary to lower standards in order to expand the system. Both men were responding to positions taken by Yard and others that, for instance, Jackson Hole should not be added to Grand Teton National Park because it had a reservoir in it or that a new Kings Canyon National Park should be opposed because it would include valleys that might later be developed for water and power. Cammerer and Albright, as well as the Sierra Club, thought that an imperfect park was better than no park at all. The Park Service stated publicly that it could do better than its principal rival in the wilderness protection game, laying claim to outdoor recreation and wilderness, but it struggled, as did its rival, with the challenges of defining and implementing a wilderness policy that went beyond rhetoric to real protection.

5 MORE FERMENT AND EXPANSION

The decade of the 1920s proved a time when an upstart National Park Service firmly established itself as a player in the public lands management game. It expanded slowly, all the while battling with the rival Forest Service for the lead role in providing outdoor recreation services to the American people. Stephen Mather proved an astute leader and politician, supported and then succeeded by an equally wily and effective Horace Albright. The idea of wilderness grew in importance as the Park Service and the Forest Service jockeyed for position, each claiming wilderness preservation as its province, yet neither quite deciding how it could and should go about that task. Debate over what should be the primary mission of the Park Service—provision of recreation or preservation of heritage—continued, fueled by outside voices such as that of the National Parks Association. As the "roaring twenties" came to a close, expansion of the national park system went on, and the issues of the 1920s continued to occupy national park interests both inside and outside the government.

THE DRIVE FOR "WILDERNESS" PARKS

A major battleground over wilderness between the Park Service and Forest Service at this time involved proposals for more new parks. The Park Service had achieved partial victory at the Grand Tetons in 1929. Struggles between the agencies over park proposals for the Olympic Mountains of Washington, the Sawtooth Mountains of Idaho, Kings Canyon in the southern Sierra Nevada, and other areas continued and, in the 1930s, increased in intensity. A central issue in all these cases was wilderness and who could and should manage it.

Before describing the two principal new park initiatives from the national park wilderness perspective—Olympic and Kings Canyon—authorization of two other parks deserves mention. John Ise, in his history of national park policy, concluded that all new parks added in the Cammerer administration were wilderness parks. The first of these was Everglades. Ise's analysis did not suggest that the wilderness emphasis of new park proposals in the 1930s was a consequence of changes in Park Service policy. He thought it came from the nature of the landscapes involved and from forces outside the Park Service. In Ise's view, "There is no clear line dividing wilderness parks from others; it is always 'more or less.'"[1] Albright had contended that since only a small portion of national parks was developed, all the nature parks were wilderness parks. In the proposed new parks the land was wild, with few roads, and the Park Service decided to keep it mostly that way, motivated in part by Secretary Ickes's conviction that this was how the national parks should be. As repeated pronouncements by Cammerer and others suggested, the Park Service was feeling the pressure to keep parks wild, a pressure that came from growing preservation activism on the part of the Emergency Conservation Committee, the National Parks Association, the Sierra Club, and The Wilderness Society. Park Service spokesmen claimed they could protect wilderness better than the Forest Service and felt compelled to prove this assertion. Voices inside the Park Service were raised in support of keeping the parks as roadless as possible. Last but not least, the development-oriented initiatives of Mather and Albright and the infusion of money and manpower from New Deal programs had achieved accessibility to the parks. The park constituency had grown, the agency was more secure, and the argument that roads in parks were necessary to achieve those goals was not as persuasive as it had been earlier. Ise was correct in his assertion that landscape and outside forces were at work to increase the wilderness emphasis in the push for new parks, but that was not the whole story. Internal Park Service change and debate were also present and would contribute to a shift in policy regarding park wilderness.

Everglades National Park was the first of two national parks authorized in the mid-1930s that would be established when the land for them was acquired and transferred to the federal government. Concern for the fate of birds and wetlands in South Florida, an area long besieged by commercial hunting, drainage, and development, had generated interest in a national park there as early as 1920. In 1930 Interior Secretary Ray Lyman Wilbur appointed a committee that included Horace Albright and Arno Cammerer to study the national park potential of the Everglades. They reported that the area of concern was of national park quality and recommended that a park be established to preserve the wildlife and primitive character of the region. Legislation was introduced and, in the give and take over proposals, new Park Service director Cammerer agreed to an amendment to a 1934 bill that the park should always remain a wilderness. Debate over the Everglades bill included the argument in its favor that as a wilderness park it would not cost much. Keeping the park in a primeval condition, argued its supporters, was sensible because of the obstacles to development inherent in park terrain. And, since wildlife preservation was a major reason for the park, modification of habitat would be counter to the very purpose for which the park was being established.

The National Parks Association, generally skeptical of new park proposals at this time and opposed to most of them, appointed trustees Frederick Law Olmsted Jr. and William P. Wharton to study the Everglades. They examined the site of the park proposal and reported positively on it. As Alfred Runte has pointed out, their report was notable because it made the case that, while the proposed park did not offer the sort of scenery traditionally associated with national parks, it offered other qualities. They noted that while "the quality of the scenery is to the casual observer somewhat confused and monotonous," the beauty of "the great flocks of birds . . . the thousands upon thousands of ibis and herons flocking in at sunset" could be "no less memorable than the impressions derived from the great mountain and canyon parks of the West."[2] The other quality was wilderness. In the Everglades, the visitor would find a "sense of remoteness" and "pristine wilderness." They found there a mangrove forest "not only uninhabited and unmodified by man, but literally trackless and uninhabitable."[3] The National Parks Association, self-appointed keeper of national park standards, could support the park proposal if it were conceived as a wilderness park.

The NPA and other park proponents insisted that the enabling act for Everglades stipulate that its wilderness would be preserved. Cammerer and Ickes were willing to go along, and on May 30, 1934, the Everglades National Park Act, amended to include a mandate for a more complete conservation than stipulated in other congressional national park legislation to that time, was approved by Congress. Section 4 of the enabling act began: "The said area or areas shall be permanently reserved as a wilderness." No development of the park must "interfere with the preservation intact of the unique flora and fauna and the essential primitive conditions" of the park.[4] The legislation provided for a park of 1,280,000 acres. Consistent with the approach Congress had used with Shenandoah, Great Smoky Mountains, and Isle Royale parks, land for the park was to be acquired and presented to the federal estate by the state of Florida. After a prolonged and difficult land acquisition process, this was accomplished and the park was finally achieved in 1947.

Everglades was established as a wilderness park because its advocates insisted that it be so. The Park Service went along. Commenting on opposition to specific bills for the Everglades park by groups like the NPA, Arno Cammerer said in 1934 that "such opposition as has been evidenced among organizations to the Everglades Bill has been directed to the form of the bill and not to the project, and solely to the alleged insufficiency that the future wilderness character of the areas was not fully provided for."[5] Cammerer shared the Mather-Albright view that the Organic Act provided sufficient direction for preservation. He would not press for a more protective mandate, but if that was helpful to passage of legislation for a park the service wanted, he had no objections to specifying that it be a wilderness park. Thus was another nudge given the Park Service toward overt and declared wilderness preservation. The Everglades enabling act language was, of course, open to interpretation, but its specific mention of wilderness brought the concept more to the foreground. It would influence decisions regarding what should or should not be done to manage the new park.

The next park authorized continued this trend toward stipulating wilderness quality for new parks. Big Bend National Park was authorized by Congress in 1935 and established in 1944 when land was acquired by Texas and deeded to the federal government. While it did not break new ground on wilderness as Everglades had, it reaffirmed the wilderness orientation in the establishment of new parks. The National Park Service decided when the park was established to keep most of it as wilderness, taking steps toward recognizing wilderness quality as a resource to be actively, rather than passively, managed and protected. Thus a big natural area like that of the Big Bend of the Rio Grande would be dedicated primarily to preservation rather than recreation. In no small part, as Ise noted, the landscape made this possible because, unlike some other potential park landscapes, the forbidding, inhospitable, but gorgeous area with its unique natural history was not in high demand as a recreational resource at this time and was largely wild. Keeping it wild would not be as difficult or controversial as doing so in some other places.

THE PARK SERVICE WINS IN THE OLYMPICS

Storms parading onshore off the North Pacific make the Olympic Peninsula a unique place, a land of rocky glacier-clad mountains, deep forested valleys, numerous lakes, and the most spectacular temperate rainforest in the world. Its giant trees have always been one of its great attractions, both to those who would admire some of nature's largest plants and to those who saw great fortunes to be made by cutting them down. The peninsula offered inaccessible if relatively low-elevation mountains and abundant herds of elk, among other wildlife. The resource wealth of the area was recognized early, but settlement of this very wet and stormy area was slow. It was still largely a wilderness when, in 1897, it became a forest reserve administered by the Department of the Interior and then later by the Department of Agriculture's Forest Service. In 1909 President Theodore Roosevelt proclaimed a national monument there, which would continue to be administered by the Forest Service. Elk herds were being rapidly depleted by hunters seeking trophies and elk teeth popular with the Fraternal Order of the Elks. Roosevelt exercised the power granted him under the Antiquities Act to protect the elk.

The first national park proposal for the area, Elk National Park, was introduced in 1904, followed by similar bills in 1906 and 1908. Proponents wanted to protect the elk and huge trees—some of the largest specimens of several species of trees were to be found on the peninsula. Proclamation of the monument slowed the drive for a park, though the idea was still discussed, especially when President Woodrow Wilson, responding to pressure from timber interests, reduced the monument by half in 1915. The Forest Service administered what remained of the monument until 1933, when Franklin Roosevelt's transfer order put the Park Service in charge. The monument was mostly rock and ice surrounded by rich Forest Service–administered forests, and the elk continued to suffer. Even if the monument had protected them from hunting, which under Forest Service management it had not, there was insufficient habitat to sustain the elk herd. They were forced down into the national forest and private land, where hunters exacted a damaging toll on them.

In 1928 Madison Grant, president of the New York Zoological Society and very concerned about the elk, suggested to Stephen Mather that he should move aggressively for a park in the Olympic Mountains because the Forest

Service intended to log the rainforest. According to Grant, "The forests there are magnificent and the Forest Service is considering cutting the trees down in the immediate future."[6] Grant was especially concerned about roads penetrating the still roadless core of the peninsula. The Forest Service assured him that they were planning proper development of the recreation resources there and intended that no roads be built into the higher mountains. Yet Grant knew even as he was issued these assurances that timber management plans were on the books that would require roads, even into the national monument. Mather, however, was not interested in the Olympics as a national park, commenting quite often throughout his tenure as director that he thought the forests and glaciated mountains of the Pacific Northwest were adequately represented in the national park system at Mount Rainier. Proposed new parks at Mount Baker or in the Olympics, while they would be nice, were not a priority for him.

Forest Service officials, especially in the Pacific Northwest, were outraged when President Roosevelt issued Executive Order 6166 in 1933 transferring Mount Olympus National Monument to the Park Service. Some wanted to complain to Congress or the president, but the politics of the moment discouraged a strong public response. The Forest Service needed public works funds, which were under the control of Secretary Ickes as administrator of the Public Works Administration, so officials toned down their public response. The Forest Service had, in 1927, designated a Snow Peaks Recreation Area of 316,960 acres in the Olympics that would be managed to maximize recreational potential with summer homes, hotels, and resorts. In 1930 they created an Olympic Primitive Area of 134,240 acres adjacent to the recreation area that they hoped would slow or stop the prospect of a national park in the region.

These Forest Service administrative actions were not enough for conservationists, especially for the small but active and influential Emergency Conservation Committee. In 1928 Willard Van Name, director of the American Museum of Natural History in New York, published a book titled *Vanishing Forest Reserves* in which he cast convincing doubt on whether the Forest Service truly meant to conserve any forests with what, in his view, were deceptive ploys like the primitive area program. Van Name, indefatigable activist Rosalie Edge, and Irving Brant, an influential journalist soon to be a special assistant to Secretary Ickes, were the core of the Emergency Conservation Committee, which in 1934 launched a campaign for a national park in the Olympic Mountains.

A national park bill was again introduced in Congress in 1935, and from the beginning of the debate wilderness was a central issue. The question was whether the Forest Service or the Park Service would most completely protect the area. In 1936 Robert Sterling Yard, acting as secretary of the newly established Wilderness Society, queried both the Forest Service and the Park Service about their plans for wilderness in the Olympics. The Forest Service responded that it would enlarge the national monument but would build two roads, one across the mountains. The Park Service assured Yard it would protect the wilderness, and The Wilderness Society supported the park proposal. Meanwhile, some in the Forest Service community, including former chief Henry Graves and Bob Marshall (still with the Indian Forest Service but soon to rejoin Agriculture's Forest Service), argued that if the Forest Service hoped to retain control of the Olympics (and perhaps other areas currently in contention with the Park Service), it had to give meaningful assurance of wilderness protection. This could only be done, counseled Graves, Marshall, and several others, with legislation. Graves recommended that the Forest Service "recognize the special character of the Olympic problem and ask for legislation to lock up certain portions as primitive areas. It is only by some such device that the timber will not be opened up by some later administration."[7]

The Forest Service could not take this advice, tied as it was to its multiple-use philosophy and its emphasis on timber, in time to stop the park. In 1937 President Roosevelt traveled to the Olympic Peninsula to see for himself what all the fuss was about, and he came away convinced that the interagency struggle should be resolved in favor of a national park. He asked that a meeting be called in Washington, DC, to achieve this and directed that boundaries for the new park be drawn up by top officials of the Forest Service and the Park Service. He favored a large national park. Legislation was drafted designating an 860,000-acre mountain park with a 50,000-acre coastal strip. Congress passed it, and the president signed it on June 29, 1938. In early 1940 Roosevelt added 187,411 acres to the park, including forested valleys that the Forest Service and timber interests fought to the end to keep out of the park.

This episode is important to the national park wilderness story in several ways. It was a victory for the Park Service in part because it was more convincing than its rival in its assurances that it would manage for wilderness values. Most conservationists supported the park legislation (the National Parks Association was an ironic exception) because they were con-

5.1 Olympic National Park was the first new park in which preservation of wilderness was, from its beginning, a stated policy. © 2007 Keith Lazelle Nature Photography

vinced that the Forest Service was not serious about wilderness preservation in the Olympics. By this time, that agency had shown in other primitive areas that its long-term commitment to wilderness preservation was suspect. Its management plans for the Olympics were known, and those plans included road development and logging. Only in 1938, in the face of President Roosevelt's clear favoring of a national park, did Chief Forester Silcox decide to draft a bill for legislative protection of Olympic wilderness as advised by Graves and Marshall, but he was too late to keep the Olympics under Forest Service administration.

At the Department of the Interior, the Park Service was also feeling pressure to be more wilderness preservation oriented, and it was responding. Secretary Ickes had made clear his belief that new national parks should be wilderness parks. He reaffirmed this in a speech in Seattle in 1938 referring specifically to the newly established Olympic National Park. Create a national park, said Ickes, as had just been done in the Olympics, and the people will come.

In view of this it is timely to reflect that fame has its drawbacks as well as its compensations. A national park, praised by everybody, thronged to by the great traveling public, needs the same protection from its too enthusiastic admirers that a man needs when fame descends upon him. . . . It is simpler and easier to protect a national park, provided the right kind of a start is made. In the case of a wilderness area like the Olympic National Park, the solution can be stated in four words. Keep it a wilderness.[8]

The secretary was unequivocal in this statement. He elaborated his vision for this new park. It would not follow the development pattern of many of its predecessors. "Since this is to be a wilderness park, the Department of the Interior will neither build nor approve the building of hotels on public lands."[9] The Park Service would build trails and trail shelters "for hikers and horseback parties," but those who wanted the "comforts of home" would have to find them in the communities at the base of the mountains.

Secretary Ickes indicated in his Seattle talk that he understood the history of national parks and the development that had occurred in them. In his typically blunt-spoken way, he called for a different approach to new parks. He would concede that some roads needed to be built to allow those with physical limitations to enjoy the parks. Even those who chose to drive instead of walk should be accommodated.

But let us preserve a still larger representative area, in its primitive condition, for all time by excluding roads. Limit the roads. Make the trails safe but not too easy, and you will preserve the beauty of the parks for untold generations. Yield to the thoughtless demand for easy travel, and in time the few wilderness areas that are left to us will be nothing but the back yards of filling stations.[10]

Ickes elevated the preservation mission of national parks. He said that "the greatest function of national parks is to preserve what civilization, lacking them, would destroy. The increasing destructiveness of civilization must be counter-balanced by a steady growth in our National Park System."[11] While he did not deny that recreation was important, preservation was in his view the preeminent purpose of new national parks. Ickes did not use the approach of his Interior Secretary predecessors Franklin Lane and Hubert Work and write a policy letter as they had. That was not his style. He enjoyed being front and center in policy issues of interest to him and was not reluctant to publicly state his views regardless of whether the agencies in his department agreed with him. He was not on good terms with Director Cammerer and seems to have believed that a better way to promote wilderness preservation as a goal of national park policy was to put public pressure on Cammerer and other Park Service leaders. The publication of his Seattle speech in the influential *American Planning and Civic Annual* indicates that Ickes intended his words to reach well beyond his small audience in Seattle.

The new Olympic National Park thus gave Secretary Ickes the opportunity to express his strong views on wilderness and national parks. The new parks were to be managed differently than the other parks and the Park Service seemed, in this Olympic case, to almost begrudgingly respond to Ickes's priorities. When Charles Moore of Gig Harbor, Washington, a community near the park, expressed his concern to Director Cammerer that the phrase "wilderness park" might be "taken to mean exclusion," Cammerer indicated what the goal for management of the new park would be.

> After thorough studies by the various technical branches of the Service, a master plan covering the developments of the park will be drawn up and no developments will be permitted that are not included in the approved master plan. In general, however, it is not our intention to exclude people from enjoyment and use of the park, but, rather, to develop the park in such a way as to retain its wilderness character.[12]

This seemed to be the usual tired bureaucratic rhetoric from the Park Service that had earlier frustrated wilderness preservationists, but this time the Park Service, prodded by Ickes, concluded that the management plan for Olympic should indeed be for a trail park with minimum road construction. The primary consideration was to be noninterference with natural conditions. Principles for resource management were drawn up in late July and early August 1938 by a group that included, for some of the sessions, Secretary Ickes himself, his representative and strong park advocate Irving Brant, Superintendent Tomlinson of Mount Rainier, and Preston Macy, acting superintendent of the new park, among others. They laid out an approach that Macy, in his long tenure as the park's first superintendent (1938–1951), followed carefully. He developed trails and opposed roads as he attempted to define how Ickes's "wilderness park" should be managed.

THE ARGUMENT OVER KINGS CANYON

Far to the south of the Olympics yet another wilderness park campaign was coming to a head: the long struggle for a Kings Canyon National Park in the southern Sierra Nevada. John Muir had first visited the area in 1875 and concluded that it was the equal of Yosemite. He had agitated for a national park in the region, and the Sierra Club had devoted itself to that goal since its founding in 1892. Sequoia and the tiny General Grant national parks had been a start toward protecting some of the giant sequoia groves from loggers, but beginning in 1910 the inadequacies of these parks had been recognized and calls had been made for enlargement. The Forest Service, for all of the reasons previously described, was opposed to any additional national parks in the southern Sierra (unless a new park through exchange might free up valuable timber already locked up in Sequoia National Park while costing the Forest Service only rock and ice alpine areas). Bills proposing a new park came and went, until finally the Barbour Act of 1926 more than doubled the size of the existing park. Some of the desired additions were made, but the Kings River region, a vast wilderness, remained unprotected.

This expansion in 1926 did not satisfy the Sierra Club and other preservationists, and they continued to agitate for a new park. In 1935 Secretary Ickes persuaded California Senator Hiram Johnson to introduce legislation for a Kings Canyon National Park. As with the Olympic proposal, Ickes argued that Kings Canyon be a wilderness park. He issued a statement on September 20, 1935:

1. This park will be treated as a primitive wilderness. Foot and horse trails to provide reasonable access will be encouraged, but roads must be held to an absolute minimum. The state road now being constructed should never be extended beyond the floor of Kings Canyon.
2. Responsible packers will be encouraged to conduct their parties through the park, the only restriction being their conformance to such rules and regulations as will be promulgated in the interest of the public and the preservation of the primitive character of the area.[13]

Johnson's bill was swiftly killed in the Senate by a coalition of power—recreation, tourism, grazing, and timber interests.

If any park, wilderness or otherwise, was to be established in the Kings River country, more public support for it was needed, and Ickes, the National Park Service, and the Sierra Club faced a major challenge in lack of local support. The people living near the proposed park, they found, held a low opinion of the Park Service, believing it opposed to development, callous about the economic fate of local communities, and catering to a wealthy, urban constituency. The Forest Service, which granted less-regulated access to lands it administered, was held in higher esteem. Not surprisingly, the Forest Service was doing all that it could to curry local support and encourage fear of the consequences of a new national park. Ickes and the Park Service launched a campaign to counter Forest Service criticism and agreed to conditions that would allow satisfaction of local and regional needs for water, power, and tourism development. They could do this, they thought, without compromising their goals.[14] California representative Bertrand Gearhart introduced a bill for a John Muir-Kings Canyon National Park that, after tortuous maneuvering by supporters and opponents, was approved by the 76th Congress. President Roosevelt signed the Kings Canyon National Park bill on March 4, 1940.[15]

5.2 FDR's Secretary of the Interior Harold Ickes decreed that Olympic and Kings Canyon would be "wilderness parks." National Park Service Historic Photographic Collection, Harpers Ferry Center

This new park, like Olympic, was to be managed as a wilderness park. The Sierra Club had long advocated wilderness preservation in the area and had been skeptical of whether the Park Service would or could preserve it. The Forest Service had wooed the club, and since the days of Stephen Mather and his overdevelopment of Yosemite Valley, it had considered the Forest Service at least as likely as the Park Service to do what it wanted. It was impressed by Secretary Ickes's pronouncements about wilderness, and in October 1938 he met with the club directorate and convinced them that a wilderness national park was the best option. The bill Representative Gearhart introduced included provisions "to insure the permanent preservation of the wilderness character" of the park; "no hotels, permanent camps or other similar physical improvements" should be constructed therein, "except upon ground used for public housing purposes." And there should be constructed no "new roads, truck trails, or public housing structures other than simple trailside shelters." Thus the wilderness preservation goals of the Sierra Club and Ickes would be addressed.[16]

Congress, influenced by growing public interest in wilderness and by an outspoken and powerful advocate in Secretary Ickes, began a new phase in park wilderness history that is important in several ways. The mandates in the legislation establishing these parks testify to the conviction of some, even a strongly pro–national park secretary of the interior, that the Organic Act did not provide the level of protection from impairment of national park resources that they thought necessary. Ickes and others thought the Park Service needed clearer directions regarding the purposes for which at least some parks were established and for management of them. The stories of Everglades, Olympic, and Kings Canyon reveal that by the late 1930s influential people strongly believed that a more wilderness preservationist approach in legislation was needed to prevent overdevelopment of new, mostly roadless, parks. Park Service leadership went along with this, but there is little evidence that they actively sought it.

A consequence of this stage in national park wilderness history is that, whether it wanted to or not, the Park Service began to engage in planning and management to preserve wilderness. Thomas Vint's comment in 1938 that he and his planners had given up on the idea of designating specific areas within parks as wilderness and were instead considering all areas outside of limited developments as wilderness may be seen as recognition of the new reality presented by wilderness park legislation. The Park Service was engaged in much more than wilderness preservation, but it could not avoid that aspect of its mission. Vint's comment sounds very much like Albright's earlier pronouncements that, since only a small part of the park is developed, the rest must be, by definition, wilderness. But Vint could not rest on such reassurances. At least in new natural parks and soon-to-be parks like Everglades and Big Bend, a more complex definition of wilderness was evolving, a definition beginning to be influenced by ecological science.

INTERNAL PARK SERVICE INTEREST IN WILDERNESS

At the first Conference of Park Naturalists in 1929 the topic of wilderness was discussed, stimulated in part by the group's interest in research reserves and by the issue of national park standards. Naturalists urged the Park Service to survey the parks to determine as quickly as possible what land should be "areas of intensive use," what should be "wilderness areas penetrated by trail only," and what should be research reserves. Scrutinizing the statement on national parks standards approved by the Campfire Club of America and embraced by the NPA and other conservation groups, the naturalists focused especially on the statement "that wilderness features within any park shall be kept absolutely primitive." They agreed with the goal but questioned its practicality. "We ask 'What shall be the policy adopted in control of insect infestations, tree diseases . . . and forest fires occurring under natural conditions (lightning, etc.)?' While not recommending the discontinuance of natural controls, we wish to point out that such control very definitely influences 'natural conditions.'"[17] At this meeting the naturalists were wrestling with the nature of park wilderness and raising questions that would require, for their answers, scientific critique of standard Park Service resource management policies and practices. That critique would come several years later from George Wright and his wildlife biologist colleagues in *Fauna No. 1*.

The park naturalists also anticipated issues that would rise to the top of park and wilderness management debates decades later. These would involve definitions of wilderness and policies of "naturalness." How would "absolutely primitive" be defined, or even identified? If the condition were found, how could it be maintained in a changing and developing world? They mentioned "natural" as in lightning-caused fire, asking how a policy on the "primitive" could be reconciled with the need to control forest fires. Since 1890 a minority of naturalists, among them U.S. Geological Survey Director John Wesley Powell, had argued that wildfire might be "natural," but this view had not prevailed. A policy of suppression of all fires had eventually gone into effect in national forests and parks and virtually all forest land. These park naturalists were, in 1929, raising a central question about the nature of wilderness that is still being pursued in the twenty-first century.[18]

The rise and fall of science as an influence on national park policy during this period has been thoroughly described by Richard Sellars.[19] The story he tells is relevant to national park wilderness history in several ways. As mentioned earlier, the first official "wilderness" in a national park, at Yosemite in 1927, was a small area dedicated to scientific research from which visitors were to be excluded. The term "wilderness" was then dropped and "research reserve" replaced it. As science grew in the service in the 1930s, plans for more such reserves were initiated. In 1931 Director Albright issued a policy to "preserve permanently" selected natural areas "in as nearly as possible unmodified condition free from external influences." He extended this in 1932, directing that reserves be formally designated on park master plans. Ultimately, however, the science initiative was deflated when George Wright, its leader, was tragically killed in an automobile accident. Little came of this "reserve" program.

The importance of the science initiative to the park wilderness story is that it may be seen as an admission by some in the Park Service that the agency was protecting wilderness less effectively than it claimed. If more protection was necessary for some areas to protect naturalness suitable for scientific baseline studies, then all not developed must not be wild, as Albright and others were claiming (admitting, of course, that many definitions of "wild" were held at this time). Park Service wildlife biologists became, as mentioned earlier, "a minority 'opposition party' within the service, challenging traditional assumptions and practices—in effect reinterpreting in scientific terms the Organic Act's mandate to leave the parks unimpaired."[20] Biologists challenged on ecological grounds Park Service claims that it was managing most of its land in "unimpaired" condition. Their 1933 *Fauna No. 1* report made a convincing if preliminary case that natural conditions had been altered in many supposedly natural and wild parks to the detriment of many fauna. All of this injected an ecological definition of wilderness into the discussion that was lost at the time on virtually all players in the wilderness discussion both inside and outside the Park Service. Still, from inside the agency, the seed of a critique of national park wilderness policy was planted.

WILDERNESS AT SEQUOIA NATIONAL PARK

Wilderness came up in high policy-level discussions and it also came up out in the field. Perhaps the most important example of this was in Sequoia National Park, where Superintendent John Roberts White was not afraid to raise issues with his superiors and to follow his own convictions. Stephen Mather had hired White and appreciated his independence. Mather sought men as superintendents who were "resourceful enough not to have to turn to Washington except in major crises, adaptable enough to get on with the local community, and urbane enough to handle the whole, diverse traveling public, from nobility on down."[21] White had proven to be such a man. During the 1920s White supervised the work necessary to upgrade public accommodations, including water and sewer systems, telephone lines, ranger stations, and campgrounds. He built a park staff, constructed service buildings, and even increased road mileage. As he did all of this he gradually came to the conclusion that the best development for a national park like Sequoia was the least development. In 1922 he observed in his *Annual Report* that he had been disgusted by the spectacle he encountered on the Fourth of July at General Grant Park, of which he also had charge. "Tents were jammed one against the other," he wrote, "automobiles were rioting over the grass and other vegetation and people were spread everywhere as thick as flies on molasses."[22] He made this observation at the height of Mather's campaign to attract people to the parks and accommodate them, but White concluded that concentrating people in attractions like the Giant Forest and around centralized concessions was the wrong approach. He began a conversion to the "preservation" side of the national park tradition.[23] In the late 1920s he opposed an alternate route for the Generals Highway in the park that would invade the roadless backcountry of the Middle Fork of the Kaweah River. Among his reasons for this was his conviction that roads should not penetrate the wilderness of the park. People should, he thought, climb out of their cars and walk, and the way to encourage that was to build trails rather than roads. He did just that, clashing with Director Albright over the issue but ultimately prevailing in his Sequoia domain.

5.3 John Roberts White served as superintendent of Sequoia and Kings Canyon National Parks in their formative years. National Park Service Historic Photographic Collection, Harpers Ferry Center

White built trails and opposed proposals to build roads into roadless park areas. His policy was that no roads should extend above 7,000 feet in the park. He thought that "if we hold all development to the simplest form and confine ourselves to the use of native materials, there will be little of overdeveloping in the wilderness areas—providing the roads are kept aside."[24] When the Civilian Conservation Corps (CCC) appeared, White at once saw both the opportunity and the threat. He took advantage of the opportunities and carefully controlled CCC projects in his park, guiding them according to his evolving preservationist approach. Park historians Lary Dilsaver and William Tweed attest to the success White enjoyed, describing how the CCC under White's careful oversight "gave a huge boost to infrastructure improvement while avoiding the pitfalls of sudden, uncontrolled development."[25] White could succeed as a strong, independent superintendent at this time, they argue, because the huge and rapid organizational growth and its decentralization gave superintendents, for a time at least, more autonomy than they had normally enjoyed. White's strong convictions, his seniority, his forceful personality, "and the growing suspicion [in the Park Service] that he might be right in his increasingly preservationist ideals combined to lend him exceptional authority."[26] Dilsaver and Tweed suggest that White's thinking and his example contributed significantly to increased Park Service support for wilderness at this time. In describing the defeat of a major proposal for the Sierra Way, a high-elevation highway linking Lassen Volcanic National Park, Mount Shasta, Yosemite, and Sequoia national parks, in which White played a key role, they write:

> In the evolving attitude of the Park Service, however, the concept of roadless wilderness had been enjoying ever-increasing popularity. In part this arose from rapidly amassing evidence of scenic disruption by auto traffic in the accessible portions of parks like Sequoia. In part it arose from strong statements from groups like the Sierra Club and the Commonwealth Club in opposition to mountain roads. And in part it arose from the success of trails like the High Sierra Trail [championed by White] and evidence of public need for wilderness areas.[27]

In 1941 John White was assigned the superintendency of the new Kings Canyon National Park and became architect of development policies there. He would serve until 1947. White pursued the same preservation-oriented approach to development in the new park, buttressed by the wilderness directive of the park legislation. He wrote to Francis Farquhar in 1945 that "I am having the most interesting job of planning development there—or shall we say lack of development, which actually takes planning, if not more planning than development."[28]

John Roberts White was certainly no wilderness purist. There is no evidence that he grasped ecological arguments for wilderness or even that he embraced the romantic conception of wilderness as a place for inspiration and recreation. He opposed roads because he thought they defaced the scenery and cheapened the park experience. Observing the mess involving tourists around automobile-accessible attractions and concessions, he concluded that dispersing visitors was better than concentrating them and that nothing concentrates them like a road and accompanying "improvements." Thus he championed trails and opposed roads. According to Dilsaver and Tweed,

White's campaign against roads "prevented a full third of Sequoia Park's later formal wilderness from being lost. . . . Later, it would be apparent the Sequoia National Park's greatest feature was its grand and spacious backcountry."[29]

Was John Roberts White unusual in his policy initiatives as superintendent of a major natural park? He probably was, for few enjoyed the career longevity of leading a major park that he did. Others served as many years, but few managed to stay with a particular park and landscape throughout as White did. Few had the opportunity to spend nearly thirty years shepherding a park from its early stages to maturity. And few enjoyed the special circumstances of the 1930s that allowed a very senior superintendent greater autonomy than usual. All of these factors converged to make White's experience unusual. Still, it seems likely that in other parks similar stands were taken by superintendents, though with less flair. Historians Paul Sutter and David Louter have described how roads, and arguments about roads, shaped some national parks in the 1920s and 1930s. Mather, of course, championed roads. Louter writes that "at least in the 1920s, defining national parks as wilderness areas free of roads was difficult. So much of their identity at the time was related to the notion that they could actually sustain roads and cars without losing their wilderness values."[30] Despite this, public support for wilderness preservation was growing, and some strong superintendents like White responded. When directors Albright, Cammerer, or later Conrad Wirth claimed that national parks were largely wild—taking credit for a policy stance—the extent to which some parks were wild was in no small part due to many large and small decisions made in the field by people like John Roberts White.

A BIOLOGIST SPEAKS OUT

In November 1936, Acting Park Service Director Arthur Demaray circulated a paper written by Park Service biologist E. Lowell Sumner Jr. Demaray wrote in his cover memo that "it is believed that members of the Service will be interested in this discussion and recommendations on wilderness-use and the development of primitive areas. The preservation of natural park features in the light of the pressure of increased public use is a complex problem in park planning and administration which must be recognized and receive serious consideration of all officers of the Service."[31] The paper by Sumner was an excerpt from a wildlife study that he and colleagues had done in the high Sierra of Sequoia and Yosemite national parks. Sumner's report alluded to the rising pressure of national park use in general and criticized Park Service efforts "to coax large numbers of less venturesome individuals into wilderness by the construction, even in remote places, of ready-built camp sites and extensive systems of early trails."[32] There was, in his opinion, a "saturation point beyond which further concentration of people will always destroy the very thing they seek," and that saturation point in wilderness was reached quickly. The recreation needs of the many who do not wish to venture far from their autos might be met by state and local park initiatives, while to the national parks "properly belongs the function of preserving superlative natural regions, including wilderness areas, as little changed as possible for the benefit of posterity." Sumner encouraged the limiting of development in national parks, especially roads, the promotion of other park systems to share the recreational burden, and "definite recognition of remnant wilderness areas and establishment of a code of administration designed to protect them from all but the very simplest maintenance activity." The Washington office thought these ideas important enough to bring them to the attention of field officers across the country, an indication of the level of interest in the topic.

Lowell Sumner was one of the Park Service wildlife biologists who, in the 1930s, was beginning to look at park management through an ecological lens. He wrote of wilderness from this perspective, but more than most of his biologist colleagues he expressed an interest in a broader conception of wilderness. He was concerned about the experience of visitors as well as the fate of wildlife. Two years later Sumner composed another paper that he titled "Losing the Wilderness Which We Set Out to Preserve." He expressed some of the same thoughts as earlier, strongly opposing roads, but went into some detail about what must be called "wilderness management" in the modern sense. If trails were built instead of roads (as White was doing in Sequoia) they should be narrow and minimally intrusive. A big trail could do as much harm as a small road. Managers should be alert to the problems of erosion, soil compaction, and impacts of any development on wildlife and vegetation. Even removing trees for ski trails might lead to such problems as blowdown and desiccation of vegetation. The significance of this is that Sumner argued for keeping the roads out of roadless areas but went further to point out that keeping an area without roads was not all that was needed to protect its wilderness qualities. Recreation in the roadless area should itself be carefully managed, and if this were done "we may yet avoid losing the wilderness which we set out to preserve."[33]

The influence of Sumner's ideas on Park Service policy cannot be isolated, but as Sellars has documented, the group of National Park Service scientists of which he was part affected the course of national park history over the long term. Sumner was thinking beyond the challenge of roads to wilderness to details of how, once a landscape was dedicated to wilderness, it should be managed to keep it wild. He recognized that a blanket policy for protection would not work everywhere in a system of diverse natural areas, noting that "in the case of the national parks there is urgent need for the determination of the recreational saturation point *for each threatened area* [italics added] together with the establishment of a policy for holding all developments below that point."[34] Even as Cammerer and Vint were saying that all parkland not developed was wilderness, thoughtful members of the Park Service like Sumner and White were expressing their view that this approach to wilderness was inadequate and simplistic. They understood that protecting wilderness required far more than not developing it.

The 1930s was a period of great ferment in American society, in the National Park Service, and in the outdoor recreation, park, and wilderness movements. Several generalizations about wilderness and national park history can be drawn from this stage of the national park wilderness story. One is that the decade saw a growing internal Park Service debate about wilderness and what its role should be in the national park system. The Park Service had much to occupy its attention: its new responsibilities for historic preservation and its leadership of national outdoor recreation policy and development; its use of the remarkably abundant financial and human resources lavished upon it by the New Deal; and its rapid organizational growth and the need to reorganize to administer its expanding domain. Yet even in the face of all these demands, the issue of national park wilderness kept a measure of its attention in Washington and in the field. This was in no small part because the ambitions of the Forest Service forced it to pay attention or risk losing opportunity and even part of its mission. Add to this activist Interior Secretary Harold Ickes's strong views on wilderness and the growing wilderness preservation movement manifest in the founding of The Wilderness Society, and it is clear why the National Park Service could not ignore the wilderness challenge during this period.

Even so, the leadership of the Park Service was not enthusiastic about the issue and needed to be pressured to pay attention to it. This can be explained in part as a consequence of all the other matters it had before it. At the core of the agency's reticence was the value orientation imbued in it by Stephen Mather. Directors Albright and Cammerer were "Mather men" and shared his ambitions for and insecurities about the Park Service. They shared his view that the important thing was to build a strong national park system and a strong organization to run it. If some ideals or standards were compromised along the way, they could go back and correct the problems later when the system was secure. When, in the mid-1930s, the National Parks Association attacked the service for supporting inclusion of such substandard areas as Jackson Hole (with its Jackson Lake reservoir) in the national park system and abandoning standards, Cammerer responded, "Because civilization has moved into the choicest areas faster than they could be established as national parks, some parks must now be carved out of developed areas."[35] Horace Albright, now a business executive but still a force in national park affairs, backed Cammerer, telling the American Planning and Civic Association in 1938 that it and other national park supporters must "not adopt obstruction policies" and should not "define National Parks to the point where there can never be any new parks or additions to existing parks. Once the system is completed," he added, "we must see that the non-conforming uses are abated and we must foster the reversion to a natural state of injured areas in the parks."[36] Building the system was the first order of business.

By the 1930s the rationale Mather had used for park development was not as compelling as it had been in the 1920s. The basic infrastructure of roads, water and sewer systems, and administrative facilities was in place in most parks, but then new resources for development appeared through New Deal programs. Projects that Mather had only dreamed of could be realized, so some of them were built. The Blue Ridge Parkway is a spectacular example. Such development in turn generated reaction from within and outside the Park Service. Bob Marshall and his friends were inspired to found their wilderness advocacy group. Lowell Sumner summarized the reaction when he wrote in 1938, in his wilderness paper, that "the perils of exceeding the recreational saturation point in the national parks may be avoided in large measure if the service emphasizes *quality* rather than *quantity* in the administration of its national scenic treasures."[37] The point is that the Park Service leadership had always recognized the importance of quality but had sometimes succumbed to emphasis on quantity for various political reasons. In the 1930s there is evidence that it slowly dawned on some of the Park Service leaders that the idea of wilderness, rising in the consciousness of the outdoor recreating public thanks to Leopold, Marshall, Yard, and others, was an increasingly important part of the quality of national parks. They were not ready to fully embrace the idea, but they could not ignore it.

Even as Thomas Vint seemed to give up on wilderness designation in master plans in the late 1930s, the dedication of parks to wilderness became official at Olympic, Kings Canyon, Isle Royale, and Everglades national parks. Though the Wilderness Act and designated wilderness in national parks were decades in the future, Congress took a step in that direction with the legislation establishing these new parks. What it actually would mean on the ground remained to be seen, but the Park Service was in the wilderness business in a new way.

Finally, the argument was made throughout the 1930s that the Park Service was tending very adequately to wilderness, which was true in many cases. Park Service leadership argued that it had the legal mandate it needed to do its job in the Organic Act and several secretaries' policy letters interpreting that legislation. Directors Albright and Cammerer and lesser Park Service officials spoke and wrote the word "wilderness" quite commonly during the decade, assuring the public that all was well on the wilderness protection front. They no doubt fully believed what they said. They were, in their view, minimizing development and fighting against commercial exploitation and keeping everything else wild. Yet doubts lingered in the minds of scientists, wilderness and park purists, and even some park superintendents. These doubts would be carried into subsequent decades and drive additional chapters in the story of national park wilderness.

As the decade of the 1930s closed, the national park wilderness situation was confused. On the one hand, Park Service policy was, as expressed by Thomas Vint, that there were to be no lines drawn around wilderness in the national parks. The service would limit development to what its planners saw as essential for meeting the mandates of the National Park Act and legislation establishing each park. The rest of the land in national parks would be "wilderness." On the other hand, planners working on new parks were discussing wilderness in their plans for management and development. There was no contradiction in this necessarily, but it reveals how far the Park Service was from resolving its collective mind about wilderness. In the decades of the 1940s through the 1960s the agency would continue to tentatively feel its way toward a stance on the wilderness issue.

Events well beyond park boundaries greatly influenced the path the Park Service followed in this search in the 1940s. Foremost among them was World War II, which effectively stopped all work on national park and wilderness issues for six years. Visits to parks were curtailed by urgent war work and the concentration of the nation's resources on the war effort. Park Service budgets and personnel declined sharply. National Park Service headquarters was moved to Chicago, indicating how far from the center of the nation's agenda national park matters were at this time. Then, at the end of the war, people returned to national parks in rapidly growing numbers. A park system that had been neglected for many years found itself inundated with visitors and straining to meet the demands they made upon the park system's human and physical resources. For a time Park Service leaders were unable to respond satisfactorily to this challenge. Then, in the mid-1950s, they launched a politically savvy and well-funded effort, which they called Mission 66, to repair and construct park infrastructure. These challenges were on a scale unimagined by earlier generations of Park Service leaders, but so were the resources channeled their way in Mission 66.

The conservation movement shrank to virtual dormancy during the war and, like the Park Service, recovered slowly afterward. The generation of conservation leaders too old to fight or otherwise contribute directly to the war effort kept the conservation fires banked. They fought commercial invaders who, under the guise of patriotism, attempted to log, mine, and otherwise gain long-sought access to pristine parklands. Together the Park Service and conservationists were largely successful in protecting the wilderness parks. After the war conservationists rebuilt their organizations and responded to familiar and new threats to parks and wilderness. This response, catalyzed and unified by a struggle to keep dams out of the national park system (Hetch Hetchy's fate still sharp in their memories), resulted in the growth of a conservation movement stronger, more energized, and more powerful than it had been before the war. Gradually its focus shifted to the issue of wilderness, and conservationists set their sights on achieving a level of protection for wilderness that was not provided, in their view, by discretionary policies of the Forest Service and the National Park Service. A long and epic legislative struggle for a wilderness bill was launched at precisely the same time the National Park Service won the congressional support it needed to redevelop the national parks and respond to the rapidly growing pressures of postwar America. Mission 66 and the drive for the wilderness bill began in 1956, and both efforts were to culminate in the mid-1960s.

SETTING UP THE NEW "WILDERNESS PARKS"

Wilderness parks were, as described earlier, authorized or established in the 1930s. Two meetings convened before the war, one involving Olympic National Park and the other Kings Canyon National Park, brought up issues involving wilderness that would emerge in the postwar period. One meeting, in July 1938, drew up a General Statement of Controlling Development Policies for Olympic National Park. Secretary Ickes was present at part of this meeting before relinquishing his seat to his representative, Irving Brant.

Others present were Park Service officials, biologist Lowell Sumner among them. The meeting resulted in the incorporation of a powerful prewar wilderness policy statement into a national park master plan.

The master plan opened with a statement of the three reasons the park was created, which were to preserve the virgin rainforest, protect the Roosevelt elk, and provide "protection of one of the finest remaining scenic wilderness areas of the nation, with emphasis on maintenance of wilderness conditions for the benefit of future generations."[1] Policies guiding the master plan were then enumerated. No new roads would be built into the park. Olympic would be a "trail park" with many miles of good trails but with areas totally free of trails "so the youths of future generations too may exercise their 'sense of direction' . . . in traveling cross country where only elk and deer trails now are found." Accommodations would not be constructed inside the park, and existing resorts inside park boundaries would be eliminated as opportunity for their purchase might allow. The Park Service would work with other agencies to maintain natural conditions in the management of forests and wildlife, for "within the national park all native species have a proper place in the national picture, and should not be disturbed where it is necessary for essential development or essential protection."[2] There was talk of constructing cabins in the wilderness to house trail crews, but the planners thought such cabins a bad idea. "Few things can be more destructive to wilderness qualities in a forested park than to regularly encounter . . . cabins along trails when traveling on foot or horseback." Cabins, they wrote, citing a "ruling of the Director in another case," had often been the beginning of development in national parks. Tents would be preferable, the director had stated, because they can "be located from time to time where the work requires, and leave no permanent scar in the wilderness when moved."[3]

This 1938 meeting and the subsequent Olympic National Park master plan put meat on the bones of Secretary Ickes's idea of a wilderness national park. The plan was specific and attacked directly the issues of road building and resort development that had so long bothered those who believed there had been too much emphasis in park management on accommodating automobile-oriented tourism. While Ickes had promoted the general idea, Park Service planners and even the director were moving toward defining precisely how a wilderness park would be managed. This was not inconsistent with Vint's approach of considering land not developed as wilderness. It was simply an assertion that the way to more wilderness was less development. The

Olympic plan was, however, the first clear indication of how an overtly wilderness park might be designed and managed.

The Kings Canyon meeting was convened on March 12, 1940, in the Park Service's San Francisco regional office. Attending were Sierra Club board members and other conservationists (including Newton B. Drury, soon to assume directorship of the Park Service), park superintendents, and regional Park Service officials. The first topic discussed was planning for development of the new park. With the exception of the fifty-year-old General Grant area, the new park was wild. At issue was how far the road in the South Fork of the Kings River should be extended beyond its current terminus at Cedar Grove. Nearly everyone present agreed that the ideal was the least intrusion upon the wilderness character of the area. Promises had earlier been made to local interests to reduce their opposition to the park proposal; they had been told they would be guaranteed access. The issue of where the road should end involved keeping those promises. Where should campgrounds and ranger stations be located? What should be the role of the Forest Service (which managed the lower valley of the South Fork, including Cedar Grove) and the Park Service in the area?

Discussion ranged across these issues, and there was disagreement. The Sierra Club's William Colby favored extending the road far enough so that as many people as possible could experience the highly scenic canyon, one of the principal attractions of the new park. He invoked John Muir in his argument, commenting that Muir had been farsighted enough to realize that concessions had to be made to allow most visitors to see the valley. The payoff would be, as Muir had argued forty years earlier, that visitors would appreciate both the experience of the valley and the need to protect it as a park. Colby advocated that the road go beyond the present terminus and end near Copper Creek, which is what finally came to pass. Other members of the Sierra Club, who thought Muir's arguments were no longer relevant in an era of significantly increasing visitation to most national parks, disagreed with Colby. The less road building, this faction thought, the better.

The Park Service's Harold Bryant, head of the Branch of Research and Information at this late stage of his long career, saw the mandated wilderness of the new park as an opportunity. The minutes of the meeting described his thoughts.

He brought out the fact that the Park Service is facing something rather new in the development of parks, for the Kings Canyon is the third park that has been created with the main idea behind it of making it a wilderness park. He mentioned Isle Royale, the only park with no roads at all; Olympic National Park where it is desired to have no roads through it and to consider only roads at the edge of the park which would give some access into the park; and now the Kings Canyon National Park. Dr. Bryant said he felt it was up to the Park Service to show that they know how to develop a wilderness park where people can find solitude and quiet and gain inspiration, away from crowds of people. He stated . . . that we should move slowly and study the problem and not start out as in other parks with the sole view of getting development started. He said he would like to have us proceed cautiously enough to see if we can't do something different.[4]

Bryant's remarks summarize well the park wilderness situation at this point in the story. The agency had moved (as at Isle Royale) or been moved (as at Olympic) to emphasize the wilderness values of new parks. The temptation to "get development started" in new parks was very much present, but strong voices within the agency, like Bryant, urged caution and a new approach.

The March meeting did not resolve the issue of where the road should end; not until 1946 was Copper Creek decided upon as the terminus. Debate continued not only on the road issue but also on where in the valley of the South Fork it should be located. The Sierra Club pressed for the least intrusive road, and the Park Service suffered internal division over the issue. In the end, however, pressure from the Sierra Club, aided by the opinion of eminent landscape architect Frederick Law Olmsted Jr. (at the time a Sierra Club vice president), led to a decision to follow the path of least intrusive road development. The struggle over development at Kings Canyon would continue for decades, but the concerns of Bryant from within the Park Service and Olmsted from outside assured that the interest of wilderness preservation would be at the forefront of all development discussions.[5]

Newton Drury did not have much to say at the March 1940 meeting about Kings Canyon development, but he no doubt listened carefully. Five months after this meeting he became director of the National Park Service, succeeding Arno Cammerer, who resigned for health reasons. Drury, a graduate of the University of California at Berkeley like Mather and Albright, was not a "Mather man" as directors Albright and Cammerer had been. They had served under Mather and generally embraced his philosophy and approach to building the national park system. Drury had never been in the Park Service. Leader of the Save-the-Redwoods League for two decades, he had served as executive officer of the California State Park Commission since 1929 and in that role proved himself an able administrator. He had been a National Park Service critic at times, was an honorary life member of the Sierra Club, and was a wilderness preservationist. Historian Donald Swain notes that Ickes, who had tried to recruit Drury to the post in 1933, had high hopes for the new director. "To Ickes, Drury held out the hope of new vigor in the Park Service bureaucracy and he symbolized the importance of wilderness preservation."[6]

DRURY AND THE WAR YEARS

When Drury became director in August 1940, the National Park Service was flourishing. The appropriations that had grown so much as a consequence of New Deal programs remained generous. National Park Service influence in the broad field of outdoor recreation was at its peak. Roads, trails, fire lookouts, and other construction projects were under way in many park system units. Emergency relief funds were still available and CCC crews, while waning, were still at work in the parks. The major new parks at Olympic and Kings Canyon were being organized. Isle Royale National Park was finally established in 1940, land acquisition there was proceeding well, and establishment of Mammoth Cave National Park was imminent. Secretary Ickes's choice was at the helm, and the National Park Service seemed to have prevailed in at least some of its battles with the Forest Service. Drury was heading up a strong and maturing land management agency that, while it still faced many challenges, seemed assured of long-term survival and the favor of a growing constituency. Then, just over a year after Drury assumed the directorship, the Japanese bombed Pearl Harbor, the United States entered World War II, and National Park Service fortunes changed rapidly.

In 1941, before the bombs and torpedoes did their deadly work in Hawaii, more visitors than ever, numbering 21 million, entered national parks. The shift of priorities to war led Congress to cut 1942 appropriations to the Park Service in half. Visitation that year dropped to half of what it had been in 1941 and continued down throughout the war years. All construction and land acquisition stopped. National Park Service staff, which had been developing experience, expertise, and esprit de corps for two decades, was decimated by enlistment in the military and severe budget reductions. Full-time appointments dropped between June 1942 and June 1943 from 4,510 to 1,974.[7] To gain space needed for war work, National Park Service headquarters was moved from Washington to Chicago in 1942 and would not be returned to the nation's capital until 1947.

Drury and his skeleton crew carried on in the face of all this. Master planning continued, and the first round of master plans for all 166 units of the park system was completed in 1942. Supported by conservation groups, which had also shrunk in wartime, Drury and Ickes fought to keep commercial interests from capitalizing on park resources. Loggers, miners, and stockmen maneuvered to get at the resources that park status had denied them. Their motives were cloaked liberally in the rhetoric of national need and patriotism, but they made few incursions despite constant pressure applied to the weakened Park Service. Long-simmering issues, such as Albright's goal of bringing Jackson Hole into Grand Teton National Park, heated up occasionally. When President Roosevelt invoked the Antiquities Act to proclaim Jackson Hole National Monument in March, 1943, congressional ire was piqued and Drury had a political fight to manage. John D. Rockefeller Jr., who had been acquiring Jackson Hole land for two decades with the idea of donating it to the federal government for the park, threatened to sell the land if the government would not accept it. This forced a reluctant Roosevelt, urged on by Ickes, to act. The Park Service, off in the political hinterlands of Chicago, did not relish being thrust into such a fight, but the stakes were high. Thus occasionally, during the war years, did national park issues capture presidential and national attention, if only briefly.

The general issue of wilderness also faded into the background of American consciousness during wartime, but there was some activity among those who kept a wilderness watch during this period. The question of what to do about wilderness in national parks remained unresolved in master planning. A master planning conference on Kings Canyon was held in the Washington office of the Park Service in July 1941. Director Drury told the group that "many of the basic policies of the Service are on trial in Kings Canyon National Park." One issue was maintaining the park as a "strictly wilderness area." Drury said he did "not like the implications associated with use of the term 'wilderness park' because it places the Service in a position where it must justify other parks more extensively developed." He wanted the group to come up with a clear statement as to "how far we can go in developing the park and still carry out this primary obligation" of preserving wilderness values.[8] Drury's sympathies were with wilderness preservation, but as this meeting indicates, even he was uncertain about how wilderness should be manifest in park planning and management. When the Kings Canyon Master Plan was completed, wilderness designation was present, if in a confusing way. Under "land use" in the "Development Outline" one finds "Classification of Areas," the first category of which is "primitive class" and within which falls "Wilderness Area." Then the plan stipulates that the majority of the park is designated as a "Primeval Wilderness Area, without roads; and characterized by primitive conditions of transportation." Yet on the maps of the plan, no wilderness designation is outlined. Park Service policies may, in Drury's mind, have been on trial, but treatment of wilderness in this and other master plans of this period did little to clarify National Park Service wilderness policy at this point.[9] The policy of keeping wilderness "zones" vague and indistinct continued.

Robert Sterling Yard, from his position as president and permanent secretary of The Wilderness Society, continued to press the Park Service and Forest Service about their wilderness plans and designations. He wanted clarification of definitions, and he continued the campaign for a system of "national primeval parks" that had been championed by the National Parks Association. (He also continued as editor of the now occasional National Parks published by the NPA.) In July 1940 he asked Director Cammerer to clarify the National Park Service definition of wilderness and to provide a list of wilderness areas in national parks and monuments. He was not satisfied with Cammerer's reply that the Park Service measured its wilderness by subtracting the gross area of its roads from the total areas of the park and calling the rest wilderness as he interpreted Vint's position. In 1941 Yard queried Drury on the same issue and, in the director's absence from his office, received a reply from his administrative assistant that Yard must be asking about "Research Reserves." The assistant knew that there were such reserves but did not know how many there were.[10]

Drury patiently responded to Yard's continuous stream of requests and in February 1943 penned a letter to Yard, which is the clearest statement during the war of the director's views on national park wilderness. Yard had in January written an exasperated letter that closed, "I am hoping that some day the Park Service will develop Wilderness Areas of its own."[11] In his response to this letter, Drury's opening comment echoed Cammerer's earlier statement. "Roadless areas and Wilderness areas within National Parks can only be determined by the size of the Park and the amount of area not now developed. The Parks in reality are divided into two zones, developed areas and undeveloped areas." There are no plans, Drury continued, to expand developed areas. "Briefly stated, the future development program occupies the same ground that is occupied by existing facilities. No further trespass into the wild is necessary."[12]

Drury admitted in this letter the difficulty of saying where exactly a wilder-

6.1 Newton B. Drury was sworn in as National Park Service director in 1940 under the watchful eye of Secretary Ickes. National Park Service Historic Photographic Collection, Harpers Ferry Center

ness boundary might be drawn along an existing road or park boundary. But, he asked rhetorically, what difference would drawing such a line make? "What regulations will apply to the Wilderness area that does [sic] not apply to the remaining undeveloped park land?" Yard would have appreciated an answer to this question. Drury then asked, "Shouldn't its classification as National Park land be the best protection it can have?" The reason Yard was pressing the issue was, of course, that while he might agree that such classification *should* be the best protection, he did not believe that it was. Drury continued, arguing that compared with other public lands (such as national forests), national parks provided the highest level of protection of natural conditions. Some encroachments, such as trails, patrol cabins, and "facilities for fire detection and fire fighting are necessary." The National Park Service must weigh the risk of "larger scars by fire" with encroachment on wilderness. Would Yard have excluded from wilderness classification all areas encroached upon by such necessary development? Drury concluded his letter by admitting that there were many such issues, but in the end he and his Park Service believed that "we must take the parks as they are and attempt no further encroachment on the natural, but rather work toward retrenchment." This was the policy, and he could see no point in designating "a tract within a tract" as wilderness. He closed with the statement, "It is the hope of the National Park Service that National Park status is the safest classification wild land can attain for its protection in a natural condition for future generations."[13]

Thus did the most preservation-oriented director of the Park Service to this point (and perhaps since) attempt to lay to rest the issue of special designation of wilderness in national parks. No response from Yard is extant, but he probably found Drury's comments both reassuring and troubling. The war was on, and that reduced the threat that the Park Service would develop its parks for additional recreational use. It simply lacked the resources to develop at all. Yard undoubtedly believed that Drury was sincere, but he had been around long enough to know that Park Service directors come and go. Would the next director stay with the policy on development as Drury described it? Yard was nearing the end of his long career. He was eighty-two years old and seemed obsessed with the idea of a special system of "primeval parks." Drury hoped he could quiet and reassure the increasingly strident Yard, and perhaps he succeeded. On the other hand, Yard may have quieted down because he was old, tired, and approaching the end of his life. He died in 1945.

Yard's death led to a leadership decision for The Wilderness Society that was to have profound consequences for the wilderness movement in general. To this point in its history the society had employed a single person in the roles of president and executive officer, and this had been Yard. He had done a good job in the relatively slow period of the war, but as the conflict seemed to be nearing its end, the society's council decided it would need more resources to address its goals. Two men, Olaus Murie and Howard Zahniser, were selected to staff and lead the organization. Murie would work, as director and later president, from his home in Moose, Wyoming, while Zahniser, as executive secretary and editor of The Living Wilderness, would oversee action in Washington, DC. Zahniser would tend to administrative matters and run the society's day-to-day operation. Both men had worked for the Fish and Wildlife Service and its predecessor, the Biological Survey, Murie as a field biologist and Zahniser as a writer and editor. Murie was a consummate outdoorsman who had spent years in trying field conditions in

Alaska and the West. Zahniser was urbane, an intellectual far more at home on Capitol Hill than in wilderness. Both men were independent, Murie retarding his career by fighting his Biological Survey superiors over its predator policies and Zahniser expressing ideas considered radical by many at the time. Zahniser thought modern man's manipulative and destructive behavior toward nature, epitomized by development and use of the atomic bomb, demanded some response in general and from him. "All of us can unite in a determination to do our best to understand the cosmos we now perceive before we shatter its whole into disintegrating atoms," he had once written.[14] Murie and Zahniser decided they could do the most good by taking up and building on the work of Bob Marshall and Robert Sterling Yard. They thought The Wilderness Society could lead what would likely be a long struggle for legislative protection of wilderness. They could, in this way, address threats to the cosmos.

Under its new leadership The Wilderness Society continued to focus on immediate challenges to wilderness in both national parks and forests. Murie wrote to council member Robert Griggs in 1945 that "preservation of Wilderness values is very closely akin to preservation of values in national parks. It so happens one type is largely in national forests, the other in national parks. And The Wilderness Society has certainly concerned itself with national park problems."[15] Murie was writing to Griggs about the possibility of joining forces, perhaps even uniting into a single organization, with the National Parks Association. He anticipated a need to focus on both forest and park wilderness. The two groups might work together more effectively as one, with a division of labor between park and forest issues. Ultimately they decided to remain separate but to work closely together. For a time they worked out of the same offices. Murie and Zahniser made increased cooperation with other conservation groups a major goal and achieved close relations with the Sierra Club and the National Parks Association. The two Washington-based groups joined the still California-focused Sierra Club in a successful effort to save from ski resort development the San Gorgonio Primitive Area in the San Bernadino National Forest of southern California. They worked together on the society's project of assisting groups in the upper Midwest who were fighting to keep roads and resorts out of Minnesota's Quetico-Superior wilderness. Zahniser and Charles Woodbury of the National Park Association convened a meeting at Mammoth Cave National Park with the aim of unifying the efforts of conservation organizations. This postwar generation of conservation leaders saw a need for unity. Historian Stephen Fox describes this as "the application to politics of an ecological imperative: to see each issue in context, to emphasize cooperation and interrelatedness."[16]

CHALLENGES AFTER THE WAR

As the war ended, people returned to the national parks. Visitation in 1944 was 7.4 million, rose to 8.5 million in 1945, 21.7 million in 1946, and went up steadily each year, reaching 46 million in 1954.[17] These visitors found parks poorly staffed and roads and facilities in disrepair. Harold Ickes was not happy in the Truman administration and was succeeded at Interior by Julius Krug. In April 1946 the National Parks Association's Devereaux Butcher visited the new secretary and reported that Krug was most interested in increasing travel to national parks and in particular in making them more accessible to low-income people than they had generally been before the war. Did this portend development that might damage the "primeval" parks? The watchdogs would have to be vigilant.[18] Drury, in his annual reports and annual appropriations requests, made the case for increased funding of his strapped agency, but Congress, worried about war debt, modestly and inadequately increased appropriations to the National Park Service. Despite Secretary Krug's orientation to development, this lack of funds meant that, at least for a time, the Park Service would not be pushing any new projects into wilderness areas.

Conservationists and the Park Service were confronted by other challenges in this postwar period. One was a proposal to open the entire Olympic park to logging. When that proved unattainable, timber interests tried to remove some of the most valuable timbered areas from the park. A proposal was floated to reduce the size of Joshua Tree National Monument to allow mining. The killing of wolves was advanced as a way to resolve a long-simmering conflict at Mount McKinley National Park over wolf predation on Dall sheep. Two growing threats of special concern were a push by resource interests, especially stockmen, for less federal control of land in the West and plans for dams that would affect national parks. Of the first threat writer Bernard DeVoto—who branded the whole initiative a "land grab"—wrote in 1947:

> This year, possibly counting on the postwar revulsion against government control to favor their efforts, some of them are launching a new and particularly vigorous attack. If they should manage to breach the policy that has kept the parks

inviolate, one may anticipate the ultimate destruction of the parks, both as wilderness reserves and as the "pleasuring grounds" which the act of Congress that set aside the first one called them.[19]

Ultimately this threat, which was greatest to national forests, would, with DeVoto's help, be thwarted, but not before it raised considerable anxiety among conservationists.

The threat of the dams was not so quickly blunted. Director Drury told the National Parks Association in April 1946 that "the present craze for dam building constitutes a very grave threat to the national park system."[20] The Glacier View Dam in Montana threatened Glacier National Park. The Army Corps of Engineers proposed a dam in Kentucky that would flood caverns at Mammoth Cave. The Army Corps had also begun a flood control project in south Florida that would divert water necessary to maintain the aquatic environment of the Everglades. In the West, the Bureau of Reclamation had big plans for the Colorado River and its tributaries, plans that were a potential threat to many National Park System units. The story of this dam threat has been thoroughly told and will not be detailed here, but it must be mentioned because of the profound effects it would have on the conservation movement and thus on the future of wilderness and national parks.[21]

Ironically, reservoirs created when dams were built had become part of the national park system. The Park Service had taken over management of Lake Mead behind Boulder Dam in the 1930s and had taken on recreation planning and ultimately management of the lake created by Grand Coulee Dam in Washington State. It agreed to survey the recreational potential of reservoirs that would be created by the Bureau of Reclamation's Colorado River Basin Project. Drury thought such work threatened the mission of his agency and tried to take the National Park Service out of the reservoir recreation business but lost the policy debate. Richard Sellars has described Drury's predicament:

> The Park Service tie to river basin studies and reservoir management put it, as Drury stated it, in an "equivocal" policy and philosophical position. Although committed to protecting the park's scenic landscapes from intrusions such as dams, the Service, through its reservoir work, lent support to the inundation of scenic canyons and valleys throughout the West. Moreover, Drury's fears that reservoir recreation commitments would make the national park system more vulnerable foreshadowed the troubles that arose when the expansive dam-building programs

of the Bureau of Reclamation and the Army Corps of Engineers began to threaten established units of the national park system.[22]

As the decade of the 1940s drew to its end, the dam threat grew ever more serious.

THE DRIVE FOR A NATIONAL WILDERNESS POLICY BEGINS

Despite all the immediate threats to parks and wilderness, Howard Zahniser was thinking long term. In 1946 he issued his first call for "wilderness zoning" for parts of wild America. He worked with The Wilderness Society stalwart Benton MacKaye to draft legislation that would involve congressional appropriations to agencies for the acquisition of land to be protected as wilderness. The bill was never introduced, but the effort gave Zahniser experience in drafting wilderness legislation.[23] In June 1948 Zahniser engineered a request from a congressional committee chairman to the Legislative Reference Service of the Library of Congress for a study of America's wilderness needs. The Reference Service sent questionnaires to federal agencies, states, and conservation organizations. The Park Service received one and Director Drury responded in late November.

Drury first noted that The Wilderness Society defined wilderness as "areas retained in their primeval environment or influence, or . . . areas remaining free from routes which can be used for mechanized transportation." National parks and monuments "of considerable size" would qualify as wilderness under the first part of this definition, in Drury's view, but many would be disqualified by the second part because there were roads within their boundaries. Even so, "they would contain many large wilderness areas which are not crossed by roads." With this qualifier, Drury addressed the first question, which asked for the agency's definition of wilderness:

> This Service has no official definition of "Wilderness Area." The Wilderness Society's definition, however, seems acceptable. Wilderness areas in the National Park System are not designated as such, but the establishment of national parks and monuments preserves wilderness conditions.[24]

Throughout his response Drury took the position that the questions were not really applicable to the Park Service, since it had no designated wilderness, but he answered them and gave a telling response to the question, "Are there any suggestions you would care to make as to an over-all National Wilderness Area Policy?" Drury wrote:

> The National Park Service has no particular suggestions to make regarding an over-all national wilderness area policy except that it believes that the few remaining areas in the United States qualifying for such status should be preserved and that they should be preserved inviolate by Congressional mandate rather than by administrative decision.[25]

Drury's suggestion might be read several ways. He may have been thinking of Forest Service primitive areas, which could be made and unmade by "administrative decision" and had been many times. This seems the most likely explanation of his point, since the Park Service continued to be in conflict with the Forest Service over areas in national forests they thought should be classified by Congress as parks. But he might also have been thinking of his own agency, where administrative decisions had in the past developed the wilderness. Perhaps he recognized that one way to assure wilderness in parks was to mandate that they be wilderness parks, as at Olympic and Kings Canyon. Whatever he was thinking, his was a strong pro-wilderness statement.

The Forest Service, in its response, explained its system and said it had no plans for additional wilderness areas. It replied to the question about national wilderness policy that it could take no position on the matter without further study. In its view, the secretary of agriculture should decide important land use issues, such as wilderness designation of national forests, and some additional legislation might help make that possible. Its response was far less supportive of a national wilderness policy than the Park Service seemed to be.

The survey found respondents divided on the need for legislation to implement a national policy and opinions ranged widely as to what wilderness policy should be.[26] Nevertheless it was useful to Zahniser and his colleagues in that it revealed significant support for a national wilderness policy. Of course it also revealed strong differences of opinion about what specific path should be taken to better protect America's remaining roadless areas in national forests, parks, and other jurisdictions. The upshot of this study was, however, that it "set the stage for Zahniser's first detailed proposal for comprehensive federal wilderness legislation."[27]

Before the Library of Congress study was released, the Sierra Club convened the first of a series of conferences on wilderness that would be held biennially until 1969. The idea for this first conference came from Norman Livermore, a high-Sierra packer and Sierra Club director, who thought the Sierra Club should lead in formulating wilderness management policy for the high Sierra. These conferences would bring agency managers together with conservationists and be a principal forum for discussion of wilderness through the critical early years of wilderness legislation and later creation of the National Wilderness Preservation System. The first conference marked the beginning of an inclusive discussion of wilderness management. Its focus was not on wilderness philosophy or legislation but on wilderness recreation and management of the wilderness resource. Since the Park Service was the overseer of much Sierra wilderness, it was well represented at the meeting. Lowell Sumner was the opening speaker, addressing the problem of meadow destruction by visitors and how to deal with it. Carl Russell, the superintendent of Yosemite, spoke to the need to educate wilderness users. Regional Director Owen Tomlinson chaired the session "Wildlife Management Affecting Wilderness Areas," in which Sumner strongly made the point that wildlife management in wilderness had to be different than conventional approaches that aimed to produce game animals for hunters and often involved predator control. Sumner argued that "we harm wilderness by exterminating mountain lions, for instance, in order to raise more deer (that may then find insufficient food for their increased population). In the wilderness we should try to preserve or restore the natural balance."[28]

Sumner made these remarks at a touchy moment in Park Service wilderness management, for it was embroiled in deep controversy over management of Dall sheep in Mount McKinley National Park. Russell and Sumner were both intimately acquainted with the "sheep-wolf controversy" there and knew that Drury had recently called in a scientist to be an impartial analyst in the argument about whether wolves should be controlled to maintain a larger sheep population. This adviser had made recommendations for "active control" of the wolves, and Drury had lifted the limit earlier imposed on killing wolves. Harold Anthony, the scientific consultant, had reported that "in my opinion the situation with regard to the wolves in Mount McKinley National Park is a critical one, first with respect to the uncertain future of the Dall Sheep if it must accept any wolf predation at all, and second with respect to the loss of public confidence in the Park Service as the administrator of the federal wilderness areas."[29] Park Service leadership was very worried about this perceived loss of public confidence at a time when it was trying desperately to increase its budget. They wanted the public to believe that they were doing what they should in managing wildlife and wilderness. Sumner in particular, who had a long history of struggles over national park wildlife management policy, was very worried by this development. He took the opportunity at the Sierra Club conference to express his concern about the need to manage wildlife in national park wilderness in the Sierra and elsewhere in the park system (including Alaska) with "natural balance" in mind. Discussion of wilderness nationally was heating up, and the Park Service was in the thick of it, though not always on a footing it might choose.

Michael Cohen, in his history of the Sierra Club, calls the early Sierra Club wilderness conferences a process of "constructing a system of trails between old and new ideas."[30] The conferences brought together groups with diverse ideas about what wilderness was and what it ought to be: conservationists, land managers, scientists like Sumner, economic users such as stockmen, and recreational concessionaires such as packers. They offered an opportunity for all of these diverse interest groups to explore what a national wilderness policy might be and for thinkers like Zahniser to float their ideas.

Zahniser took advantage of the opportunity to introduce his biggest idea at the second conference in 1951. What was needed, he said, was a congressionally established wilderness system in which Congress specified what the proper uses of wilderness should be. Congressional action would prohibit the Forest Service from declassifying or modifying the primitive areas and the Park Service from expanding its developed areas into wilderness portions of the parks. Zahniser's idea was that conservationists should go all out for a wilderness "system" involving all federal agencies that had any wilderness within their jurisdiction. Many of his colleagues questioned the wisdom of this approach in 1951. They thought he was reaching for too much. But Zahniser thought the time had come to lay the proposal on the conference table for critical review and debate. The issues were argued until, in 1957, a wilderness bill was finally introduced into Congress.

Before the push for wilderness could begin in earnest, other obstacles had to be overcome, and foremost among these was the growing threat to national parks and wilderness from the dam builders. The Bureau of Reclamation's proposed dams in Dinosaur National Monument became the focal point of the fight on this front. Proclaimed a monument in 1915 to protect 80 acres of dinosaur bones and enlarged to 209,744 acres by Franklin Roosevelt in 1938, Dinosaur was a little known but very beautiful and wild unit of the national park system. The Green and Yampa Rivers converged in the monument, flowing through a deep canyon that the bureau thought an ideal dam site. Advocates of dams in the monument claimed there was a provision in the 1938 proclamation that would allow dam construction there, but conservationists disagreed. They girded to fight what many thought might become the worst intrusion in the national park system since Hetch Hetchy. Newton Drury had been worried for years that the national park system was increasingly in jeopardy from the nation's growing interest in dams. Though the Bureau of Reclamation was a sister agency in the Department of the Interior, and there was no doubt that the Truman administration was in favor of the Colorado River Storage project, Drury strongly and publicly objected to the Dinosaur dam proposal. The consequence of Drury's open defiance of administration priorities was that in 1951 Secretary of the Interior Oscar Chapman asked Drury to resign as director of the National Park Service.

Drury did not go willingly, and Chapman's action drew strong objections from conservationists. Chapman claimed that he was simply rewarding long-serving Assistant Director Arthur Demaray with the appointment as director to replace Drury, but this ploy fooled no one. Drury had crossed his boss, and the boss wanted him out. Zahniser and others argued that Drury had done a fine job and should continue in his post, but the director had committed the sin of publicly criticizing the administration. He was beyond saving, and Chapman appointed Demaray, who accepted the role of honored placeholder until the administration could name its choice as Drury's replacement. After nine months, Conrad Wirth, a twenty-year Park Service veteran, took the reins in December 1951.

What bothered conservationists about Drury's dismissal was that it seemed blatant punishment for doing the job the National Park Service director was sworn to do. Drury had written in 1943, "As long as the basic law [the National Park Act] that created them [the national parks] endures, we are assured of at least these few places in the world where forests continue to evolve normally, where animal life remains in harmonious relation to its environment, and where the ways of nature and its works may still be studied in the original design."[31] If Drury was being punished for his defense of the national parks, then his assurances that "these few places" would remain sacrosanct rang hollow. His pronouncements about the wilderness policy of the Park Service might also be rendered meaningless. Writing in *National Parks Magazine*, Waldo Leland observed that "the greatest and most persistent danger to which the national parks are subjected results from the plans of other agencies of the government, such as the Bureau of Reclamation of the Department of the Interior, for the construction of an infinite number of multiple-purpose dams for the control and utilization of water resources."[32] Drury had stood up to this threat, or attempted to, and his firing sent a signal that some in the government, the interior secretary among them, thought water resources development should take precedence over protection of the national park system. Leland was well qualified to express this view. He was director emeritus of the American Council of Learned Societies and had served on the Advisory Board on National Parks, Historic Sites, Buildings and Monuments from its creation in 1935 until 1950, serving as chairman from 1946 to 1950.

Leland concluded his *National Parks Magazine* article with a challenge:

> Nature conservationists will realize that now, and in the immediate future, they must be more than ever on the alert. They have not forgotten Hetch Hetchy; if the destruction of Dinosaur, which has been conclusively shown to be unnecessary, is consummated, and if Mr. Drury is succeeded by Directors less determined to defend, without exception, the great heritage of countless generations of Americans, the friends of the national parks will resort to all means within their power to create such defenses in public opinion as cannot be broken down.[33]

In this challenge he pointed out something else that bothered conservationists about Drury's dismissal. There was concern about his successor, who, even as Leland wrote, was known to be Conrad Wirth. Wirth's dedication to preservation was suspect, and if he was being chosen by Oscar Chapman, that itself cast suspicion upon him. Would he, asked Leland, "be able to defend the Service from undue interference, already manifesting itself, from 'up-stairs'?"[34] Fred Packard of the National Parks Association observed in a letter to NPA president William Wharton that as far back as the 1930s, Robert Sterling Yard had been worried about Wirth. Yard thought Wirth "aspired to be Director, and . . . with his previous background in State Park work his policies would conflict seriously with a proper national park program." Packard thought that "under Wirth the emphasis of park policy would be on development for recreation rather than on protection."[35]

Wirth had been leading Park Service recreation initiatives since 1934 and had been very successful. He had made the Park Service the leader in outdoor recreation planning nationally, and everyone knew that his primary interest was in the recreation rather than the preservation side of the Park Service mission. The conservation community understood that national park facilities and roads had declined in the neglect of the war years and agreed that a large effort for maintenance and repair was essential. Wirth might be the man to tackle this big task, but would he favor serving the ever-growing recreation needs of the parks at the expense of protecting park resources, and would he defend the parks against development in the way Drury had attempted? Many seriously doubted that he would, and the consequences might be critical for wilderness preservation.

WIRTH TAKES COMMAND

Conrad Wirth was trained as a landscape architect and was deeply committed to the Park Service. His skill as an administrator and his political astuteness had been amply demonstrated in the 1930s when he nearly overnight built up the recreation planning effort of the Park Service to an unprecedented level. He was a leader in the mold of Horace Albright, highly organized, focused on goals, and comfortable around politicians. Unlike Albright, however, he had never seen duty in the field at any level. His entire career had been spent in Washington, DC (except when headquarters had been moved to Chicago and for a short period he spent in Germany after the war). Wirth certainly had visited many parks during his long career with the Park Service, but nowhere in his writings and speeches can passion for nature, for wilderness, or even for park beauty be found. Conrad Wirth knew that his recreation work and his organization to pursue it were important and threw his considerable energies into making his part of the Park Service run smoothly and achieve its goals. He was cut from different cloth than many members of the Park Service and conservation communities who were moved, like Muir, Yard, and Drury had been, by the mystical and inspirational qualities of nature. That Wirth was a practical man, and proud of it, is not a criticism of him, but it helps in understanding the mindset that he brought to his new job. He believed that the Park Service should protect the parks, but also that it should serve the needs of ordinary citizens who were out in the parks for "fun and excitement as well as 'inspiration.'"[36] He thought the Park Service had, at times, erred on the side of preservation at the expense of tourists, and he thought this should be corrected. Historian Michael Cohen has compared the orientation of wilderness enthusiasts and advocates like Aldo Leopold and Bob Marshall with Mather, Albright, and Wirth. Leopold and Marshall believed not in an agency and its work but in working with the land and helping people draw strength and spiritual sustenance from it. The principal allegiance of land managers like Mather, Albright, and Wirth was to their organization, their institution. Their world was that of the institution's values, attitudes, and duties. "In the extreme example, a manager like Conrad Wirth saw a national park as the sum of its facilities, roads, and buildings built for visitors, saw a different reality from those engaged in the wilderness movement."[37] Drury's views of the national parks had been more akin to those of Leopold, Marshall, Yard, and other preservationists than to Albright's and Wirth's. He had expressed this in the 1940s in his writings and talks to the National Parks Association and other conservation groups. Now Wirth's appointment was, it was feared, a move away from aestheticism and preservation.[38] It was, thought wilderness advocates, a likely move away from wilderness in the national park system.

The fight over Dinosaur lasted five years, four of them during the Wirth directorship. The National Park Service stayed officially on the sidelines, publicly supporting the Colorado River Storage Project while conservationists fought with all of their resources to keep dams out of Dinosaur and the national park system. Yet even as they publicly stayed out of the fight, the Service at the same time encouraged rafters to float the Green and Yampa rivers, thus quietly feeding ammunition to dam opponents. These opponents ultimately prevailed and did so by unifying and coordinating their efforts to an unprecedented degree. They formed a coalition of seventeen conservation groups under an emergency committee of the Sierra Club's David Brower, Zahniser, Ira Gabrielson of the Wildlife Management Institute, and William Voigt Jr. Ultimately the anti-dam campaign grew to involve seventy-eight organizations. As Mark Harvey has noted, the success in the Dinosaur campaign was especially important to the organizations most interested in parks and wilderness—the Sierra Club, the National Parks Association, and The Wilderness Society.[39] These groups were small but recruited larger organizations like the National Wildlife Federation and the Izaak Walton League to their cause. As Harvey observes, "The threat of Echo Park provided them with an excellent opportunity to laud 'primeval parks' and to incorporate their agenda into the broader conservation movement."[40] The fight over Dinosaur revealed to a wider public the nature of threats to wilderness and parks. More important, success in the campaign, fueled by a public outpouring for preservation, demonstrated that the public cared about protecting the few remaining wild and beautiful places in the public domain. Zahniser understood this and wasted no time—he introduced the first wilderness bill in Congress two months after the battle over Dinosaur ended.

While they marshaled their forces in the Dinosaur struggle, conservationists continued to shape their position on wilderness. They needed to come to some consensus as to what the goal should be. Were they protecting wilderness for its own sake in the sense that wildness is manifest in creatures like wolves and grizzlies that are dependent upon it? John Muir, back in 1875, had thought about this, commenting that "I have never happened upon a trace of evidence that seemed to show that any one animal was ever made for another as much as it was made for itself."[41] Or were they aiming to protect it for the people's sake, for the type of recreation that Leopold and Marshall had extolled? If they hoped to wield their newfound power to protect wilderness, they would have to explain their aims to the public, and to do that required a greater degree of clarity as to their goals than had yet appeared in their discussions.

The Sierra Club wilderness conferences provided a forum in which to wrestle with such issues. At the 1953 conference Zahniser addressed the abstract issue of defining wilderness. Forest Service speakers and Sequoia-Kings Canyon National Park superintendent Eivind Scoyen brought discussion down to earth. The Sierra National Forest supervisor said he thought the issue of wilderness would rapidly go from "philosophical and spiritual considerations to the cold realities of administration."[42] He shared statistics on the huge increase in visitation to wilderness in his forest. Scoyen argued that the impact from visitation could be managed, but the National Park Service hardly had the resources to do it. Wilderness recreation and its impacts on the wilderness resource were growing, the managers argued, regardless of how wilderness was defined. Views were shared and nothing was resolved, but the issues continued to be clarified.

Discussion ensued at the wilderness conference in 1955. One session focused on park wilderness, and Scoyen sang the familiar Park Service refrain. "We should consider the parks as a whole as wilderness and tag the exceptions rather than classifying special portions of the parks as 'wilderness.'"[43] Other park officials spoke to projections of national park visitation—they were expecting 75 million by 1975. While they knew most of the visitors would stay on park roads, pressure would also grow on the backcountry. Zahniser reiterated the ideas for wilderness system legislation he had laid out back in 1951 and joined Harold Bradley of the Sierra Club in a session devoted to classifying wilderness areas. In his history of the Sierra Club, Michael Cohen observes that this alliance was important for its symbolism. The Sierra Club had moved from the idea that compromised wilderness was better than none to a consideration of wilderness "zoning" and had committed itself to The Wilderness Society's idea of legislation. This discussion "marked a significant shift in emphasis for the conference, as well as growth in the strength of the idea [of wilderness]."[44] As the legislative battles to come would reveal, all conceptual issues had not been resolved, but matters had progressed among the conservationists to the point that, when the time was right, the drive for wilderness legislation could begin. That time would come before the next conference.

MISSION 66

Meanwhile, back at the Park Service, other issues were the focus of attention. Foremost among them were the challenges posed by rapidly rising visitation. The budget was lagging far behind demand and the pressures it brought. Drury had lobbied for increased appropriations but had been frustrated—appropriations increased but not at the rate he thought necessary. Little progress was made during Demaray's brief tenure, and when Wirth became director his efforts also failed initially to win appropriations adequate to meet needs. Annual visits in 1951 were 37 million and rose to 46 million in 1954. In his annual report that year, Wirth pointed out that there had been no new facilities to meet this increase. The backlog of road, trail, building, and utility projects continued to grow. In 1955 Wirth recorded increased funding, but still "the system has been allowed to deteriorate because of necessarily lowered standards of maintenance, protection and development."[45]

Wirth and his colleagues were not the only people concerned about this funding situation. Bernard DeVoto used his column in Harper's to bring the problem to national attention. Writing in his usual hard-hitting style, he stated that "Congress did not provide money to rehabilitate the parks at the end of the war, [sic] it has not provided money to meet the enormously increased demand. So much of the priceless heritage which the Service must safeguard for the United States is beginning to go to hell."[46] DeVoto detailed the fiscal woes and consequent problems of the national park system and argued that what needed to be done was as clear to Congress as it was to him—appropriate large sums of public money to improve the parks and the Park Service. But, since no such funding seemed likely, DeVoto advocated an extreme measure:

The national park system must be temporarily reduced to a size for which Congress is willing to pay. Let us, as a beginning, close Yellowstone, Yosemite, Rocky

Mountain, and Grand Canyon National Parks—close and seal them, assign the army to patrol them, and so hold them secure till they can be reopened.[47]

DeVoto's column did not result in park closings, but it helped bring much-needed public attention to the growing national park crisis.

Wirth was inspired, in 1955, to mount a new approach to the park funding challenge. He had for three years been submitting budget requests and making the case piecemeal for various projects and programs. Why not, he asked, estimate what it would cost to bring the entire park system up to "satisfactory conditions"? Why not propose to Congress an "all-inclusive long-term program for the entire park system"? He organized the Park Service to study this, and the program he called "Mission 66" was born. The goal would be to seek all funding necessary to complete the upgrade of park protection, staffing, interpretation, development, and financing by the golden anniversary of the Park Service in 1966. Rather than continue the piecemeal approach to appropriations, he would go for the whole package in one large program request.

Wirth was a politically savvy bureaucrat. He knew how to marshal his resources toward agency goals, had a solid grasp of what needed to be done internally to prepare his case, and had good political skills. As he explained to a skeptical National Parks Association, he thought Congress would more readily fund a systemwide program than a park-by-park approach. The Park Service had solid master plans and could gather plenty of evidence to make the case for a sustained program. He convinced the association and went on to persuade the Eisenhower administration that this approach would be a good one politically. With administration backing he lobbied Congress, and after fifteen years of neglect the park system finally received a large infusion of funding. Its budget started growing in fiscal 1956, rising from $33 million in 1955 to $49 million in 1956, ultimately reaching a high of $128 million in 1965. Mission 66, before it ended, brought to the park system more than $1 billion for operation and capital improvement.[48]

Wirth appointed a Mission 66 committee that drew up fourteen guide-lines for the program. One dealt specifically with wilderness, stating that "large wilderness areas should be preserved except for simple facilities required for access, back-country use and protection, and in keeping with the wilderness atmosphere."[49] Brower and Zahniser described later how they met in 1955 with Wirth and an assistant to discuss conservationists' concerns about Mission 66. They convinced the Park Service to add to the stated objec-

6.2 Conrad Wirth directed the Park Service during the drive for the Wilderness Act. National Park Service Historic Photographic Collection, Harpers Ferry Center. Photo by Abbie Rowe, 1960

tives of the program one that would read, "Provide for the protection and preservation of the wilderness areas within the national park system and encourage their appreciation and enjoyment in ways that will 'keep them unimpaired.'" There was some resistance to stating this objective in Mission 66, Wirth insisting that it was to be assumed, but he finally relented.[50] Lemuel Garrison, National Park Service chief of conservation and protection, was named to chair one of the lead Mission 66 committees. He later reflected in his memoir, *The Making of a Ranger*, that he was surprised to learn, in gathering information on needs and plans for Mission 66 in 1956, that concern for wilderness among Park Service people in the field was very high. Many endorsed park preservation as the major goal of national park management.[51] This was, thought Garrison, a good thing, but why was he surprised by this response? Later he commented that the Park Service was managing the parks "according to wilderness precepts already," so he and others thought "the Wilderness Bill was redundant as it related to National Parks."[52] Perhaps Garrison was out of touch with people out in the wilderness parks, since he had been in the East for several years. At about this time Wirth selected Eivind Scoyen as associate director rather than Hillory Tilson, who had been serving him as assistant director. Wirth chose Scoyen over Tilson because he knew he needed someone with field experience, and Tilson, like Wirth, had been in the Washington office throughout his career.[53] Scoyen would not have been among senior officials surprised to learn of the high level of interest in wilderness and preservation among Park Service field people. His duties in Yosemite had placed him at the center of the wilderness discussions at Sierra Club conferences and in his region and park. The consequence of all of this was that wilderness made its way into the stated goals of Mission 66, which, as will be seen, was a mixed blessing.

Mission 66 began with support from conservationists. They had been working with the Park Service for years to increase congressional appropriations. Everyone agreed that park facilities and infrastructure had deteriorated and needed to be repaired and upgraded. They also agreed that rapidly increased use required investment in projects that would assure visitors a quality experience. In 1956 Devereaux Butcher of the National Parks Association, a persistent Park Service critic, commented about Mission 66 that "it is gratifying to comment [on] a program the Park Service has developed that is so excellently conceived and so far-reaching in its implications as to encourage the belief that the national parks and their administration are going to improve for a long time to come."[54] If such a critic viewed Mission 66 this way, then so did most of his colleagues at this time. Still, just as Yard worried back in the 1930s about what the infusion of New Deal money might do to the parks, so Butcher and others intended to watch the Park Service carefully as it launched its new initiative.

Wirth asked a respected scholar of natural resource issues, Marion Clawson of Resources for the Future, to review Mission 66 projections for the future use of national parks, and Clawson thought their projections low. He thought visitation would reach 80 million by 1963 and might reach 120 million by 1966 (it actually reached over 133 million during that golden anniversary year).[55] Garrison remembered that Park Service planners thought that "we had to get visitors on the roads, flowing easily through 'travel tubes' that we had created, diverted as needed at intersections through multiple lanes and modern signs, sidetracked occasionally for scenic views or a roadside moose."[56] The trickle of automobile visitors that had begun back in Mather's day had become a flood, and the Park Service needed to respond. That meant development, and Congress, in approving Mission 66, agreed. Furthermore, the National Park Service idea that development was in fact a method of conservation—first seen back in the Mather era—was a part of the Mission 66 thinking. Garrison expressed it, writing that "appropriate development of facilities such as roads or trails actually could be viewed as a conservation and protection measure, as it tended to channel and restrict use."[57] This might well be so, but conservationists worried, as they had earlier, that this excuse might be used to build roads that reduced park wilderness. Their concern about this was a motive for wilderness legislation. Despite all the assurances in the Mission 66 guidelines and other official pronouncements, preservation-minded conservationists like Zahniser did not trust the National Park Service to protect wilderness.

Wirth had, in his long career, advanced the recreation side of the Park Service mission. Would he continue to do this at the expense of preservation? Some thought he might, and some now think he did. Richard Sellars has written that Mission 66 "was a high point of what might be termed the 'landscape architecture approach' to national park management, when, under landscape architect Wirth, development of the parks for recreational tourism dominated national park concerns and went largely unfettered by natural resource concerns."[58] In his memoir Wirth touted the "construction accomplishments" of Mission 66, and the list is long. Among accomplishments, of which he was very proud, are 1,197 miles of new roads, 577 miles of new trails, 1,502 new parking areas, 575 new campgrounds, 221 new administrative buildings, and so on. Many of these were undoubtedly necessary to meet basic needs of increasing visitation, yet all of this construction eventually resulted in criticism of Mission 66. Conservationists thought that some projects, such as the widening of the Tenaya Road in Yosemite, crossed the line between needs and wants, justified and not. Some, they thought, were blatant invasions of wilderness.

At the same time as it enjoyed huge support and realized its funding goals, this "Golden Age," as Sellars notes, brought major changes to Park Service programs. It lost control of natural resource planning to a new agency, the Bureau of Outdoor Recreation. Its support from conservationists eroded and, most important for the story being followed here, it lost its "administrative discretion over the parks' backcountry" to the wilderness bill.[59]

Howard Zahniser, the struggle over Dinosaur nearly behind him, turned his attention back to the idea of a congressionally established wilderness preservation system. On May 24, 1955, he spoke in Washington, DC, to the National Citizens Planning Conference on Parks and Open Spaces for Americans. He called for protection of areas of wilderness that remained, not only from "exploitation for commodity purposes" but from the managers themselves. "Their [wilderness areas] peculiar values are also in danger from development for recreation, even from efforts to protect and manage them as wilderness."[1] After reviewing the values of wilderness, he repeated the proposals he had introduced at the Wilderness Conference in 1951. Minnesota Senator Hubert H. Humphrey, who had become an ally in the fight over Dinosaur, placed the speech in the *Congressional Record* and was so impressed by the case Zahniser made for wilderness that he asked him to draft a bill he could introduce in the Senate. Zahniser began this task the following February, circulating drafts among fellow conservation leaders for their comment.

Zahniser believed success in this new initiative would require the sort of cooperation that had enabled victory in the Dinosaur struggle. He wanted a bill that could be supported by the members of the Dinosaur coalition and collaborated closely on the bill with the Sierra Club, the National Parks Association, the National Wildlife Federation, and the Wildlife Management Institute. The purposes of the bill, as summarized by long-serving Sierra Club leader Mike McCloskey, were fourfold: to "provide clear statutory authority for the maintenance of wilderness areas," to "remove the administrative authority of Forest Service officials to decrease the size of or to declassify wilderness-type areas," to "protect national forest wilderness areas against mining and installation of water projects," and finally to "require designation of wilderness zones in units of the National Park System, the federal wildlife refuge and range systems, and within Indian reservations."[2] As early as 1951, Zahniser had suggested that any legislation to create a National Wilderness Preservation System should respect the existing management jurisdictions—land designated wilderness would stay under its current manager. The hope was that this would reassure agencies and blunt their opposition. Zahniser also hoped to reduce opposition from commodity interests by assuring them that existing uses would be respected. Language in the bill about "nonconforming uses" and "equitable" termination of such uses did not, however, reassure that group, nor did language that could be used to enforce condemnation if negotiations to end such uses failed to achieve that goal.[3]

KEY MOTIVES FOR DRAFTING A WILDERNESS BILL

While the focus here is on national park wilderness, the introduction of the wilderness bill brings the Forest Service back into the story. As McCloskey's overview of the bill's purposes reveals, the issue of national forest wilderness seems to have been of deeper concern to Zahniser and his colleagues than national park wilderness. While recreational development might threaten national park wilderness, extraction of resources by mining, logging, and grazing were all prohibited in most parks. All of these activities, on the other hand, were possible "multiple uses" in national forests. National Parks were established by Congress (though national monuments were not), and a few national parks even had wilderness language in the legislation creating them. In this the national park wilderness was not in as critical a condition as that in the national forests.

National forest wilderness areas had proven to be more vulnerable to administrative fiat than national parks. The 1939 U-regulations issued by the Forest Service were intended to at least partially remedy this, but it was clear to many that they had not done so. The U-regulations required that all primitive areas be reevaluated before reclassification by the secretary of agriculture as "wilderness areas" (100,000 acres or more) or "wild areas"

(5,000–100,000 acres). They would in the meantime be protected. The Forest Service got off to a slow start on its reevaluation and did little work on it during World War II. After the war, pressure grew for timber harvest, and the Forest Service seemed very reluctant to reclassify the primitive areas. It had, by the late 1940s, reclassified only 2 million acres as wilderness, and it seemed on a path toward excluding from wilderness, wherever possible, areas that had valuable timber standing on them.

In its response to the 1948 wilderness survey, the Forest Service reported it had no plans to designate any additional wilderness. This was of concern to Zahniser and his colleagues because there was still much de facto wilderness—roadless areas with no protection except their isolation—in national forests, but it was disappearing rapidly in the postwar timber and road-building boom. If there was any hope of preserving some of this de facto wilderness it would lie in congressional action. There was little hope the Forest Service would take the initiative.

As for the national parks, the hope of conservationists was that the wilderness bill would force the Park Service to formalize its long-held approach that park land that had not been developed was wilderness. This was the "zoning" to which McCloskey referred in his summary of the bill's purpose. The Park Service was zoning the parks in an informal and unofficial way. What worried Zahniser and his allies about this was that nothing, in their view, bound the Park Service to keep the wilderness zones in place. Even as Zahniser was struggling to draft his bill, Wirth was mounting Mission 66. While Wirth was not setting out to invade park wilderness zones, what was to stop him if he were to decide that new roads should be built into roadless areas somewhere? What was to keep the Park Service from expanding its "developed" zones in order to meet the needs of its growing mass of visitors? The Park Service enjoyed its administrative discretion just as much as the Forest Service. Zahniser and his conservationist colleagues made clear that they were looking for ways to reduce this discretion.

In late February 1956, Zahniser sent a draft of the bill to Wirth and to the chief of the Forest Service. He followed this with a visit. Sierra Club Executive Director David Brower and Charles Woodbury of the National Parks Association joined him for his call on Wirth. Following this meeting, Wirth wrote to Zahniser rejecting the idea that national park wilderness would be better protected in the proposed National Wilderness Preservation System. He cited the National Park Service Act of 1916, which he was certain gave "primeval areas of national parks and monuments" all the protection they needed. "In these circumstances, it is our view that nothing would be gained from placing such areas in the National Wilderness Preservation System as provided in the bill."[4] He thought protection of parks and monuments might be diminished by the proposed legislation because so many types of areas were lumped into the bill that the "degree of preservation which could be afforded" might well "settle to the lowest level applicable to any of the types of areas involved." Wirth was convinced that the inevitable compromises with water development interests, miners, grazing, and timber interests necessary to get the bill through Congress "can only mean that the standards which are now set so high by law for the National Park System will be lowered." While Wirth was interested in the objectives of the proposed legislation, "I feel that we cannot afford to run this risk." Wirth pledged to have Eivind Scoyen explore ways to guide the Park Service operations "so that the wilderness preservation groups will feel that their interests are better protected." He closed with assurances that "no further encroachment on the primeval wilderness is the overriding policy of this Service."

As this letter so well indicates, the leadership of the Park Service and the wilderness preservationists saw the situation quite differently at this point. There is no reason to think that Wirth and his colleagues were not sincere in raising their concerns. He raised exactly the same issues in an internal memorandum urging the Interior Department to submit "adverse reports" on the versions of the wilderness bill introduced in 1956.[5] The bill's drafters certainly wanted no lowering of wilderness protection in the national park system and would accept no compromise that would bring such a result. Wirth should have understood that, but he could not be sure of the outcome of the wilderness bill debate that he knew would be long and contentious. As had the National Park Service directors before him, he believed that his agency had all the authority it needed to protect wilderness and that it had been doing so in a responsible way. He saw no need for additional legislation that at best would reduce the management flexibility of his agency and at worst weaken the protection that he believed park wilderness already had.

Despite Wirth's rejection of the whole idea and concerns raised by the Park Service, Zahniser continued to circulate the bill. He presented it to the Twenty-First Wildlife Conference in New Orleans in March and to the Federation of Western Outdoor Clubs Northwest Wilderness Conference in April. Sigurd Olson, veteran wilderness advocate and president of the National Parks Association, had, as a resident of Senator Humphrey's state of Minnesota, worked with the senator on other conservation measures, principally efforts to protect the Quetico-Superior wilderness. He wrote to the senator in April 1956 about the wilderness bill:

> In short the bill will give approval to policies the Services have inaugurated and have fought for against tremendous odds for a long time. It will enable the departments to say "now for the first time, the preservation of wilderness has assumed the stature of a congressional mandate. Above political or industrial pressures, it is no longer subject to the vagaries of administrative change."[6]

Olson was undoubtedly aware of the National Park Service response to the bill (Wirth had sent a copy of his letter to Zahniser to the NPA's Woodbury), and here he states that whatever Wirth might think, he and other advocates of the National Wilderness Preservation System thought a mandate specifically for wilderness preservation in national forests and parks was necessary. The National Park Act was not sufficient protection.

WIRTH ATTEMPTS TO CHANGE THE BILL

As Zahniser pressed on, Wirth seems to have been doing a bit of behind-the-scenes work to change the wilderness bill to a form more acceptable to the Park Service. While no documents link him directly to such an effort, he is implicated in some complex machinations. The vehicle for this effort was the Council of Conservationists, an umbrella organization that appeared in 1954 and had been an important player in the final stages of the drive to defeat the Echo Park dam proposed for Dinosaur National Monument. Founded by a wealthy St. Louis businessman and led by Fred Smith, a savvy public relations expert from the insurance industry, the organization recruited the top leaders of conservation groups onto its board, including David Brower, Zahniser, Ira Gabrielson, and Joe Penfold of the Izaak Walton League. Zahniser was the group's Washington, DC, representative. In April 1956 Zahniser received a letter from Fred Smith, with whom he had recently discussed the wilderness bill and who was, he thought, a solid supporter of it. Smith objected to various provisions of the proposed legislation. He thought the bill would never pass and that "the Park Service is completely justified in its opposition." Smith asserted that he had been in close consultation with Horace Albright about the bill, and Albright, whom Smith thought a great friend to conservationists, was in an awkward position. In a revealing paragraph Smith says:

In order to go along with us he [Albright] would have to break with Wirth. . . . In the end, he might have gone along even at that cost, but if he did, Wirth would have twice as much reason to buck us the next time around—he would not only be disturbed at interference in his preserves but would be sore because we took away one of his staunchest allies. Since it will be extremely difficult to pass a wilderness bill in spite of Wirth, this would have proved an unwise eventuality.[7]

Horace Albright still believed national park wilderness was well protected (as he did to the end of his long life). He and Wirth were in agreement on that point. As Albright wrote Brower later in April, he was for wilderness preservation in the national forests, "but I certainly shy away from the bill that has been prepared and which embraces the national parks."[8] He felt this way because he thought the wilderness bill would add nothing to protection in national parks and monuments and because the bill "would unnecessarily limit the power and authority of the Secretary of the Interior and the Director of the National Park Service over areas that, except for exceedingly small sections, are in wilderness condition." Albright's last point was fundamental. His and Wirth's public objection to the wilderness bill might claim that new legislation was redundant or take issue with particular technical points in the bill, but underneath it was an unwillingness to give up Park Service authority and administrative discretion. In a December memorandum to the Council Executive Committee, Smith and Albright suggested that the bill should include "a formula by means of which administrators can change the borders (with considerable difficulty, but) without requiring Congressional approval."[9] This was of course unacceptable to bill supporters. The whole point was to remove the administrator's discretion on adjustment of wilderness boundaries. No bureaucrat gives up power without a fight, and Wirth undoubtedly was using the still considerable influence of Horace Albright to try to deflect what he saw as an assault on Park Service authority over its domain.

Zahniser was open to suggestions to improve the wilderness bill, but this dissension among former colleagues went beyond constructive criticism. In January 1957 Zahniser wrote journalist John Oakes, "I am afraid I am in Fred Smith's dog house, but I couldn't help it. He seems to be in volunteer command of a flank maneuver in behalf of the Park Service."[10] A month later Smith "dismissed" Zahniser, Brower, and Penfold from the council, and Gabrielson resigned. In May Brower wrote Sierra Club colleague Howard Elliott explaining how, in his view, Wirth had attempted to drive wedges among wilderness supporters. "The difficulties arose from the combined efforts of Wirth, Albright, and Smith to undercut the wilderness bill and pry supporters away from it."[11]

This episode is described here to reveal that, while in public the exchange between Wirth and Zahniser was polite and both openly discussed issues, Wirth and Albright were not above attempting to get national parks out of the wilderness bill with a little backdoor maneuvering. They damaged the conservationist's unanimity a bit, isolating Smith, who went along with them for his own reasons. They did not, however, knock the campaign off course. Zahniser had a response to all of the concerns expressed by Smith. In a one-page statement he sent to the governing council of The Wilderness Society at the height of the exchange with Smith, Zahniser states as clearly as he ever did why the national parks must be included in the bill:

> The national parks and monuments containing areas of wilderness should be included in the proposed National Wilderness Preservation System both for the sake of making the system complete and for the sake of making more secure the preservation of the wilderness back country of the Park System itself. Existing legislation does not insure the preservation of areas within the parks and monuments as wilderness. Under the existing legislation all of the roads and buildings now in the national parks have been constructed, and more and more could be built. There is nothing in our legislation now to protect future administrators from mounting pressures to use more and more of the back country for developments that would destroy them as wilderness.[12]

Zahniser could not have been clearer about why national park units should be included in the wilderness bill. Rather than threaten park wilderness, the bill "provides a new and further opportunity for extending the influence of the national park principle and for developing further the cooperation and leadership of the National Park Service in helping to preserve our heritage of wilderness."[13] Zahniser would work to lessen the concerns of the Park Service, but he was adamant about inclusion of the parks in the bill. Maneuvering would continue for years, but Wirth and Zahniser had staked out their positions.

CONGRESS CONSIDERS THE WILDERNESS BILL

Senator Humphrey and eight other senators introduced the first wilderness bill in 1956. Five identical bills were introduced in the House, and the legislative struggle was on. Nine years of argument, sixty-five bills, eighteen hearings, and thousands of pages of testimony would be necessary before a

Wilderness Act would be signed into law in 1964. The fascinating and complex history of this legislation has been described in detail elsewhere.[14] While much of the opposition to the bill and reason for the protracted fight involved national forests, the lens here remains focused on national parks. Forest Service historian Dennis Roth rightly points out that if the bill concerned only parks it would have faced less opposition.[15] National forest issues prolonged the legislative struggle. The National Park Service continued for years to search for ways to minimize the impact of the legislation on their operation, their objections slowly being met. Finally they would come to a politically necessary, if grudging, acceptance of the wilderness bill, which is the next phase of this story.

The wilderness bill was reintroduced in the 85th Congress, its earlier appearance having served merely as an introduction to the proposal. The Sierra Club convened another wilderness conference in March, and Wirth spoke at length to the idea that "wilderness and its preservation involve far more than roadlessness."[16] He cited National Park Service reduction of grazing, acquisition of private inholdings in parks, fire control, new approaches to trails and roads, even "recognition of the place of predators as a part of the natural fauna" as evidence that the National Park Service was contributing to wilderness preservation. He tried to sell Mission 66 as "a magnificent and challenging opportunity to augment wilderness values of the parks." Park interpretation was focusing on wilderness use and appreciation, and the National Park Service was contributing to a "comprehensive analysis of the wilderness and wild land needs of the country, and a systematic plan for the preservation of wilderness and wild lands required to meet those needs."[17] All of this was evidence, Wirth argued, that the National Park Service could be trusted to care for its wild lands. Further, with analysis and planning, the Park Service would work toward new park wild lands. Wirth announced that the service had prepared a statement on wilderness preservation in national parks that would elaborate on what he could say in his talk and that would be distributed to those in attendance.

Prior to the meeting, Senator Humphrey had written to Sierra Club president Alexander Hildebrand expressing his disappointment that "some people we have come to count upon as friends of conservation have raised ... unjustified doubts about it [the wilderness bill]."[18] The senator mentioned Chief Richard McArdle of the Forest Service and Wirth as among these wayward friends. He undoubtedly knew that the agency leaders would attend the wilderness conference now that legislation had been introduced and their discretionary powers threatened. This was the first wilderness conference that any agency heads attended. Hildebrand replied, after the conference, that neither administrator had openly opposed the legislation during the meeting. Wirth had never mentioned it in his long speech, though most in attendance undoubtedly knew of the stance he had taken in opposition to the legislation. Zahniser, in his summary remarks to the conference, stated the point he had made to his governing council three months earlier when he had said, "We owe the leaders of the National Park Service a great debt for the way in which they have fostered the wilderness idea, but we must recognize that the wilderness concept is compatible with, not identical to, the national park idea—an enrichment certainly of the national park purpose, but not the genesis."[19]

The first hearings on the wilderness bill were scheduled for May 1957. Prior to the hearings, the Public Lands Subcommittee of the House heard testimony on another important and related piece of legislation—a bill to establish an Outdoor Recreation Resources Review Commission (ORRRC) that would do an inventory of outdoor recreation resources in the United States. Such a comprehensive inventory had not been done since the Park Service conducted one in the 1930s. Everyone agreed that the proposed review was a good idea, and wilderness advocates viewed it as a companion to the wilderness bill. The Fifth Biennial Wilderness Conference had unanimously endorsed it and recommended "that the legislation establishing the survey not be misinterpreted so as to interfere with the adoption of other legislation to provide for the immediate protection of wilderness."[20] In his statement at this hearing Zahniser expressed his support for the measure and noted that wilderness bill opponents were already using the review as a delaying tactic. They should not, he argued, be allowed to do this.

When, a month later, the same subcommittee heard testimony on the wilderness bill, the delaying tactic Zahniser anticipated was attempted by bill opponents. Director Wirth read the Department of the Interior statement to the committee. His earlier views and concerns were repeated: the Park Service was already doing what was needed to protect park wilderness; protection would not be improved and current levels of protection might be threatened by the proposed legislation; the council was redundant and would increase administrative cost. The Interior Department opined that, in particular, "a thorough and objective study should first be made of each area" suggested for wilderness status, and the proposed Outdoor Recreation Resources Review Commission "should review not only public recreation

7.1 Howard Zahniser and Olaus Murie, co-leaders of the Wilderness Society during the push for the Wilderness Act at National Jewish Hospital, Denver, 1950s. Wilderness Society Records, CONS130, Conservation Collection, Denver Public Library

resources but also wilderness areas and the need therefor."[21] The National Park Service was recommending delay. The Forest Service submitted a substitute bill. Conservationists testified, of course, for the wilderness bill, and the usual opponents were heard. The public debate of the wilderness bill was launched, and the Park Service position was clear: it was against it.

Commenting on the hearings afterward, Zahniser thought they had been useful. He and other supporters had "smoked out the opposition" and heard their concerns. Conservationists had stood together and done nothing to antagonize the opposition.[22] The Interior Department concerns could, he was sure, be refuted and at least some of the concerns lessened by revision of the bill. Wirth himself had said at the May hearing that there was no conflict between the Outdoor Recreation Commission bill and the wilderness bill. In a Park Service statement released to supplement Wirth's speech at the wilderness conference in March, it had inadvertently confirmed wilderness proponents' concern that the wilderness protection approach of the National Park Service was a matter of administrative discretion and thereby inadequate. The Park Service release had stated:

There would be little wilderness and much less of the natural beauty of the national parks left had the National Park Service been development-minded, promotionally inclined, and unrestrained by conservation principles. Acquiescence by the National Park Service, plus a little promotion, could have extended the road system, at least in prospect, up the Kings River, across the Olympics, around Mount Rainier, or into almost any wilderness area.[23]

This was a remarkable if unintentional admission that conservationists' claims for the necessity of statutory protection of park wilderness were legitimate. With statements like this on the record, how could the Park Service continue to claim that park wilderness was adequately protected? Zahniser thought the hearings had clarified what needed to be done to bring Interior and the National Park Service behind the wilderness bill.[24] He was underestimating Wirth, who had other initiatives in the works.

THE PARK SERVICE MOUNTS A PUBLIC RELATIONS CAMPAIGN

The mimeographed paper distributed at the March wilderness conference had, by September, become a thirty-seven-page color brochure titled *The National Park Wilderness*. The statement, quoted above, that agency discretion, not the Organic Act as claimed by Wirth and others before him, had preserved wilderness had been removed from the glossy version of the Park Service statement. There were other edits, but on the whole the new brochure was a slick version of the March release. Its target audience was the public, and its goal was to convince the public that the Park Service had always protected park wilderness and would continue to do so. The wilderness bill was never mentioned, but there was no doubt that the Park Service considered the publication a potent tool in its campaign against the legislation. It would, in subsequent years, be cited repeatedly by Wirth and others as an indicator of how committed the Park Service was to wilderness preservation.

The *National Park Wilderness* not only touted the Park Service record as protector of wilderness but promoted Mission 66. It cast Mission 66 as a wilderness preservation program. "MISSION 66 is in a position," stated the brochure, "to use development as a means of better preservation."[25] Mission 66 was much more than a wilderness program, of course, but the Park Service tried to make the point that because Mission 66 was long range and involved planning "on a scale large enough to overtake today's problems and to prepare for future ones before they develop," the program would allow development that would be constantly advised by a concern for the protection of wilderness. The pronouncements about wilderness in the brochure sounded very good, but some people thought them mostly rhetoric. David Brower, in particular, expressed his skepticism in a caustic article in *National Parks Magazine*. He recalled the trouble he and Zahniser had experienced just two years before when they had tried to convince the Park Service to include in Mission 66 goals one to the effect that "the entire Mission be directed so as to provide for the continued preservation, unaltered and unimpaired, of the areas of wilderness within the national park system."[26] Now here was a brochure claiming that wilderness was the central value of the national park system. What had brought about this big change? There was also the excised passage quoted earlier, which suggested that the discretion of Park Service leaders had really preserved the wilderness. This, thought Brower, tipped off the real intent of the brochure. It was pure public relations. Brower, Zahniser, and their colleagues knew that the National Park Act was not sufficient for protection of park wilderness. So, presumably, did Wirth aide Howard Stagner, who wrote the brochure, and Wirth himself.

The National Park Wilderness was the most extensive statement the National Park Service had ever made about wilderness in national parks. Only a few years earlier it could not even bring itself to use the term "wilderness" except in the broadest descriptive way. Events over the past five years had made an enormous difference in the seriousness with which the Park Service considered the idea of wilderness. They had decided to go on the offensive about it. To one not aware of the struggle over the wilderness bill—the casual reader of the brochure—it presented the Park Service as a strong defender of wilderness. The American public could rest assured that the Park Service was protecting wilderness. Also, the brochure was not entirely a response to the wilderness bill. As Mission 66 got under way, criticism of it grew stronger. The linkage in the brochure of wilderness preservation and Mission 66, the Park Service hoped, would reassure the public that the much-needed development to meet growing visitation would be no threat to park resources such as wilderness. The public could have both accessible parks and wilderness parks.

Meanwhile, as the public relations campaign was mounted, there were internal discussions as to how the Park Service should be responding to the wilderness bill. Associate Director Scoyen sent a memorandum to Wirth in January 1958 sharing his analysis of the bill. In it he argued that the National Park Service's view that the bill would lower park standards was not valid grounds for opposition. He thought the provision requiring the Park Service to identify wilderness and areas to be developed "carries out our contention that all of a park area is wilderness under the law and that the exceptions are our road corridors and developed areas." Parts of parks not designated for development should reasonably become part of the National Wilderness Preservation System. He suggested language that would make the point more clear about not lowering standards along with other thoughts on how the Park Service could contribute to better legislation. Scoyen concluded, "I think we will improve our public relations by changing from a position of outright opposition to one proposing acceptable change."[27]

In this memo Scoyen said he did not think passage of the wilderness bill was very likely, but he thought the Park Service would be well advised to contribute to improvement of the measure, not simply oppose it. The Forest Service, he pointed out, at least attempted to be constructive. They had proposed a substitute bill in which proponents found useful ideas for future drafts of the legislation. There are indications that Wirth took Scoyen's advice. At the end of January Zahniser wrote his Wilderness Society colleague Harvey Broome that "Conrad Wirth has assured Sig [Olson] and me that if certain safeguarding additions can be made (and Sig and I think they can be rather readily) he will go along with us on the Wilderness Bill and when it comes up in the Department of the Interior he will be 'in our corner,' to use his expression."[28] Also, the Senate bill, S. 4028, contained provisions, including the stronger statement regarding protection of standards, that Scoyen suggested be proposed. The Park Service had decided to be at least a little less obstructionist.

Veterans of politics like Wirth and Scoyen understood that they might more effectively achieve their ends by playing the game rather than simply stonewalling a popular idea. They did not become converts but took a more constructive approach while raising legitimate concerns. Zahniser and his bill-drafting and revising team were encouraged by this and responded in good faith. Scoyen ended his memo to Wirth on a cynical note regarding "public relations," but this too was a legitimate concern. Wirth, with his Mission 66 well under way, was acutely concerned about public relations. With new wilderness bill hearings looming, the Park Service needed to be concerned about both the image and the substance of its stance on the wilderness bill.

The Senate Committee on Interior and Insular Affairs held hearings on S. 4028 in July 1958. This time the secretary of the interior, in a letter to committee chairman James Murray, did not oppose the legislation as he had the previous year, but he continued to stall. Many of the questions he had raised "have been substantially resolved." The department recommended "early action by the Congress to attain the immediate basic objectives" of the legislation. In particular, it now believed the time had come to grant statutory recognition to wilderness, at least in principle. It supported Congress setting up a timetable for establishment of future wilderness, and it thought Congress should resolve the issue of authority for designating future wilderness.[29] Zahniser and his colleagues had responded to Park Service concerns in redrafting the wilderness bill. It now stipulated, for instance, that "the inclusion of any National Park System area within the Wilderness System pursuant to this Act shall in no manner lower the standards evolved for the use and preservation of such National Park System areas" established by other applicable laws.[30]

At this point the Interior Department and the National Park Service had softened their opposition but were not ready to support the bill as written. The struggle was renewed in 1959 when the bill was reintroduced in the 86th Congress. The Park Service continued its refrain that all was well with national park wilderness. Eivind Scoyen addressed the California Academy of Sciences in March, contending that 98 percent of the parks were wilderness, and even in the face of growing pressures he projected the parks would not lose more than 1 percent of their wilderness in the next fifty years. "Is this a fair amount?" he asked the group.[31] Later that month he reported to Wirth's "squad meeting," a regular gathering of the director's top Washington staff, that a new round of hearings on the wilderness bill was scheduled. The Department of the Interior was considering its report on this latest bill, and it would again take a position favoring the bill in principle. In early April the Park Service began its first formal backcountry management planning, choosing Sequoia-Kings Canyon National Park as the place to do it. The service would begin this planning process, to be extended to all wilderness parks "to bring under control the use of wilderness areas in the National Park System."[32] In August Wirth told a squad meeting that, whether or not the legislation passed, "we should proceed on our own with analysis of the areas to find out which areas we will want to define as 'developed areas' to meet the terms of the bill." Scoyen said that master plans would show developed areas and road corridors as zoned, and in establishing these zones planners should look well into the future. "If this bill goes through and parts of the parks go into the National Wilderness Preservation System then we will have considerable difficulty if we want to designate additional developed areas or road corridors." Wirth thought that one-half mile on each side of a road would be ample corridors.[33]

Here, in Wirth's inner circle, Scoyen expressed the fundamental reason behind the Park Service's reluctance to support the wilderness bill. Its hands would be tied in the future as it faced growing pressures from visitation. All it could do, thought Wirth and Scoyen, was plan far ahead and zone developed areas to meet some of the anticipated need for development. Howard Stagner, a member of this inner circle and author of *The National Park Wilderness*, recalled that the Park Service was "very cold" toward the wilderness legislation. Richard Sellars has observed that "to the Service it was kind of a 'turf situation'—a desire to maintain full control of the national parks backcountry without additional, burdensome regulations."[34] In the summer of 1959 Wirth decided to begin backcountry planning and a master planning approach that would keep his options as open as possible. Once again, however, no action was taken in Congress on the wilderness bill, so the threat of losing control of its backcountry was still not an immediate threat to the Park Service.

THE FINAL PUSH TO THE WILDERNESS ACT

By this stage in the effort to pass a wilderness bill, the proponents suspected that the opposition, especially the commodity interests, would go to any length to defeat the legislation. In February 1960, Wyoming Senator Joseph O'Mahoney, a member of the Interior and Insular Affairs Committee, introduced amendments and then, with Senator Gordon Allott of Colorado, a substitute bill. O'Mahoney's amendments were unacceptable to wilderness proponents and to the Park Service. Then Senator Richard Neuberger, a staunch advocate of the bill, died and Senator Murray announced that he would retire. Congress passed the Multiple Use Sustained Yield Act of 1960 (MUSY), which formalized policy the Forest Service had long been following on its lands. Outdoor recreation stood at the head of the multiple uses cited in the MUSY bill, and the Park Service was not pleased that its rival now seemed to have the authorization it needed to fend off efforts long under way by the Park Service and preservationists to carve new wilderness parks out of such areas as the North Cascades of Washington and the Three Sisters of Oregon. The MUSY Act also statutorily sanctioned wilderness preservation in the national forests for the first time. It stated that "the establishment and maintenance of areas of wilderness are consistent with the purposes and provisions of this act."[35] The MUSY Act gave hope to both opponents and proponents of wilderness. Its passage, the O'Mahoney amendments, and the substitute bill all required further modification of the wilderness bill, so once again action was postponed.

The Park Service was quiet through 1960, but when Senator O'Mahoney's amendments were introduced it became concerned. Eivind Scoyen read the amendments to a squad meeting in February. One of the amendments would empower the president to authorize prospecting, reservoirs, roads, and other developments in wilderness areas "upon his finding that such use or uses in the specific area will better serve the interests of the United States . . . than will its denial." If such amendments should be approved, Scoyen declared, the Park Service would "bitterly" oppose the bill. "At the time the conservationists first suggested a wilderness bill, we tried to point out to them that what could happen would be to bring the Park Service wilderness areas down to Forest Service level—and that is just what would happen if these amendments are enacted into law."[36] O'Mahoney's amendments went nowhere, but this illustrates that some Park Service officials continued to be justifiably concerned about how this wilderness bill might turn out. The agency proceeded with its work on backcountry management plans and its zoning in master planning, watching and waiting to see what would happen next.

The 87th Congress convened in January 1961, and the new chairman of the Senate Committee on Interior and Insular Affairs, Clinton Anderson, introduced S. 174 on January 5 with thirteen cosponsors, including Senator Humphrey. Anderson was, as Murray had been, a strong supporter of wilderness preservation, and his bill was substantially like its predecessor. As the new Congress convened, the Kennedy administration came into office with a different stance on the wilderness bill than that held by the Eisenhower administration. One month after he became president, Kennedy addressed Congress on natural resource policy and endorsed the wilderness bill. Senator Anderson moved to quickly hold hearings, and Agriculture and Interior secretaries Orville Freeman and Stewart Udall strongly recommended passage of the wilderness bill. The Forest and Park services found themselves in a new political environment in which they would be expected to support wilderness system legislation rather than oppose it.

A critical article about the national parks was published in *Atlantic* in February 1961. Written by Devereaux Butcher, it analyzed what Mission 66 was doing to selected parks and described examples of where Butcher thought the Park Service was crossing the line between necessary and excessive in its efforts to accommodate more visitors. Butcher concluded:

> This sampling of Mission 66 in action shows the trend that is occurring throughout the national park and monument system and emphasizes the extent to which the taxpayer unknowingly is taking part in the impairment of those masterpieces of nature's handiwork. To popularize and commercialize the national parks is to cheapen them and reduce them to the level of ordinary playgrounds. To cherish them for their primeval splendor and give them the kind of protection the pending Wilderness Bill would afford is to realize the enduring value they have for us and those who will follow us.[37]

Butcher's article touched a nerve in the Park Service. As Mission 66 projects progressed, criticism from conservationists increased. Wirth's effort to sell Mission 66 development as protection of wilderness had not convinced Park Service critics, and Butcher's article expressed a widely held view. Wirth wrote a long and detailed memo to his new boss, Stewart Udall, defending Mission 66 and casting Butcher's criticism as representing "the view of a small but vocal minority which would insulate the parks from the people and preserve them from the obviously mounting pressures and demands of our rapidly expanding and increasingly mobile population."[38] Wirth claimed that no new roads were being built (though later, in his autobiography, he proudly summarized the achievements of Mission 66 and listed roads first, including "1,197 miles of new roads, mostly in new areas").[39] Udall's response was, "Personally, I am a strong believer in wilderness preservation and you can depend on me to scrutinize all programs and activities of the National Park Service with this point clearly in mind. On the other hand, I feel very strongly that the people do have a right to visit and enjoy their parks."[40] Wirth was still feeling out his situation, and Udall's response, while sympathetic to the Park Service dilemma of serving increasing visitors while protecting wilderness, indicated that he definitely thought wilderness needed to be preserved in the national parks and elsewhere. Udall wrote:

> I agree with the concept that areas set aside and developed for mass public use are zones of civilization in a wilderness setting, and that our park roads are corridors through the wilderness reaching or connecting these zones. I can see no other acceptable way that can be found to meet all of the responsibilities placed upon the National Park Service by existing laws. As a matter of fact the situation is specifically recognized in the current bill establishing a National Wilderness

Preservation System. Under provisions relating to the National Parks, the developed and road areas will be described and then what is left will be wilderness. Under the standards established by the Act, at least 98% of park lands will qualify as wilderness.[41]

The secretary's response was both good and bad news to Wirth and his colleagues. On the one hand it agreed with their contention that most national parks had protected wilderness, yet on the other hand it supported formal wilderness designation and consequent reduction of Park Service discretion for 98 percent of park lands.

Thus was a clear message sent to the Park Service, early in the new administration, that the Interior Department position would be very different on the wilderness bill than it had been during the Eisenhower years. Wirth already knew that Interior had reported favorably on Senator Anderson's S. 174 in February, but Udall's response to his letter left no doubt where the new administration stood on the wilderness bill and park wilderness.[42]

In July Anderson's committee reported favorably on S. 174, and the wilderness bill finally reached the Senate floor in September. After a floor fight, with opposition led by Senator Allott, a wilderness bill was finally approved by the Senate on a vote of 78–8 and sent to the House. The key committee there was chaired by another Colorado politician and enemy of the bill, Wayne Aspinall. He held field hearings in the fall and then, after delaying ostensibly to wait for ORRRC *Study Report 3*, which dealt with wilderness, he held hearings in Washington, DC, in May 1962. The ORRRC report recommended for wilderness legislation, as Congressman John Saylor read into the *Congressional Record*. "There is a widespread feeling, which the Commission shares, that the Congress should take action to assure the permanent reservation of suitable areas of National Forests, National Parks, Wildlife Refuges, and other lands in Federal ownership."[43] The report concluded that "it is difficult to avoid the conclusion that new legislation, specifically directed at and with clear mandates toward preserving wilderness units both in the National Forests and in the National Park System, will be necessary if wilderness areas are to be maintained."[44] The commission had been studying the wilderness issue since 1960, and it had not been convinced by the Park Service that congressional action to protect park wilderness was unnecessary or redundant.

Quite to the contrary, *Study Report 3* concluded that the Forest Service and Park Service differed greatly in their concepts of wilderness and that "the concept of wilderness employed by the National Park Service appears to weaken the security of wilderness lands in parks and monuments." This in part derived, in the commission's view, from the fact that "in the language of analysis: the Forest Service defines wilderness in constant and objective terms; the Park Service (which considers it both an ecological condition and a 'state of mind') defines wilderness in variables involving subjective judgment." This had led to "the somewhat anomalous condition . . . where wilderness is more secure in the national forests (except for permission of livestock grazing) than in the national parks—so far as the respective agency's jurisdiction is concerned." The Forest Service had a prescribed classification procedure, wrote the commission, but:

> The Park Service, on the other hand, has been reluctant to impose formal allocation procedures. There is some disagreement on this point within the Department of the Interior; but the basis for this reluctance appears to be that it would modify the power of management by subsequent administrations. Part of the purpose of wilderness legislation . . . has been to force the Park Service to impose formal zoning which would bind subsequent administrations.
>
> From the point of view of administrative action only, the Forest Service places its wilderness reserves in a more secure state by committing itself to a formal zoning procedure than the "stroke of a pen" security which in fact exists throughout the national park system.[45]

This conclusion should not have surprised the Park Service, which had so recently admitted that its wilderness was there because its directors had not exercised their pens to reduce wilderness. One can imagine how the Park Service responded to being compared with the Forest Service as offering less protection than had its rival. Neither the Outdoor Recreation Resources Review Commission nor wilderness bill proponents disagreed with the Park Service contention that a very high portion of the national parks were in a wilderness condition. But the ORRRC report zeroed in on the problem that had so long been of concern to wilderness preservationists. The irony of the ORRRC report concluding that the Forest Service approach offered more protection to wilderness than the Park Service must have chagrined many Park Service people. They knew it was not really true on the ground, yet in the procedural sense it could not be denied. If there had been any hope by Park Service opponents of the wilderness bill that their cause would be helped by the report, they were disappointed.

Opponents still thought they had a chance of defeating the bill in the House, where the leadership was hostile to it. When the 88th Congress convened in January 1963, the combatants stood on familiar ground. Senator Anderson introduced S. 4 on January 14. It was identical to the bill passed by the Senate in 1962. Brief hearings were held at which secretaries Freeman and Udall again endorsed a strong wilderness bill. The Senate once again passed the bill, this time 73–12, and the action moved again to the House. The opponents were ready for it there, and by the time hearings began in Washington no fewer than twenty-four versions of the bill had been introduced. The most important one was, once again, John Saylor's H.R. 9070, the last in a long series of revisions drafted by congressional wilderness advocates in close consultation with Howard Zahniser and his allies. Some concessions were made on issues raised in the previous session, but Saylor's bill was a strong one. After yet more hearings, H.R. 9070 was amended to allow prospecting and the filing of claims in national forest wilderness for twenty years after the legislation was approved. Aspinall's full committee further amended it, and in a floor debate their amendments were defeated. Finally, on July 30, 1964, the House passed the wilderness bill. Final points of disagreement were ironed out between House and Senate, and the Wilderness Act was signed by President Lyndon Johnson on September 3, 1964.

Howard Zahniser spoke to the final public hearing on the bill in late April 1964. He spoke, as he so often had over the years, to the need for wilderness and, as Craig Allin has observed, "summarized his own efforts."[46] Zahniser said, "It may seem presumptuous for men and women, who live only 40, 50, 60, 70, or 80 years, to dare to undertake a program for perpetuity, but that surely is our challenge."[47] Six days later Zahniser died at the age of 58. He had met the challenge but sadly did not live to know it.

The first legislative phase of the effort to establish a national wilderness policy was over. The Park Service and Forest Service had been competing since 1917 over who would provide outdoor recreation services and wilderness protection, and this decision in 1964 asserted that both agencies would do so. Each had, at one time or another, thought they should have exclusive responsibility for this work, but the approach of each had been flawed. Right up to the end of the fight over the wilderness bill, there was ambivalence among conservationists about who would be the better wilderness caretaker and manager. The Park Service seemed inclined to cater to motorized tourists too much, at the expense of wilderness. On the other hand, the Forest Service had a multiple-use mission and a worse record of wilderness preservation than the Park Service. In the end, as Zahniser seems to have known from the start of the long campaign for a wilderness bill, conservationists did not have a choice between the agencies. The only politically possible approach would be to maintain administrative control of both agencies over their lands and set up a process for review of wilderness in national parks, forests, and wildlife refuges that might comprise the National Wilderness Preservation System. That is what the Wilderness Act did, and thus it was not the end of the process of congressional protection of wilderness, but the beginning.

Throughout the tortuous process that led to passage of the Wilderness Act, the Park Service remained convinced that it was doing what was necessary to protect park wilderness. Thomas Vint's decision back in the late 1930s not to attempt to designate what was wilderness and what was not in the parks was the agency line until 1964 and even, to some extent, after that. All park land not developed, in their view, was wild, and that was enough. Yet as the nearly two and a half decades of this period elapsed, the world changed and forced change on the Park Service. People came to the parks in unprecedented, even unimaginable, numbers. The automobile made the parks accessible as never before. Nearly everyone had a car, and with the building of the interstate highway system, begun in the late 1950s, the national parks were accessible to ever more people. Americans had always loved their national parks, and they loved them in the post–World War II era as never before.

Conrad Wirth was a recreation planner and landscape architect. He saw both challenge and opportunity in the growing pressure of visitors to the national park system. Mission 66 was an ambitious program in tune with its times. The parks needed a huge infusion of cash just to make them safe and accessible, and where Newton Drury had failed, Wirth succeeded. He brought in the financial resources to do the job. Yet almost simultaneously, as the Mission 66 development effort got under way, so did the drive for a national wilderness system. These two projects seemed to be moving at right angles to each other. In the case of national parks, it was as if there was a convergence of the two forces that had been pushing and pulling at national parks from their very beginnings, as if two factions, driven by ideals, had been skirmishing for forty years, and the battle finally broke out in earnest—preservation versus recreation. The battlefield moved for a time from the parks to the halls of Congress, and in 1964 the struggle was not over. Preservationists had won a significant victory, but even as they were doing so, the national park system was moving in new directions. These new directions were not necessarily at cross purposes to preservation because they often involved initiatives, such as finding national recreation areas close to urban centers where wilderness preservation was not an issue. Nonetheless, the struggle over wilderness in parks would continue, even as Secretary Udall moved to make the national park *system* more accessible to the American people.

The legislative struggle for the Wilderness Act might be over, but the park wilderness story was merely entering a new stage that would challenge the Park Service in different ways. Now the service could not, as it had for so long, avoid the issue by pronouncing that everything not developed was wild. That approach had been forcefully rejected. Law now required that it examine the land under its management and decide what should be officially designated as wilderness. And having done this, the decision on whether or not its recommendation would be accepted and the wilderness boundaries established was largely out of its hands. Interest groups and the politicians who listened to them would decide whether a park would or would not be wilderness and where the boundaries would lie.

To this point in its history the Park Service had developed a fierce pride in its professionalism. It had faced many challenges and had done its best to deal with them. Many in the leadership and rank and file of the agency were certain they had done what was right and proper, and they regretted what they perceived as a great, or at least a potentially great, loss of autonomy from the Wilderness Act. Never before in its history had the Park Service suffered a loss like this. Now the "park men" might lose what they considered their professional prerogatives—managerial control of part of their domain. Zahniser and the other Wilderness Act advocates had tried hard to reassure agency managers that designated wilderness would remain under their control, but many had not been convinced. Now that legislation was on the books, all would learn what its consequences would be.

THE WIRTH ERA ENDS

Conrad Wirth would not be in charge of this new phase of the park wilderness story. Events had overtaken him, and he had retired nine months before President Johnson signed the Wilderness Act. Wirth's selling of his Mission 66 program to the Eisenhower administration and Congress, and the launching of it, had been the high point of his years at the Park Service helm. He had enjoyed the support of nearly everyone concerned about national parks as he campaigned for the funds to upgrade the long-neglected infrastructure of the system. When the work began, however, critics began to appear. He found himself increasingly at odds with conservationists over some Mission 66 projects, and his support from that sector eroded. The Sierra Club and National Parks Association clashed sharply with him over upgrading the Tioga Road in Yosemite, a project long sought by commercial interests east of the park. They offered him advice on how the project might be modified to be less intrusive, and he ignored them. He was, at least in their view, more interested in recreational tourism than in resource protection. His stance on national park wilderness seemed another indicator of this. The issue of hunting in national parks came up, and Wirth vacillated on this most emotionally potent of national park issues. His suggestion in 1961 that hunting be explored as a way to manage deer in the proposed Great Basin National Park brought a strong retort from conservationists. Ultimately he pronounced that hunting was not reconcilable with national park values, but his flirting with the idea only increased doubts about him in the conservation community.

Wirth no doubt would have liked to see Mission 66 through to its conclusion, but politics made that impossible. The transition to the next director, National Park Service veteran George B. Hartzog Jr., was orderly, and Wirth "retired." His departure was not entirely voluntary, since Stewart Udall considered him out of step with the times and encouraged his retirement. It is an understatement to say that Wirth was not enthusiastic about the move toward a National Wilderness Preservation System, while the Kennedy administration and Secretary Udall were solid backers of it. Wirth also thought that he and the National Park Service could and should oversee the national outdoor recreation agenda, but the Outdoor Recreation Resources Review Commission and Secretary Udall did not agree. A new Bureau of Outdoor Recreation would do that work. The Kennedy people, led by Udall, embraced a "new conservation" that broadened the vision of the conservationist mission of past decades and raised questions about conventional definitions of progress. Ron Foresta, in his study of the post–World War II National Park Service, has written that the Mission 66 program "reflected a great faith in progress rather than a healthy distrust of it. Its building program reflected assumptions about the harmony of development and wilderness which were no longer in fashion."[1] In the mid-1950s Wirth had responded to the challenge of repairing park system damage inflicted by the war, and he was succeeding in this work. But even as he was doing this, a sea change swept the conservation movement and he found himself increasingly at odds with it. This ultimately brought an end to his tenure.

An emergent and growing ecological consciousness in the early 1960s began modifying the goals of conservation and contributed to Wirth's problems. His stumble over the hunting issue led Secretary Udall to request a study of the wildlife management policies of the National Park Service. Wildlife in national parks had generated many issues over the years, arguments about predators foremost among them. The Park Service had begun by eliminating predators and managing for animals the public loved to see, such as elk and bison. Biologists like Joseph Grinnell, Harold Bryant, George Wright, Carl Russell, Ben Thompson, Adolph Murie, and Victor Cahalane, all but Grinnell with the Park Service, had for nearly four decades advocated with little success a park management based on ecological concern for the viability of natural communities in the parks. As the decade of the 1960s opened, with conservationists' growing interest in wilderness and ecology, views on the purpose and nature of national parks changed. Scenery and recreation continued to be important park values, but as Richard Sellars has so thoroughly explained, the ideas of wildlife biologists who "focused on preserving ecological integrity in the parks while permitting development for public use in carefully selected areas" were finally given more credence. As support for wilderness grew, the idea of national parks as areas intended primarily for "recreational multiple use" eroded. The view that national parks should be minimally developed gained support. For decades the management ideas of the wildlife biologists had been overwhelmed by those of landscape architects and recreation-oriented managers. The wilderness movement contributed to a change in this. Biologists, as Sellars points out, "defined 'unimpaired' in biological and ecological terms, a concept more compatible with that expressed in the 1964 Wilderness Act."[2]

Udall in 1962 called for scientific assessments of the situation. He asked the National Academy of Sciences to review the "natural history research needs and opportunities" in the parks. He also appointed the Advisory Board on Wildlife Management. The chairman of this board was wildlife biologist A. Starker Leopold. On March 4, 1963, the committee submitted its report to Secretary Udall. The Leopold report argued that the primary goal of national parks and monuments should be "to preserve, or where necessary to recreate, the ecologic scene as viewed by the first European visitors." Achievement of such a goal would require new levels of historical and ecological understanding that could be achieved only by scientific work on a scale exceeding anything the Park Service had done before. It should conduct research "oriented to management needs," which should then guide management policy. Roadless sections of the parks should be "permanently zoned," and nonconforming uses, most of them associated with recreational development, should be "liquidated as expeditiously as possible."[3] While this report did not figure materially in the drive toward the Wilderness Act, it certainly pointed toward changes in national park management priorities that would be served by designating "permanent" wilderness zones in the national parks.

The National Academy Report, released five months after the Leopold report, was not as directed at management but severely criticized the Park Service's failure to support science. It emphasized the ecological challenges of national park management that could be addressed only by more and better science. These two reports initiated a new phase in national park history that involved a protracted struggle over the role of science in management, a new emphasis on "naturalness" in management, and a new casting of the nature and purpose of national park wilderness. Conrad Wirth, in Stewart Udall's view, was not the man to preside over the National Park Service response to this new set of challenges.

George B. Hartzog Jr. became director on January 8, 1964. He was a lawyer who had risen from the ranger ranks to become superintendent of Jefferson National Expansion Memorial. In this position he resurrected a nascent Gateway Arch project and saw this monumental effort through to completion. He met Secretary Udall in 1961 when the secretary visited the Ozarks, where Hartzog's work on a proposal for an Ozark Rivers National Monument impressed him. In 1962 Hartzog left the Park Service thinking that his opportunities lay elsewhere, but in a casual meeting with Udall in August the secretary sounded him out about becoming director. With Eivind Scoyen retiring, the search was on for a new associate director to Wirth, and this job would go to Hartzog with the understanding that when Wirth retired he would become director. Wirth was to announce his retirement at the superintendents' conference in Yosemite in October 1963.

The ambitious Hartzog was delighted at the opportunity and embraced it. Wirth announced his retirement at the conference, but this was overshadowed by controversy generated by the keynote speech of Assistant Interior Secretary John Carver, who blasted the Park Service and by inference its outgoing director. Carver's remarks were leaked to the press and appeared nationally the day before he delivered them at Yosemite. The story suggested that Wirth was being forced out, and Carver's remarks seemed to confirm this. The Park Service was shocked at this whole development, not so much because Wirth was leaving but because of the way in which the administration was handling the situation. Udall denied that Wirth was being forced out and eventually the storm blew over, but many suspected that Hartzog was being brought in to oversee a change in direction, to carry out an agenda that people in the Park Service had not developed. This, to Park Service veterans and knowledgeable park observers, seemed to be high-order political meddling.

Undoubtedly Udall wanted a man in the director's chair more supportive of the directions he thought appropriate for the national park system than Wirth had been. He also wanted a young, dynamic leader more in the mold of the Kennedy team, and George Hartzog seemed to fit this bill. So much suspicion was generated by the Carver speech that Scoyen wrote an account for his Park Service colleagues of the change in the directorship, documenting the history of Wirth's decision to retire and the process of Hartzog's selection. He assured his Park Service colleagues that Hartzog had been chosen on his merits and had played no role in Wirth's ouster. Scoyen thought the whole episode had seriously affected Park Service morale, and he hoped his assurances might help improve it.[4]

George Hartzog was no wilderness hand. Born and raised in the East, his park experience had been primarily in eastern, urban settings, and he was devoted to the idea of bringing the parks to the people. Conservationists in general and wilderness advocates in particular expressed no strong concern at Wirth's departure as they had a decade earlier when Drury was forced reluctantly into retirement. While Wirth had not proven as disastrous to preservationist interests as some had predicted when he was appointed in 1952, most were not sorry to see him go. They viewed him at best as an obstructionist to their wilderness protection goals. One reason conservationist concern may

8.1 Director George Hartzog and Horace Albright were key figures in park wilderness history, though a generation apart. National Park Service Historic Photographic Collection, Harpers Ferry Center

have been muted about Hartzog's appointment despite his lack of a record on wilderness issues was that Secretary Udall seemed a strong supporter, and with prospects for the wilderness legislation brightening, advocates appeared to be in a much stronger position than when Wirth became director. If the legislation passed, they would have a potent tool to force the National Park Service to live up to its long-espoused wilderness protection ideals.

One of the new director's first major policy changes was the establishment of a three-part classification system for the national parks. There would be recreational, historical, and natural areas "so that resources may be appropriately identified and managed in terms of their inherent values and appropriate uses."[5] Robert Sterling Yard would have approved of this, for while the "natural area" category was not called "primeval" as he would have preferred, it constituted recognition that the national park system consisted of parts with quite distinct resource values that required different management priorities and skills. Most significantly, it seemed to recognize that in some parts of the system "recreation" would not be of paramount concern. This policy decision held out the possibility that in some areas preservation of natural values would not compete with recreational values. It might promise a resolution of the perennial conflict between the "conserve" and "provide for the enjoyment of" elements of the National Park Service Act of 1916.

Foresta and others regard this new approach as a "milestone in park management policy because it prompted the Park Service to adopt a preservationist orientation in a large number of parks."[6] It was, in their view, a response to the criticisms of Mission 66 that the service was sacrificing natural park values to accommodate visitors. Roads had been the greatest concern, and Hartzog publicly disavowed support for road building in parks where natural values were paramount. Addressing the crowding in Yosemite Valley and alternatives to automobiles for transportation in the parks, he proclaimed that "people want some alternative. No more roads will be built or widened until these alternatives are explored. . . . We need to limit access to parks and wilderness. We've simply got to do something besides build roads in these parks if we're going to have any parks left."[7] Under Hartzog the Park Service view of roads took a turn that has been maintained since. There would be new roads and new euphemisms for roads such as "motor nature trails," but the era of extensive road building in national parks was over.

The new classification system, conveyed as a directive from Udall to Hartzog in July 1964, was a response to the growing environmental concern soon to be called "environmentalism" in contrast to an earlier "conservation." Udall's memo to Hartzog notes that "in recent decades, with exploding population and diminishing open space, the urgent need for national recreation areas is receiving new emphasis and attention." The Park Service would, he directed, address this with recreation areas where provision of access would be a central goal. In natural areas, the recommendations of the Advisory Board on Wildlife Management would be implemented. Physical developments would be limited "to those that are necessary and appropriate." As for wilderness, "Park management shall recognize and respect wilderness as a whole environment of living things whose use and enjoyment depend on their continuing interrelationship free of man's spoliation."[8] The secretary declared that "the concern of the National Park Service is the wilderness, the wildlife, the history, the recreational opportunities, etc., within the areas of the System and the appropriate uses of these resources." He thus directed the agency and its new leader to respond to the emergent ecological concerns reflected in the Leopold and National Academy reports as well as to the soon-to-be-passed Wilderness Act. It was, at the same time, to respond to the growing demand for outdoor recreation. Hartzog may not have been primarily interested in preservation of wilderness and wildlife, but his instructions were clear. He would have to find a way to manage parks as both playgrounds and preserves.

THE WILDERNESS ACT

President Lyndon Johnson signed the Wilderness Act on September 3, 1964, and the federal agencies began analyzing what would be involved in its implementation. They needed to start immediately because Section 3(c) stipulated that the Department of the Interior review every roadless area of 5,000 contiguous acres or more in the national park system within ten years and report to the president on the suitability or unsuitability of those areas for preservation as wilderness. Similar instructions and deadlines were issued for national forest primitive areas and wildlife refuges. The Park Service was to complete one-third of the reviews within three years, not less than two-thirds within seven years, and the remainder by the ten-year deadline. The president, in turn, was required to convey his recommendations based on these reviews to Congress, which would then decide whether or not an area would become part of the National Wilderness Preservation System. The act required that "nothing . . . shall, by implication or otherwise, be construed to lessen the statutory authority of the Secretary of the Interior with respect to the maintenance of roadless areas within units of the national park system." Here was the provision, inserted to allay Park Service concerns expressed early in the debate over the legislation, assuring that no action under the act would lessen protection of parks mandated by earlier legislation. This was restated even more specifically in Section 4(a). Should any change be made in a wilderness established by Congress, it could be made only by affirmative action of that body. Thus was all discretion for setting wilderness boundaries removed from agency purview once a wilderness had been congressionally established. An agency could recommend but not decide.

Another reason for the Park Service and other agencies to get to work was that Section 3(d) required that the public be involved in agency wilderness reviews. This would involve public hearings and the processing of the information gathered at these hearings and from all other public officials with an interest in proposed wilderness designation. Such public participation was up to this time unheard of in the practices of the federal land-management agencies, and it would prove to be a large, politically charged, and time-consuming process. Congress expected the agencies to listen to the people on wilderness proposals and to incorporate what they heard into those proposals.

The review to determine which roadless areas to recommend for the National Wilderness Preservation System would require application of a definition of wilderness, and agreement on a definition had always been and would continue to be a problem. Section 2(c) provided a definition:

A wilderness, in contrast with those areas where man and his own works dominate the landscape, is hereby recognized as an area where the earth and its community of life are untrammeled by man, where man himself is a visitor who does not remain.[9]

This was a definition of an ideal, and Congress recognized that the ideal was rare if it existed at all. Attempting to balance the ideal with the real out on the federal lands, the drafters of the legislation further defined areas to be considered as land "which *generally appears* to have been affected *primarily* by the forces of nature, with the imprint of man *substantially* unnoticeable" (italics added). The intent of Congress was to create a system that incorporated the ideals of wilderness philosophers like Muir, Leopold, and Marshall but without adding too many qualifications to the definitions.[10] Still, anticipating that too pure and ideal a definition would impose severe limitations on what might qualify for the wilderness system, drafters left some room for interpretation, which would lead to other problems.

The opening statement of the act was a clear and unambiguous refutation of the Park Service's long-held position that it was providing, under existing law, all the protection necessary for wild parkland. Section 2(c) begins,

> In order to assure that an increasing population, accompanied by expanding settlement and growing mechanization, does not occupy and modify all areas within the United States and its possessions, leaving no lands designated for preservation and protection in their natural condition, it is hereby declared to be the policy of the Congress to secure for the American people of present and future generations the benefit of an enduring resource of wilderness.

Congress agreed with Zahniser and others that, with growing visitation and responses to it like the road building of Mission 66, the long-term protection of national park roadless areas was by no means assured. More protection was needed, and one intent of the Wilderness Act was to provide that protection.[11]

Use of wilderness areas was taken up in the act's Section 4. Its purpose was to be "within and supplemental" to the purposes for which existing units of the national park and other public land systems were established. Wilderness was to be devoted to recreation, scenic, scientific, educational, conservation, and historical use. Prohibited uses were catalogued with qualifications such as "except as necessary to meet minimum requirements for the administration of the area for purposes of this Act." This and other qualifications would lead to difficulty later when areas had been designated and management policy was developed. Specifically, the act stated that "there shall be no temporary roads, no use of motor vehicles, motorized equipment or motorboats, no landing of aircraft, no other form of mechanical transport, and no structure or installation within any such areas." As the Park Service proceeded to develop its wilderness proposals during the review period, many questions would arise regarding "chalets," shelters, and docks, which the Service often ruled excluded an area from wilderness and thus must constitute an "enclave" if within a proposed wilderness unit. Section 4 also stated that some uses that might affect national parks were expressly permitted, including established uses of aircraft and motorboats, actions to control fire, insects, and disease, and "commercial services . . . to the extent necessary for activities which are proper for realizing the recreational or other wilderness purposes of the area." Mining was addressed at length in Section 4(d) but applied primarily to national forests, since most national park lands were withdrawn from mineral entry. There were at the time of the act's passage six national park system units that were open to mineral entry, and they posed a problem that would be addressed later. As implementation of the act unfolded, all of these provisions would raise a flock of issues that would slow progress and lead to many conflicts between the Park Service and conservationists.

The act specified that national forest "wilderness," "wild," and "canoe" areas would by its approval be designated wilderness, thereby creating fifty-four national forest wilderness areas totaling 9.1 million acres. It stipulated that national forest primitive areas were to be managed according to regulations in effect when the act was approved until Congress determined whether they would be designated as wilderness. Nothing was said about management of Department of Interior lands to be reviewed, thus creating some confusion.[12] The Department of the Interior was thereby given more latitude than the Department of Agriculture in managing the roadless areas it must review. Park Service road plans would consequently be closely watched by conservationists during the review period. A proposed road in Great Smoky Mountains National Park would, right at the start, be a very contentious issue.

To this point in its history the National Park Service had managed to avoid what it saw as the conceptual constraints of "wilderness" as defined by people outside the service. Robert Sterling Yard had wrestled mightily with terminology, but while he might have been unsure what term to use, he knew what he wanted it to mean—preservation in roadless condition of the as yet pristine and mostly unchanged backcountry of the national parks. Aldo Leopold and Bob Marshall conceived of wilderness similarly but added the idea that such land would serve a particular recreational approach—primitive travel on foot or horseback without modern amenities. The Park Service had recognized these ideas and catered to them to some extent, but it was also engaged in what came to be called "industrial tourism." It would protect the wilderness as long as it could—most Park Service people thought (and hoped) that would be a long time, perhaps forever in some places—but if the public demand grew so as to require development even of remote places, it wished to be free to exercise its professional judgment on how that development might be done. The Wilderness Act defined the purpose of wilderness preservation in a more clear and restrictive way. It established "a national policy of maintaining a system of areas where natural processes could operate as freely as possible. Recreational use was an appropriate use of these areas only so long as it was consistent with this purpose."[13] This policy should pose no problems for the Park Service, which had for so long claimed to be protecting nature in its parks, but it would continue to have difficulty as it attempted to comply with the act.

THE DEVELOPMENT OF REGULATIONS AND PROCEDURES

With passage of the Wilderness Act, the land management agencies' first job was to establish policies and procedures for implementating it. How should the new mandate to review roadless areas and recommend wilderness designations fit into the ongoing planning the Park Service was doing? How should the Wilderness Act implementation relate to the many other initiatives under way in the park system, such as implementation of the Leopold report, development of management guidelines for "natural areas," new area studies (and politics) in places like the North Cascades and Sawtooth Mountains, and the National Recreation Plan being developed by the Bureau of Outdoor Recreation? How would the new work be accomplished with no new resources to dedicate to it? The National Park Service was required to develop and apply a complex, bureaucratic procedure involving public input on a new scale for review of fifty-seven areas.

The Park Service did not swing into immediate action on this. Minutes of Director Hartzog's staff meetings make no mention of wilderness until a February 1965 discussion of master planning, where it was noted that master planning would have to be accelerated because of the schedules of the

Wilderness Act and the National Recreation Plan. In late 1964 Hartzog had sought answers to several questions from Secretary Udall. He proposed to develop no special organization within the National Park Service for wilderness and would incorporate planning for wilderness into established master planning procedures. Udall thought that would be fine. Should a moratorium on development and road construction be put in place while park system lands were classified? Udall did not think this would be necessary. Should the Park Service proceed with efforts to upgrade national monuments such as Death Valley, Glacier Bay, and Organ Pipe Cactus to national park status while wilderness review and associated mining studies were being done? Udall thought they should. Hartzog told the secretary that the Park Service review would begin with those parks having the most clear-cut wilderness sections, such as Great Smoky Mountains and Yellowstone. Udall thought that a fine approach and requested that a schedule for review be prepared and submitted to him as soon as possible. Hartzog was satisfied that the Park Service was set to proceed.[14]

As the Park Service launched this effort it was several years into its new role as partner to the Bureau of Outdoor Recreation. The bureau had taken over national recreation planning and as part of that was applying a national land classification system that had been developed by the Outdoor Recreation Resources Review Commission. The Park Service was attempting to use this system in its planning, adapting it as necessary to suit its special needs. It was mapping existing land uses and ORRRC land classifications for each park as well as in the region adjacent to the park, which required delineation of various land classifications within the parks and rationales for these classifications. All of this was being fitted into master planning.

The classification system included the following categories:

Class I, or High-Density Recreation Areas, were places such as Camp Curry in Yosemite Valley or Grand Canyon Village at Grand Canyon National Park that featured a road network, parking, stores and shops, and administrative facilities, among others things. A high level of development was the defining characteristic of this category.

Class II, General Outdoor Recreation Areas, encompassed less intensively developed areas of a park that received heavy recreational use. These were developed areas with two-way roads, parking and picnic areas, campgrounds, marinas, even administrative facilities, but in a less dense pattern than Class I.

Class III, Natural Environment Areas, included lands used for activities dependent on qualities of the natural environment, such as sightseeing, hiking, nature study, and mountaineering. The Park Service Master Plan Handbook stated that the primary objective of such areas was "to provide for traditional recreation experience in the out of doors." Acceptable development might include "motor nature trails," trails, interpretive shelters, and "minimum" sanitary facilities. The Park Service considered this category to be the "wilderness threshold," about which more will be said later.

Class IV, Outstanding Natural Features, were unique areas, usually of limited size, of exceptional or irreplaceable nature such as Old Faithful or Devil's Tower. They might be developed only for research, though the actual features might be surrounded by Class I or II (as at Old Faithful). This category was reminiscent of the "sacred areas" of early park master plans.

Class V, Primitive Areas, were the wild and undeveloped lands, those free of commercial use and mechanization of any kind, and large enough for visitors to have a "wilderness experience." These were the areas to be studied for wilderness classification (at least in Park Service plans; conservationists thought large portions of Class III should also be considered).

Class VI, Historic and Cultural Sites, were places of historical or cultural significance. Management's aim was preservation and restoration, with all development governed by these goals.

This, then, was the system the Park Service would have to work into its master planning and wilderness review, with Class V most important to carrying out the review mandate of the Wilderness Act.[15]

Speaking to the National Park Service Superintendents Conference in Gatlinburg, Tennessee, in September 1965, Assistant Director Theodore Swem addressed the general subject of master planning and the challenges to it posed by the Wilderness Act. He pointed out that for the first time "we will have to consider wilderness as a *very precise thing* and recommend it on that basis" (italics added). Master planners, said Swem, could no longer think of wilderness as what was left over after planning for development but must precisely define and designate it as a land allocation unit. This must be done thoroughly and carefully, and "it will be necessary by the time we propose lands for wilderness classification that our planning thinking be refined enough that we may recommend the commitment of lands to basic types of use for what we must assume for all practical purposes to be in perpetuity."[16] Swem made clear to his colleagues the importance of the decisions they would be making—once the recommendation for wilderness went to the president from National Park Service planning teams, decisions regarding what would or would not be wilderness would be out of agency control. Swem was personally a supporter of wilderness and a sitting member of the governing council of The Wilderness Society, but he refrained from any advocacy in this speech. Still, he strongly stated the importance and nature of the wilderness review that was beginning in 1965.

Director Hartzog addressed the same conference and spoke directly to the wilderness review. He noted that the Bureau of Outdoor Recreation had directed that wilderness be a subdivision of Class V.

> There is not an overwhelming difference in the day-to-day management of primitive lands and wilderness lands. There is, however, an all-important difference in the *legal significance* of primitive lands and wilderness lands. Primitive lands may be classified and re-classified through administrative procedures. Wilderness lands, on the other hand, may be classified and re-classified only by legislative enactments of Congress. We can no longer lump wilderness lands and primitive lands together.[17]

One year after the Wilderness Act was signed, the general was informing his troops of the nature of the work to be done. "Our responsibilities for wilderness management are strengthened and heightened under the Wilderness Act," Hartzog continued. "We are cognizant that more than ever we must evolve new and dynamic concepts of management to attain the goals that have been laid down." If any of his listeners thought that it would be business as usual in regard to wilderness, he put that idea to rest. "We are not satisfied that we have yet developed adequate wilderness management programs."[18] Hartzog told the superintendents that doing this job would likely involve more regulation of visitors and more and differently trained rangers and naturalists. Then he brought up an idea that went back to Wirth:

> We intend to experiment further with the concept of the wilderness threshold. The wilderness threshold implies both a physical location and a kind of experience. It can serve not only as a buffer for the wilderness but also as a zone of orientation where the newcomer may explore the mood and temper of the wild country beyond that beckons him. . . . The wilderness threshold provides unequalled opportunity for interpretation of the meaning of wilderness.[19]

Hartzog also announced that the first wilderness review and proposal—the pilot for this program—would be the master plan and wilderness proposal for Great Smoky Mountains National Park.

A process to prepare a wilderness proposal for Great Smoky Mountains and other parks had to be developed. In February 1966 the secretary of the interior formally delegated authority to the Park Service to make the wilderness studies and approved procedures for doing them. The first task was to conduct a "field study," which involved examining the master plan and the purposes and management of the park under study. A land classification plan, using the Bureau of Outdoor Recreation system, was then prepared, followed by a wilderness proposal drawn on a map of the area. The wilderness review team applied the definition of "roadless area" as in the federal regulations, which specified that it was a "reasonably compact area of undeveloped federal land which possesses the general characteristics of a wilderness and within which there is no improved road that is suitable for public travel by means of four-wheeled, motorized vehicles intended primarily for highway use."[20] A wilderness report was written by the team, incorporated into the master plan, then reviewed by the park superintendent and regional director. This was then passed on to the Washington office, where it was analyzed "in terms of its wilderness threshold concepts, ecological implications, regional planning, legislation, inholdings, water rights, and grazing and contiguous lands."[21] Next it was passed to the Wilderness Committee (which comprised six Park Service Washington office specialists in relevant fields), the director, and finally to the assistant secretary of the interior for fish, wildlife, and parks. If the proposal got by all of this scrutiny, it was then released to the public, a public hearing date was set, and the hearing was held. After the hearing the Park Service analyzed letters received and statements heard and prepared its wilderness proposal, which went to the secretary and last to the president, who, after tweaking it, would send it on to Congress.

This eighteen-step bureaucratic process would have to be repeated at least fifty-seven times if the Park Service was to comply with the mandate of the Wilderness Act. The agency would be very slow in doing its reviews and would be accused of intentionally dragging its feet. This may have been a fair accusation, since one would expect that the Park Service would be able to go through the early stages of the process fairly quickly with the intimate knowledge of its parks derived from long management of most of them. At the same time, scrutiny at so many levels prior to public hearings and then afterward surely contributed to a nearly glacial slowness in review of all fifty-seven park units. Finally, the sheer scale of the task indicates what a strain this must have added to the staff of the Park Service. Congress had given them a huge task, with no additional resources with which to carry it out. At a director's staff meeting in August 1966 devoted to wilderness review, Park Service Associate Director Clark Stratton remarked, "So far, I might say that we haven't received the first nickel to help us out financially in preparation of all the data that's necessary [to do the reviews]."[22]

Had the Park Service been willing and able to get right to work on its review, it would have been delayed while waiting for regulations governing application of the Wilderness Act to come from the Department of the Interior. These were not forthcoming until February 17, 1966, seventeen months after passage of the legislation. Thus nearly a year and a half of the ten years allowed for the work passed before the Park Service could begin its review. Why did it take so long to draw up the regulations? Proposed regulations were published in the Federal Register on July 28, 1965, with a revised draft circulated in November. Conservationists had many issues with the original draft: the definition of "roadless area" was too restrictive; a regional planning approach was absent; there would be inadequate access to information about agency proposals; the public notice period for hearings was too short; issues involving mineral surveys were unresolved. The November draft responded to many of the conservationists' concerns, but they were still unhappy. They especially feared that the Interior regulations might open the door to mineral exploration of the national park and refuge systems. They argued that the regulations did not reflect the language of the Wilderness Act. These concerns were raised and some were resolved, but the process of resolving them took time. Definitions from the act were included in the regulations, terms such as "roadless area" were clarified, and the public notice period was increased from six weeks to sixty days.[23] Finally, after months of wrangling, the regulations were issued and the "pilot" national park wilderness hearing, for Great Smoky Mountains National Park, could be held.

EARLY STAGES OF THE REVIEW

The Great Smoky Mountains proposal would be a test for everyone. Conservationists would be primed to judge whether the Park Service was applying the law as rigorously as they thought it should. The Park Service would be testing its procedures, but more important would be attempting to blend its interpretation and application of the Wilderness Act with its other duties as it perceived them. Great Smoky Mountains National Park, as the largest intact mountain wilderness east of the Great Plains, offered much potential as a candidate for inclusion in the National Wilderness Preservation System. How would things go there?

Hearings were held in Gatlinburg, Tennessee, and Bryson City, North Carolina, in June 1966. The Park Service presented its plan, and a hearing officer took testimony. "Conservationists the world over are looking to our National Park Service for exemplary leadership in the field of safeguarding the beauty and character of natural lands and sites," said Stewart Brandborg of The Wilderness Society in his testimony. "It would be most unfortunate if the Park Service were unable to fulfill this role in the Smokies."[24] Testimony quickly revealed that many thought the Park Service fell far short of this role with its proposal.

The proposed wilderness would include 247,000 acres in six blocks ranging from 5,000 to 110,000 acres. The wilderness was chopped up by a proposed new trans-mountain highway across the park from North Carolina to Tennessee. The main line of the road and inner loop roads were excluded from proposed wilderness. Conservationists knew this was coming, since George Hartzog (despite his protestations about no new roads) had announced the proposed road in 1965. The road was not a new scheme and had been debated in one form or another since the mid-1940s, but here was a classic confrontation of the two forces central to the park wilderness issue from the beginning—roads for recreation versus protection of primeval landscapes. The Park Service seemed to confirm the worst fears of its critics and to throw down the gauntlet on the issue of development versus wilderness. It seemed arrogant because it could hardly have begun the review process with a more controversial case. Earlier, in his exchange with Udall, Hartzog had characterized the Great Smoky Mountains proposal as a straightforward one. He could hardly have been more wrong.

Conservationist opposition to the proposal was unified and vocal. Testimony was heard from 184 people (52 in favor and 132 against), and 5,400 letters were received. Those testifying for the proposal were primarily local officials and boosters happy at the economic prospects that would come with the new road. The Appalachian Trail Conference, National Audubon Society, Izaak Walton League, National Parks Association, Nature Conservancy, The Wilderness Society, and Sierra Club were all opposed. Conservationists thought no new road should bisect the park's wilderness, which should be at least 350,000 acres. Three major counterproposals were brought forward. When the Park Service completed the transcript of the hearing, it totaled 992 pages.

Two months after the hearing on the Smokies, a director's staff meeting was devoted to discussion of wilderness review. In Director Hartzog's absence, Associate Director Clark Stratton presided. Lessons learned from the Great Smoky Mountains experience were discussed. One obvious lesson was that conservationists were doing their homework and would challenge any weaknesses they perceived in agency proposals, which surprised no one. One participant in the meeting said that "we are in sort of an adversary position with the conservation groups who are our friends." John Reshoft, in charge of the whole wilderness review process at this point, observed that most people involved in the hearing wanted "more wilderness, not less."[25] Perhaps most revealing was a comment by Stratton that "we had the Transmountain Road which practically overshadowed the Wilderness Proposal that we were trying to put forward." This seemed to him a "complicating factor" unique to the Great Smoky case. In Stratton's mind the road and wilderness proposals seemed separate issues, a remarkably naive view for a senior Park Service official at this stage in the wilderness game. No one in the long discussion that August day, except perhaps Reshoft, seemed to grasp that the central lesson from the Smokies experience might be that any effort to minimize wilderness in the national parks would be seen as such and strongly challenged. Stratton summed up what he thought the Park Service had learned:

> Since many of the conservation organizations are already studying these same areas that we are coming up with, it necessitates us having all of our ducks in a row and really doing a good job, or the summaries that come in are going to result in overwhelming proposals, in some cases, against what the Park Service is proposing.[26]

To Stratton, the problem seemed procedural. If the "ducks" were lined up—that is, if the plans and rationales were well organized and procedures dutifully followed—all would be well. He would be proven very wrong in this assessment.

Ten days before this director's meeting, Hartzog had issued planning procedures for national park wilderness that would prove the seed of much conservationist discontent. The seed had been planted by the Bureau of Outdoor Recreation's classification system and would grow to cast a shadow over nearly the entire national park wilderness review process. Hartzog made the grand claims that the "wilderness concept has under-girded the management of national parks for nearly a century" and that the national park movement had been "a focal point and fountainhead for an evolving wilderness philosophy within our country." He went on to say that "the basic philosophy influencing the use and management of the parks is one of preserving large areas of wilderness, while at the same time providing it with a surrounding natural setting or environment—or 'wilderness threshold.'"[27] The Park Service had, of course, used the term "wilderness threshold" since 1962 (before the Bureau of Outdoor Recreation classification system) when Wirth's Long Range Requirements Task Force had introduced the term into the planning lexicon. It had been presented in the National Park Service Plan at the Conference of Challenges, the superintendents' conference convened at Yosemite in October 1963. The three-category national park system scheme had also been unveiled at that time. Of the "Goals for Scenic and Scientific Parks" presented at this meeting, one was, "To continue to reserve the primitive, roadless wilderness for all visitors willing to use the wilderness on its own terms." A second was, "To encourage wider enjoyment of the less rugged portions of the back country by making more accessible the 'Wilderness Threshold' lying between developed areas and the primitive wilderness."[28] Nearly a year before final passage of the Wilderness Act, the Park Service was embracing an intermediate concept of land use that it hoped would allow it to locate wilderness boundaries to assure more management flexibility than if there were just two categories of land use, or "zones" as it called them—developed and "wilderness." There is surely irony here, since the Park Service had so long insisted that there were only developed and undeveloped or "wilderness" areas of the parks.

Back in 1959 Wirth had decided that regardless of whether a wilderness bill was ever to be approved, "we should proceed on our own with analysis of the [national park] areas to find out which areas we want to define as 'developed areas' to meet terms of the bill." The aim was to look far ahead and project where new roads and other developments would be needed and put them in the master plans. If a wilderness bill was passed and parts of the parks went into a National Wilderness Preservation System, it would be difficult to designate any new roads and developed areas. Discussing how wide road corridors should be, Wirth thought that a half mile on each side of a road should be enough.[29] Some work was done on this in the context of master planning, but the significance of Wirth's approach is that well before the Park Service found itself faced with wilderness reviews, it was trying to figure out how it might reduce the impact of a wilderness act on its ability to accommodate the increasing numbers of automobile-borne visitors that were coming to the parks. This was not an unreasonable approach, but the idea of "wilderness threshold" that came out of it was to be a big headache when the Wilderness Act was approved and the Park Service maneuvered to retain some of its management autonomy through the use of "thresholds" and other stratagems.

There is no doubt that, in addition to pushing back the boundary of wilderness defined by the Wilderness Act, some in the Park Service thought they could define their own concept of wilderness. At the director's staff meeting in August 1966, John Reshoft commented that one "important thing to keep in mind on wilderness threshold is that the Wilderness Act does not require all agencies to necessarily have the same kind of wilderness. There might be a different kind of wilderness, in one sense, in some national parks."[30] Exactly what Reshoft meant by this is not clear, but this remark in the context of their exploration of the threshold concept suggests that there was interest in floating such ideas to see if they might give their agency some room to maneuver in its balancing of the preservation and recreation missions as it did its wilderness reviews.

The Great Smoky Mountains wilderness hearing was followed by hearings for Craters of the Moon National Monument in August, Lassen Volcanic National Park in September, Sequoia and Kings Canyon in November, and Isle Royale at the end of January 1967. The trans-mountain highway controversy in the Smokies eclipsed all other issues there, but the wilderness threshold became a high-profile issue at these subsequent hearings. Sierra Club Conservation Director Mike McCloskey devoted much of his Lassen testimony to it. He pointed out that since the 1920s the Park Service had been claiming that the national parks were "seas of wilderness with merely occasional threads of development running through them; 'step back ten feet off the road,' they said, 'and you are in the wilderness that runs back miles.'" Now, with the Park Service applying the Bureau of Outdoor Recreation classification system and the threshold idea in its planning, it seemed to view wilderness not "as the sea within the park boundaries—but rather as a series of islands within a sea of various levels of development."[31] The threshold, McCloskey argued, was a wilderness buffer as the Park Service was proposing it at Lassen and elsewhere, and it was a buffer *outside* the wilderness rather than within it. The Sierra Club believed the wilderness boundary should be adjacent to roads, not some distance back from them as the Park Service was proposing.

> In defining the boundaries for its wilderness islands, generally the Washington office has withdrawn wilderness boundaries by a mile or more from existing roads to place

the buffer outside the wilderness. Generous Class III areas for light development are reserved. Because the current master plan does not indicate that development is planned or approved in these areas, the areas serve merely as an unspecified hedge against the future to allow greatly expanded development. This is what the Wilderness Act was designed to prevent.[32]

The Sierra Club thought the Park Service proposal designating less than half of Lassen as wilderness was far short of what it ought to be. It considered the wilderness threshold as nothing but a ploy to allow for "light development."

The same opinion about thresholds was held by at least one National Park Service veteran. S. Herbert Evison had enjoyed a long career with the Park Service, serving as its chief of information services from 1946 to 1958. Initially he had thought the threshold a good idea—it would allow the uninitiated to be introduced to wilderness. But as the wilderness hearings began, he changed his mind. He had been disappointed, he wrote, to learn that "though the threshold of a house is part of the house, the Service considers the wilderness threshold not a part of the wilderness and is willing, in the Great Smokies at least, to build so-called 'motor nature trails' into it at half a dozen or more points—thus greatly reducing the area within that park that would meet the wilderness standards established by the Wilderness Act."[33] Evison was chagrined to find provision for thresholds even in the wilderness proposal for Isle Royale National Park. In a letter to the hearings officer, he wrote that "service policy seems to be to provide for public use of 'wilderness threshold' by construction of 'motor nature trails,' but, since motor vehicles are not used on Isle Royale, even this poor excuse for the exclusion of de facto wilderness seems to be lacking."[34] Not only was his revered agency misguided in its policy, but it seemed to be engaged in sloppy preparation of its proposals.

Evison tried to convince George Hartzog to reconsider the approach he was taking. Thresholds in parks were one thing, but to propose "motor nature trails" in them was quite another. This confirmed suspicions of conservationists long skeptical of the Park Service commitment to wilderness that it would use any way it could to reduce park areas eligible for protection under the Wilderness Act. Evison wrote Hartzog that motor nature trails in wilderness thresholds "seemed to justify doubts of the validity of the Service assertions that areas not included in designated wilderness could continue to get adequate protection."[35]

Hartzog's mind was not changed. In April he addressed the Tenth Biennial Wilderness Conference in San Francisco and claimed that from the begin-

TABLE 1 Acreages Proposed for Inclusion in the National Wilderness System after Hearings in the First Review Period

Before Congress	Park or Monument Total Acreage	Preliminary Agency Proposal	Citizen Proposal Presented at Local Hearing	Revised Agency Proposal Following Review of the Public Hearing Record
Craters of the Moon National Monument (ID)	53,545	40,800	40,800	40,785
Lassen Volcanic National Park (CA)	106,933	48,587	101,000	73,333
Pinnacles National Monument (CA)	14,497	3,720	13,000	9,197
Lava Beds National Monument (CA)	46,238	8,792	37,000	9,197
Petrified Forest National Park (AZ)	94,189	43,010	60,400	50,260
Still under Review				
Great Smoky Mtns. National Park (NC and TN)	512,700	247,000	350,000	————
Sequoia and Kings Canyon National Park (CA)	841,200	740,165	826,000	————

(continued on facing page)

ning of the national park system Congress had intended there to be "enclaves of development" for the accommodation of visitors and "transition zones" between development and "untrammeled, primeval wilderness." He reiterated Albright's claim that since the beginning "wilderness preservation has under-girded the management of our National Park System," that the national parks have remained wild and, in some cases, such as Sequoia, had become even more so. He described the classification system and explained the rationale for wilderness thresholds; they would be invaluable for research, interpretation, and to provide a "foretaste of the wilderness beyond." He mentioned the light development planned for the thresholds, including "one-way

(continued from previous page)

Before Congress	Park or Monument Total Acreage	Preliminary Agency Proposal	Citizen Proposal Presented at Local Hearing	Revised Agency Proposal Following Review of the Public Hearing Record
Still under Review (cont.)				
Isle Royale National Park (MI)	539,347	119,618	130,000	————
Cumberland Gap National Hist. Park (KY, TN, and VA)	20,170	8,980	15,250	————
Shenandoah National Park (VA)	193,531	61,940	91,000	70,000 (tentative)
Bryce Canyon National Park (UT)	36,010	17,900	23,800	————
Cedar Breaks National Monument (UT)	6,154	4,600	5,300	————
Capitol Reef National Monument (UT)	39,173	23,074	30,150	————
Arches National Monument (UT)	34,010	12,742	28,417	————

SOURCE: Stewart M. Brandborg, "The Wilderness Law and the National Park System in the United States," Conference on Canadian National Parks, Calgary, Alberta, October 11, 1968, 17. Box 2:203. TWS.

motor nature trails." Visitors to the national parks, he concluded, would find them "unimpaired" and "enjoy the finest wilderness in our Nation—lands and waters that meet the highest standards yet devised for wilderness preservation."[36] His audience was not convinced.

The Wilderness Society's Stewart Brandborg also approached the podium at this conference. He praised the Park Service in general for its planning procedures, especially its pledge to open its master planning to more public involvement. He complained of "confusion introduced by the classification system and the use of thresholds." Brandborg said that "there continues to be an underlying basic question as to whether any land in the National Parks should be designated for high density, recreation use."[37] Brandborg, in this comment, revealed a fundamental issue of the wilderness review. Some conservationists believed that no further development of national parks should occur and would try to use the Wilderness Act to achieve this goal. Many in the Park Service, on the other hand, believed that pressure of visitation on the parks would continue to grow, and one way to address this demand was to keep open as many options for development as possible. This was, on one level, a clash between some who thought that the only way to protect the parks was to close them to further development and those who felt that national parks were the people's parks and as more people came to them there would of necessity be more development to meet this demand. On the other hand, nearly everyone could agree that another way to meet growing demand was to create more parks and to create them as close to the people as there was parkland available. This work was ongoing and was common ground for all parties interested in the future of national parks. Drives were under way both for new wilderness parks and for recreation areas close to the people.

The first review period during which the Park Service was to review one-third of its wilderness ended September 3, 1967. The review fell short of the goal because of slow development of regulations and procedures. Only ten field hearings had been held by this date. The goal had been nineteen. No penalty was exacted for falling behind schedule, but this meant the schedule would be more crowded during the next review period. Every National Park Service wilderness review proposal except one had been smaller than conservationists thought it should be. A tally prepared by The Wilderness Society reveals this (see table 1). The Park Service revised its proposals after hearings, usually adding acreage, but it continued to designate thresholds and its proposals continued to be controversial.

For forty years the Park Service had successfully avoided drawing boundaries around the portions of the national park system that were "unimpaired." As the reviews mandated by the Wilderness Act revealed, it had succeeded in keeping large parts of the system sufficiently unimpaired to qualify as wilderness according to Wilderness Act definitions. Now, when it faced a legal mandate to draw wilderness boundaries, or at least recommend to Congress where it thought wilderness boundaries should be, it found itself unprepared for the task. Reluctant to even now yield any of what it perceived to be its professional prerogatives, despite the long and politically complex debate that led to the Wilderness Act, it tried many tactics to minimize what it perceived as damage to its authority and autonomy.

The Park Service conducted field hearings late in 1967 on four units in Utah and for only two small New Mexico areas (Chiricahua and Chaco Canyon national monuments) in 1968. The pace of review, slow to begin with, ground to a halt. The few proposals aired were, as usual, controversial by the areas excluded from proposed wilderness. No wilderness field hearings were held in 1969, and they did not resume until late in 1970. The review process stalled for nearly two years while the 1974 deadline drew ever closer. Why did progress on wilderness reviews virtually stop for so long?

At the time, many conservationists thought the Park Service was deliberately stalling because it still hoped to find ways to reduce the impact of the Wilderness Act on its managerial discretion. The service indeed continued to explore ways to exclude portions of the wilderness-eligible roadless areas from Class V. Master planning and the complex, ever-changing wilderness review procedures were the excuses for the slower pace. Regional planning, advocated by both conservationists and park planners, complicated master planning and slowed things even more. Whether or not master planning was intentionally used to stall the review process is difficult to establish, but linkage of wilderness review to it certainly had that effect. In 1970 a frustrated congressman, John Saylor, long among the strongest congressional supporters of wilderness, attacked this master plan–wilderness review linkage.

These master plans are each taking three or four years to prepare. There is no reason why decisions as to what portions of a national park shall be recommended for wilderness designation should be held up while somebody argues over each parking lot, how many campsites in each automobile campground.[1]

The linkage of master planning and wilderness designation was not an unreasonable idea, but Saylor was stating the obvious. The Park Service did not have all the time it might wish to develop wonderful plans. Congress had given it a specific job to do and a limited schedule within which to do it.

TACTICS OF EXCLUSION

The Park Service had sent up trial balloons in its early wilderness proposals and had been roundly criticized on several fronts. Now, in 1968 and 1969, it was working on other approaches that proved similarly controversial. One of these, akin to thresholds, was enclaves. These were non-wilderness islands identified for various reasons that were surrounded by proposed wilderness. Both the Park Service and Forest Service were, at this point, holding to a policy of "purity" in determining what qualified as wilderness. They were very narrowly interpreting Section 2(c) and definitions of "permanent improvements" and "substantially unnoticeable" impact of human activity. This led the Park Service to claim that such "developments" as snow gauges, campsites, aircraft landing sites, sanitation facilities, fire towers, and ranger patrol cabins should be excluded from wilderness proposals. Some of these claims were appropriate and some were not. Purism was also manifest in the threshold concept in the view that if there might be any sights, sounds, or smells of civilization, the wilderness boundary should be moved back to avoid these intrusions on the wilderness experience.

Inside the Park Service at this time there was debate about the purity issue. National Park Service planner John M. Kauffmann, for instance, wrote a memo to the chief of the Division of Wilderness Studies in 1968 about an issue that had arisen in wilderness review. He asked which facilities might be appropriate in wilderness and concluded that facilities needed for resource protection would be allowable. This would require a careful definition of what was really necessary for such protection, and he offered his informed opinion of this issue. In his view, the Park Service was using facilities far more than it should as excuses to establish enclaves and buffers. The many islands within wilderness created by these exclusions would only make wilderness protection and management more difficult in the future.

Park Service planners were also excluding areas from proposed wilderness because of uses they considered incompatible with it, and Kauffmann thought this too was ill advised in many instances. If, for example, the problem was a lifetime grazing allotment, it should simply be considered a nonconforming use within the wilderness. If it were a nonconforming use allowed by Congress, then the Park Service should include it in its proposal "until Congress acts otherwise." In Kauffmann's view this "does not compromise and weaken the effect of the Wilderness Act by causing the administrators to designate less wilderness than their best judgement dictates."[2] Kauffmann's memo is an example of substantive debate within the Park Service about controversial wilderness review approaches. Such debate may have been a factor in slowing wilderness review at this stage.

Kauffmann's views on enclaves did not prevail. The 1971 wilderness proposal for Isle Royale National Park exhibited the "Swiss cheese" qualities that bothered Kauffmann, as did the proposal for the new park in the North Cascades. In the latter case there were to be eighteen enclaves to accommodate visitors, including trail shelters and even "chalets." Finally, at the May 5, 1972, wilderness hearing in Sequoia and Kings Canyon National Parks, the issues raised by Kauffmann and others were forcefully addressed. Assistant Secretary Nathaniel Reed, presenting the Park Service proposal, was told by Senator Frank Church, floor manager of the Wilderness Act eight years earlier, that the "test of suitability of an area for wilderness designation is simply and solely in the definition of wilderness in Section 2(c), which is a reasonable, flexible definition, resting basically on a balancing judgment of the imprint of man's work being 'substantially unnoticeable' within the proposed wilderness entity." Church saw no reason why, under the Wilderness Act, minimal management facilities could not be present in wilderness.

> The issue is not whether necessary management facilities and activities are prohibited; they are not—the test is whether they are in fact necessary. Nothing in the Act or the legislative intent requires or forces the National Park Service or the Bureau of Sports Fisheries and Wildlife to carve out these kinds of non-wilderness enclaves. . . . the concept of non-wilderness enclaves, at least as embodied in these proposals, is undesirable, dangerous, inconsistent with the letter and intent of the Wilderness Act, and altogether unjustifiable.[3]

This was not the end of the matter, but the Park Service was notified that its narrow and purist interpretation of the Wilderness Act that had resulted in many proposed enclaves was not what Congress had intended.

The Park Service also wrestled with another sort of enclave—the inholding. New parks were often pocked with small pieces of private land acquired as homesteads or mining claims. The intent was always to eventually acquire these inholdings and add them to the parks, but for political and fiscal reasons this had often not been possible. The definition of wilderness in Section 2(c) contained the phrase "an area of undeveloped federal land," which the Park Service interpreted to mean that non-federally owned land could not be included in a wilderness proposal. Conservationists thought that where the service intended to acquire inholdings they should be included within the boundaries of a proposed wilderness. In February 1969 the Park Service decided to take what it called a "wilderness escrow" approach, whereby it would exclude holdings and areas of "adverse use" such as grazing and stock driveways and mineral claims but would prepare supplemental wilderness reports on these areas.[4] A detailed procedure was set up to do this. Here was yet another complication and more work in preparing wilderness proposals.

There was also the issue of grazing. While this activity was limited to only six national park system units, it had to be dealt with. Two of the affected areas were Grand Canyon and Sequoia. The Park Service decided to exclude from wilderness proposals areas where grazing was permitted, which led once more to charges of excess purity. At Lava Beds National Monument, for instance, a significant portion of possible wilderness was excluded from the proposal because of a rancher's lifetime grazing permit. Conservationists thought the proposed wilderness far too small; when the proposal reached Congress in 1972, the House Interior Subcommittee on National Parks and Recreation, and then the full House Interior Committee, agreed with them. The committee stated in its report that it "did not concur in the conclusion that grazing per se, precludes designation of lands as wilderness."[5] It tripled the size of the wilderness from the Park Service's proposed 9,197 acres to 28,460. Here was another signal to the Park Service that it needed to rethink its approach.

These were a few of the issues occupying the Park Service wilderness review teams and planners at this time that explain some of the slowdown in the review process. While they worked on all of these complications, there was a change in national administration when Republican Richard Nixon won the presidential election of 1968. A new secretary of the Interior was installed—Walter J. Hickel. As secretaries before him had done, Hickel sent a policy memo to the Park Service director suggesting what park policy should be. Several points in Hickel's memo related to wilderness review. While he thought it should proceed expeditiously, he favored some development for visitors to the back country.

> You should . . . emphasize a program of providing low cost and rustic back-country facilities such as the chalets in Glacier National Park and the High Sierra Camps in Yosemite National Park. . . . Such operations . . . enable an urban society—growing numbers of which are not prepared to cope with wilderness camping—to enjoy the scenic grandeur and re-creative values of a quality park experience at minimum cost and with minimum intrusion in the physical environment.[6]

The secretary's statement gave hope to those advocating enclaves in wilderness. Hickel favored the effort already under way to identify parks close to urban areas that could bring "parks to people," thought it important to figure out how the crush of vehicles could be reduced in many parks, and advocated cooperative regional outdoor recreation planning with other agencies. All of these were initiatives already taken by Director Hartzog. As to wilderness, Hickel wrote, "I am also interested in preserving the wilderness of our National Park System. In this connection, I note that you are behind schedule in your wilderness studies of roadless areas of the National Park System. It is important we get this program on track."[7] Adjusting to the agenda of a new administration, with its inevitable changes in politically driven priorities and procedures, could not be expected to speed up the progress of wilderness studies.

The program did not, at the secretary's urging, move any faster along the track. There is no evidence that the change in administration made any difference in the wilderness review process, though it probably added more work to the already stretched agency workforce. Transition to new administrations always involves a new cast of politically appointed characters in the Interior Department, all of whom must be informed and educated about programs under way. New people always bring with them new ideas about how agencies should address their missions and often different ideologies that affect priorities. They also usually want to review programs under way, and all of this involves work and slows progress of ongoing work. So while there might have been some stalling by reluctant Park Service officials, there were also legitimate reasons why progress was slow and halting at this juncture.

Conservationists became increasingly frustrated with the Park Service. They pressed Leslie Glasgow, assistant secretary of the interior for parks, to pressure the Park Service to speed its work, but to little effect. The minutes of The Wilderness Society Executive Committee meetings during this period, for instance, reveal extensive discussion of Park Service wilderness review and its shortcomings. Leaders of The Wilderness Society understood the difficulties the Park Service was facing: changes in master planning and wilderness review procedures; desire of the new administration to review proposals already prepared; inadequate proposals sharply opposed by conservation organizations. The Park Service faced real challenges, but consensus among conservation leaders was that it was not trying hard enough. Early in 1970 a call was issued to increase pressure on the Park Service by bringing the problem of lack of progress in wilderness review to the attention of Congress. Lobbying of National Park Service field people would also be increased.

The spring 1970 issue of The Wilderness Society's *The Living Wilderness* carried a long article by Ernie Dickerman in which he lambasted the Park Service for its "foot dragging." "Not a single acre of national parks has been placed in the National Wilderness Preservation System," he wrote, "more than five and one-half years after the signing of the Wilderness Act on September 3, 1964." In his opinion, both the Forest Service and the Bureau of Sports Fisheries and Wildlife had been making "serious efforts to move forward," but not the Park Service. Twelve national park wilderness hearings had been held, but the proposals that came out of them were "somewhere in limbo," and "meaningful information as to the status of any of them is virtually impossible to obtain." He described the factors that had, in the opinion of conservationists, made many proposals inadequate: wilderness thresholds, roads, grazing exclusions, inholdings and general exclusions, and the connection of wilderness review to master planning. This last he thought an especially serious problem. He urged his readers to let Secretary Hickel, Congress, and the Park Service know of their concerns. Dickerman concluded that what was needed was for the Park Service to "adopt a positive wilderness philosophy and decide that in accordance with the specifically stated policy of the Secretary of the Interior as well as Congress it is going to get on with the job and accomplish the objective of the Wilderness Act as written."[8] Dickerman's point about "positive wilderness philosophy" was a telling one. As one reviews both the Park Service rhetoric and its actions during this period, the rhetoric sounds positive (as Park Service rhetoric about wilderness always had), but its actions belie any enthusiasm about its wilderness review task. Its "wilderness philosophy" was not negative, but it certainly was not positive either. Perhaps the best description of it is "continually conflicted." In the hearing regarding the first wilderness proposal, at Great Smoky Mountains National Park, Stewart Brandborg had made the point that if any government agency should set the standard and embrace the opportunity presented by the Wilderness Act, it should be the Park Service. Several years later Brandborg's hope, dashed from the beginning by the Trans-mountain Road fiasco, could be seen as a vain one.

Dickerman's article seemed to have some effect. Congress heard from many people, and the Park Service in turn heard from Congress. Still, the Park Service continued to brush off criticism. Acting Director Harthon Bill responded to one congressman's inquiry by saying that the Park Service shared Dickerman's desire to speed things up and was "looking toward means of accelerating the process." But, he continued, linkage to master planning was not the problem. Such linkage was essential and "insures that wilderness recommendations are firmly based on sound comprehensive planning for all aspects of park development and management." As evidence, Bill pointed out how such planning for Lassen Volcanic National Park and Pinnacles National Monument had revealed a need for "additional interpretive roads to meet visitor needs." Such roads "are not by any means major highways but are designed to low standards to minimize their impact on the land."[9] Such roads, which he called "interpretive (motor nature) roads," would be only fourteen feet wide.

Ever since Wirth had called, in the early 1960s, for a study of parks to determine what areas should not become wilderness because they might be needed for development, the Park Service had been finding excuses to keep areas out of wilderness proposals. Here Bill cited another—"motor nature" roads (also euphemistically called "trails" by some). No one was challenging the wisdom of comprehensive master planning—Dickerman conceded this in his article—but the fact that such master planning kept producing new schemes for potential development like these "motor nature roads" was at best annoying to wilderness advocates and at worst confirmation of their suspicions that the Park Service would find every device it could conjure up to minimize wilderness in its parks. The fact that it kept coming up with new excuses for roads—the symbol of damage to wilderness regardless of their width or purpose—indicates how far many in Park Service leadership seem to have been from understanding the nature of the response they were getting from wilderness advocates in Congress and elsewhere.

Acting Director Bill characterized Dickerman's article as "an overstatement aimed at a specific audience." The National Park Service had been making "considerable progress" in its reviews though "there has been little visibility associated with it." He assured the congressman that "our record, or visible record, for the next 18 months will be much more to the Wilderness Society's liking." Bill's claim that the Park Service had been making progress but that its critics had just not seen it raises several questions. Why, if they had been progressing, had they not simply explained what they were doing to those accusing them of doing little or nothing? There were, in the conservation community, strong advocates of regional planning like Anthony Wayne Smith of the National Parks Association, and why had they not used Smith's advocacy of the approach they were taking to reassure other conservationist critics? Smith, in fact, was as concerned as everyone else about lack of agency progress on wilderness review. The Park Service could perhaps, for good reasons, not reveal all the details of its work, but it could surely explain what it was doing better than it had. And why, if it were the strong protector of wilderness that it had so long claimed to be, did it keep coming up with excuses and new ways to "develop" the wilderness, such as these "motor nature trails"?

Two months after Bill claimed that the Park Service was making acceptable progress, he presided over a meeting that suggests he was being disingenuous in his earlier response to Dickerman's article. The meeting was about the "accelerated wilderness program" that had been ordered by Leslie Glasgow and for which the assistant secretary had requested a schedule for completion of wilderness reviews. In attendance were deputy directors Bill and Thomas Flynn, Mike Griswold as head of the Washington office branch overseeing new parks and wilderness reviews, and Cortland Reid, head of the wilderness review program. Glasgow had asked for a list of areas that would be reviewed in conjunction with a master plan and, of those, which would be reviewed without master plan studies. Wilderness studies could and where necessary should, according to Glasgow, be done without linkage to a master plan.[10] This would cost money, and Glasgow stated that "it is understood, in light of the money now allocated to wilderness studies, that it will be necessary to reprogram funds from master planning, and possible new area studies, in order to get this work accomplished." He urged Hartzog to get on with this reprogramming.

Glasgow did not think the Park Service was making adequate progress and ordered it to get moving. It should change its priorities and its budgeting of resources if necessary. He did not agree with Bill's claim that the Park Service was on track in its reviews. In late July Hartzog informed his people that they were to expedite wilderness reviews. This would, he wrote, speed the process but not change the approach.

> This accelerated wilderness study schedule—without Master Plan—does not change in any way our need for land classification of the entire park . . . provision for buffer zones, and provision for future developments in the park, especially one-way motor nature trails, group and high mountain camps and chalets, as indicated in the Secretary's Policy Guidelines of June, 1969.[11]

A plan to expedite review was presented to the group in Bill's office, with several steps previously involving the Washington office removed. More responsibility would be passed to the regional offices, and since there would be less thoroughness the wilderness proposals should be "safe" and "conservative." The meeting record states that "for the sake of meeting the deadline, the Service will put together general proposals. There will be no pretense that wilderness proposals were developed through detailed planning studies."[12] This was a major change. Glasgow had directed that the last recommendations for national park wilderness needed to be submitted to the president by December 1973 (a goal that would not be met), and he wanted a plan for how this would be achieved.

The Interior Department was responsible for wilderness review of national parks and wildlife refuges. The Bureau of Sports Fisheries and Wildlife was making progress and, by comparison, the Park Service was far behind. Political pressure was being applied to the administration to get things moving on national park review, and in the summer of 1970 it finally had an effect. Glasgow's directive was an admission that the Park Service needed to move faster. The meeting in Bill's office belies his assurances that all was well and confirms that major procedural changes would be required to accomplish the wilderness review goal. In an August director's staff meeting it was noted that the president had ordered a speedup of wilderness reviews and would back this up with a supplemental appropriation to do the job. At the same meeting the staff reviewed "preliminary wilderness suitability reports" for Black Canyon of the Gunnison National Monument, Mesa Verde National Park, and Crater Lake National Park.[13] Perhaps the "dragging of feet" was ending.

What inspired this push from Interior to speed up the national park wilderness reviews? Pressure from many sources probably yielded this result, but one likely nudge came from a House Interior Committee hearing in June 1970. John Saylor of Pennsylvania, a member of the committee and a congressional wilderness advocate, expressed his concern about lack of progress on national park wilderness at the hearing. He had introduced an omnibus bill that would designate wilderness in twenty-three national wildlife refuges, two national parks, and one national forest primitive area. The hearing dealt with his bill, which was ultimately approved in the closing days of the 91st Congress and produced the first congressionally established wilderness in the national park system. The park wilderness areas were in Arizona's Petrified Forest National Park (50,260 acres) and Idaho's Craters of the Moon National Monument (43,243 acres). This achievement set off no wild celebrations, though it was a significant moment in the history of national park wilderness. More than forty years of effort had finally yielded the level of protection for wild lands in national parks that had been the dream of Robert Sterling Yard, Howard Zahniser, and many others. Only Congress could now change the status of these wilderness areas. This was affirmative wilderness, not just wilderness by virtue of the fact that it had not been penetrated by a road or some other development to accommodate visitors. Congressman Saylor called passage of the omnibus bill "a conservation achievement of the highest order through which the Congress has set the precedent for effective implementation of the Wilderness Law."[14] He wanted to move toward more congressional approval of wilderness, and this was being retarded by the slowness of national park reviews.

Saylor and his conservationist colleagues could not afford to celebrate because the balance of their work still lay ahead. The administration was sending forward three more wilderness proposals for congressional action, and the Park Service informed Leslie Glasgow that twenty-six wilderness recommendations that had been developed through master planning studies would be forwarded to the Interior Department. Twenty more, including such large parks as Glacier, Rocky Mountain, Mount Rainier, Everglades, and Olympic, would be prepared without accompanying master plan studies. The schedule would have all forty-six of the required recommendations made before December 1973 as directed. Glasgow assured Saylor that "such a speedup will meet your request to move forward rapidly. Accelerated activity is already becoming evident all along the wilderness study line."[15]

Two wilderness field hearings had been held by the Park Service in the summer of 1970, and four more were held in December. Nine field hearings were convened in 1971 and seven in 1972. In late October of 1970 Stewart Brandborg could report that eight wilderness proposals for national parks were in the final stages of executive branch approval.[16] Brandborg and his allies were pleased at the prospect of moving park wilderness proposals to Congress where they could address some of the deficiencies they saw in Park Service recommendations. In most cases the Park Service had responded to comments in the public hearing phase and modified their proposals. This usually resulted in a larger proposed wilderness, but in few cases did the conservationists win all the improvements they sought. They would take their fight to Congress.

The North Cascades wilderness field hearing in June 1970 revealed that, while political pressure might be motivating acceleration of the review schedule, the Park Service was still intent on enclaves, buffers, and other exclusions to which conservationists objected. The North Cascades proposal contained three exclusions so that tramways could be built to give tourists unable or unwilling to hike to viewpoints an overview of this spectacular mountain park. Exclusions for "management zones," which was the latest Park Service name for thresholds, and for enclaves were present in most new wilderness proposals. "Nonconforming uses" excluded large areas, as at the Grand Canyon, where grazing and motorboats on the Colorado River reduced the size of proposed wilderness. At Yosemite conservationists protested that inholdings should not preclude some areas from becoming wilderness. The Park Service, they argued, should acquire inholdings, or plan to do so, and write the statute for the wilderness so that when acquisitions were made the areas acquired would automatically become part of the wilderness.

Within the Interior Department and the National Park Service, maneuvering around wilderness review was still evident. Rogers C. B. Morton replaced Hickel as secretary of the interior. Morton sent a memo to Hartzog in June 1971 asking him for a statement of his philosophy and a long-range plan. The Park Service was about to launch a celebration of the national park system's centennial year, and Morton laid out for Hartzog what he thought should be in a plan for the next century of that system. Morton wrote of wilderness that "the National Park Service must do everything possible to get and keep the wilderness reviews on schedule." His principal concern, however, was wilderness management. The Park Service should have symposia and do research on wilderness use problems and solutions to them.[17] The Wilderness Act had fueled a rapidly growing interest in wilderness recreation, and ever more people were venturing into wilderness whether it was congressionally designated or not. The Park Service was increasingly concerned about managing this growing wilderness visitation. Also, it now had its first congressionally designated wilderness and needed to draft management plans for it. Not only did the service face growing pressure to expedite reviews; as managers of congressionally designated wilderness, they faced challenges of what to do in the field that would differ from their previous practices. The agency's wilderness responsibilities were growing.

WILDERNESS IN NEW PARKS

In addition to wilderness reviews and wilderness management, the Park Service at this stage was a partner in major initiatives for new parks. Several long campaigns to make major additions were coming to fruition. Among them were the North Cascades and Redwoods national parks (1968), Sleeping Bear Dunes National Lakeshore (1970), authorization of Voyageurs National Park (1971), change of status of Arches National Monument to a national park (1971), Buffalo National River (1972), Cumberland Island National Seashore (1972), Big Cypress National Preserve (1974), and authorization of Big Thicket National Preserve (1974). All of these were considered additions to the natural area category of the system (though that categorization system was fading in importance by this point), and in all but Redwoods the park legislation directed a wilderness review. For the North Cascades park, for instance, the secretary was directed to "review the area within the North Cascades National Park [and] . . . report to the President . . . his recommendation as to the suitability or nonsuitability of any area within the park for preservation as wilderness" within two years.[18] Similar provisions were written into the legislation for the other parks mentioned above, with duration of the review period ranging from two to five years. This wilderness review provision in new park legislation extended the Wilderness Act to new park areas. Congress did not act to create wilderness at the outset, though some thought it should do so and avoid much work and possible conflict later. Others thought the new parks should be studied in exactly the same manner as the rest of the system. Many issues were unresolved at the time the parks were created. The North Cascades National Park provides examples. It was essentially a de facto wilderness park with very little access except for those willing and able to hike. Since many national park visitors could not or would

9.1 Mount Shuksan in the North Cascades National Park displays the wild, glacier-clad nature of this Northwest landscape. Photo by John Miles

not hike, how would the "public use and enjoyment" part of the mission be accomplished there? Many ideas were floating around, such as the tramways and enclaves mentioned earlier. Various road schemes were being touted. Yet here was an opportunity to plan and manage a wilderness park in the new era of wilderness preservation. How might this be accomplished? All such questions needed resolution before wilderness boundaries could be drawn, and Congress passed the job of sorting them out to the Park Service. Not until 1988 would wilderness be designated in the North Cascades.

Wilderness parks like the North Cascades offered both new opportunities and new challenges. As with all the new parks, opponents had lost their fight to keep the lands in the North Cascades open to commodity production and multiple use, but they were still in action. Mining and logging interests had fought long and hard to defeat a park in the North Cascades. They failed but still won many concessions. For the first time Congress established, as a compromise addressed to hard-fought issues, a national park "complex." Along with the national park, which was virtually roadless and one of America's wildest landscapes, the North Cascades legislation established two national recreation areas. These were adjacent to the park—the Ross Lake and Lake Chelan National Recreation Areas—and would be places where "public use and enjoyment" could be provided without impacting the wilderness park. Ross Lake was created by a hydroelectric dam. The North Cascades Highway would traverse the Skagit River corridor, often paralleling transmission lines, and cross the mountains. Campgrounds would be developed along the highway and a visitor center would eventually be constructed. The isolated and unique village of Stehekin at the head of Lake Chelan would be maintained, a tourist destination close to the heart of the range. The wild park itself could be managed as wilderness because the visitor pressure could be accommodated in the already developed national recreation areas. Thus did Congress allow—perhaps "require" would be a more accurate term—the National Park Service to do its master and management planning and wilderness review for the complex, while making the task of identifying wilderness a bit easier by the very design of the new national park system unit.

Each new park had its own special needs and challenges, but the North Cascades example indicates a congressional commitment to national park wilderness. Hot battles were waged over every new addition, but if a new park of the natural-area type could be added, then Congress intended that its wilderness, whatever there might be of it, should be considered for protection. During the period when North Cascades entered the park system, sixty-nine new areas were added, only five of them classified as natural areas. The late 1960s and early 1970s was a time of growing support for environmental protection as well as for bringing parks to the people. Even as national recreation areas were being planned for the gateways of New York and San Francisco and the urban regions of Cleveland and Los Angeles, wild remnants of America were being preserved in parks and assessed for even greater protection as wilderness.[19]

MORE STARTS AND STOPS

The National Park Service and the Department of the Interior seemed, in late 1971 and early 1972, to be true to their assurances that they would expedite the park wilderness reviews. Field hearings were held in 1971 for ten parks and monuments, including Yosemite and Grand Canyon, and seven more were held in the first three months of 1972, Yellowstone among them. Then things stalled again. In 1971, President Nixon sent wilderness proposals for seven national parks to Congress, including North Cascades, Isle Royale, Sequoia and Kings Canyon (treated as one unit), and Shenandoah national parks, and Cedar Breaks, Capitol Reef, and Arches national monuments. All proposals were, in the view of conservationists, flawed by exclusions of areas they thought should be included in wilderness. The Park Service continued to justify the exclusions with all of the rationales it had been using for years. Congress held hearings on Lava Beds National Monument and Lassen Volcanic National Park and approved wilderness for both of them in October 1972. Controversy continued to swirl around Park Service insistence on enclaves, management zones, and motor nature trails. When the Subcommittee on Public Lands of the Senate Committee on Interior and Insular Affairs held hearings on the administration's park proposals in May 1972, these and other Park Service rationales for wilderness exclusions were attacked by committee members. Senator Frank Church of Idaho expressed the strongest views.

Church had been floor manager of the wilderness bill when it first passed the Senate in 1961 and had been keenly interested in the bill ever since. At the May 5 hearing, after citing specific legislative history of the Wilderness Act, he tackled the Park Service policies one by one. He opened with several broad points about the Wilderness Act. He and his colleagues had specifically provided for established grazing and, as in the case of Yellowstone Lake, even use of motorboats. Such established uses were not sufficient to justify exclusions. There was no justification in the law for buffers and thresholds as the Park Service was drawing them. "Sights and sounds from outside the boundary do not invalidate a wilderness designation or make threshold exclusions necessary, as a matter of law."[20] So much for the Park Service's purity argument. "In the absence of good and substantial reasons to the contrary," Church continued, "and I am specific, case by case reasons—the boundaries of wilderness areas within national parks should embrace all wild lands."[21] Enclaves, present in several proposals before the committee that day, were of special concern. He saw no need or justification for them. In his opinion, "The concept of wilderness enclaves, at least as embodied in these proposals, is undesirable, dangerous, inconsistent with the letter and intent of the Wilderness Act, and altogether unjustified."[22] As wilderness proposals for each park and national wildlife refuge were examined in the hearing, Church continued to use legislative history as grounds for clarifying congressional intent. On the snow gauge issue, for instance—the Park Service had drawn 9-acre enclaves around these installations, arguing that they did not meet the test of necessary for administration of the park and thereby were not allowed in park

9.2 Frank Church was among the strongest supporters of wilderness in the Senate and influenced the National Park Service wilderness review at a crucial point in the early 1970s. Frank Church collection, Boise State University Library

wilderness—Church cast the service's interpretation as "very forced." The gauges had been located carefully and for good reason, he said, and "you can't administer that area without taking into reasonable account the impact on other land. The snow up there is going to melt and in my experience when the snow melts the water goes downhill and affects all the land."[23] Church's sarcastic tone here indicates his level of exasperation at the Park Service. Later, in addressing buffers in the Sequoia-Kings Canyon proposal, he sharply interrupted the park superintendent's explanation of why buffers were needed, saying, "You can control inside of the wilderness, you don't have to have a buffer zone." Assistant Secretary for Fish and Wildlife and Parks Nathaniel Reed responded that the Park Service field study teams were merely abiding by a directive from the director, and Church retorted, "I wish you would revise the bill and take all of these cheese holes out of it."[24] The senator did not have the final word on any of this, but he was very influential and his exasperation reflected that of the conservation community and many of his congressional colleagues.

Following the May 5 hearing, Park Service officials thought Church had confused rather than clarified issues. The Wilderness Society's Ernie Dickerman met with Stanley Hewlett and Mike Griswold and was told that it might now be necessary to hold up further wilderness proposals until Congress clarified its intent on enclaves, buffers, and other issues. This, thought Dickerman, was a new National Park Service "alibi for obstructing and deferring the review process layed [sic] down under the Wilderness Act."[25] At the same meeting, Assistant Secretary Reed expressed a sharply different view. According to Dickerman, Reed said that "he regarded Mr. Church's remarks as being helpfully clear and definite in furnishing guidance as to what is and is not acceptable within wilderness candidate areas."[26] Reed said he was ready to move forward "along the lines indicated by Senator Church," and indeed he was. On June 24, in a memorandum to the directors of the Park Service and

Bureau of Sports Fisheries and Wildlife, he issued new "Departmental Guidelines for Wilderness Proposals." These guidelines reflected Church's positions very closely. Regarding visitor use structures and facilities, the guidelines stated that "an area that contains man-made facilities for visitor use can be designated as wilderness if these facilities are the minimum necessary for health and safety of the wilderness traveler."[27] When there exist "prior rights and privileges" such as stock driveways and grazing or "limited commercial services" appropriate for recreational and wilderness use of an area, areas so affected should be included. Unimproved roads that might be removed need not disqualify an area. If plans drawn up for an area involve future development inconsistent with a wilderness, they should be excluded, but with exceptions. When small boat docks and primitive shelters are present in an area being studied for wilderness that might otherwise qualify, "a specific provision may be included . . . giving the wilderness manager the option of retaining and maintaining these structures."[28] Necessary management practices such as controlled burning should also be specifically mentioned in proposals as allowable in wilderness, as should hydrologic devices. There would be no more enclaves around snow gauges. Even lakes, created by water developments, and underground utilities should not disqualify areas for inclusion in wilderness proposals. Finally, when areas did not qualify as wilderness at the time of review because they were an inholding but were surrounded by wilderness, "A special provision should be included in the legislative proposal giving the Secretary of the Interior the authority to designate such lands as wilderness at such time he determines it qualifies."[29]

Thus did the Department of the Interior reject the Park Service purism in its wilderness reviews. Conservationists had objected strenuously over the past seven years to what they considered at best a Park Service misinterpretation of congressional intent and at worst a deliberate strategy to evade that intent. Key congressional leaders had agreed with their position, and in turn the Nixon administration had decided that the Park Service should take a new approach. Nine months after he issued these guidelines, Reed was interviewed for a Park Service newsletter. When asked about buffers and enclaves, he replied sharply. "Buffer zones. No more buffer zones. Buffer zones are out. . . . there are to be no more buffer zones, and there are to be damn few enclaves, and the enclaves will have to have terribly close scrutiny by me to make it."[30] Reed left no doubt as to the approach he thought should be taken on these issues. Senator Church's words had made an impact, at least on Assistant Secretary Reed, and he was the boss.

As Interior was formulating these new guidelines, the Park Service was moving forward with wilderness proposals that contained recommendations formulated under the old guidelines. Glacier National Park field hearings were held in late June, and the service proposal included twenty-nine enclaves within three proposed wilderness units. There were management zones ranging from one-eighth to one-half mile wide along all exterior park boundaries, roads, and lakeshores where there were established motorboat use and facilities. Inholdings, interpretive trails, and a glacier research installation were all excluded from the wilderness. On the other hand, the impact of the new guidelines could be seen on other proposals. March hearings on a preliminary proposal for Yellowstone wilderness revealed management zones, fifty-eight enclaves, and exclusions for grazing and water rights. The Park Service released its revised proposal in August and had eliminated most of the buffers, reduced the enclaves from fifty-eight to six, and otherwise implemented the new guidelines. The revised proposal added 34,381 acres, deleted 400 acres, and recommended 6,040 acres of "potential wilderness." Conservationists had been striving for years to see such a wilderness proposal, and here was certainly a sign of the long-desired change in approach.

THE FINAL PUSH

As 1972 drew to a close The Wilderness Society issued a status report on the Wilderness Act. "In its ninth year the Wilderness Review process . . . is at last hitting full stride."[31] It could report that two additional national park wilderness areas had finally been established by Congress at Lassen Volcanic National Park and Lava Beds National Monument. Field hearings had been held for thirty-three areas and it expected that in 1973 they would be held for all remaining national park areas except so-called second-generation parks—those established since passage of the Wilderness Act. The legislation for these parks included special requirements for wilderness study but not within Wilderness Act deadlines. By 1973 the Park Service had retreated from its earlier approach of using various devices to keep portions of roadless areas out of wilderness status. It had substantially accepted Senator Church's clarifications of May 1972 that "in the absence of good and substantial reasons to the contrary . . . the boundaries of wilderness areas within national parks should embrace all wild land."[32] The Park Service had tried to find ways around, as Church said, "surrendering their full administrative discretion over such areas" but had finally accepted that Congress had intended that they do just that. With an assistant secretary for parks and wildlife committed to finishing the review and carrying out the intent of Congress, the service was finally forced to get down to business, revise its procedures and approach, and make its final push toward the deadlines set by Leslie Glasgow and, missing that, the Wilderness Act.

George Hartzog, never a champion of wilderness and in no small part responsible for the Park Service's dilatory approach to wilderness review, was fired and left his post in December 1972. No official reason was given by the Nixon people for his dismissal, but speculation was that he had crossed one or more of Nixon's principal advisers and thus had to go.[33] He was replaced by Ronald Walker, whom the deposed Hartzog later described as "in the vanguard of White House assistants appointed to a number of strategic positions in the bureaus and departments to make the career bureaucrats toe the line, although no one seemed to know where the line was."[34] Nathaniel Reed became, in the view of some, surrogate National Park Service director during Walker's brief tenure (he resigned in January 1975). Ron Foresta describes Reed as "by background and inclination . . . an environmentalist" and characterizes his involvement as "ensuring that the agency managed the Park System in accord with the Wilderness Act."[35] What this means is that the Park Service strove to make up ground and complete wilderness reviews within the mandated schedule.

Field hearings were held in 1973 for Glacier, Olympic, and Zion national parks. The final ten parks, including Mount Rainier and Rocky Mountain, rushed through field hearings and preparation of recommendations to the president in 1974. Conservationists took issue with details of every Park Service proposal but in general were more supportive than earlier. Assistant Secretary Reed seemed to be making good on his pledge to reduce or eliminate buffer zones and closely scrutinized all enclaves. There was still argument over what the Park Service considered necessary "management exceptions" to the management standards of the Wilderness Act, but the attention of the conservation community was gradually drawn away from the park wilderness issue by what it perceived as more pressing challenges. The showdown over park wilderness had been the hearing of May 5, 1972, and this was the high point of the decade of struggle over park wilderness review. People who were invested in parks decided that they had done what they could at this stage. They would continue to keep an eye on how the Park Service did its reviews, but their energy was increasingly devoted to Alaska, where a new prospect for truly vast and ecologically designed wilderness might be achieved.

The world outside of national parks also played a role in reducing attention by conservationists to national park wilderness at this time. The Watergate crisis distracted anyone involved in the federal political world. Conservation groups suffered from identity crises brought on by the emergence of environmentalism. On the one hand environmentalism increased public interest in wilderness and strengthened the wilderness preservation current of conservation, but on the other the established groups found themselves broadening and diluting their efforts. The classic case of this was the National Parks Association (now the National Parks Conservation Association), which began a decline in the early 1970s as it drifted away from its focus on the national parks.[36] The Sierra Club and The Wilderness Society both suffered crises in leadership that focused them inward for a time.

Another reason for the reduction in activity around park wilderness was simply that wilderness in national parks had always enjoyed a greater measure of protection than that in national forests, and in the early 1970s there was need to invest ever more effort in protecting national forest wilderness. Conservationists realized that there was a great opportunity to extend wilderness protection on national forests well beyond the primitive area system mandated for review by the Wilderness Act. They began a prolonged campaign to protect de facto wilderness in both the east and the west, areas that had received no classification under earlier Forest Service initiatives but that were roadless and wild. Out in Montana a new development in the wilderness protection effort had occurred—a strictly citizen wilderness proposal had led to the addition of the Lincoln-Scapegoat Wilderness to the National Wilderness Preservation System in 1972. Conservationists could now see that their wilderness preservation efforts need not be confined to those national forest areas mandated for review by the Wilderness Act, and wilderness preservation entered a new era. From 1972 to 1980 the issue of de facto wilderness in national forests would occupy center stage in wilderness politics.[37] All of this reduced the conservation community's attention to park wilderness, smoothing the process as the Park Service raced to meet its Wilderness Act deadline.

By late 1973 the Department of the Interior had made wilderness recommendations on twenty-nine National Park Service managed areas, still well short of its goal. Congress had acted on only four of these recommendations, and the total national park portion of the National Wilderness Preservation System was 201,000 acres. In late November the president sent to Congress wilderness recommendations for six additional areas totaling nearly 1 million acres, including large wilderness proposals for Big Bend National Park and Joshua Tree National Monument. In the final year of the review period there was a fury of activity involving wilderness proposals for all the agencies with hearings on fifty-eight areas, involving eighty-six field hearings in twenty-eight states. As might be expected, many proposals were less complete than they might ideally have been had there been more time and more careful planning, but the die had been cast, especially for the Park Service, through the long period of stalling and fussing that had characterized the early stages of the process.

In the end, the National Park Service studied and reported to Congress on wilderness in fifty-six units of the national park system. Five units were found not to have suitable wilderness, wilderness recommendations were made for forty-eight units, and no action was recommended for two. Of the forty-nine units that met the requirements for study under the Wilderness Act, only Mount McKinley National Park had no recommendation for wilderness at the end of the review period. A final recommendation for this park was deferred because the park was proposed for enlargement under the d-2 provision of the Native Claims Settlement Act and there were issues yet to be resolved. During the ten-year review period fourteen new units had been added to the national park system, and in each case wilderness study had been required by the congressional act creating the unit. Wilderness review had been completed for only one of these new units—the North Cascades National Park Complex. By the time the park wilderness reviews under the Wilderness Act were completed there were proposals pending in Congress that would establish nine new park units and enlarge two existing parks, all in Alaska. All of these would require wilderness study. Finally, there was a group of ten existing units that for various reasons—because they were less than 5,000 acres or had been created without a wilderness study requirement in establishing legislation—had not been on the original list for review but that the Park Service decided possessed areas of wilderness potential and deserved study.[38] Recommendations on them would come later.

At the congressional deadline ten years after the Wilderness Act, the story of park wilderness was, as this summary indicates, far from over. In December 1974 the National Wilderness Preservation System comprised 125 areas encompassing 12.6 million acres. Of this, 11.9 million wilderness acres were in national forests, 563,000 acres in the thirty-six national wildlife refuge wilderness areas, and 201,000 acres in the four national park wilderness units. The majority of the total National Wilderness Preservation System at this stage

(9.1 million acres) had been established by the "instant wilderness" provision of the Wilderness Act. At the end of the review period, the action on national park wilderness (and much of that under other agencies as well) moved to Congress, where a huge amount of wilderness legislation was under consideration, not the least of which was that dealing with Alaska lands. The Alaska situation was catapulting the Park Service into yet more wilderness review on a scale that would have boggled the mind of even the most optimistic wilderness advocates of earlier times.

The Wilderness Act had launched a decade of fits and starts by the Park Service. As this chapter has revealed, the agency continued to struggle with the wilderness idea. Even in the face of decisive congressional action it could not let go of the conviction that designation of national park wilderness was a superfluous and unnecessary step. But, pressured from many directions, it had done what it was legally mandated to do and passed the issue back to Congress. How well had it done the work? It had not, in the minds of many conservationists, lived up to the great potential that some, like Stewart Brandborg, had hoped that it would. In almost every case its recommendations had fallen short of what wilderness advocates thought they should be. Still, given the system that Congress had established with the act, an important step had been taken. Congress obviously did not intend that the Park Service would have the final word in wilderness designation, and it would now weigh the concerns of conservationists along with those of the other interests that might be concerned about wilderness in national parks, forests, and wildlife refuges. As will be seen, a new era of wilderness politics would now commence in which the Park Service would play a role, but a politically reduced one. Other forces beyond the control of park managers or even conservationists would shape the wilderness system both within and outside national parks.

To many Americans in the mid-twentieth century, the very word "Alaska" connoted the romance of wilderness. Remote, far to the north, land of the Inuit and northern Indians, arena for trappers, miners, and other adventurous types, Alaska was the "last frontier" and the "platonic ideal" of romantic wilderness.[1] Few roads traversed the Alaska landscape (compared with the "Lower 48," as Alaskans called the rest of the United States; Hawaii was not yet a state), and many species banished from the rest of the country were there—wolves, bear, moose, caribou, wolverine, and countless others. Alaska, the "Great Land," was a remnant of what America must have been before pioneers and settlers and developers had advanced the frontier and changed it. The territory was vast—570,374 square miles, 365 million acres. People were few, the census of 1950 counting a mere 128,643 residents, or 284 acres per Alaskan.[2] These people were scattered across the vast landscape, concentrated in a few cities like Anchorage, Fairbanks, and Juneau, but many also lived in small villages and isolated homesteads. Indians and Inuits traveled the bush in search of salmon and caribou while, as the population grew in the 1950s and 1960s, sportsmen from the Lower 48 sought trophy fish and game, their floatplanes touching down in even the most remote corners of the Great Land. Even so, it seemed to many that Alaska was empty, a place that evoked the feeling of "a truly virgin land, a wilderness on a continental scale."[3] Alaska was, in the popular imagination, wilderness.

The world changed nearly everywhere after World War II, and Alaska was not exempt. The war came to Alaska as the Japanese invaded the Aleutian Islands in 1943 and the U.S. military responded with a defensive buildup and ultimate repulse of the invaders. The Alaska Highway, built as part of this defensive effort, linked Alaska to the Lower 48 in 1942 and was opened to the public in 1948. Tourism in Alaska began, only a trickle at first. The normal boom-and-bust economy of the territory was stabilized by a continuing postwar military presence. The Cold War demanded a northern line of defense against the Soviet threat, and this led to the development of a chain of early warning stations across the wilderness north. The 1950s saw the culmination of a long push for Alaska statehood, which finally came in 1958. When Congress created the new state, it granted land that the new government could use to build its economy and its system of public education and to meet other needs, as had always been its practice in enabling statehood. In Alaska's case, Congress was especially generous: 102,550,000 acres could be selected from the public domain as state land, to join a million acres earlier granted to the territory. Alaska officials slowly began to select land, hampered by limited knowledge of what portions of this land might be most economically useful and by a limited financial ability to manage the land selected. With twenty-five years under the statehood act to choose its land grant, the state was in no hurry to make its selections.[4]

There was, however, a problem. Alaska Natives were scattered across the state, living in small, isolated villages and supporting themselves to a large extent with a subsistence lifestyle. They hunted, fished, and gathered to meet many of their needs, as they had for millennia. As the state proceeded to claim what it thought the most productive land, conflict with these people grew. Natives feared that development of state land claims would threaten their subsistence way of life. Native claims to land had been ignored since cession and throughout Alaska's history as a territory. Congress continued to ignore them in the statehood act. Alaska Natives had not been organized enough to press their case in these earlier times, but as concern among them grew over the threat of state land claims after statehood, they organized and their political voice grew too loud to ignore.

In 1966 the Alaska Federation of Natives requested that Secretary of the Interior Stewart Udall impose a freeze on the transfer of lands to the state pending resolution of conflicts over land claims. While he had been resisting such a freeze for three years, the growing political power of the Alaska Natives led Udall in 1966 to stop transfer of all land until the issue could be resolved. How might such resolution be achieved? Some thought it should be through the courts, while others favored legislation. When, in 1968, oil was discovered on the North Slope at Prudhoe Bay and plans were drawn up to transport that oil across Alaska in an 800–mile pipeline, resolution of the conflict seemed imperative to all involved, especially the oil interests. Another Alaska economic boom depended on it. A quick legislative solution was necessary.

The interest of a third party was at stake in this dispute: the American public. If land was to be allocated to the state and to Alaska Natives, which part of the public domain was it in the "national interest" for the federal government to retain and protect? What rationales might be used to "reserve" some portions of Alaska's public domain lands from selection by either the state or Alaska Natives? Proposals had appeared over the years for national parks in Alaska, and one park (Mount McKinley) and two monuments (Katmai and Glacier Bay) had been established. Park proposals had been forwarded in the 1930s and 1940s for Admiralty Island, Lake George, and portions of the Wrangell-St. Elias mountains. In 1950 the Park Service initiated the Alaska Recreation Survey, which yielded extensive knowledge of potential Alaska parklands and, among other ideas, the first proposal for an Arctic Wilderness International Park in the area that was ultimately to become the Arctic National Wildlife Refuge. Other studies in the early 1960s, some under the aegis of the Park Service, yielded knowledge of preservation and recreation potentials in Alaska. National Park Service planner Ted Swem made his initial visit in 1962, returning in 1963 with wilderness advocate and writer Sigurd Olson. All of this contributed to a rudimentary and limited information base that the Park Service would tap when the question was posed as to what areas should be protected in the national interest.

When George B. Hartzog Jr. replaced Conrad Wirth as director of the Park Service in 1964, he realized that the greatest and perhaps only potential for significant growth of the national park system was in Alaska.[5] He selected Ted Swem as his assistant director for cooperative activities and placed him in charge of planning and new area studies. He also appointed a special task force to analyze "the best remaining possibilities for the Service in Alaska."[6] Over the next several years, the Park Service extended its effort and presence in Alaska. An Alaskan field office opened and teams studied potential new areas for the national park system. In 1970 the service set out to determine how adequately the system illustrated the nation's human and natural history and, where there were gaps, to recommend how to fill them. As part of this national effort, the Alaska office developed a National Park System Alaska Plan that identified a long list of historical, natural, and recreation areas in the state that should be studied for possible inclusion in the National Park System.

A GREAT OPPORTUNITY

As the Park Service worked to assess the potential for parks in Alaska, Congress attempted to resolve the impasse over land claims as quickly as possible. A bill passed the Senate in 1970 that contained a provision directing the secretary of the interior to conduct "detailed studies and investigations of all unreserved public lands in Alaska . . . which are suitable for inclusion as recreation, wilderness or wildlife management areas within the National Park System and the National Wildlife Refuge System." The secretary would advise Congress of such areas and withdraw them from land selection pending Congress's decision as to whether to add them to the park and refuge systems.[7] The bill died in the House. The following year forces again mobilized to pass a bill settling the land claims issue. An Alaska coalition was formed by conservationists, and Stewart Brandborg, testifying before the House Committee on Interior and Insular Affairs, argued that the native claims legislation should include a provision like that in the earlier bill for identification, preservation, and establishment of "areas of national significance as units of the National Park and National Wildlife and National Wilderness Preservation Systems."[8] Intensive lobbying by conservationists of Senator Alan Bible, chairman of the Senate Subcommittee on Parks and Recreation, Hartzog, and others resulted in Bible sponsoring a national interest land amendment to the Alaska Native Claims Settlement Act (ANCSA). After much maneuvering the ANCSA of 1971 was passed and signed by President Nixon. It authorized withdrawal by the secretary of the interior of up to 80 million acres for study for possible inclusion in one of the conservation systems.

The section of ANCSA significant to national parks and wilderness was 17(d)(2). It directed the secretary to withdraw up to 80 million acres within nine months. Lands withdrawn but not recommended for inclusion in the conservation systems would be available for selection by the state and native regional corporations; areas recommended for inclusion would remain withdrawn until Congress acted, not to exceed five years from the date of recommendation. Approval of ANCSA thus launched a nine-year campaign that would result in "one of the most significant pieces of conservation legislation in American history" and vastly enlarge the national park system and national park wilderness.[9]

As the work on the Alaska d-2 withdrawals began, wilderness preservation was not an overt and principal concern. Conservationists and many Park Service people engaged in Alaska work simply assumed that protecting land of national significance in Alaska would protect wilderness. Few land areas in the United States (or anywhere in the world outside of Antarctica) were wilder and less affected by human activity than these Alaska lands. Since the Park Service was under a congressional mandate to review parkland everywhere else in the system for potential inclusion in the National Wilderness Preservation System, it expected that the issue of wilderness would be addressed, if not in whatever legislation established new Alaska parks, then in the way Congress had recently stipulated for new parks outside Alaska such as North Cascades.

The first task was to identify the lands for withdrawal. Hartzog appointed Ted Swem to coordinate the effort, and Swem called in Richard Stenmark from the Alaska office. The recently completed National Park System Plan with its history and natural history themes was applied as a way to identify areas that would form a system in Alaska consistent with goals of the national system. Within days, drawing upon the information gathered in the Alaska park studies of the past several decades, Stenmark had a list of candidate areas (including twelve natural and ten historical and archaeological areas). These were sent forward by Assistant Secretary Reed to Secretary Rogers C. B. Morton, who announced on March 15 that he was signing public land orders for 273 million Alaska acres. Of these, 33.5 million acres were to be studied as additions to the national park system. The Park Service was generally, though not entirely, pleased with Morton's recommendations, for he had modified the agency proposals to satisfy political interests. Some areas identified by the Park Service were excluded, such as parts of Gates of the Arctic in the Brooks Range, portions of the Wrangell Mountains, and Kenai Fjords.

Still, these March recommendations were preliminary, and with final recommendations due in September, the federal agencies continued to work furiously to assure that the best lands were being recommended for withdrawal. Under the overall direction of the indefatigable Ted Swem, five Park Service teams took to the field to fine tune the recommendations, the final versions of which were due in the secretary's office in late July. When the secretary announced final withdrawals in September, included were

41,685,000 acres of potential park additions. Since any new park unit would be established by Congress, detailed legislative recommendations had to be drawn up, and this would, over the next four to five years, involve a herculean effort. By 1978 the Park Service and its consultants had completed 176 studies, with 61 still in progress.

Conceptual master plans and environmental impact assessments had to be prepared, and in the process National Park Service planners realized that Alaska posed special problems and opportunities. Among the usual problems was the tight time frame. They could not be as thorough in their analysis as they would like. The Park Service could not proceed slowly as it had in wilderness reviews because it had clear congressional deadlines and a one-time opportunity for massive expansion of the national park system, and would do nothing to jeopardize that opportunity. A unique problem was that people used some of the potential parkland for subsistence. Throughout American national park history the guiding policy had been that people did not inhabit national parks (except of course the park managers and concessionaires judged essential to provide the park experience to the public). When indigenous people hunted and gathered or otherwise "inhabited" a potential park, they were removed before the park was established.[10] This would not be acceptable in Alaska for various reasons, principal among them that the indigenous people there had achieved an unparalleled level of political clout that had forged the very opportunity at hand. Also, by the 1970s, a sense of social justice had emerged in Americans that simply would not tolerate massive dispossession of people in the United States even for such a cause as wilderness preservation. Some Alaska park planners saw the possibility of a new kind of park, a chance to affirm an indigenous heritage value. A new concept of national park was necessary that could include inhabitants.

At one stage of the exploration of Alaska park potentials, Alaska Natives offered a proposal unique in the history of the national park wilderness story. In April 1973 the Arctic Slope Regional Corporation (ASRC) proposed a park that would be co-managed by natives and the Park Service and would protect wilderness and thus the subsistence base of native people in the Central Brooks Range. The natives would combine their land selections with federal lands, thus creating both a wilderness and a cultural park, which they proposed be called the Nunamiut National Wildlands. Emboldened to make such a proposal by the guarantees of subsistence hunting and gathering in ANCSA, they seem to have thought that their interests would be served by a wilderness park that would protect subsistence resources. According to park planner John Kauffmann, "Retention of wilderness conditions, for the local people or for visitors, was the underlying management principal" that would be applied to this "Nunamiut National Wildlands."[11]

The Park Service authorized Kauffmann to discuss this proposal with the Nunamiut, and the ensuing negotiations changed the ASRC proposal and fleshed it out. The national park, which would be divided into an east and a west unit, would be called Gates of the Arctic National Park. The Nunamiut National Wildlands would lie between the two units and would include the native village of Anaktuvuk Pass. Management of the park would institute new approaches: subsistence hunting would be allowed; "fair-chase hunting" by sportsmen would be permitted, strictly limited to travel on foot, with no high-tech air and radio aids, with a wilderness stay of ten days minimum required; visitors could fly in, landing only in designated places, with reservations and permits required; the Nunamiut National Wildlands would be similarly managed, but it would be co-managed by the service and the natives, with subsistence hunting given priority over any sport hunting. No development for visitors would be allowed anywhere in the complex.[12]

This radical proposal was dead on arrival in Washington, DC. The Office of Management and Budget (OMB) rejected the Nunamiut National Wildlands designation, stating that it would not accept a proposal that relinquished some of the federal authority to parties outside government. The idea that national and native interests might coincide within a wilderness park appealed to some in both the Park Service and the native community. In the end it was not seriously considered, and even John Kauffmann, who was initially intrigued by the possibility of a much larger park with the native lands included, grew cool to the idea, fearing that the wildlands designation might be an invitation to later development. He knew that the natives were hardnosed negotiators who sought a proposal that would in every way maximize their situation, and granting them co-management of any part of the area posed at least the potential of future erosion of wilderness. Kauffmann moved on to other plans.

Theodore Catton, in his study of the relationship between national parks and native people in Alaska, argues that this episode was an important step toward the realization that new models of national parks might be necessary in Alaska. Could there be "inhabited wilderness" parks in which indigenous people could practice their traditional lifestyle, even though it clashed with long-established canons of national park manage-

10.1 John Kauffmann was on the
Master Survey Team and was a key
planner of Alaska National Parks.
National Park Service Historic
Photographic Collection,
Harpers Ferry Center

ment? The very idea of hunting of any sort in national parks had been taboo
since the 1890s. Yet in Alaska, subsistence hunting had been practiced for
millennia, and was the land not still wild? Some conservationists came to
the position that humans belonged, in the subsistence sense, in Alaska wilderness. Catton writes that some "sought to broaden the primitivist wilderness aesthetic so as to include an appreciation of contemporary native life.
One spoke to the NPS's mandate of preserving natural conditions, the other
to the service's mandate to provide for the enjoyment of national parks by
wilderness users."[13] In the end, Catton concludes, the National Park Service
"indicated that it did not want the law to declare subsistence to be a park purpose (as the Nunamiut National Park proposal did) but only a permitted
use."[14] When legislation was finally approved in 1980, the question of
whether subsistence was a purpose of new Alaska parks was unclear. But
what was clear was that the parks were to be both wilderness and subsistence landscapes.

Another opportunity in Alaska, the Park Service saw, was that it might be
possible to draw boundaries to encompass entire watersheds, intact habitats
for wildlife, or even ecosystems. Development and the politics of park designation elsewhere in the United States precluded such possibilities, but vast areas
in Alaska were undeveloped. Achieving protection on such scales required extensive data to support rationales, more data than the park planners had yet available. Details of boundaries and rationales for drawing them according to
"ecologic" criteria would have to appear in legislative proposals. All of this
required exploration of literal and figurative new ground by the Park Service.

On December 17, 1973, Secretary Morton forwarded proposed "final"

10.2 Ted Swem at an Alaska Task Force meeting in Anchorage as the National Park Service prepared its Alaska strategy. National Park Service Historic Photographic Collection, Harpers Ferry Center

Alaska land legislation to Congress. He recommended that 83,470,000 acres be added to the conservation system, 32,600,000 of which would be new park system units. If approved, the recommendation would double the size of the national park system. Traditional subsistence uses would continue in all d-2 areas. All park areas except Yukon-Charley National Rivers were placed off limits to appropriation, and a three-year wilderness review was required. Morton's proposal to continue sport hunting in six of the proposed park areas was especially controversial.

This legislation proposed by Morton pleased no one. The state complained that it would "lock up" too much land and cripple its economic prospects, and it pledged to sue to stop the proposal from going anywhere. Conservationists thought too much land of national significance had been left out. They drafted alternative legislation proposing 119,600,000 acres, 62 million for national parks. The Park Service saw the Morton package as "bitter sweet."[15] While the park system would double in size, some areas the Park Service thought of park quality were to be managed by other agencies or not included in a conservation system at all. The sport hunting provision, included by Morton to mollify the politically powerful Alaska hunting lobby, troubled them greatly. The Morton proposal thus set the stage for an epic conservation struggle that was to stretch over the next seven years and generate national controversy.

This first stage of the Alaska national interest land process had not been about wilderness preservation. The issue of what might be in the national interest had been raised because of the likelihood that some of America's finest scenery and wildlife might be lost to the state and native corporations that were more interested in development for their own benefit than in the interest of the people of America as a whole. As in the earlier stages of national park history in the Lower 48, the wilderness quality of the new parks was assumed. John Kauffmann, in describing how he and many of his Park Service colleagues saw their work in Alaska, affirms their strong commitment to wilderness preservation:

> For National Park Service planners, preservation with use was an ideological inheritance of our profession at a time when there was much talk about recreational demand—practically imperious demand. Yet here were resources, fragile and finite, physical but also experiential, dependent upon our devising a management strategy that would allow them to endure forever, forever in the finest quality, offering discovery and solitude no matter how many people might seek recreation in the Great Land. It was, in a way, a wilderness trust fund, capable of yielding unforgettable dividends only if the capital were not invaded.[16]

The Alaska Park Service crew in this hectic time believed they had an opportunity unequaled in the history of their agency and that opportunity lay not only in providing for recreation but in protecting a unique part of the American heritage—truly vast wilderness.

The Morton bill launched a national debate about what Alaska lands should remain in the public domain and to what purposes they should be allocated. While this was being played out, the tide of interest in wilderness preservation was flowing strongly in the conservation community, and the issue was before Congress as the wilderness reviews mandated by the Wilderness Act progressed in the stop-and-go way that has been described. The Alaska lands at issue were wilderness, and protection of them would be de facto wilderness preservation. The first task of all concerned—the Park Service and conservationists—had been to retain as much of the land they judged of national significance in the public domain by keeping it closed to selection. Whether it would be park, wildlife refuge, wilderness, or some other designation would be the focus of the next stage of the process.

The deadline Congress had given itself approached inexorably after this rush of effort, but for various reasons Morton's proposal languished for three years. During this time Nixon resigned the presidency and Gerald Ford succeeded him. Neither administration seemed to have an inclination to push the Alaska legislation. The Park Service, conservationists, and interests opposed to the proposals prepared in the meantime for the day when the issues would be engaged. Movement finally came with the election of Jimmy Carter as president in November 1976. Conservationists met within a week of the election to begin the process of drawing up a new Alaska Lands bill.[17] Working with the staff of the House Committee on Interior and Insular Affairs, chaired by Democratic Arizona congressman Morris Udall, the Alaska Coalition prepared a bill quite different from the Morton proposal—it adopted park and refuge boundaries identified as areas of ecological concern by the agencies back in 1973.[18] On January 4, 1977, Udall and seventy-five cosponsors introduced H.R. 39.

This bill was a conservationist wish list: set aside more than 115 million acres in the four national systems, over 64 million in the National Park System; create twenty-three wild and scenic rivers with the National Park Service administering them; add 46 million acres to the wildlife refuge system; and authorize millions of acres of "instant wilderness," including virtually all national park areas in Alaska. This last proposal, which proved to be among the most controversial of the bill, would exempt d-2 lands from the wilderness review procedures established by the Wilderness Act.[19]

The sponsors of this legislation knew it would not be approved as introduced but intended that it define the issues for the debate. Opposition came from many directions—native corporations, Alaska politicians, and especially development interests. Alternative bills were drawn up and introduced by these opponents. In September President Carter's secretary of the interior, Cecil Andrus, offered amendments that scaled back H.R. 39 and reduced "instant wilderness" to 31 million acres. Over the next eight months the debate raged in the House. The Park Service analyzed the proposal, and Director William Whalen recommended amendments that slightly reduced recommended new park acreage to 51 million acres. He supported the "instant wilderness" designation in some proposed parks, including Gates of the Arctic, Wrangell-Saint Elias, Admiralty Islands, Lake Clark, Glacier Bay, Kenai Fjords, and Denali. Other national park system areas should, in his view, be studied for wilderness designation.

The new House Committee on General Oversight and Alaska Lands held hearings on H.R. 39 in spring and summer of 1977 and revised the bill. Overall acreage added to the four systems was reduced slightly to 104.7 million acres, with National Park System acreage increased to 45.7 million. Instant wilderness was proposed for 81,700,000 acres. The full Committee on Interior and Insular Affairs considered the bill in March 1978, making additional revisions, though 75 million acres of instant wilderness remained. Since the Committee on Merchant Marine and Fisheries had responsibility for wildlife refuges, the bill was then referred to it. Several differences between the committees were resolved and a compromise bill was drafted. It was introduced to the House floor on May 17, 1978. After three days of debate the House passed the bill by a considerable margin of 279–31. Ten new national park units would be created along with additions to three existing areas totaling 42,720,000 acres.

With the ANCSA deadline for d-2 legislation fast approaching at the end of the year, action shifted to the Senate, where the strategy of Alaska Senator Ted Stevens was to delay the process in hopes that as the deadline approached the opportunity for compromise in his direction would increase. He was successful; the Senate Committee on Energy and Natural Resources reported an Alaska bill on October 5, just eight days before Congress was set to adjourn. This bill, which recommended 88 million acres to the conservation systems, including over 43 million acres to the National Park System (of which 30 million would be instant wilderness), was not acceptable to the Carter administration, conservationists, or supporters of H.R. 39 in the House. Despite eleventh-hour efforts for a compromise, the Alaska bill died.

Anticipating the possibility that this might happen, the administration had been studying how it might protect the d-2 lands in the face of congressional inaction. In mid-November the state of Alaska forced federal action by filing for selection of 41 million acres, including more than 9 million acres of d-2 land. Two days later Secretary Andrus, invoking the Federal Land Policy and Management Act, withdrew 110,750,000 acres. On December 1, President Carter designated seventeen national monuments in Alaska that included 41 million acres to be added to the National Park System. Before he was finished, Carter found a way to protect every acre being considered for protection by Congress.[20]

The 96th Congress would next engage the issue. If it did not, the executive action would stand, which no one, including the Carter administration, thought would or should be the result of all this maneuvering. Everyone wanted congressional resolution of the issues. Midterm elections had changed the composition of Congress, with seventy seats in the House changing hands and the party out of power (the Republicans) making gains. Morris Udall reintroduced H.R. 39 with ninety-one cosponsors, his bill affirming the Carter administration actions and deleting compromises made to pass the earlier version. Over 85 million acres of instant wilderness were now proposed. After much wrangling, H.R. 39 again passed the House on May 15.

The Senate did not begin work on a bill until October, and that bill was the one considered the previous year that had been unacceptable to supporters of H.R. 39. The Senate Energy Committee reported this bill, and efforts began to strengthen it on the Senate floor. The effort stalled, and floor debate was postponed until the following year. When Congress reconvened in January 1980, hope for quick action was again stymied and the prospect loomed of yet another stalemate in the 96th Congress. Finally, in July the Senate took up the bill, but Senator Stevens blocked progress with many amendments. His stalling tactics were buttressed by a filibuster by Alaska colleague Mike Gravel. Finally, on August 19, 1980, the Senate passed the Alaska National Interest Lands Conservation Act by a vote of 78–14. Supporters of the House bill, led by conservationists, considered the Senate bill weak and hoped to strengthen it in conference, but this could not be accomplished before the November elections. Ronald Reagan won the White House and Republicans gained control of the Senate. The House then approved the Senate bill as the best possible under the circumstances, and on December 2, 1980, President Carter signed the Alaska National Interest Lands Conservation Act of 1980 (ANILCA).

ANILCA

While ANILCA was less than many conservationists had sought and was, in their view, flawed in many ways, it was a massive and historic statute—the largest ever in the scale of resource values being protected. It added over 53 million acres to the National Wildlife Refuge System, added parts of twenty-five rivers to the Wild and Scenic Rivers System with others designated for study, and created two national monuments to be administered by the Forest Service. A whopping 56,400,000 acres were added to the National Wilderness Preservation System and 43,600,000 acres to the National Park System, a large portion of which were instant wilderness. National park units included in the legislation are detailed in Table 2.

TABLE 2 National Park Service Units in Alaska

Before 1971[a]		As of December 2, 1980[b]	
Name	Acreage	Name	Acreage
		Aniakchak N. Monument & Preserve	514,000
		Bering Land Bridge N. Preserve	2,457,000
		Cape Krusenstern N. Monument	560,000
Mount McKinley N. Park	1,940,000	Denali N. Park and Preserve	5,696,000[c]
		Gates of the Arctic N. Park & Preserve	7,952,000
Glacier Bay N. Monument	2,748,000	Glacier Bay N. Park and Preserve	3,328,000[c]
Katmai N. Monument	2,923,000	Katmai N. Park and Preserve	4,268,000[c]
		Kenai Fjords N. Park	567,000
		Kobuk Valley N. Park	1,710,000
		Lake Clark N. Park and Preserve	3,653,000
		Noatak N. Preserve	6,460,000
		Wrangell-Saint Elias N. Park and Preserve	12,318,000
		Yukon-Charley Rivers N. Preserve	1,713,000
Total Acreage	7,611,000		51,196,000

SOURCE: The Wilderness Society

[a] Section 17(d) (2) of the Alaska Native Claims Settlement Act (ANCSA) authorized the withdrawal of unreserved public lands by December 1978. However, Congress failed to meet the deadline, so late in 1978 these lands were withdrawn by the secretary of the interior under emergency authority prescribed by the Federal Land Policy and Management Act of 1976 and were designated by the president as national monuments.

[b] In December 1980, the Alaska National Interest Lands Conservation Act established these lands as monuments, parks, and preserves.

[c] Includes pre-1971 acreage.

Monument	ACREAGE CLASSIFICATION		
	Park	Preserve	Wilderness
		(includes land classified as wilderness)	(land within parks & preserves)
138,000		376,000	
		2,457,000	
560,000			
4,366,000	1,330,000	1,900,000	
	7,052,000	900,000	7,052,000
	3,271,000	57,000	2,770,000
	3,960,000	308,000	3,473,000
	567,000		
	1,710,000		190,000
	2,439,000	1,214,000	2,470,000
		6,460,000	5,800,000
	8,147,000	4,171,000	8,700,000
		1,713,000	
698,000	31,512,000	18,986,000	32,355,000

The total National Park System wilderness instantly established in Alaska was 32.4 million acres (later determined to be close to 33 million). By this time Congress had established twenty-five wilderness units elsewhere in the National Park System totaling 2,975,353 acres. The National Park Service found itself manager of nearly 36 million acres of congressionally designated wilderness, the government agency charged with the management of more official wilderness land than any other in the world.

The 179 pages of ANILCA were divided into fifteen titles, the first of which explained the goals of the legislation. Titles II through VII described the specific units to be protected and for what purposes. Title II(4)(a), for instance, dealt with Gates of the Arctic National Park and included the following statement of the park's purpose:

> The park and preserve shall be managed for the following purposes, among others: To maintain the wild and undeveloped character of the area, including opportunity for visitors to experience solitude, and the natural environmental integrity and scenic beauty of the mountains, forelands, rivers, lakes, and other natural features; to provide continued opportunities, including reasonable access, for mountain climbing, mountaineering, and other wilderness recreational activities, and to protect habitat for populations of fish and wildlife.[21]

Boundaries of park, preserve, and wilderness were described. The purposes of all new National Park System units were stipulated, as were wilderness areas where there were any, and other specific provisions were made, such as, "Subsistence uses by local residents shall be permitted in the park, where such uses are traditional, in accordance with the provisions of Title VIII."[22]

This matter of subsistence was a significant departure from traditional national park policy. Title VIII added a third dimension to the mandates under which the Park Service had managed its domain since its beginning. In addition to the charge "to conserve the scenery and national and historical objects and the wildlife therein and to provide for the enjoyment of same," the Park Service in Alaska would have "to provide the opportunity for rural residents engaged in a subsistence way of life to continue to do so." Elsewhere in the national park system the policy was that people could not harm or remove any park resource under penalty of law, so Congress worded this provision carefully. Section 803 defined subsistence as "the customary and traditional uses by rural Alaska residents of wild, renewable resources for direct personal or family consumption as food, shelter, fuel, clothing, tools or transportation; for making and selling of handicraft articles out of non-edible by-products of fish and wildlife resources taken for personal or family consumption; and for customary trade . . . by administratively designated local rural people."[23] People would be consuming national park resources, especially wildlife. They would also be doing this in designated wilderness using tools banned elsewhere in the National Wilderness Preservation System, such as motorized vehicles, and constructing and maintaining cabins. The Park Service would have the authority to regulate or limit such activity when it was judged a threat to the wilderness character of a park, but this discretion would, given the history of Alaska, ANCSA, and ANILCA, require extremely careful exercise and would be subject to great political pressure.

These first eight titles stipulated how the national interest lands were to be allocated, and the final seven specified the rules and implementation procedures that Congress thought necessary to achieve the first eight. These latter titles were the product of compromise in which Alaska development interests and Alaska Natives fought for their causes. ANILCA must be consistent with the Alaska Statehood Act and ANCSA regarding oil and gas development, transportation access and planning, and federal and state cooperation. There were twenty-eight separate and detailed administrative provisions. Considering all its provisions, ANILCA had greatly enlarged the National Wilderness Preservation system, but in doing so had posed many new and complicated challenges for wilderness planners and managers.

The legislation set deadlines for the agencies to start work on their new responsibilities in Alaska. The Park Service was instructed to prepare management plans for all its new areas within five years, with explicit orders to describe how it would manage these vast new areas. Congress recognized, in its instructions, that there were "unique conditions in Alaska" that should be considered and thus activities forbidden elsewhere—principally motorized access and cabins—might be allowed. The Park Service was also instructed in Title XIV to review, in the same period, the suitability for wilderness designation of all national park lands in Alaska not designated as wilderness by the act. This was application to Alaska of the policies and procedures of wilderness review elsewhere in the National Park System.

The Park Service was delighted to achieve some of its dreams for Alaska, but now it faced some serious challenges. Foremost among them was politics, for even as it set out to implement the provisions of ANILCA an administration hostile to the legislation's goals came into office. During his presidential campaign Governor Ronald Reagan sharply stated his opinion of the Carter-Andrus withdrawals of 1979:

> Our government in the last year or so has taken out of multiple use millions of acres of public lands. . . . It is believed that probably 70 percent of the potential oil in the United States is probably hidden in those lands, and no one is allowed to even go and explore to find out if it is there. This is particularly true of the recent efforts to shut down part of Alaska.[24]

When Reagan became president he appointed James G. Watt, a pro-development conservative, as his secretary of the interior. The new secretary was, to say the least, not helpful as the Park Service and other agencies tackled the mandates and challenges of ANILCA. The service went about its work under several severe handicaps. First, the administration saw to it that the effort was inadequately funded. The Park Service had to staff the new areas, carry out wilderness suitability studies, and prepare general management plans, among other tasks, with few new resources. By the middle of 1983 the Park Service had been allocated only twenty full-time employees to staff the more than 50 million new acres of national park and preserve land in Alaska. Whatever the shortcomings of its efforts might be, they were not the result of the stalling that had marked Park Service wilderness review efforts elsewhere in the National Park System. Here the agency was enthusiastic and committed to setting up new wilderness parks, and its problem was an administration that did not want such parks. The Reagan people could not repeal ANILCA, but they did everything they could to slow its implementation by pinching the resources necessary to achieve it.

A second problem involved the regulations necessary to implement ANILCA. Broad guidelines were set up in the legislation—the executive branch had to promulgate the detailed regulations necessary to achieve the goals of the legislation. Here was another opportunity for administration stalling and reducing, and the Watt people took advantage of it whenever they could. Yet another opportunity lay in the discretionary parts of the legislation that they could use to achieve their goals. The Reagan administration was oriented to development, as had been ANILCA opponents. It leaned toward development rather than preservation wherever it could in addressing the discretionary parts of the act. This put the Park Service on the defensive when it needed to be on the offensive in the sense that it needed to be planning for long-term management of its new areas. The new parks in Alaska might be different in some respects from those elsewhere in the system, but the mission to protect the park resources was well established. The Park Service had plenty of precedent and legal authority to preserve its parks, and it needed all of it. It found itself in this period protecting the Alaska parks from the government rather than for it, though it could not, of course, say so.

On the wilderness front, the service faced two immediate tasks: to set up management of the vast wilderness units created instantly by ANILCA and to do the wilderness suitability reviews as directed by Section 1317. Doing the wilderness management was both a short-term, on-the-ground challenge and a long-term planning problem. ANILCA had drawn lines on the maps and stipulated that areas within those lines would be managed the same as the rest of the National Wilderness Preservation System as stipulated by the Wilderness Act, except where otherwise directed (as with subsistence hunting). So the Park Service needed to put people into the field to see that this was done. The planning task involved the preparation of general management plans for all the areas, which would include planning for wilderness management.

11 A NEW SORT OF NATIONAL PARK WILDERNESS

When the new wilderness boundaries were drawn on the maps of Alaska, not much changed on the ground. This was the case partly because little management was actually under way or even possible in most of the new park areas and because, while the Park Service might have had an inclination to launch its management there, it lacked the means to do much. As mentioned earlier, few new personnel were allocated to "manage" the vast new wilderness areas. Ten years after ANILCA, The Wilderness Society's T. H. Watkins, writing in *Wilderness*, noted that the staffing of new park units had been hopelessly inadequate for a decade. He reported that in 1990 Yellowstone National Park had one full-time employee for every 4,436 acres while the Alaska parks had one for every 297,332 acres. This discrepancy was a bit misleading in that the use pressure on Yellowstone was vastly greater per acre than that in any Alaska park; thus the problems associated with the discrepancy might not be as acute as Watkins suggested. On the other hand, it did reveal a problem—the Park Service in Alaska could do little to actively manage its vast domain with the level of staff it had available. Watkins also reported that a persistent problem in these parks was poaching, and in 1990 the Park Service had, for instance, one ranger-pilot to patrol the huge Wrangell-St. Elias National Park. It could hardly monitor hunting or the condition of wildlife populations with one plane to cover an 8.3 million acre park.[1] Even had resources been showered on the new parks, the policy of the Park Service in Alaska and elsewhere was not to take action that would have a lasting effect on resources until a general management plan was developed and approved.[2]

The Park Service knew quite a bit about the land it now had to manage. It had been studying the landscape for years and during the d-2 period had worked with the Bureau of Land Management (BLM) on interim management of proposed park areas. When President Carter proclaimed the national monuments in 1978 the service was thrust into management more precipitously than it had expected to be, and this brought challenges. For one thing, the proclamations brought no new budget and personnel with them. For another, everyone knew the monument status was intended to be temporary, allowing time for Congress to work out a more permanent arrangement. Thus the Interior Department did not even request a supplemental appropriation but asked instead to reprogram existing funds, which was denied. Not much could be done during the first winter the monuments had been established, though Park Service officials set out to build a relationship with communities they knew to be opposed to the monuments. They also responded successfully to the Great Denali Trespass, a protest in early January.

The following summer, in the face of congressional inaction on Alaska legislation, twenty-one rangers, all commissioned law enforcement officers from various parks and offices in the system, were dispatched to Alaska, with the home parks picking up the cost. The detail was called the Ranger Task Force. Seven task force members were assigned to the field, the rest to the Anchorage office. Out in the monuments, Alaskans had assumed that, given their temporary nature, the new units would allow "business as usual," whatever that business might be. When they learned that the Ranger Task Force meant to enforce rules that forbade some of their long-established activities, they became hostile. The rangers encountered this hostility in many forms but went about their business of patrolling, answering questions, conducting search and rescue operations, and issuing citations for illegal hunting in the monuments. During the summers of 1979 and 1980, the task force established a Park Service presence in prospective Alaska parklands and indicated that it would protect the resource values that defined them as resources of national significance, including wilderness.[3] Hostility was not entirely dissipated over these two seasons, but it lessened as the local people came to know the park personnel. The rangers knew that a big part of their job was establishing relationships with neighbors, and they went about this delicate task carefully and effectively.

11.1 Some Alaskans did not welcome the prospect of national parks in their state, as this sign in the early 1980s at Yukon-Charley River's National Preserve clearly states. Courtesy of Bill Paleck

"INSTANT WILDERNESS" MANAGEMENT

When ANILCA was finally approved, the process of permanent staffing went forward, handicapped not only by a dearth of resources but also by a lack of infrastructure. Back in the 1970s the Park Service had appointed what it called "keymen" for each projected park with the intention that these experienced and knowledgeable hands would play a key role in setting up new area management, but the d-2 process dragged on so long that by 1980 most of them had moved on to other assignments. This meant that most of the staff of the new parks were new to Alaska and had much to learn about the parks and the people. Moving to Alaska has been likened by historian G. Frank Williss to moving back in time to the days of early national parks when rangers lived isolated, often rather primitive lifestyles on the "frontier." In Alaska in 1980 park personnel found themselves living a lifestyle far removed from the modern world they were accustomed to. They were far from the few urban centers of Alaska, the winters were long, cold, and dark, and amenities were few. Williss describes one case:

Jim Hannah, district ranger at Chitina in Wrangell-St. Elias, typifies the experience of the new Park Service employees in Alaska. Hannah, who came to Alaska from Big Bend National Park in Texas, found himself living with his wife and two teenaged daughters in a cabin with no indoor plumbing, and heated only by a woodstove. For the entire family, a considerable amount of energy would be spent in simply surviving.[4]

Thus park managers, charged with establishing mostly wilderness parks, found themselves living very close to that wilderness.

ANILCA established thirteen new areas, eight of them with "instant wilderness" totaling over 32 million acres. A complete description of how the Park Service approached the huge task of "managing" this vast and diverse area is beyond the scope of this book, but it is important to get some sense of how it went about this work. Consider, for instance, Katmai National Park and Preserve, a 4.2 million acre unit with nearly 3.5 million acres of instant wilderness. A national monument since 1918 when its unique volcanic landscapes were protected, it lay approximately 250 miles southwest of Anchorage at the beginning of the Alaska Peninsula. The monument had been expanded several times in its history to include 2.7 million acres and was already popular for sport fishing, river trips, and sightseeing. It had a concession that operated two lodges and a fishing camp. A tent camp at the Brooks River was a popular destination for people intent on viewing some of the exceptional population of brown bear that inhabited the area. Katmai was not then a new area to the Park Service, but ANILCA greatly enlarged it and made it mostly wilderness. It consisted of nearly 4 million acres of park and 308,000 acres of preserve, with sport hunting allowed in the latter.

The Park Service had begun deploying backcountry rangers at Katmai in 1972, their primary responsibility being to protect wildlife during the spring and fall hunting seasons. Summer backcountry duty had begun in 1978. ANILCA brought modest increases in budget and staff. In 1979 the monument's budget had been slightly under $300,000, with three permanent staff: a superintendent, a chief ranger, and a maintenance foreman. Fourteen seasonal staff came in during the summer. By 1983 the budget had grown to $680,000, three new permanent staff had been added, and seasonals were up to twenty. Budget growth stalled in the mid-1980s, but by 1992 permanent positions had increased to thirteen.[5] The biggest problem for the new park was poaching, since ANILCA had extended the Katmai boundary to include areas used by trappers and hunters who would not stop their activities unless they were required to do so. Rangers were sent to patrol areas of potential problems and, in most cases, the locals responded to the Park Service presence by moving to areas outside the boundaries where they could hunt and trap legally.

Park Superintendent Dave Morris moved his rangers throughout the year to where they were needed most, usually where visitor concentrations necessitated some enforcement of park regulations. In 1982, for instance, a ranger camp was established at the outlet to Nonvianuk Lake, a popular launch point for float trips on the Nonvianuk River. Here rangers offered advice and education about the park rules. As in other wilderness areas the principal way wilderness rules were enforced was simply by establishing presence and explaining good wilderness behavior and the reasons for it. At other times a ranger presence was established along the Big River and the Kamishak River during big salmon runs. Here again the presence of the Park Service increased the likelihood that visitors would behave themselves and observe the wilderness regulations.

Dave Morris tried, in the early 1980s, to put in place interim regulations to address access issues in Katmai. The principal mode of access all over Alaska was (and is) the airplane. Powerful and maneuverable planes with big tires or floats could land in many remote areas, accessing fish, wildlife, scenery, and other resources. Traditional modes of access like this were guaranteed by ANILCA, but there were times and places where landings were so disruptive of wildlife or visitor experiences that the Park Service thought them inappropriate or even a danger to resources. The issue of airplane access was, in Alaska, a major wilderness management issue for the Park Service, different than anywhere else in the National Wilderness Preservation System where planes were simply forbidden to land (with some, though few, exceptions to the rule). Morris's attempt in 1981 to restrict aircraft landings was intended to protect areas with heavy bear populations. He also tried to deny and restrict motorboat access in some areas of the park, again for protection of wildlife and secondarily to protect the wilderness experience of visitors. His efforts were vigorously opposed by natives and sportsmen, and he ultimately dropped the effort. The issue of aerial access would come up again in the planning that would soon be undertaken as required by ANILCA.

Alaska was no different than anywhere else in the National Park System in that visitors concentrated around a limited number of attractions and amenities. This was true at Katmai, where the primary visitor point had for many years been the Brooks River, a rich fishery popular with sportsmen and brown bears. All the attention paid to Alaska in the long fight over the d-2 lands had attracted national interest, and with passage of ANILCA, visitation to the new areas began to grow. This meant that in places like Brooks River the encounters between bears and visitors increased, which could be serious for both visitors and bears. Improved concession services were achieved, with concessionaires offering package tours that added to the growth in visitation. Fly-in anglers and others on day trips to visit the Valley of Ten Thousand Smokes increased pressure in a few areas. Most of the park, however, was relatively unaffected by growing visitor pressure. All of this meant that the Park Service had to marshal its limited resources very carefully, focusing them where they would do the most good. With relatively few people in the Katmai backcountry and potentially serious crowding at places like the Brooks River, most Park Service effort was spent dealing constantly with managing the most accessible areas, at least during the times of heavy visitation, sending rangers into the wilderness majority of the park only when a problem occurred or was anticipated. Out on the ground, then, the enlargement of Katmai and designation of much of it as part of the National Wilderness Preservation System did not result in major changes in management, but it did increase pressure on some park resources and staff.

New parks like Gates of the Arctic and Wrangell-Saint Elias posed an altogether different challenge, since they had no previously established Park Service management except the skeletal cooperative effort of several years working with the Bureau of Land Management. The Ranger Task Force had initiated a small Park Service presence, and the long process of study of these areas had given the service knowledge of the land, resources, and some sense of use patterns, but management had to start from scratch. The Bureau of Land Management approach had been to manage loosely, if at all, so there was much creative work to be done. At Gates the staff spent the entire 1981 season living out of briefcases and backpacks in their effort to figure out what proper management might involve. Patrols were dispatched to the remote northwest areas of the park about every ten days to determine levels of use, develop information about resources, and provide visitor services to people traveling the Kobuk and Noatak Rivers.

Young, ambitious, and adventurous Park Service professionals jumped at the opportunities offered by the new Alaska parks. Bill Paleck was one who responded. He moved to Alaska in 1979 from his position as chief ranger of Wupatki and Sunset Crater Volcano national monuments in Arizona. Paleck's first Alaska jobs were in the regional office, but he soon found himself one of the two initial staff at the vast Wrangell-St. Elias National Park and Preserve where he wore the hats of chief ranger, deputy superintendent, and chief of operations. He had hoped to go to Kenai Fjords National Park, but Regional Director John Cook thought him a better fit for the challenges of Wrangell-St. Elias. Paleck was a big, imposing man who had considerable experience in the field. He would, thought Cook, be able to stand up to any troublesome locals he might encounter, and that would be important at this stage of asserting a Park Service presence. Cook instructed Paleck and Chuck Budge, the superintendent, that they were to establish "custodial management" of the new park and preserve and equipped them with a Chevrolet Luv pickup truck, one four-wheel-drive vehicle, and a Cessna 185 aircraft. Paleck had earlier, on his own initiative, earned a pilot's license knowing it would be an invaluable asset in Alaska, and it would indeed be essential to ranging over more than 13 million acres of park and preserve. Of this area, 8.7 million acres had been designated as wilderness, and most of the rest was de facto wilderness.

Paleck and Budge first had to learn the geography and become acquainted with a local community that hardly welcomed them. In the BLM days prior to the park a ranger station had been burned. The plane being used by the 1979 task force members in the area was also burned. During the first two years of park operation a ranger was beaten so badly that he was forced to retire, and yet another ranger station was set afire. At first the locals would not even sell Paleck aviation fuel he needed for his plane. Hostility was so great that some Alaskans went so far as to say that "the only good parky is a dead parky." This may have been bluster and bravado, but these early Alaska park staff found themselves in a situation not for the faint of heart. To counter such primal emotion, Paleck and Budge spent their first months driving around introducing themselves to as many locals as they could find. They worked to identify the problems that needed immediate attention and to determine what initial management priorities should be. In their meetings with people they tried to explain how the new parks and preserves could be assets to local communities by offering them search and rescue services, EMTs and pilots who could assist in emergencies, and an eventual infusion of tourism dollars that would be a sustained economic benefit. Most locals were doing what they enjoyed doing and were not impressed, but the public relations effort that continues to this day had begun.

One of the biggest challenges was learning the ANCSA and ANILCA leg-

11.2 Bill Paleck (at -10° F) trying to unstick the skis of his Cessna patrol plane on a November day in 1981 at Carden Lake in Wrangell-St. Elias National Park. Courtesy of Bill Paleck

islation and the regulations that emerged from them. Another was applying these regulations in a situation involving airplanes, snow machines, and hunting, all of which were largely alien to traditional national park culture. Paleck and his colleagues—the staff grew from two to twenty-eight during his six years there—had to be careful not to declare an approach to management that could not be enforced. Initially the Park Service took a light-handed approach to enforcement. Paleck describes how, during the 1979 and 1980 task force periods, they could have prosecuted dozens of hunting cases but chose instead to develop three airtight cases that would stand up in court. Rangers at Wrangell-St. Elias worked for two years to figure out how to chase and stop cagey hunting guides engaging in illegal activity. When they finally caught one they did not issue a citation but gave a warning that they had the game figured out and next time would crack down on the offenders, which they subsequently did. When rangers located illegal traplines they would spring the traps and leave a business card. If they found the line a second time, they would confiscate the traps.

In these early post-ANILCA years the Park Service also wisely made local hires, men who knew their way around in the bush. Professional rangers may have been strong and tough and skilled, but they needed expert help dealing with the extreme conditions of the Alaska winter. Local people needed the jobs, and they proved invaluable in establishing the "credentials" of the Park Service in the field across rural Alaska. Further, they understood the nature of subsistence to a degree impossible for anyone from "outside." Members of the Alaska community gradually began to make important contributions to the infant park management enterprise.

As to wilderness management in these early days of the new parks, the field people saw the challenge as becoming adept at managing in the wilderness as much as managing for it. Vast wilderness surrounded small human communities that literally derived their livings from those wild lands. All park and preserve regulations merited enforcement, but some activities threatened the wilderness more than others and needed more attention. Mining, long the principal human activity in the new park, topped the list of threats to park resources. In 1976 Congress had passed the Mining in the Parks Act, which authorized the secretary of the interior to establish stringent regulations governing mining in the National Park System. Production of minerals was not widespread in the park system, but there were areas such as Death Valley and Glacier Bay national monuments where mining was present. The new Alaska parks raised the mining problem as never before on national parklands. The number of mining claims in Wrangell-St. Elias alone exceeded the total number of claims in all the parks outside Alaska.

The Mining in the Parks Act resulted in regulations to protect natural features when valid mineral rights were exercised on parklands and prohibited further mining entry. It required that acquisition costs and environmental consequences of working all patented claims be determined and that the validity of unpatented mining claims be established before any further mining activities proceeded. Further, recommendations were to be developed for acquisition of claims or boundary adjustments to minimize the impacts of mining on park resources. The heyday of mining in most Alaska parks, including Wrangell-St. Elias, had passed, but there was still scattered activity that added up to much work for the skeletal Park Service resources that could be allocated to carry out the mandates of the act. First the level of threat to park resources had to be assessed and strategies developed for enforcement of the inevitably unpopular regulations governing mining. Most miners were back in the Alaska bush because they wished to be far from the complex constrictions of less remote places, and mining was what they did for a living. Their options were very limited. Decisions painful to both the miners and federal agents had to be made. Because all of this was taking place in the 1980s, the pain for the Park Service was worse than it might have been at some other time, since it was being pressured from one political direction to tread lightly on the public while pressure from the other side called for strict enforcement of environmental protection laws. In 1985, for instance, a federal court found that the Park Service was violating its own regulations in approving plans for mining operations. It ordered closure of mining in all Alaska national parks until adequate environmental studies could be done and proper permits could be issued.[6] The early park stewards at Wrangell-St. Elias and elsewhere in Alaska did what they could, with limited resources, to "manage" issues and problems like this in the wilderness. Strongly proactive management for the wilderness would have to wait for a while.

National Park Service veterans of these early post-ANILCA years, like Paleck, look back fondly on their Alaska service. The work in an often uncomfortable, cold, remote, and hostile environment was hard on families. It was sometimes dangerous. The area was so vast—the Yakutat Ranger Station was 240 miles from Wrangell-St. Elias headquarters at Glennallen—that sometimes the idea of "managing" such a landscape seemed absurd. Paleck figures that in the first couple of years he achieved no more than a 20–25 percent success rate in even traveling from one place to another in the huge park. Still, the work was rewarding. They were on a frontier physically, socially, and historically in the sense of new types of parks and new ideas of wilderness. Administrators back in civilization at the regional and federal headquarters allowed them to push park ideas rather than papers to an unprecedented degree in a federal bureaucracy—at least for a while. Their work initially was on the ground rather than in the office, a delight to people who often were in the Park Service because they loved to be out in the country. These people were, in many ways, pioneering. As Paleck, now a recently retired senior superintendent nearly twenty years after his Alaska service, summarizes his experience, "It was like being in a Jack London novel." Most of these post-ANILCA "pioneers," having proved themselves in this frontier crucible, went on to senior Park Service posts and long careers in the agency.

The stories of both old and new Alaska park units reveal how high the learning curve of the National Park Service had to be in Alaska in the early 1980s. Its experience managing land under the dictates of the Wilderness Act was, to this point, relatively little anywhere, since few areas elsewhere in the National Park System outside Alaska had been placed in the system by Congress, and most of those were very recent. The Alaska situation was complicated by the special provisions that made the Alaska wilderness management challenge different than elsewhere in the National Wilderness Preservation System. The scale of the challenge in terms of sheer area was beyond anything early wilderness advocates had even imagined. Add to this the relative scarcity of resources available to actually manage on the ground, and the challenge that faced the initial group of post-ANILCA Alaska park managers was daunting.

On the other hand, at least initially, several factors buffered the challenge. One was the fact that visitation to Alaska park units was, compared with that elsewhere in the National Park System, very light. The cost of going to Alaska parks from the Lower 48 was high, and it was even more costly to go into the backcountry by the usual means, which was by air. Relatively few visitors could or would go to the expense of traveling to the Alaska parks, though the number who did rose each year after ANILCA. The visitation pattern was different from the Lower 48 in another way. While a park and preserve like Katmai might be over 4 million acres in extent and Gates over 8 million, tourists visited only a tiny fraction of this area (though subsistence users traveled much more of some units). Thus park managers did not have to "manage" for the whole park in this initial stage. They could focus on the known areas of highest use and do what was minimally necessary to protect park resources until staffing and management plans could be developed that would allow a more thorough approach to carrying out the mandates of the various laws under which they had to operate.

"Wilderness management" in Alaska was initially and would continue to be different in some ways from that in the rest of the National Wilderness Preservation System. The most obvious difference was that in Alaska the wilderness was "inhabited." That is, ANILCA allowed subsistence use of wilderness there, which meant that some hunting and motorized travel was allowed even in the most remote areas. Initially the Park Service could only study and monitor what went on as it tried to figure out how to handle this unique situation. What would be the impact of subsistence use on visitors who came for the ultimate wilderness experience? How could any conflicts that might arise around this situation be minimized? A second difference was that in Alaska, wilderness was accessed by a most modern vehicle—the airplane. In the Lower 48, the only place airplanes were allowed in wilderness on a regular basis was in the Boundary Waters area of Minnesota. Airplanes would be everywhere in Alaska wilderness. What limits, if any, should be placed on use of planes? As Dave Morris had learned at Katmai, efforts to restrict access by air would meet strong resistance, and of course air was the only way that most people could even gain access to places they wished to visit. There seemed a built-in contradiction in the Alaska wilderness experience—it was viewed by many would-be visitors as the ultimate wilderness experience since it involved travel into vast areas that had been changed little by humans, yet getting to this "ultimate" experience required modern technology that was itself intrusive on that experience. This dilemma seems to symbolize the nature of the challenge facing Park Service wilderness managers in Alaska.

WILDERNESS IN GENERAL MANAGEMENT PLANS

The Park Service had to be extremely careful in addressing wilderness management challenges on the ground in the initial stages of setting up under ANILCA. Moving too aggressively could bring retribution from the hostile Alaska congressional delegation, which could significantly set back the work. Regional Director John Cook took the approach of doing what was necessary to protect resources and facilitate visitation while tackling the policy issues in the planning mandated by the act.[7] The Park Service was given five years to develop general management plans for its thirteen ANILCA areas. The act stipulated that "within five years from the date of the enactment of this Act, the Secretary shall develop and transmit to the appropriate committees of the Congress a conservation and management plan for each of the units."[8] These plans should specify the management practices and programs to address the goals of the parks and preserves. Wilderness was singled out as the key resource.

The Park Service had extensive experience at management planning and was quite expert at it. Further, it had been gathering information about the lands that were in the new parks and preserves over nearly two decades. It had much to work with in this planning effort. As the keymen worked at early plans in the 1970s they became aware that, while traditional park planning approaches and concepts applied in Alaska, the unique opportunities and challenges there required, or at least offered, an opportunity for new management regimes. They "recommended a more flexible, experimental, and evolutionary approach to Park Service planning and management in Alaska, one that would not have an irrevocable effect on new parklands."[9] They envisioned what one planner, Bill Brown, called a "wealth of landscape mosaics," which included parks meeting traditional Park Service expectations, an intermediate type of park "where access and visitor aids are rudimentary" as in wilderness parklands in the Lower 48, and "outback spaces where visitors will be entirely on their own—wilderness in the absolute sense, compounded by size, weather, and terrain factors only approximated elsewhere."[10] Only the few developed areas in existing parks would fit the first category, parks relatively close to Anchorage or to the limited Alaska road system would be in the second, and most of the park system would be of the third category. Not everyone in the Park Service agreed that Alaska required new approaches—the long debate about recreation versus preservation continued, though at relatively low volume—but the opportunity to preserve large ecosystems and the growing interest among scientists and conservationists in doing so influenced the planning in Alaska. G. Frank Williss describes this as a "shift away from recreational development" that reflected a similar shift elsewhere in the National Park Service's approach to its work, but "the movement toward preservation was . . . considerably more pronounced in Alaska."[11] Complications for planning came from the need to preserve traditional uses of the land, from the constant anti-preservation pressures of the Alaska community and its congressional delegation, from an administration in power in Washington, DC, that did not believe wilderness was a good idea, and from severely limited resources. The Park Service, in the face of all this, set to work on its management plans.

Initially, with the shortage of resources in Alaska, the regional office there passed the key responsibility to the centralized planning arm of the Park Service, the Denver Service Center. Alaska personnel had all they could do to establish initial management. The responsibility for plans would devolve back to the regional office in 1983. The decision was also made to take an approach that would propose such small-scale actions that an environmental assessment would be sufficient in the planning process rather than a full-scale environmental impact statement (EIS).[12] The service had already prepared such detailed environmental impact statements back in the 1973–75 period. The assessment would determine whether the action proposed by the agency was significant enough to require an EIS as mandated by the National Environmental Policy Act (NEPA) or would have no significant impact. This was an important decision for wilderness because it meant that the impact of proposed management upon the wilderness resource when it was primary (as it was in most of the new parks) would be minimal. In this early decision the Park Service signaled that it meant to minimally change the status quo for most of the land.

The management planning process for parks in Alaska, as elsewhere, followed the NEPA dictate that the planning process would determine the scope and significance of issues to be addressed in assessing the environmental impact of a proposed action. This involved collecting public comments, drafting management alternatives, holding public meetings, and, on the basis of input gathered, selecting a preferred management alternative. This final plan was then submitted through the various bureaucratic levels of the Park Service and the Department of the Interior to the president and ultimately to Congress, as required by ANILCA. The Park Service was well schooled in this long and involved process, as has been seen in examining the wilderness reviews that had been done in the Lower 48.

The Park Service followed this process, with minor variations dictated by the circumstances of each area. So how did wilderness factor into all of this, and what does the way they handled this indicate about the Park Service stance on wilderness in Alaska? Plans were developed for thirteen areas, and the individual stories of each area cannot be described or even summarized here. Gates of the Arctic National Park and Preserve (which was nearly named Gates of the Arctic Wilderness Park but for the objections of the Office of Management and Budget to another park classification) provides an interesting and informative example. ANILCA placed most of this park in the National Wilderness Preservation System as instant wilderness and specified that its management emphasize wilderness. First in the legislation's statement of purpose for the park was that it should be managed "to maintain the wild and undeveloped character of the area, including the opportunity for visitors to experience solitude."[13] In its legislative deliberations on ANILCA the Senate Committee on Energy and Natural Resources "recognized that the wilderness values of Gates of the Arctic are paramount and provide a special value to the National Park System."[14] Remote, with relatively little visitation and over 7 million acres of designated wilderness, Gates offered the best opportunity the Park Service would ever have to develop and implement a model wilderness management plan.

The process began for the park and preserve with a Draft Statement for Management that was circulated in May 1982, which was built on an earlier such statement prepared in 1978. In that 1978 statement Gates keyman John Kauffmann had written that "the greatest resource of this park is space: unique recreational space for wandering and solitude and adventure. It is a major reserve of wilderness, the last of such caliber among America's dwindling wilderness resources."[15] The challenge was how to preserve this resource while providing for visitation and accommodating the provisions of ANILCA regarding access and subsistence.

The 1982 draft statement identified several issues. Management would, because of the vast area involved, require use of aircraft. Some areas of the park, such as Arrigetch Peaks, Walker Lake, and the Noatak and North Fork Koyukuk rivers, had already experienced concentrated use and resource damage, yet options for controlling use and encouraging restoration without interfering with the wilderness experience were limited. Should access by air to wilderness, which ANILCA permitted, be restricted and, if so, how? How much regulation of visitors for their safety or for resource protection was too much? To what extent and in what ways could traditional National Park Service approaches to management and the park experience, such as interpretation, be used? All of these issues derived from the challenge of maintaining both the wilderness experience and the wilderness resource. The draft statement proposed management objectives:

- Allow wilderness recreation with "minimal formal regulatory requirement."
- Base resource management on research and monitoring with the goal of maintaining "a primitive environment where natural processes regulate the ecosystem."
- Determine optimal use levels that would not damage physical resources or cause "serious disturbance to the wilderness experience."
- Provide "adequate and feasible" access to visitors.
- "Monitor the effect of aircraft use on the wilderness experience and modify that use as necessary to minimize impact on the wilderness experience."
- Use visitor programs and interpretation as tools to insure safety and resource protection but not to intrude or promote.[16]

Thus the Park Service identified key issues related to management in general and wilderness in particular and suggested how it might address them.

This statement solicited considerable comment. A letter from the Fairbanks Environmental Center counseled the Park Service to recognize Gates "as the Park unit on the farthest end of the 'paved to pristine' spectrum." It should be the "most protective of natural values" of anywhere in the National

Park System. Nothing should be done to promote visitation or to accommodate "convenience-oriented use."[17] Roderick Nash, who had recently visited the park, concentrated many of his suggestions around the management of aircraft, which he saw as the biggest challenge in making access and the wilderness experience compatible in this and other Alaska parks.[18] A resident of Bettles, a village on the edge of the park, wrote to say, among other comments, that the Park Service was already promoting too much with a brochure on fishing that "will pave the way for over-fishing of the Gates' low productivity lakes."[19] Destry Jarvis of the National Parks Conservation Association offered a comment that summarized the views of many about the Draft Statement for Management and the plan the Park Service should develop.

> People should not be a dominating subjugative presence and should adapt themselves in such a way that enables them to become an integral part of the whole wilderness and natural resource experience. These resources should not be manipulated and compromised to suit the demands of people.[20]

Superintendent Dick Ring and the planning team digested these and other comments and proceeded to the next stage.

The Draft General Management Plan for Gates was released in March 1985. It addressed how the Park Service would manage a range of issues over the next ten years, protection of the wilderness resource foremost among them. The draft offered a preferred alternative and three others. Alternative C was the proposed management approach. These alternatives ranged from minimal Park Service action to protect resources to active management.[21]

Under the proposed alternative the Park Service would "as necessary prescribe visitor behavior or use limitations to ensure that outstanding wilderness opportunities and natural resources remain undiminished."[22] Visitors would be encouraged to register voluntarily, group size would be limited to twelve for river running and six for backpacking, and visitors could stay only three nights in a campsite. Further limits would be placed on groups around heavily used areas like the Arrigetch Peaks. No limits would be placed on fixed-wing aircraft landings within the park, though routes and minimum altitudes would be recommended. Use of snow machines and motorboats could continue for subsistence and access to private lands. No recreational use of snowmobiles would be allowed, and recreational motorboats could be used on only one lake. No structures, permanent camps, roads, or trails would be built.

11.3 Middle of the Killik River Valley, June 1972, was to be included in Gates of the Arctic National Park with passage of ANILCA. National Park Service Historic Photographic Collection, Harpers Ferry Center. Photo by Jules Tileston, June 1972

The Park Service recognized, in this draft, that while Gates had been designated to protect wilderness, "its designation is also a magnet that will attract an increasing number of visitors." It continued:

> Future land use changes around the park and preserve will delineate the now indistinguishable boundaries. These pressures necessitate active management by the National Park Service, although it is recognized that National Park Service actions can also diminish wilderness. Many major factors are beyond the control of the National Park Service; thus, the proposal and alternative vary only slightly in the future scenarios of the wild and undeveloped character of the area.[23]

The Park Service concluded that its proposal would maintain the wilderness status quo, "neither significantly improving it nor allowing it to deteriorate."[24]

Comment on this proposal, as on all such draft general management plans for Alaska parks, ranged across the spectrum from complaints that the proposal was too restrictive of use and too anti-people to concern that the wilderness resource would be placed at risk by too lax an approach to controlling visitation and, in particular, use of aircraft. John Kauffmann, now retired, wrote that the preferred alternative "is only a palliative for the erosive problems that are appearing in the park or that can be anticipated." He thought the most restrictive alternative the only one that "stands a chance of holding on to the present wilderness quality of the park and restoring it from some of the wear that has already occurred."[25] He was especially concerned that no visitor permits would be required. How could visitation be effectively controlled, or even monitored, without mandatory permits? He and other protection-oriented critics wondered if all the reference to protection of wilderness in the draft plan was merely rhetoric. The goals were good, but the means to achieve them, they thought, were lacking.

After comments were reviewed, a revised draft was circulated for still more comment, and in 1986 the General Management Plan (GMP) was finalized and published. There were no major changes from earlier drafts, only more detail. The plan stated that "Gates of the Arctic is destined to be America's premier wilderness, and it will remain a wild, undeveloped land" and that "visitor use will change the wilderness experience and the natural environmental integrity, yet the National Park Service must continue to provide opportunities for wilderness recreation. Thus managers must contend with the question 'What degree of change is acceptable?'"[26] The Park Service intended that Gates be the ultimate wilderness in the national park system, thus its management would be the ultimate attempt to manage *for* wilderness. But the service admitted that it had a limited understanding of how it could achieve its goals. As always, even in the most remote and wild park in the system, the Park Service had to balance use and resource protection. At this stage in its Alaska experience it faced many unanswered questions about wilderness management, some specific to Alaska, some general across the roadless and wild areas of all the parks. What was the carrying capacity of a wilderness park in Alaska or anywhere? What was "carrying capacity" anyhow? How much regulation of use of the wilderness resource, which many visit to experience a freedom not possible elsewhere, was too much? The GMP attacked these and other questions. One objective for Gates, for instance, was to "maintain the wild and undeveloped character of the park and preserve." A standard for judging whether this was achieved would be that "disturbed/impacted campsites and fire rings do not occur along lakeshores or river/hiking corridors."[27] The Park Service offered a list of objectives and standards for visitor use management and indicated that it would attempt to apply the standards but fully expected that they would be modified and new standards developed as their experience grew. "If monitoring and research indicated numerous standards are being exceeded . . . despite reasonable management actions, a new approach to recreational visitor use management may be needed."[28] Clearly the Park Service planners recognized their limitations here. Even as the managers in the field were struggling with challenges of managing wilderness on the ground, the planners, advised by this field experience, were trying to look ahead and decide what needed doing in the long term.

Several years after the GMP for Gates was completed, John Kauffmann published a book about the Brooks Range in which he commented that though the plan "honored nearly all of the precepts planned for this ultimate wilderness park," prevention of damage, the "cornerstone of all park planning," had been abandoned. Reasons for this, he thought, were political pressure and the fact that the Park Service "does not like to say no to visitors." The consequences would be great, for if damaged resources increased (and Kauffmann thought they already had) and capacities that led to such damage were established, "the politics of trying to roll back use will be horrendous." He continued, "With no policies or mechanisms for control short of disaster, the National Park Service apparently had to adopt the management principle known as acceptable rate of change, with use and development patterns left to evolve without strict adherence to standards."[29] Commenting on a draft of Kauffmann's book, Boyd Evison, who as Alaska regional director had presided over the general management planning process, revealed the complexity of the environment in which the agency was trying to plan and implement the plans.

> "Acceptable rate of change" sounds a little like "rate of acceptable change." I don't believe either has been established as policy for Gates—but the latter is not necessarily bad. It would require definition . . . and probably regulations. "Acceptable rate of change, and evolutionary development" was, in effect, what Alan Fitzsimmons (Horn staffer) tried to force into National Park Service management policy, but he didn't make it. We don't accept it for Gates.[30]

The Horn to whom Evison referred was William Horn, assistant secretary of the interior for fish, wildlife, and parks, who had led the Reagan administration drive to frustrate implementation of ANILCA in Alaska since the days of James Watt. Kauffmann and Evison and other Park Service staff past and present in Alaska seem to have been working hard to promote a strong wilderness resource preservation approach there. But, as Evison indicated, those in power had other priorities.

Review of the general management plans for Gates and other Alaska parks indicates that in the mid-1980s the Park Service was taking the wilderness planning and management challenges there very seriously. In the face of strong political pressure from Washington to do less protection rather than more, it was trying to implement the vision developed in the 1960s and 1970s of a flexible, experimental, and evolutionary approach to management. It was not following the recreational development approach that had led to controversial encroachment on wilderness in earlier episodes of the national park wilderness history. On the other hand, as John Kauffmann repeatedly pointed out, it was not doing all that it should do to protect wilderness, though perhaps it was all that it could do under the political circumstances. Another Evison comment to Kauffmann suggests this conclusion:

> Your vision of Gates of the Arctic as it might be is a nice one. I guess I'm being defensive when I say I'd rather you didn't seem to be suggesting that the NPS can actually achieve it by unilaterally undoing what is provided for by ANILCA. Senator Stevens told the [Alaska] legislature that he got 80% of what he wanted in ANILCA. I suspect that's about right. Bureaucratic fiat won't overcome it.[31]

There were limits to what the Park Service could do no matter how much it might be committed to objectives of wilderness protection in Alaska.

The case of Gates of the Arctic National Park and Preserve is offered as one example of how the Park Service addressed its general management planning challenges in Alaska. Each park was different, but the process was the same, and the issues were also generally similar. Emphasis on wilderness was, both legislatively and managerially, a higher priority at Gates than at other areas, but wherever there was "instant wilderness," the Park Service took the general stance toward future management of it that is manifest in this Gates case. Evison's comments were applicable across the Alaska national park system.

WILDERNESS SUITABILITY STUDIES

As it worked on its management plans, the Park Service also did the wilderness suitability reviews mandated by Section 1317(a) of ANILCA. The act directed the agency to examine all lands in the Alaska parks and preserves not designated as wilderness, decide which were suitable for wilderness designation, and make recommendations to the secretary and thus to the president, who in turn was required to make his recommendations to Congress before December 2, 1987. The suitability reviews were included in general management planning, with recommendations presented in the draft and final GMPs. After the general management plans were approved in 1986, the next step was to prepare an EIS to evaluate the impacts of designating additional wilderness in the parks and preserves.

Since a detailed explanation of what happened for each of the thirteen areas is too much to describe, Gates of the Arctic National Park and Preserve once again offers a good example of this process. First the Park Service had to specify criteria to be used to decide what would qualify for wilderness designation. ANILCA stated that the definition of wilderness should be that of the Wilderness Act, with special wilderness provisions that would apply only to Alaska: existing public use cabins could remain and new ones could be built under certain conditions; navigation aids and research facilities could be constructed (no enclaves in Alaska wilderness); and aircraft and motorboats could continue to be used for traditional activities. To qualify as wilderness in Gates the area must be greater than 5,000 acres and be federal land. Minor disturbances from past activity and little-used, unimproved roads and off-road vehicle trails could not disqualify an area, nor could uninhabited cabins or minimally improved landing strips (no "purity" here either).

The draft GMP reported that the Park Service found 1,009,638 acres in Gates that met the criteria and 190,023 acres that did not. Subsurface mineral rights, all-terrain-vehicle easements, and heavy subsistence use disqualified some places as wilderness. The draft GMP was revised, and the wilderness suitability recommendation did not differ in the final plan. This final GMP stated that "all lands determined suitable for wilderness designation will be managed under the terms of ANILCA to maintain the wilderness character and values of the lands until designation recommendations have been proposed and Congress has acted on the proposals."[32] This policy was important, since pressure was always present to allow activities in de facto wilderness that would depart from the strongly preservation-oriented management line that the Park Service was taking.

Next came the impact assessment process and wilderness recommendation. The Park Service had found 80 percent of nonwilderness land suitable and now had to recommend all or part of that area for possible addition to congressionally designated wilderness. The draft EIS was released for comment on April 15, 1988, with comment accepted until the middle of July. The final EIS was issued in August. Much to the surprise and chagrin of conservationists, the recommendation was for 330,846 acres, or 31 percent of the area judged suitable. Four alternatives were considered: no action, which the Park Service said would result in fragmentation of wilderness-suitable areas and loss of wilderness values; the preferred alternative; a "majority wilderness" alternative that would recommend 90 percent of the suitable area; and a maximum wilderness recommendation that would include all of the study area found suitable.

The alternative selected was on the side of less protection and raised the question of why the Park Service, which had so far seemed to take a protective stance, would settle for less rather than more additional wilderness. The EIS stated unequivocally that the preferred alternative would have significant negative impact on wilderness values.

> Because no wilderness would be designated by law in these [southwestern and northeastern] areas, policy over the long term would vary and competition between the objectives of preserving park values and allowing and providing for recreational use would result in trade-offs in values. . . . The integrity of the area would decline as the parts became disconnected by corridors of activity and development nodes. . . . The overall character of the area would gradually change and much of it would become essentially nonwilderness in character.[33]

Not surprisingly, no answer appears in the EIS to the question of why the Park Service would recommend less rather than more wilderness.

Someone preferred that new wilderness be minimized, and judging from the language in the EIS it was not the Park Service. The agency said all it could about the consequences of its recommendation. What it could not say, of course, was that it was being pressured by the politicians to recommend less wilderness than it might. Among these were the Alaska congressional delegation, which had always opposed any wilderness, and their friends and allies in the Reagan administration. In April 1981 then Secretary of the Interior James Watt issued a directive forbidding the Bureau of Land Management to consider any wilderness in its domain (it was not mandated to do so by ANILCA but could have if it chose to). Next, in 1985, the director of the Fish and Wildlife Service instructed the Alaska regional office to consider only minimal wilderness recommendations in the refuge planning process. Bill

Horn in 1986 instructed the National Park Service to consider only unique resources or characteristics that might have been overlooked by Congress. His memo stated that "in view of the thorough review conducted by Congress, I would not anticipate there to be a significant amount of land proposed for wilderness designation."[34] This seemed to contradict the congressional intent. The wilderness review provision of ANILCA had originated in the House, where the Interior Committee had expressed its expectation that reviews would result in more wilderness. "It was recognized that essentially all of the public lands within these [conservation system] units possess high wilderness value and that significant additions to the National Wilderness Preservation System should be made to protect those values. Therefore . . . the Committee included provisions for study of such areas in conservation system units."[35] So the Park Service did what it was instructed to do, but politics put it in the position of subverting its own analyses and the recommendation it had to make at Gates and elsewhere. Writing to John Kauffmann, who was keeping a watchful eye on this whole business and letting his thoughts be known, Boyd Evison confirmed this strategy. "It appears that our subversion is working—at least on people who read with care. This is off the record, but you should be aware that the specters of development on non-wilderness were inserted to make clear the mischief that could be done by the concerted efforts of . . . another very pro-development administration. The 'recommended' alternatives were imposed directly by Bill Horn . . . and used some phony criteria given us, in writing, by him."[36] Evison expressed his hope that the Washington office of the Park Service would recommend a Record of Decision for maximum wilderness in all units, but he doubted that Secretary of the Interior Donald Hodel would sign off on it.

This situation reveals a strong pro-wilderness bias in the Park Service right to the top in Alaska. It believed that the intent of ANILCA was to protect wilderness in Alaska parks and that opening any of the wilderness for development was to be avoided if possible. They continued to hope for additional congressional help, as Evison told Kauffmann, and knew they were running some risks. In his comment about the Record of Decision, Evison observed that if Secretary Hodel did sign off on such a decision, "It will put us on record [for maximum wilderness] (and probably incense the Alaska Congressional delegation, at cost to the National Park Service that can't be predicted)." Quite a battle went on behind the scenes over the wilderness recommendations, but whatever the outcome, it showed that in Alaska the Park Service was deeply committed to protection of wilderness. If it had been ambivalent about wilderness in its past (and no doubt it was still so in some of its areas else-where), in Alaska it embraced its mission of preservation with determination and resolve. In the end, though, this wilderness review came to naught, as Table 3 indicates.

The suitability reviews of all Alaska parklands concluded that 16 of nearly 19 million acres qualified for wilderness designation. Assistant Secretary Horn cut the proposed figure to 7 million, then to 4.7 million acres. In one park, Wrangell-St. Elias, the suitability review found that 3,174,000 acres qualified. The recommendations then dropped precipitously until, in 1989, Secretary Horn had reduced the proposal there to a mere 60,960 acres, even proposing that 109,000 acres of existing wilderness be removed from the system.[37] The secretary of the interior, by directive of ANILCA, was to report on wilderness suitability in five years and the president was to submit his recommendation in seven, but these deadlines passed and no action was taken. The hostility of the Reagan administration to any additional wilderness continued through the first Bush administration. Bill Clinton was elected in 1992 and conservationists hoped for action, but his administration failed to act in its first two years. Then in 1994 the Republicans took control of Congress, dashing any hopes for movement toward additional wilderness. Alaska congressman and dedicated foe of wilderness Don Young became chairman of the House Resources Committee, and the archenemy of ANILCA, Alaska Senator Ted Stevens, assumed the chair of the Senate Interior Committee. Though an administration more sympathetic to wilderness preservation occupied the White House, no progress could be made toward any additional Alaska wilderness designation.

Meanwhile, the Park Service followed a generally preservation-oriented management strategy for potential wilderness in its domain.[38] Its policy nationally was to maintain the integrity of wilderness study areas throughout the National Park System, and it applied that policy to Alaska. Despite this, conservationists feared that precisely what the Park Service suggested in its environmental impact assessments, the gradual degradation of wilderness under a multitude of pressures, might happen. Lack of action on any wilderness recommendation because of politics was, in effect, the "no action" alternative described in all the impact assessments. In concluding its assessment of this alternative for Gates the Park Service wrote, "Over the long term this alternative would result in major deterioration of wilderness character, reduction of wilderness size, and destruction of some wilderness values that would be irreparable. A large part of the study area

TABLE 3 Status of Wilderness in Alaska National Parks

National Park Unit	Alaska Acres[a]	Designated Wilderness[a]	Remainder of Lands	Lands in Wilderness Inventory[b]	Qualifies as Wilderness[b]
Aniakchak	602,779	0	602,779	602,779	602,779
Bering Land Bridge	2,784,960	0	2,784,960	2,690,179	2,690,179
Cape Krusenstern	659,807	0	659,807	633,587	633,587
Denali	6,028,091	2,124,783	3,903,308	3,726,343	3,726,343
Gates of the Arctic	8,472,517	7,167,192	1,305,325	1,052,561	1,052,561
Glacier Bay	3,283,168	2,664,840	618,328	62,790	62,790[c]
Katmai	4,124,075	3,384,358	739,717	643,448	643,448
Kenai Fjords	669,541	0	669,541	668,165	668,165
Kobuk Valley	1,750,421	174,545	1,575,876	1,494,500	1,494,500
Lake Clark	4,045,300	2,619,550	1,425,750	1,240,280	1,240,280
Noatak	6,574,481	5,765,427	809,054	757,175	757,175
Wrangell-St. Elias	13,188,024	9,078,675	4,109,349	3,174,000	3,174,000
Yukon-Charley	2,523,509	0	2,523,509	2,220,576	2,220,576
Total	54,706,673	32,979,370	21,727,303	18,466,383	18,446,383
Percent	100%	60.3%	39.7%	33.8%	33.8%

SOURCE: National Park Service

[a] Based on 1998 EIS information and surveys made subsequent to ANILCA's passage. This shows an increase or decrease in all protected areas as a correction to acreage in National Parks, Preserves, Monuments, and Wilderness Areas shown in ANILCA.

[b] Sec. 1317 ANILCA Wilderness Reviews.

[c] Includes some proposed wilderness deletions and additions.

would become semi-wilderness, and some non-wilderness in character."[39] This eventuality was precisely the goal of opponents of additional wilderness designation.

A DIFFERENT AGENCY ATTITUDE ABOUT ALASKA WILDERNESS

The National Park Service, in this ANILCA stage of its history, stepped up to the mission of wilderness management and planning as it never had before. It was less conflicted than it had ever been about overt designation of and management for wilderness. There were several reasons for this new stance. First, congressional directives regarding wilderness—the Wilderness Act and ANILCA—had been superimposed on the Organic Act. Throughout its history the Park Service had wrestled with the problem of balancing recreation and preservation, as has been amply demonstrated. The Organic Act had not elevated one mission or the other but left it to the Park Service to strike the proper balance. The Wilderness Act and ANILCA removed the responsibility for such balancing. Thus in Alaska the issue for the Park Service was not whether parks should be designated wilderness but how they should, as wilderness, be properly managed in the short and long term. The wilderness suitability reviews were, of course, the same challenge in Alaska as elsewhere, but the experience of the landscape up there and the obvious wilderness value of park and preserve areas not designated as wilderness in ANILCA made wilderness advocates out of most Alaska Park Service planners and managers.

Second, in most of the Alaska parks, the pressures for development and recreation were less than elsewhere in the system. They were certainly not absent but simply not as strong. Some areas, like Brooks Camp in Katmai and the Kantishna and George Parks Highway areas of Denali, felt strong pressure, but on the whole the Park Service could comfortably embrace wilderness values without running into the level of conflict with its constituency that it might elsewhere. It had time to embrace wilderness without the prospect of a rapidly rising tide of visitors overwhelming it. Visitation would certainly grow, but because of the remote location of Alaska, its climate, and its economy, the future of use in Alaska seemed to be quite different than in the more accessible areas of the Lower 48. The prospect of meeting the expectations and needs of visitors into the foreseeable future with modest development of services seemed good.

Third, many of the attractions of the Alaska parks for these visitors required wilderness. At few parks in the Lower 48 was wildlife the major attraction. With the exception of Everglades National Park, no parks there had been established with wildlife protection and presentation as primary values. If people wanted monumental scenery, glaciers, spectacular geological features, and the challenges and thrills of mountaineering and river running, they could find all of them in parks in the Lower 48. If they wanted a reasonable assurance of seeing free-roaming brown bears, caribou, wolves, musk oxen, humpback whales, sea otters, Dall sheep, and moose in their natural habitats, they must go to Alaska. If these creatures were to remain viable and "viewable," they needed wilderness, and large expanses of it. The Alaska parks offered experiences that depended on wilderness in this way, even if visitors only rode the bus at Denali, took a cruise in Glacier Bay, or flew into Katmai for a few days of bear and salmon watching. With attractions like these the Park Service should not, it thought, have difficulty selling its visitors on the need to contain development and maximize wilderness.

A fourth reason some in the service embraced wilderness in Alaska was that they saw the opportunity to preserve a part of the American heritage in ways impossible elsewhere. As long ago as the 1820s a pioneering scientist on the Stephen H. Long expedition to the Great Plains had reflected on the possibility of protecting bison and the plains Indians and their relationship. Thomas Say wrote that the plains, "unfit for tillage of civilized man . . . may for ages afford asylum to the cruelly persecuted Indian and its immense herds of Bisons."[40] A few years later artist George Catlin expressed a similar idea when he wrote, "What a beautiful and thrilling specimen for America to preserve and hold up to the view of her refined citizens and the world, in future ages! A nation's Park, containing man and beast, in all the wild and freshness of their native beauty!"[41] Despite such ideas, when the national park system was constructed, no such preservation of indigenous life in the "wilderness" was possible, for by the time parks were made the Indians and most of the wildlife were gone or, in the case of the Indians, banished to reservations. Yet in Alaska, late in the twentieth century, indigenous people still roamed the wild lands, making a living off them. The concept of "inhabited wilderness" would require adjustments for many both inside and outside the Park Service, but the opportunity to preserve a part of the heritage of all Americans, indigenous and otherwise, was a great opportunity that would never come again.[42] While park planners and conservationists were thinking mostly about preserving wildlife and wilderness, some saw the opportunity in the necessity of preserving the subsistence lifestyle of native Alaskans. Thus, ironically, the Park Service could at the same time help protect the rights of a people while protecting wilderness, though how they might do both there together was a puzzle and a challenge.

Another "last chance" for the Park Service was the opportunity to protect "ecosystems." This goal emerged early in Park Service studies for possible Alaska parks. When planners realized that ecosystems remained intact and relatively unchanged by human activity to a degree greater than anywhere else in the United States, they saw an opportunity. They were studying this in the 1960s and 1970s when an ecological awareness was beginning to penetrate national park management as never before. The environmentalism that emerged in the 1960s was heavily influenced by ecological ideas, and people began to think about parks and their values in new ways. As work on the d-2 lands progressed, the Park Service was realizing the value of trying to consider ecosystem processes in drawing boundaries for new parks. In the Lower 48 they were struggling with problems, as at Everglades National Park, that might have been avoided by a more successful ecological drawing of that park's boundaries. The water necessary to bathe the "river of grass" was unreliable because much of it came from outside the park. At Redwood National Park logging outside the park was severely threatening the resources within it. Alaska offered the opportunity to design parks with attention to ecological systems. If wildlife populations, which were such a central feature of many Alaska parks, were to be maintained, such protection was imperative.

A final and obvious reason for its pro-wilderness stance in Alaska was that the Park Service was responding to a real if intangible shift in national values. These had appeared in the 1960s and had been manifest in the directives of Secretary Udall. By the late 1970s the Park Service had everywhere shifted to a more resource-protective orientation than in earlier periods. The debates over balance between use and protection raged on, but in the "age of environmentalism" of the 1960s and 1970s, protection had been more strongly embraced. In Alaska, for all the reasons previously mentioned, the Park Service could further this protection in a relatively remote and as yet undeveloped region. Alaskans and their politicians might rage, but the public generally supported wilderness protection in Alaska. Boyd Evison and others like him could honor their convictions about what the right course should be while sending a signal to the conservation community that the Park Service was, in a political environment hostile to environmental protection, with them.

All of these reasons, to a large or small degree, can be offered to explain why the Park Service embraced wilderness in Alaska as never before. The central park resource there was wilderness on a scale beyond anything it had experienced before. People like John Kauffmann understood this from the beginning of the park planning process, and by the time ANILCA was finally approved, the centrality of the wilderness resource in Alaska had come to be fully appreciated by most in the Park Service.

Throughout its history the Park Service interpreted its mandates and addressed them as it thought right for the time and place. Sometimes this meant it emphasized recreation more than preservation; at other times it was the other way around. In the 1980s in Alaska, in the service's initial management and planning, it embraced wilderness preservation. It had little choice in such a wild and remote place where the principal resource was wildness itself. In this remote corner of the National Park System there was more parkland than everywhere else combined, so the Park Service could not have thought its stance on wilderness there would go unnoticed.

laska wilderness might have seemed to many conservationists an annoying distraction in the early 1970s if the stakes there had not been so high. The period was called by some the "environmental decade," with great strides being taken toward environmental protection on many fronts. Wilderness advocates, though frustrated by many bureaucratic delays, were riding the wave of environmentalism. This meant that the workload for everyone involved in environmental protection, both inside and outside government, was demanding as never before. A result was the need to prioritize how time and other limited conservation resources were allocated, and wilderness advocates after 1974 moved national park wilderness back on the priority list behind national forest wilderness and Alaska. This is not to say that no attention was paid to national park wilderness but rather that achieving wilderness in national parks seemed less urgent than other priorities. The need to protect wilderness portions of national parks had been well established, but in the mid-1970s the most immediate threats were elsewhere.

After 1974, action for wilderness was intensely focused on national forests and Alaska, but even so work was done on park wilderness, if at a slower pace than previously. The Park Service had prepared wilderness recommendations for forty-eight units as mandated by the Wilderness Act and had completed its recommendation on one new area, the North Cascades, established during the review period. In 1975 it was working on wilderness recommendations for thirteen other new areas. The main park wilderness action for the next several years would be in Congress.

PARK WILDERNESS IN CONGRESS

The 94th Congress convened in January 1975. Gerald Ford was in the White House and Rogers C. B. Morton was secretary of the interior. By April 30 no fewer than 124 bills dealing with wilderness had been introduced, 38 of them involving units of the national park system. Congress had, to this point, added seventy-one areas totaling more than 3 million acres to the National Wilderness Preservation System, bringing the total to 12.6 million acres. Four national park wilderness units had been approved, a mere 201,000 acres.[1] During the next eighteen months some of the long-fought battles over wilderness would finally be resolved.

A big step forward for national park wilderness was made in the closing days of the 94th Congress when the Omnibus National Park Wilderness Act was passed. The House approved a bill, H.R. 13160, on September 22 that included ten national park system units and special management language. This language, which allowed the secretary at his discretion to authorize use of motor vehicles for certain projects in the wilderness areas, construction of boat docks, and other measures outside normal procedure under the Wilderness Act, was of concern to conservationists.[2] The Senate, responding to these concerns, removed some of the offending provisions, added three more park units, and passed a bill much more to conservationists' liking. The addition of these thirteen park areas, totaling 919,828 acres, was hailed as a significant step forward, since to this time only 4 of the 127 wilderness areas established had been in national parks.

At this point action had been taken on thirteen of the forty-eight proposed national park wilderness areas before Congress. Some of this new wilderness had been relatively uncontroversial, while for other areas the legislation ended long, heated struggles. For instance, the 25,370-acre wilderness at Point Reyes was a compromise between 38,700-acre conservationist and 10,600-acre administration proposals. In Colorado's Great Sand Dunes National Monument conservationists won a slightly larger wilderness than the administration had recommended. Wilderness advocates came nowhere near their goals at Mesa Verde, where only 15 percent of the area was approved for wilderness. The main issue there was the possible effects of wilderness designation on future archaeological exploration. Ten years of effort finally resulted, in the Omnibus National Park Wilderness Act, in a significant eastern national park wilderness at Shenandoah National Park. Altogether the bill established nearly 920,000 acres of national park wilderness; it also classified 52,944 acres as potential wilderness that would automatically be added to the system when nonconforming uses ceased.

Each park wilderness created in this omnibus bill had its story, and some of them were long and involved. The history of one case, that of Isle Royale National Park Wilderness in Michigan, gives a sense of what came to fruition in this legislation. The wilderness qualities of this park had been prized and protected from its earliest days. Twenty miles from the mainland, this island in Lake Michigan had no roads and few other developments and was thus relatively easy to keep wild, though, as mentioned earlier in the discussion of enclaves, proposals for development projects had been advanced from time to time. The park was authorized in 1931 and established in 1940. Adolph Murie, Harold Bryant, and others had from the beginning advocated for protection of its wildness, and the Park Service had generally followed their advice.

The Park Service carried out its mandated wilderness review of Isle Royale and presented its wilderness recommendation in 1967, touching off a ten-year battle. The Isle Royale wilderness was to include 90 percent of the park with enclaves and buffer zones. John Little, in his history of the park, characterizes the proposal as "clearly designed to conform to the 1964 act in a manner least detrimental to the management flexibility of the Park Service."[3] A classic debate about the need for buffers and enclaves ensued with conservationists, led by Doug Scott, then a University of Michigan graduate student and later a master wilderness tactician for The Wilderness Society and the Sierra Club, demanding more wilderness. The Park Service proposal was for a 119,600-acre wilderness. Scott and his associates thought it should be 130,000 acres. The debate ranged along these lines for years.

President Nixon made the formal Isle Royale wilderness proposal to Congress in 1971 along with recommendations for thirteen other National Park System units. Attempting to move on these recommendations, a park omnibus bill was introduced that, along with Isle Royale, included North Cascades, Shenandoah, Sequoia, and Kings Canyon national parks, among others. There were controversies over every proposal, which led to Senator Frank Church's strong statements described earlier about enclaves and buffers at the May 5, 1972, hearing on the omnibus bill. The administration proposal for Isle Royale contained enclaves and buffers, and the Park Service revised the proposal over eight months, increasing the wilderness recommendation to 129,573 acres.

By this time a coalition of preservationists, the Northern Michigan Wilderness Coalition (NMWC), had its sights set on a wilderness of 132,700 acres with no wilderness thresholds or enclaves. Congressional maneuvering continued over the next several years, with some members of the state's congressional delegation supporting the bill while others offered alternatives. All agreed that there should be a significant wilderness, and the argument at this stage amounted to fine tuning. In the end, the coalition bill was reduced by slightly over a thousand acres, with management provisions written into the bill involving boat dock maintenance and construction, power line maintenance, and prescribed burning for preservation of natural conditions. This was folded into the 1976 omnibus bill, which finally approved a 131,800-acre wilderness with 271 acres identified as potential wilderness.

The Isle Royale wilderness case typifies several aspects of park wilderness politics at this stage. First, by 1976 the contentious issues of enclaves and buffers, among others, had been largely resolved. Second, conservationists were, as they had said they would, using the congressional debates to advance proposals that had failed during the wilderness review process. Sometimes they were successful, as at Isle Royale, and sometimes they were not. Third, when the congressional delegation of a state was behind wilderness protection, wilderness designation could be successfully prosecuted there. Michigan politicians gradually came to agreement on what they could support, and it was nearly the maximum desired by wilderness advocates. Fourth, where the issues were rather marginal, as in the struggle over roughly 10,000 acres or slightly less than 8 percent of potential wilderness, a compromise could be reached. This is not to minimize the issues but to recognize that at this stage the battles were sometimes over only small differences. Related to this last point was the fact that opposition to wilderness on a remote island in Lake Michigan had, by the 1970s, diminished to very little. In other regions, such as the Northern Rockies, opposition to park wilderness remained strong and proposed wilderness could not be achieved. Finally, the Isle Royale case confirmed the Park Service expectation that implementation of the Wilderness Act would significantly reduce its managerial discretion. Management provisions were written into the legislation. On the other hand, the provision for Isle Royale regarding prescribed burning was a recognition of new management challenges facing national parks, and it also recognized that Park Service discretion on some aspects of resource management should be preserved.

One other feature of the Omnibus National Park Wilderness Act was important. In it Congress introduced the category "potential wilderness" into its decisions on park wilderness. This was wild land that was usually surrounded by or adjacent to land proposed for wilderness designation but that did not qualify at the time of the review. The condition that disqualified it might be temporary. It might be an inholding or harbor a nonconforming condition such as an inhabited structure that could eventually be acquired and removed. Congress stated that such areas could become designated wilderness upon determination by the secretary of the interior that the nonconforming use had been removed or terminated. This determination would be announced in the *Federal Register* and no further congressional action would be necessary. This approach, articulated by Assistant Secretary Reed back in 1972 in response to Senator Church's pointed remarks at the hearing on park wilderness proposals, has continued since it first appeared in the 1976 legislation.

THE NATIONAL PARKS AND RECREATION ACT OF 1978

The Omnibus National Park Wilderness Act cleared only a small part of the congressional logjam of park wilderness legislation. At this point California congressman Phillip Burton, chairman of the Interior Subcommittee on National Parks, introduced another omnibus bill, the largest single national park bill in history, which among its many provisions included more park wilderness. Fourteen new national park wilderness areas were proposed, among them a 2,022,221-acre Yellowstone wilderness, in what would ultimately become the National Parks and Recreation Act of 1978. Burton did not include all pending park wilderness proposals in his bill because, as Craig Allin has pointed out, "The politics of omnibus legislation is a politics of expediency and, therefore, a politics of consensus and congressional courtesy."[4] Burton's bill was huge, running to 157 pages and seven titles, with 150 projects affecting more than 200 congressional districts in forty-four states. Some of his congressional colleagues referred to it as "park barrel."[5] The wilderness provisions in the bill, including eight for acreages larger than those recommended by the administration and three larger than citizen proposals, were among its less controversial features.

Even so, some of the wilderness proposals ran into immediate opposition. Wyoming and Montana congressmen were not yet to the point reached earlier by their colleagues from Michigan. They opposed any wilderness for Yellowstone and Grand Teton national parks. Montana's Max Baucus, on the floor of the House, argued for his amendment to eliminate the wilderness recommendation for Glacier National Park. "Our national park system contemplates motorized use; that is, people are permitted—indeed encouraged—to drive through the parks. Also, the National Park Service sets aside certain areas for development in the wilderness. . . . Wilderness is a separate system from the national parks. I do not think we should mix the two."[6] His Wyoming colleague Teno Roncalio agreed. "To do this to Yellowstone or Glacier National Park, where our two states lead the nation in visitors, is to set back the wilderness concept itself. There has got to be some place where people can go in a car."[7] Such statements reinforced the conviction of park wilderness advocates of the need for wilderness designation in the parks. The House extended the courtesy of not approving wilderness if congressmen from affected districts were in opposition and passed amendments deleting the recommendations for such major parks as Yellowstone and Glacier.

The House passed Burton's bill on July 12, 1978, and action shifted to the Senate, which approved a somewhat different bill. Eventually, after wily maneuvering and negotiating by Burton, reconciliation of differences was achieved and the legislation was passed by both houses. President Carter signed the bill on November 10. Eight national park wilderness areas totaling 1,974,000 acres were established, more than doubling national park wilderness. The bill also added fifteen new units to the national park system, most of them of historical and recreational importance. The National Trails System was increased substantially, as was the National Wild and Scenic Rivers System.

The 96th Congress was a good one for wilderness. Along with the Burton bill, more than 4.5 million acres were added to the National Wilderness Preservation System. Congress had approved the Endangered American Wilderness Act and the Absaroka-Beartooth, Great Bear, and Indian Peaks wilderness areas in the national forests. It was, of course, also wrestling with the Alaska lands issues. At the conclusion of the 1978 session Congress had established 110 units for a total of 15,591,142 wilderness acres in the national forests; 53 units in the National Wildlife Refuge System, totaling 718,087 acres; and 2,974,537 acres in 25 units of the national park system. In 1974 Congress had received administration wilderness recommendations for forty-eight national park areas. It had, as 1978 closed, acted on twenty-one of them.

The 97th Congress, which convened in 1979, also had a full wilderness plate. It was dealing with the Alaska National Interest Lands Conservation Act. With the failure of the Forest Service to resolve the issue of which national forest roadless areas qualified for consideration as candidates for wilderness designation, wilderness advocates increasingly turned their attention to national forests. Also, back in 1976 Congress had passed the Federal Land Policy and Management Act, which had directed the Bureau of Land Management to review the lands under its jurisdiction for suitability for wilderness designation. This review was under way and, as with earlier wilderness reviews by the other agencies, was resulting in heated controversy. This became another focal point for conservation activism, also drawing attention from national park wilderness. One small national park wilderness measure was acted upon by the 97th Congress when it established the 1,363-acre Fire Island Wilderness in New York's Fire Island National Seashore. Other than this, the 97th Congress was quiet regarding national park wilderness in the Lower 48.

CALIFORNIA PARK WILDERNESS

The shift to primary focus by conservationists on national forest and BLM wilderness continued into the 1980s. Additional state-by-state omnibus wilderness bills, principally for national forest wilderness, were approved for eighteen states in 1984, including California. A small wilderness was designated at Cumberland Island National Seashore in 1982. The principal additions to national park wilderness at this time were at Yosemite and Sequoia-Kings Canyon in the California Wilderness Act of 1984. Argument had been heated during the wilderness reviews as to what parts of these two California parks should become designated wilderness. At Sequoia-Kings Canyon, the original Park Service proposal in 1966 included 740,165 acres, or 87 percent of the parks. The Sierra Club campaigned vigorously for a much larger wilderness encompassing 98 percent and, responding to overwhelming calls at public hearings for more wilderness, the Park Service proposal grew to 761,515 acres in 1967. It held at this level during the late 1960s lull in the review process, and during this period a master plan was prepared in which a rigid interpretation of the Wilderness Act was applied. The result was a 1971 proposal that featured the infamous buffers, enclaves, and all the features characteristic of "Swiss-cheese wilderness" so infuriating to conservationists. Here matters stood for many years until 1980, when a "final" agency recommendation much more to conservationists' liking was made. No congressional action was taken on any of the proposals.

At Yosemite the history was similar, with agency proposals considered by conservationists to be low and fragmentary but that grew in successive revisions. The original 1969 Park Service proposal was for 615,000 acres in five units, while the Sierra Club and The Wilderness Society sought nearly 700,000 acres in two units. By 1973 the Park Service had enlarged its recommendation, but still in five units. Disagreements over how nonconforming uses should affect wilderness resulted in the difference in the number of wilderness units in the various proposals. In 1975 California Senator Alan Cranston introduced a Yosemite Wilderness bill that embraced conservationist proposals. Argument over this bill, which was reintroduced several times, continued for years.

Then, flush with success on the National Parks and Recreation Act of 1978 and with growing interest in omnibus wilderness legislation, Phil Burton and Senator Cranston, with conservationist backing, began pushing for a California omnibus bill. Burton got his House bill approved in 1980 and 1981, but the legislation was stalled in the Senate. The problem there was an overtly anti-wilderness campaign, one of the champions of which was the other California senator, S. I. Hayakawa. He had introduced legislation that would essentially prevent additions being made to the National Wilderness Preservation System by barring the Forest Service from considering wilderness as a management option in the future and by setting deadlines for congressional consideration of proposed wilderness areas. This measure was aimed primarily at preventing more national forest wilderness, but since park wilderness in California was tied up with national forest omnibus legislation, the effect was to stall progress toward wilderness for Yosemite and Kings Canyon. Further, with a California senator opposed, wilderness legislation for that state would not be approved, out of congressional courtesy, by his colleagues.

The House passed California wilderness legislation again in 1982 and 1983. Senator Pete Wilson was elected to replace Hayakawa and was less anti-wilderness, but his proposal fell 600,000 acres short of the House bill. Negotiation and compromise ultimately resolved the differences sufficiently to allow passage of the bill, and President Reagan signed the California Wilderness Act of 1984. The Yosemite Wilderness was 677,600 acres, or 89 percent of the park, and wilderness in Sequoia-Kings Canyon was 456,552 acres, or 85 percent of those parks.

Thus were two major additions made to the national park portion of the National Wilderness Preservation System. These California cases indicate why it has often taken so long to approve national park wilderness and, in some cases, why large wild parks remain outside the system to this day. The politics of park wilderness is to no small degree local politics, as Congressman Burton well knew and had seen in the loss of the Montana and Wyoming park wilderness proposals from his 1978 legislation. Writing in 1976, Brock Evans, at the time leader of Sierra Club wilderness lobbying efforts in Washington, DC, wrote that "unlike most other issues, a wilderness bill, by definition, is attached to a particular place, and by long tradition, if a local member of Congress is opposed to a proposed wilderness in his district, that ends the discussion."[8] A local congressman can block a wilderness if it is in his district, and the same holds for a senator for a state. Hayakawa's effect on the California wilderness bill is an example of this. Also, with the shift to use of omnibus legislation to address the plethora of wilderness proposals, arguments over national forest wilderness, which had often been far more contentious than those over park wilderness, could hold up park legislation even though issues involving them had been resolved.

Another major success for park wilderness during the 1980s was achieved at Mount Rainier, Olympic, and North Cascades national parks in Washington State. Wilderness recommendations had been prepared for these parks by the end of 1974 and submitted to Congress, but no congressional action was forthcoming. In 1984, after years of debate, Congress passed an omnibus Washington Wilderness bill that established eighteen new national forest wilderness areas, added to four existing wildernesses, and designated one BLM wilderness. Since this indicated delegation support for wilderness, advocates of long-stalled park wilderness decided to press their case. A Washington Park Wilderness bill was introduced by Senator Daniel Evans in March 1988. It proposed more than 1.7 million acres of wilderness within the three parks. Three Washington congressmen introduced identical legislation in the House. Evans said of his bill that it was the "first attempt to designate wilderness in national parks on a statewide basis." He observed that "all of Washington parks were established and are managed as wilderness parks. We want the national parks in Washington to remain wilderness parks," and his bill "would prevent development from encroaching further into the wilderness areas of the parks," thereby ensuring that they would be managed for their "original purposes."[9] The Washington Park Wilderness Act passed quickly with virtually no opposition and was signed into law on November 16, 1988.

Its smooth path was testimony to the strong statewide support for wilderness that made politicians comfortable in pushing for the legislation.

The final major addition to national park wilderness in the twentieth century came in the California Desert Protection Act of 1994. Stretching back nearly thirty years, the long struggle to protect portions of the California desert finally reached fruition when President Clinton signed the legislation on October 31, 1994, after it had been blocked in congressional committees for the previous seven years. At the stroke of Clinton's pen, some 7.6 million acres of desert became congressionally designated wilderness. Of this, 3.5 million acres would be administered by the Bureau of Land Management, 95,000 acres by the Forest Service, 9,000 by the Fish and Wildlife Service, and 4 million by the National Park Service. Death Valley and Joshua Tree national monuments were enlarged and upgraded to national parks, with Death Valley growing to 3.4 million acres and becoming the largest national park outside of Alaska. Congress also shifted administrative responsibility for 1.6 million acres of BLM land, placing it under the Park Service and designating it the Mojave National Preserve, half of which was preserved as wilderness. All of this was, of course, a huge addition to national park wilderness and a major success for wilderness preservationists.[10]

UNSUCCESSFUL PARK WILDERNESS INITIATIVES

Nineteen national park wilderness areas proposed by past presidents, and twenty others proposed by the National Park Service but not yet forwarded to Congress by a president, still await final congressional action as this is written in the first decade of the twenty-first century. What has held them up? Each case is different, and it would take a book to tell just this part of the park wilderness story. The case of Grand Canyon National Park, mostly wild but without designated wilderness, reveals many of the reasons why some major wilderness proposals have yet to be achieved. The Park Service began its wilderness review there in 1970 and made its wilderness recommendation in 1972. It proposed that 512,870 acres in the park and the Grand Canyon and Marble Canyon national monuments be designated as wilderness (the two monuments, along with portions of Glen Canyon and Lake Mead national recreation areas, were combined into the current national park in January 1975). The centerpiece of the Grand Canyon is the Colorado River, which courses 277 miles through the park. From the beginning, the river and its use complicated wilderness designation.

One of the conclusions of the original wilderness suitability study was that "the plan for the continued use of motors [on the Colorado River] precludes wilderness classification for the river itself."[11] The exclusion of the river cut through the heart of the proposed wilderness—some said it cut out its heart. Separately from the wilderness review, the Park Service was working to manage a dramatically increasing visitation and its growing impact on the river and the river experience. It released in 1972 a Colorado River Management Plan (CRMP), which called for freezing use at 1972 levels, and pledged that "use of motors on these [river] trips will be phased out by 1977, and the river will be proposed for wilderness status."[12] This so enraged commercial river rafting companies, which were largely responsible for the increasing river traffic, that they filed a lawsuit to thwart these proposals. The suit was dismissed.

Legislation to enlarge the park by including the adjacent monuments and portions of Glen Canyon and Lake Mead national recreation areas introduced in 1973 included a Park Service request that the Colorado River be included as "potential wilderness."[13] National Park Service Director Ron Walker thought this designation should be included in the bill since motors would be phased out in 1977, thus removing the nonconforming use that had precluded its wilderness designation. Politicians from the area opposed this provision, and no "potential wilderness" made it into the bill. The western regional director of the Park Service then announced that the decision to eliminate motors would be deferred until more studies could be done. The only explanation for this quick about-face by the Park Service was that it had, in the opinion of wilderness advocates, caved in to political heat brought to bear upon it.

When the Grand Canyon Enlargement Act was finally passed in 1975, it included an amendment calling for the secretary of the interior to conduct a wilderness review and report a recommendation—standard procedure at the time for new parkland. Another round of wilderness review began that led, in 1977, to a final wilderness recommendation calling for 1 million acres of Grand Canyon wilderness, including the Colorado River. This recommendation in turn stimulated more studies of the use of motors on the river and a revival of the Colorado River Management Plan. The Park Service saw the management plan through another round of environmental review and public comment and in 1980 finalized another version of the CRMP. This time it proposed that motorized rafts on the river would be phased out over a five-year period.

The Professional River Outfitters Association (PROA) reacted again with a lawsuit and heavy lobbying. The Mountain States Legal Foundation, a public interest law center dedicated to preserving individual rights, filed suit on behalf of PROA against the director of the National Park Service and the secretary of the interior alleging that "the National Park Service implemented an arbitrary, elitist policy in the Grand Canyon National Park, without environmental justification, which will deprive the public of its right to use and enjoy this park in an ecologically safe, reasonably accessible manner."[14] The chief legal officer and president of the Mountain States Legal Foundation was a former federal bureaucrat named James G. Watt.

As the lawsuit proceeded, PROA pressed its case in the political arena and found a supporter in Utah Senator Orrin Hatch. The senator's cousin, Bus Hatch, had founded the oldest motorized rafting company operating in the canyon. PROA argued that banning motors from the canyon would be a blow to the economies of southern Utah and northern Arizona and urged that Senator Hatch act to stop the phaseout recommended in the 1980 CRMP. Hatch complied and attached an amendment to the 1981 Interior appropriations bill stipulating that:

> None of the funds appropriated in this Act shall be used for the implementation of any management plan for the Colorado River within Grand Canyon National Park which reduces the number of user days or passenger-launches for commercial motorized watercraft excursions, for the preferred use period, from all current launch points below that which was available for the same period of use in the calendar year 1978.[15]

Though some of Hatch's senatorial colleagues questioned the legitimacy of addressing a policy issue in an appropriation bill (not an uncommon practice), the body accepted assurances that the matter would be given a hearing later and passed on November 17, 1980, what became known in Grand Canyon circles as the "Hatch amendment." This meant there would be no wild river and a bisected wilderness until the promised hearing was held.

Other political winds were blowing down the canyon that forestalled the promised hearing. In December 1980 President-elect Ronald Reagan named the aforementioned James G. Watt his choice for secretary of the interior and the Senate confirmed him in 1981. An appropriations bill amendment like the Hatch amendment would legally be binding for only one year, but during that fiscal year (1981), buffeted by heavy political wind from the secretary's office, the Park Service revised the Colorado River Management Plan to once again exclude the phaseout of motors. Conservationists had supported an approach to managing the number of river users with calculations of total number of users. The Park Service had incorporated this approach into its 1980 CRMP. Commercial outfitters preferred a "user day" approach that would give them more flexibility and a way to increase the number of trips (and profits). Since motorized trips through the Grand Canyon took only half as long as oar trips, outfitters had an incentive to use motors, moving clients further per user day and thus being able to pack more clients into their user day allotments. The result was growth of a motorized rafting industry that put increasing pressure on the fragile riverine landscape of the canyon. This situation prevailed through the 1980s and into the 1990s. The conservation community would not press for a wilderness designation as long as Grand Canyon wilderness was bisected by a nonwilderness river corridor. They labored on other more fruitful fronts. The Park Service managed potential wilderness land as wilderness but worked in a political environment described earlier in the discussion of Alaska—one not amenable to growth of park wilderness. The commercial rafting industry successfully maintained its favorable situation at Grand Canyon.

In 1997, with the more supportive Secretary of the Interior Bruce Babbitt in office, the Park Service decided to revise the CRMP, raising the hopes of wilderness advocates. All the dormant issues were stirred up again in the public process, most prominently the unequal allocation of river permits among private boaters and outfitters and the continued use of motors and helicopters in the backcountry. A decision date for CRMP revision was missed. Then, to everyone's surprise, the park superintendent abruptly halted the process. Robert Arnberger, in explaining his decision, stated that discussion had become too contentious, too many park resources were being used, and the Park Service lacked sufficient direction from Congress regarding wilderness designation. Exasperated wilderness advocates thought the Park Service had again succumbed to the same political pressures that had halted the push for wilderness nearly two decades earlier. Arnberger had, they noted, suffered a heavy grilling about possible wilderness designation by Utah congressman James Hansen in the fall of 1999. Hansen had strongly stated his opposition to wilderness designation.

This time the lawsuit came from the other side. In July 2000 the Grand Canyon Private Boaters Association, supported by the National Parks Conservation Association and other parties, filed suit with the aim of putting

TABLE 4 Wilderness Approved by Congress as of 1996

Year	Park	Acres	Cumulative
1970	Petrified Forest	50,260	50,260
1970	Craters of the Moon	43,243	93,503
1972	Lava Beds	28,460	121,963
1972	Lassen Volcanic	78,982	200,945
1976	Point Reyes	25,370	226,315
1976	Chiricahua	9,440	235,755
1976	Saguaro	71,400	307,155
1976	Joshua Tree	429,690	736,845
1976	Pinnacles	12,952	749,979
1976	Black Canyon Gunn.	11,180	760,977
1976	Great Sand Dunes	33,450	794,427
1976	Mesa Verde	8,100	802,527
1976	Haleakala	19,270	821,797
1976	Isle Royale	132,018	953,815
1976	Bandelier	23,267	977,082
1976	Shenandoah	79,579	1,056,661
1976	Badlands	64,250	1,120,911
1978	Buffalo River	10,529	1,131,440
1978	Organ Pipe Cactus	312,600	1,444,040
1978	Everglades	1,296,500	2,740,540
1978	Hawaii Volcanoes	123,100	2,863,640
1978	Gulf Islands	4,080	2,867,720
1978	Theodore Roosevelt	29,920	2,897,640
1978	Carlsbad Caverns	33,125	2,930,765

(continued on facing page)

the Park Service back in the public planning process halted by Arnberger. They sought to challenge motors in the wilderness backcountry and to force an environmental review of contracts with river outfitters.[16] In January 2002 a settlement was reached. The Park Service would restart planning efforts to update the CRMP, perform an environmental review, distribute any unused commercial user days to private boaters, and revise its backcountry management plan. Celebrated as a victory by the plaintiffs and other conservationists, this decision renewed the possibility that the issue of motors might someday be resolved and a wilderness designation achieved for Grand Canyon.

This Grand Canyon case is an example of how a host of political issues,

(continued from previous page)

Year	Park	Acres	Cumulative
1978	Guadalupe Mountains	46,850	2,977,615
1980	Denali	2,124,783	5,102,398
1980	Gates of the Arctic	7,167,192	12,269,590
1980	Glacier Bay	2,664,840	14,934,430
1980	Katmai	3,384,358	18,318,788
1980	Kobuk Valley	174,545	8,493,333
1980	Lake Clark	2,619,550	21,112,883
1980	Noatak	5,765,427	26,878,310
1980	Wrangell-St. Elias	9,078,675	35,956,985
1980	Rocky Mountain	2,917	35,959,902
1980	Fire Island	1,363	35,961,265
1982	Cumberland Island	8,840	35,970,105
1984	Sequoia-Kings Canyon	736,980	36,707,085
1984	Yosemite	677,600	37,384,685
1988	Congaree Swamp	15,010	37,399,685
1988	Mount Rainier	228,488	37,628,183
1988	Olympic	876,669	38,504,852
1988	North Cascades	634,614	39,139,466
1994	Death Valley	3,158,038	42,297,504
1994	Joshua Tree add.	131,780	42,429,284
1994	Mohave N. Preserve	695,200	43,124,484

SOURCE: Compiled by the author from information in *The National Parks: Index 1999–2001* (Washington, DC: National Park Service, Division of Publications, 2001).

often involving commercial interests, has affected park wilderness designation. The wilderness experience as well as the designation have clashed with a lucrative commercial industry with powerful political supporters. That industry uses boat motors and even helicopters, which are incompatible with wilderness and the Wilderness Act. The helicopters are used for "passenger exchanges" allowing short, four-day float trips, which, outfitters claim, is what the busy public demands. The struggle over Grand Canyon wilderness is, in some ways, an example of the classic dilemma the Park Service has faced since its beginning—the use-versus-preservation problem. In this case the Park Service has seemed to favor preservation in the form of wilderness designation for the Colorado River and thus the Grand Canyon, but it has been unable to stand up to the considerable political pressure against a wilderness river that opponents have brought to bear upon it.

This pressure, experienced by the Park Service for over thirty years at Grand Canyon, has been the most consistent element in the story of national parks where wilderness designation remains to be achieved. One issue or another has been used by congressmen to oppose park wilderness outright or even a process that might lead to it. This is not new, of course. The entire story of national park wilderness is one of political pushing and pulling of national park ideals. National parks are public parks and thus by their nature, with a diverse public, are buffeted by various public values. The Grand Canyon case is in some respects extreme. During the entire period chronicled here, the political environments of Utah and Arizona have been conservative. These states' congressional delegations have not been supportive of wilderness (with notable exceptions such as Morris Udall of Arizona). Orrin Hatch, still in the Senate in 2006 with three decades of seniority, has stood firm in his opposition. James Watt's tenure as secretary was brief, but his views reflected the underlying convictions of an increasingly influential element of the Republican Party. These conservatives could not support any measures that might interfere with markets and individual freedoms, even if those constraints were imposed on the highly regulated landscapes of the national parks. Where they held power, as in parts of the intermountain west, wilderness designation was blocked. It might be possible in California and Washington, more liberal regions, to designate park wilderness, but not in Arizona, Utah, Montana, and Wyoming.

Three decades of politics of national park wilderness had, as of 1996, resulted in the Park Service becoming the world's largest overseer of designated wilderness, with over 44 million acres in its jurisdiction. A complete accounting of wilderness approved by Congress as of that date can be seen in Table 4. Additional acres were added to previously designated areas when "potential" wilderness was converted according to the procedure established by Congress. By 2003 the park wilderness had grown to forty-six areas totaling 44,103,184 acres.[17] The 107th Congress designated wilderness in Lake Mead National Recreation Area in 2002.

Despite this inventory of designated wilderness, the roster of unfinished business is large. As of this writing, nineteen areas encompassing 5,741,593 acres of recommended wilderness and 134,602 acres of potential wilderness await congressional action.[18] Some of these recommendations were made to Congress by the president as long ago as 1974.[19] Twenty-six additional proposals, totaling 19,326,800 acres, have been completed but not yet recommended to Congress and are in some stage of National Park Service and Department of Interior review. The Park Service recommendations that came out of the Alaska wilderness suitability studies for thirteen park units in the late 1980s, described in the earlier chapter on Alaska, along with the Grand Canyon, await decisions in the Office of the Director of the National Park Service. The remaining proposals have been forwarded to the Department of the Interior for its decision on a recommendation to the president.[20] All of this adds up to possible additions to national park wilderness, as of 2003, of 27,682,886 acres.[21]

Yet even this huge backlog of recommendations does not tell the whole story. Some park units are in the process of conducting formal wilderness studies for the first time, including parks that were in existence at the time of the passage of the Wilderness Act but were not included in the review process at that time. New parks came into the system after the act was passed, many of which were reviewed and recommended for wilderness, even approved by Congress. Some, however, have not yet done wilderness studies, such as Great Basin National Park in Nevada. Additions have been made to other parks that need to be evaluated for wilderness, among them parts of Big Bend, Crater Lake, Joshua Tree, and Sequoia-Kings Canyon national parks. Finally, in some parks where the wilderness review was completed long ago, changes have occurred that have removed conditions that disqualified areas from wilderness consideration. The Park Service has committed to revisit the wilderness review process in those areas.[22] Clearly there is much work yet to be done on park wilderness designation, but that is only part of the challenge. Designation merely moves everyone on to another set of challenges.

W hen the first national park wilderness was designated in 1970 the National Park System officially entered a new era in policy and practice. To this point the Park Service had taken its policy directives primarily from the Organic Act and the legislation for each park. Now it had to begin managing under the Wilderness Act. For decades it had insisted that it was a wilderness manager, though it resisted any official des-ignation of such and still in the 1970s preferred to use the term "backcoun-try" rather than wilderness. Now that Congress had begun designation of park wilderness, what must the Park Service do differently?

The agency could rightfully claim it had long been a wilderness manager, so moving into this new era should not have been difficult. Managers at Isle Royale, Olympic, and Sequoia-Kings Canyon, among others, had been devel-oping policy in the field for managing wilderness since the early 1940s. But even as the Park Service practiced such management, it resisted the trend toward emphasis upon it. The Wilderness Act and congressional action in 1970 made it officially a wilderness management agency and required that it develop and practice wilderness management more openly and positively than it had previously done.

Much pioneering work on how to manage wilderness had been done at Sequoia and Kings Canyon national parks, which in 1960 produced a back-country management plan. By the early 1970s such plans began to be included in master plans for parks that contained wilderness. At North Cascades, for example, such a plan was approved in 1974. It was, stated the introduction, "a bridge between that conceptual framework [the master plan] and management action for this wilderness park." It was "a statement of philosophy in managing backcountry resources."[1] The goal was to manage for the "optimum level of use" while minimizing the damage to resources. At Lassen Volcanic National Park, where 78,982 acres of wilderness were designated by Congress in 1972, the 1975 Backcountry Management Plan stated that the goal of wilderness management was "to protect and maintain the resources and to provide a quality experience for the visitor." This would be achieved, according to the plan, "by imposing use restrictions in relation to carrying capacity with backcountry patrols and various limitations on access."[2] Thus the Park Service was developing a wilderness policy both from long experience and from its interpretations of what the Wilderness Act now required of it.

The Park Service in the 1970s also initiated a new approach to organizing and standardizing its management policies across the national park system. Back in 1964 Secretary Udall had directed that the system be divided into three categories of natural, historical, and recreational areas with different management policies for each. The Park Service had attempted to implement this approach, producing in 1968 three policy handbooks. Within the handbook for the natural area category was a brief section titled "Wilderness Use and Management." Since there were as yet no congressionally designated wilderness areas, the handbook briefly listed standard policies on various management topics and stated that, when Congress acted, it would not lower the current standards and would prescribe additional standards as directed by the Wilderness Act. This section was essentially unchanged in revised administrative policies in 1970.

Revisions of the management policies were made in 1975, 1978, and 1988 in which wilderness policies were elaborated. The 1978 policies also contained a statement of great importance to subsequent national park wilderness history. It stated that "roadless study areas subject to review for wilderness designation will be protected from activities which would endanger or alter their natural, primitive character until administrative study or the legislative process determines their suitability for wilderness designation."[3] The significance of this was that at this stage the majority of park wilderness recommendations awaited congressional action, and many would be waiting for years. In the meantime, the Park Service would make these areas off limits to development of any kind. This amounted to a de facto national park wilderness system, which has been kept intact for decades in such units as Glacier, Yellowstone, the Grand Canyon, and Great Smoky Mountains national parks, where wilderness recommendations still await congressional action. This approach has been maintained in the face of the hostility toward wilderness of Republican administrations and wilderness-averse congressmen. Since establishing this policy, some wilderness recommendations have grown larger as nonconforming uses have been phased out.

As various iterations of management policies have been issued, the section devoted to wilderness has evolved and expanded. The 1988 edition reiterated the policy protecting roadless study areas and made it even more explicit.[4] This revised policy statement contained recognition of the need to achieve "consistency in wilderness management objectives, techniques, and practices" throughout the system and in coordination with other agencies. It pledged to share ideas on wilderness management with these other agencies. To these ends *Management Policies 1988* assigned responsibility within agency structure and stipulated that each park containing wilderness was to develop and maintain a wilderness management plan "to guide the preservation, management, and use of that wilderness."[5] This could be a separate document or part of a general management plan. Policy on how management would be done, as with minimum tools, was elaborated. The condition of the wilderness resource would be monitored using indicators, standards, conditions, and thresholds established in wilderness management plans. Not only would physical and biological resources be monitored, but so would impacts on wilderness "values" and the experience of visitors. Presumably this monitoring would lead to decisions on management technique. Sections of *Management Policies 1988* on facilities, research, fire management, and other topics were elaborations of sections in earlier versions.

Park Service Director Robert Stanton issued *Director's Order No. 41: Wilderness Preservation and Management* in August 1999, accompanied by *Reference Manual No. 41* on the same subject. This was another elaboration of the earlier policy statements but was a very extensive expansion of them. Still another management policy was issued in December 2000. *Management Policies 1988* had stated that "the National Park Service will continue to review areas that qualify for wilderness study, consistent with provisions of the Wilderness Act and subsequent legislation directing that wilderness studies be made."[6] *Management Policies 2001* (dated thus though issued in late 2000) issued a stronger directive regarding the Park Service's ongoing obligation for wilderness review. It required that all lands within the national park system be reviewed to determine their suitability for inclusion in the National Wilderness Preservation System. Further, it directed that lands not considered suitable in earlier reviews be reevaluated "if the non-conforming uses have been terminated or removed."[7] This assessment was to be completed within a year of issuance of the policy in parks where no wilderness suitability studies had ever been done. Procedures were specified and criteria for suitability were described at length.

Management Policies 2001 can be seen as an admission that the Park Service had not, despite all its earlier policy statements, done what it should to meet the requirements of the Wilderness Act. It stated:

> Lands and waters found to possess the characteristics and values of wilderness, as defined in the Wilderness Act . . . will be formally studied to develop the recommendations to Congress for wilderness designation. The NPS will continue to undertake wilderness studies of all lands that have been determined to be suitable as a result of the wilderness suitability assessment. Also, studies will be made of lands for which subsequent legislation directs that wilderness studies be completed.[8]

Once again the policy of maintaining wilderness status of recommended lands is stated and extended to categories of "suitable, study, proposed, recommended" wilderness and to "potential" wilderness.[9] The policies on wilderness management in *Management Policies 2001* are those stated earlier in the director's order and the accompanying reference manual.

PROBLEMS WITH THE WILDERNESS PROGRAM

A National Park Service task force was convened in 1985 and concluded that there were serious problems with the Park Service's wilderness program. Its report stated:

> Management of individual wilderness areas of the National Park System is not carried out in a systematic, consistent basis Service-wide. This lack of consistency is true for designated, potential, proposed, and de facto wilderness. The primary reasons for lack of consistent management appear to be:
>
> - Varying interpretations of, or failure to follow, the Service's Management Policies;
> - No central coordination of Service-wide wilderness management policies;

- Different concepts of wilderness between eastern and western parks;
- Lack of guidance on specific management issues (e.g., aircraft use);
- Insufficient exchange of information about wilderness management techniques among National Park System areas and among the different bureaus that manage wilderness areas.[10]

Park Service managers in the field were trying to implement the policies on wilderness that were emerging in the multiple versions of management policies, but the task force found a serious lack of coordination and guidance. This situation was reminiscent of the conditions back in the period prior to the Organic Act when national parks as a whole suffered from inconsistent management. This time the national park system was in no jeopardy, but the wilderness resource was not being managed as effectively as it should be.

What led to this situation? One factor was that after the wilderness reviews were completed in 1975 the attention of Park Service leadership, which was even then reluctantly focused on wilderness, turned elsewhere. Much was happening to occupy them, not the least of which was the challenge of Alaska. Resources had been allocated to wilderness review, but after the pressure of that process was off and Congress's attention seemed to be mostly on national forest wilderness, Park Service resources allocated specifically to wilderness were reallocated. The job was done. Another factor was the reality that wilderness was a cross-cutting management function. There were problems to be solved, such as impacts of increasing visitation on backcountry resources, but was that a wilderness management or resource management problem? Was funding allocated to visitor management specifically an allocation to wilderness management? It was to some extent, but could parks that had not yet received wilderness designation by Congress allocate resources to protecting or restoring backcountry and count that as investment in wilderness management? Many personnel were, in fact, involved in wilderness management, but their effort was not officially recognized as such. This was as true in parks with designated wilderness as in those awaiting a decision on wilderness recommendations. Further, there was no standardization—measures taken often came from the initiative of rangers and others. Finally, upper-level management often did not think it worth worrying whether they were managing wilderness or not. They had millions of visitors to deal with, and if some of that involved dealing with wilderness, so be it. What was new about that?

The 1985 task force report revealed that, despite the furor over national park wilderness so far described, in the mid-1980s the Park Service still had no wilderness program. It had policies, but these had not been translated into any coherent national program of planning, training, and management. Guidelines for implementation of the policies nationally were lacking. The task force was an internal Park Service group. Its report was a self-examination rather than a critique from outsiders. Would anyone listen to the concerns raised by such a group?

After release of the task force report, the Ranger Division tried to respond to concerns raised, but it could do little. Wilderness was not a priority of the Reagan administration, which thought the Park Service should be concentrating on upgrading facilities and visitor services. Park Service veteran Russell Dickinson had been director from 1980 to 1985, during the Watt years, and had not pressed any wilderness agenda. He had his hands full on many other fronts: the Alaska situation; a wholesale reorganization of senior Park Service officials; politicization of park management directed by Watt and his minions; a Watt agenda of emphasizing park facilities repair and development; and a report released in 1980 that identified no fewer than 4,345 specific threats to park natural resources. Many of the threats described in the 1980 report could not even be documented by the Park Service because only 100 of its 9,000 employees were scientists, and only 200 were trained in resource management.[11] Dickinson thus had many challenges, not the least of which was that he reported to an interior assistant secretary for fish, wildlife, and parks who was philosophically opposed to a strict preservation approach to national parks. Assistant Secretary Ray Arnett supported efforts to open park areas to commercial fishing, snowmobiles, and other off-road vehicles.[12] Director Dickinson had a senior Washington staff full of political appointees in an administration philosophically opposed to the idea of wilderness. Little wonder that wilderness, despite its presence in management policy statements, was not high on the agenda of the Park Service Washington office.

Dickinson retired and was replaced by William Penn Mott, who had headed the California State Park system under Governor Ronald Reagan. The status of wilderness remained low in the political environment of Washington, DC, park politics. Out in the parks the managers continued to follow the policy of managing as wilderness the areas that might one day be eligible for wilderness designation. In some parks true wilderness management specialists emerged, often of their own initiative.

Wes Henry, an outdoor recreation planner and natural resource specialist, was charged in 1989 with coordinating the wilderness program in the Washington office, small though it might be. He had other duties overseeing the park overflights program that limited the time he could spend on wilderness. Nonetheless, Henry's hiring was an important, if small, step in that it was recognition by Park Service leadership that some central coordination of the wilderness program was necessary.

A wilderness workshop was convened by the Park Service in 1989 and out of it came recommendations for the improvement of wilderness management across the system. Little improvement was evident in the next several years, which led to calls from conservationists for legislation to establish a dedicated wilderness management organization within the Park Service and the Bureau of Land Management. A bill to this effect was introduced in Congress, with some activists going so far as to call for the formation of a "national wilderness service." These ideas went nowhere and faced strong opposition from the Park Service and other agencies. Such proposals did, however, indicate the level of dissatisfaction with the wilderness management situation and prompted new Park Service Director Roger Kennedy to request yet another task force. Tapping field people, he charged the group to suggest how wilderness management could be improved consistent with other national park goals of the Clinton administration. The group convened in November 1993 and produced another report.[13]

This task force concluded that "the most important missing ingredient in improving National Park Service wilderness management was thought to be strong and consistent wilderness leadership." The report admitted that the agency needed to improve its performance:

> Several field groups . . . have provided recommendations on how to improve wilderness management in the NPS. The NPS response to these field advisory group recommendations has been ineffective at best. Past agency leadership has not met its responsibilities in wilderness management.[14]

It prepared a long list of recommendations to improve leadership, training, and planning. A work plan and target dates were established. The Park Service was again restructuring and streamlining (it seemed to be constantly reorganizing itself), and the task force recommended ways that wilderness leadership could be part of these initiatives. A centerpiece of this would be the National Wilderness Steering Committee.

A conference to celebrate the thirtieth anniversary of the Wilderness Act was sponsored by the Park Service and convened in Santa Fe, New Mexico, in November 1994. Director Kennedy addressed the meeting. He talked of wilderness as a "religious concept" because "it requires reverence from us and also because it is a deeply serious idea." All of the wilderness legislation passed in the previous decades "is an acknowledgement of our sins—our delinquencies as managers of those portions of wild land over which we have presumed to take control."[15] Kennedy recognized what the Wilderness Act added to the Organic Act and pledged increased effort to manage wilderness responsibly:

> The Park Service Organic Act and the Wilderness Act have differing requirements—compatible but different. The Wilderness Act shifts the test of appropriate use beyond the place it was set by the Organic Act. Wilderness standards are more severe. The Wilderness Act says specifically that certain activities will not occur in national parks. The Organic Act has no such limitations.[16]

Noting that most national parks that were not wilderness contained developments of many types, Kennedy asserted that "we support further wilderness designations within national parks. In the meantime, whether wilderness lands have been designated by Congress or not, we are committed to insuring that the National Park Service protects all lands qualified as 'wilderness' until such time as Congress does act on designation."[17] This 1994 speech was perhaps the strongest commitment to wilderness ever stated by a director of the Park Service. No director since Newton Drury had taken such a positive public stance on national park wilderness. Kennedy's talk indicated that he was taking the task force recommendations to heart and suggested that a new day was dawning for national park wilderness.

Even as Kennedy was speaking, Republicans were celebrating their midterm election victories of 1994. Republican control of Congress affected the ability of the Park Service and other agencies to pursue more aggressive policies aimed at protecting wilderness resources. The Park Service drew up a Wilderness Strategic Plan in 1995. A National Wilderness Steering Committee was formed and first met in Denver in March 1996. It laid out another ambitious work plan and generated many good ideas as to what needed to be done. Among them were establishment of wilderness performance measures for superintendents, a wilderness education program, guidance in development and implementation of a coordinated wilderness management program, and a stepped-up training program using the Arthur Carhart National Wilderness Training Center, a national interagency center established in Missoula, Montana. Various people were assigned to work on these tasks.[18]

The committee met again at Death Valley National Park in February 1997. Subcommittees reported progress on various initiatives. The group was informed, however, that the national strategic plan, "which included strong wilderness language, had been tabled and that parks were now required to produce individual strategic plans."[19] The bureaucratic machinery was moving erratically and glacially and, despite the inspiring rhetoric of Director Kennedy's speech, there had been little improvement, though a few products were emerging from the steering committee's work. Extensive guidance for wilderness management across the system that appeared in *Reference Manual No. 41* was one outcome. Training programs for line officers and others were initiated at the Carhart Center. A team was working on a wilderness education program. Yet all of this did not, in the opinion of some critics, constitute major progress.

Richard Sellars, as a member of the National Wilderness Steering Committee, criticized the Service's wilderness program. He addressed his concerns to his committee colleagues, and later the larger national park community, in a statement published in the *George Wright Forum*, a journal devoted to scholarship on national parks. Sellars lamented the state of the program, calling it "erratic, poorly defined, and vaguely implemented." He noted its "organizational invisibility," pointing out that "although the wilderness resource affects approximately 84% of all National Park System lands," wilderness management in the Washington office fell to one person who also had other duties.[20] He summarized the history of the Park Service's long indifference to wilderness, its resistance to the Wilderness Act, and its slowness in implementing it. This history reflected an attitude, he concluded, that "remains strong today." One manifestation of this was reluctance to draw up wilderness management plans, for "a key requirement in the Park Service's wilderness management policies is for approved wilderness management plans in all parks having wilderness resources. Yet," he continued, "more than three decades after passage of the 1964 act, wilderness management plans have not been completed in most wilderness parks: approximately 12 out of 75 parks containing wilderness resources have approved plans."[21] The Wilderness Act was a consequence, he argued, of public distrust of agencies' management of pristine portions of public land, yet that public had put the very agencies they distrusted in charge of managing wilderness. Thus, in his view, "it should be no surprise that these agencies have been ambivalent about changing their traditional management practices once designated or potential wilderness areas became a reality." He finished with a challenge:

> Perhaps more than any other natural-area program, the Park Service's wilderness management puts to the test NPS's belief in itself as a preservation agency. This belief is in everyone's heart, but is still not reflected in everyone's action. As we know, wilderness is statutorily different from typical backcountry, and the law requires very special treatment of wilderness. . . . Let the Park Service now live up to its belief in its preservation mission, and match the nobility of national park wilderness— and of the Wilderness Act itself—with a strong and decisive wilderness management program that is institutionalized throughout the National Park System.[22]

Sellars raised a point in his critique that drew a response from a colleague, which was also published in the *George Wright Forum*. Sellars had written that "no single organization within the Service is earnestly committed to excellence in wilderness management according to existing law and policy."[23] He had thought that resource management might be the place for it, but after his experience with the National Wilderness Steering Committee, he was no longer sure if that was where it might find a home.

Bob Krumenaker, a park superintendent who succeeded Sellars as president of the George Wright Society, which publishes the *Forum*, agreed in his response to Sellars that many in the Park Service community have not taken their wilderness mandates seriously, and that they should. Wilderness management could, in his opinion, be part of resource management, but even if it was, that would not necessarily solve the problem. It would be a solution only if "our legal mandates for wilderness are taken seriously and field staff are provided the fiscal, personnel, and leadership support to do the job." Further, resource management could do the wilderness management job well in many parks, "but the real need is to integrate resource management fully into park operations. If we accomplish that, wilderness can work well anywhere."[24]

This exchange suggests that the same old problem plagues park wilderness today as in the past—lack of overt recognition of the centrality of wilderness in national park management regardless of who has the responsibility for it. Much of the initiative that resulted in Park Service activity on wilderness in the 1980s seems to have come from the Ranger Division, perhaps because its members were in the field and could daily see threats to wilderness and the need for a consistent and comprehensive wilderness management program. Krumenaker argued that resource managers could develop wilderness management skills just as rangers did because "interpreting the Wilderness Act on the ground is not a technical proposition, but one of managerial direction and the will and skills to implement it." The real problem, in his view, has been that "in too many parks we still think of natural (and cultural, for that matter) resource management as separate from park operations." Wilderness management as an integral part of resource management could be seen in parks where wilderness was an important resource and resource management was integrated with other operations like visitor services. Krumenaker did not disagree with the core of Sellars's critique but thought the problem larger than wilderness. The real problem, he said, is that natural resource management of any sort, whether the resource be wilderness, wildlife, water, forests, or something else, has not been adequately integrated with park operations. Here again is the perennial problem of priorities, with both men suggesting that the Park Service still places so much priority on recreation and visitor services that the resources the visitors come to use in their recreation are at risk.[25]

All of this indicates that early in the twenty-first century the problem of wilderness continues to be the same as it always has been, a tug of war between satisfying the park-visiting public and protecting park resources. Congress has acted on many Park Service wilderness proposals, and 86 percent of the national park system lands were, in 2004, being managed as wilderness either by law or as policy. The issue is how well this vast wilderness acreage is being managed, and for nearly two decades there has been steady testimony from within the Park Service that it was not being managed as well as it might be. Task forces and internal critiques have contended that responsibility needs to be more clearly assigned. Good wilderness managers need to be rewarded for their work. Training in wilderness management should be improved. Above all, resource management should be elevated in priority, with wilderness being recognized as a key resource. If the Park Service raised the priority of resource management, critics argued, improved wilderness management would follow.

The three decades since the wilderness review period mandated by the Wilderness Act have been packed with activity on national park wilderness.

The politics, policy, and practice of national park wilderness have evolved, and the consequence is a national park wilderness system of over 43 million acres. Yet the story is far from over. Major wild parks such as Grand Canyon and Yellowstone are not congressionally designated as part of the National Wilderness Preservation System. Policy debates continue as to what the Park Service should be doing to effectively manage wilderness. The tension between large visitation to the "front country" with its necessity for development and the mandate to leave the parks "unimpaired for the enjoyment of future generations" continues and will always be present. The decision to place portions of the national park system in wilderness reduces this tension somewhat, adding an additional layer of congressional directive on top of that present in the Organic Act. Even so, the people come in their automobiles and recreation vehicles expecting services and amenities, the agency budget grows but not fast enough to keep up with demand, and agency resources flow to where the greatest perceived needs are. This is often the front country rather than the backcountry. The struggle over priorities, which is the central theme of this national park wilderness history, continues.

EPILOGUE

Despite the challenges and problems facing park wilderness in the twenty-first century, the level of protection for nature in a national park with a congressionally designated wilderness is as high as protection provided for any landscape in the world. This generalization is defensible when one looks at the national park wilderness situation as a whole. Some argue that defining a chainsaw as an appropriate tool in a park wilderness is far from ideal. There is no denying that the Park Service should have wilderness management plans in place for its wilderness areas. Nor can it be claimed that any park wilderness is entirely protected from the effects of activities beyond the park boundaries. The National Park Service can and must do a better job of managing its wilderness. Still, in a world of burgeoning human population and technological power, national park wilderness is as "natural" as any place can be.

The story told here offers several insights into this achievement. Historians have made much of the fact that wilderness preservation was not the driving force behind the original national park idea. Yet from the beginning there were those who thought that parks should protect wild nature. Beginning with Yellowstone National Park, many visitors traveled to national parks to enjoy and seek inspiration and insight into nature from the experience of wildness, and many thought the primary purpose of the parks should be to protect that wildness. The seed of the wilderness preservation movement was planted before the first national park appeared, and national parks proved fertile ground in which the idea could grow.

The politics and bureaucratization of conservation in the early twentieth century fertilized the soil of wilderness preservation, adding a healthy dose of competition over the idea of wilderness to the emerging seedling. Arthur Carhart, Aldo Leopold, Robert Sterling Yard, and Bob Marshall—all from outside the National Park Service—cultivated the idea of wilderness. Bureaucratic competition gave impetus to exploration of it, and gradually the idea that wild nature could and should be given long-term protection gained strength. People and organizations often talked around each other about the idea, bandying about terms like "wilderness" and "primitive" and "primeval" in their efforts to claim the wilderness as their own. Wilderness has always meant different things to different people. Gradually a consensus on what "wilderness" should be emerged, at least sufficient to result in the political will to legalize the designation. The Park Service played a role throughout this process, reluctantly at times. From its beginning, people in the agency believed in the wilderness idea as a goal of national parks, though they might not have been in the leadership of the wilderness preservation movement. The most prominent wilderness philosophers have not come from the Park Service, yet many dedicated park professionals have worked behind the scenes, within the organization, to further the wilderness idea. John Roberts White, George Wright, Harold Bryant, Lowell Sumner, Tom Vint, Ted Swem, John Kauffmann, Boyd Evison, and Wes Henry are a few of the Park Service heroes of this story. Over the years, many were drawn to the ranks of the Park Service by their attraction to wild nature, and most spent their careers quietly working to protect wilderness while doing all the other work that rangers, interpreters, managers, scientists, and landscape architects must do. Collectively they met the recreational needs of the American public while maintaining the wilderness quality of much of the national park system.

Conservationists have always been critics of the Park Service and also often its friend and advocate. Conservationists are idealists while government agents are of necessity less so. Public servants have multiple constituencies to serve. Throughout the park wilderness story, conservationists pushed the Park Service to be more protective of the parks they—the conservationists—were usually instrumental in bringing under Park Service stewardship. Since conservationists had fought the hard political fight to achieve the park, they had an interest in its management. They were not always as sympathetic to the service's political and bureaucratic constraints and difficulties as they might have been. A cursory reading of park and wilderness history and of the conservation archives yields the impression that the Park Service was opposed to wilderness, and this is not the case. Sometimes it was complacent about its role. At other times it was confused, and often its priorities were skewed in other (some would say wrong) directions, but it always attempted to hew to its mandate to "leave unimpaired" the resources in its care. If it often failed at this task, it was because the world changed faster than it could, and it was always subject to political pressures from above. This is not an excuse for its less than stellar performance on the wilderness front but an explanation of it.

Sometimes the Park Service leadership had legitimate reasons for what seemed its anti-wilderness stance. Conrad Wirth's initial rejection of the Wilderness Act made sense. He was rightly concerned that the politics of wilderness preservation might threaten protections already provided by the Organic Act. But that was not his principal concern, and he was disingenuous in his claims that it was. What he and many others were concerned about was the loss of agency autonomy, the lessening of bureaucratic discretion and power that would come with congressional wilderness mandates. He and his Park Service colleagues honestly believed that they knew, from their years of professional experience, what was right for the national park system. Politicians and conservationists should not, they thought, dictate to them how they should manage the lands under their care. When Howard Zahniser responded to Wirth's legitimate concerns, the director could not bring himself to soften his resistance.

As one studies the history of the Wilderness Act and of ANILCA, admiration grows for the stalwarts who, wherever they fell on the issues, worked with incredible dedication toward their goals. Fortunately, in the opinion of this author, some of the most intelligent and persistent of these stalwarts were on the side of wilderness preservation. Some were in the Park Service and many were not, but together they prevailed in a high-stakes fight for a part of the American heritage that was at very great risk. This fight continues.

At the end of this story new challenges to national park wilderness are appearing, and they are very different than in earlier periods. It seems likely that all large, wild national parklands in the United States have been designated as national parks. Few new national parks, wild or otherwise, seem in the offing. A few major national parks still lack action on wilderness recommendations, as at Yellowstone, Glacier, and Grand Canyon. There are many conventional wilderness battles yet to be decided. The new challenges are conceptual. Can there be different types of wilderness that move away from the romantic ideals of "untrammeled" wilderness so dear to the hearts of Howard Zahniser and, before him, Robert Sterling Yard and John Muir? Can measures to protect wilderness values be achieved outside wilderness boundaries when those boundaries fail to protect the values? The park wilderness story so far suggests that the idea will continue to evolve. As the human population grows, demand to bring all natural resources into the marketplace will increase. The struggle over parks and wilderness will continue, and the National Park Service will be in the middle of it. No one can predict how this struggle will turn out, but if there are more wilderness advocates in the mold of Muir, Yard, and Zahniser in that future in alliance with park people like White, Sumner, Swem, and Evison, then there will be park wilderness for many generations of Americans to enjoy.

NOTES

INTRODUCTION

1. Alfred Runte, *National Parks: The American Experience*, 2nd ed. (Lincoln: University of Nebraska Press, 1987), 48–64.

2. "An Act to Set Apart a Certain Tract of Land Lying Near the Headwaters of the Yellowstone River as a Public Park," approved March 1, 1872 (17 Stat. 32), in Lary M. Dilsaver, ed., *America's National Park System: The Critical Documents* (Lanham, MD: Rowman and Littlefield, 1994), 28.

1 WILDERNESS AND THE ORIGINS OF NATIONAL PARKS

1. See Paul Schullery and Lee Whittlesey, *Myth and History in the Creation of Yellowstone National Park* (Lincoln: University of Nebraska Press, 2003).

2. Roderick Frazier Nash, *Wilderness and the American Mind*, 4th ed. (New Haven: Yale University Press, 2001), 108.

3. Quoted in Hans Huth, *Nature and the American: Three Centuries of Changing Attitudes* (Berkeley: University of California Press, 1957), 135.

4. Henry David Thoreau, *Walden*, Jeffrey S. Cramer, ed. (New Haven: Yale University Press, 2004), 306.

5. Henry David Thoreau, cited in Nash, *Wilderness and the American Mind*, 102.

6. Nash, *Wilderness and the American Mind*, 108.

7. Alfred Runte, *Yosemite: The Embattled Wilderness* (Lincoln: University of Nebraska Press, 1990), 13–27.

8. Schullery and Whittlesey, *Myth and History in the Creation of Yellowstone National Park*, 95.

9. Runte, *National Parks: The American Experience*, 11–47.

10. Robert M. Utley, "Commentary on the 'Worthless Lands' Thesis," *Journal of Forest History* 27, no. 3 (July 1983): 142.

11. John Muir, *To Yosemite and Beyond: Writings from the Years 1863 to 1875*, Robert Engberg and Donald Wesling, eds. (Madison: University of Wisconsin Press, 1980), 159.

12. Ibid., 138.

13. Stephen Fox, *John Muir and His Legacy: The American Conservation Movement* (Boston: Little Brown, 1981), 86–99.

14. John Muir, "The Treasures of the Yosemite," in William R. Jones, ed., *The Proposed Yosemite National Park—Treasures and Features* (Golden, CO: Outbooks, 1986), 1.

15. Ibid.

16. Michael Cohen, *The Pathless Way: John Muir and American Wilderness* (Madison: University of Wisconsin Press, 1984), 264.

17. Ibid., 267.

18. Ibid.

19. Ibid., 287.

20. John Muir, *Our National Parks* (Boston: Houghton Mifflin Co., 1901), 1.

21. Ibid., 100–101.

22. Muir to Howard Palmer, December 12, 1912, in Terry Gifford, ed., *John Muir: His Life and Letters and Other Writings* (Seattle: Mountaineers, 1996), 360.

23. Nash, *Wilderness and the American Mind*, 113.

24. Ibid., 115. See also Chris J. Magoc, *Yellowstone: The Creation and Selling of an American Landscape, 1870–1903* (Albuquerque: University of New Mexico Press, 1999).

25. Nash, *Wilderness and the American Mind*, 121.

26. Ed Zahniser, "The Adirondack Roots of America's Wilderness Preservation Movement" (unpublished manuscript), 2.

27. *Congressional Record*, 49th Cong., 2nd Sess., December 11, 1896, 94; December 14, 150. Quoted in Nash, *Wilderness and the American Mind*, 115.

28. Aboriginal people had changed these and other landscapes that were to become national parks and wilderness. See Robert H. Keller and Michael F. Turek, *American Indians and National Parks* (Tucson: University of Arizona Press, 1998), and Mark David Spence, *Dispossessing the Wilderness: Indian Removal and the Making of the National Parks* (New York: Oxford University Press, 1999). For discussion of the concept of the "sublime," see Marjorie Hope Nicolson, *Mountain Gloom and Mountain Glory: The Development of the Aesthetics of the Infinite* (Seattle: University of Washington Press, 1997; first published 1959 by Cornell University).

29. Magoc, *Yellowstone: The Creation and Selling of an American Landscape*, 6, 9.

30. Theodore Catton, *Wonderland: An Administrative History of Mount Rainier National Park* (Seattle: National Park Service, 1996), 53.

31. See Samuel P. Hays, *Conservation and the Gospel of Efficiency: The Progressive Conservation Movement, 1890–1920* (New York: Atheneum, 1980).

32. James P. Gilligan, "The Development of Policy and Administration of Forest Service Primitive and Wilderness Areas in the Western United States, Vol. 1" (PhD diss., University of Michigan, 1953), 54–55.

33. For a history of the park, see C. W. Buchholtz, *Rocky Mountain National Park: A History* (Boulder, CO: Associated University Press, 1983). The definitive biography of Enos Mills is Alexander Drummond, *Enos Mills: Citizen of Nature* (Niwot, CO: University Press of Colorado, 1995).

34. Quoted in Drummond, *Enos Mills: Citizen of Nature*, 174.

35. Ibid., 381.

36. Roderick Frazier Nash, *The Rights of Nature: A History of Environmental Ethics* (Madison: University of Wisconsin Press, 1989), 41.

37. Gifford Pinchot, *Breaking New Ground* (New York: Harcourt Brace, 1947), 116.

38. Carsten Lien, *Olympic Battleground: The Power Politics of Timber Preservation* (San Francisco: Sierra Club Books, 1991), 31.

39. Frederick Law Olmsted Jr., "The Distinction between National Parks and National Forests," *Landscape Architecture* 6, no. 3 (April 1916): 114–15.

40. Ibid.

41. Throughout this discussion, the term "conservationists" will be used to refer to those advocating preservation of wilderness. A distinction is made in much of the conservation literature between utilitarian conservationists of the Gifford Pinchot school of conservation thought and preservationists associated with John Muir. Throughout the research on park wilderness, the author found the activists for park wilderness referring to themselves as "conservationists." In view of this, they will be called "conservationists" here.

42. Hays, *Conservation and the Gospel of Efficiency*, 192–98.

43. Donald C. Swain, "The Passage of the National Park Service Act of 1916," *Wisconsin Magazine of History* 50 (Fall 1966): 5.

44. U.S. Department of the Interior, *Proceedings of the National Park Conference Held at Yosemite National Park, October 14, 15, and 16, 1912* (Washington, DC: Government Printing Office, 1913), 33.

45. Ibid., 139.

46. Horace M. Albright and Marian Albright Schenck, *Creating the National Park Service: The Missing Years* (Norman: University of Oklahoma Press, 1999), 59.

47. Ibid., 127.

48. Ibid.

1. Gifford Pinchot, *The Fight for Conservation* (Seattle: University of Washington Press, 1967; originally published 1910), 40–52.

2. *U.S. Statutes at Large*, 34 (1906): 225.

3. See Hal Rothman, *America's National Monuments: The Politics of Preservation* (Lawrence: University Press of Kansas, 1989).

4. Ibid., 89–118.

5. For an overview of the standards debate, see John C. Miles, *Guardians of the Parks: A History of the National Parks and Conservation Association* (Washington, DC: Taylor and Francis, 1995), 71–93.

6. Robert Sterling Yard, *National Parks Portfolio*, 6th ed. (Washington, DC: U.S. Government Printing Office, 1931), 7.

7. Ibid., 9.

8. *U.S. Statutes at Large* 39 (1916): 535.

9. Richard Sellars, *Preserving Nature in the National Parks: A History* (New Haven: Yale University Press, 1997), 43.

10. For an account of this period, see Albright and Schenck, *Creating the National Park Service: The Missing Years*, and Horace M. Albright and Robert Cahn, *The Birth of the National Park Service: The Founding Years, 1913–33* (Salt Lake City: Howe Brothers, 1985), 53–93.

11. This comes through in Albright's memoirs, though he does not state it outright. An example: writing in *Creating the National Park Service* of Yellowstone in 1918, "I told the commissioners that for the time being, and probably the foreseeable future, Yellowstone would get along just fine with General Chittenden's army roads. . . . All the wondrous sights were on Chittenden's loop route, which left the vast majority of the park in wilderness. That could be visited on horse or on foot" (294–95).

12. Paul S. Sutter, *Driven Wild: How the Fight against Automobiles Launched the Modern Wilderness Movement* (Seattle: University of Washington Press, 2002), 21.

13. Ibid., 27.

14. Earl Pomeroy, *In Search of the Golden West* (New York: Alfred A. Knopf, 1957), 125.

15. Hal K. Rothman, *Devil's Bargains: Tourism in the Twentieth-Century American West* (Lawrence: University of Kansas Press, 1998), 146.

16. Ibid., 147–48.

17. Ibid., 149.

18. U.S. Department of the Interior, National Park Service, *Report of the Director of the National Park Service to the Secretary of the Interior for the Fiscal Year Ended June 30, 1925* (Washington, DC: Government Printing Office, 1925), 64–65.

19. U.S. Department of the Interior, National Park Service, *Report of the Director of the National Park Service to the Secretary of the Interior for the Fiscal Year Ended June 30, 1921* (Washington, DC: Government Printing Office, 1921), 120–21.

20. Albright and Schenck, *Creating the National Park Service*, 299.

21. U.S. Department of the Interior, National Park Service, *1923 Annual Report* (Washington, D.C.: Government Printing Office, 1926), 48–49.

22. Sellars, *Preserving Nature in the National Parks*, 61.

23. Ethan Carr, *Wilderness by Design: Landscape Architecture and the National Park Service* (Lincoln: University of Nebraska Press, 1998), 86–87.

24. Ibid., 146.

25. Ibid., 148.

26. Harold K. Steen, *The U.S. Forest Service: A History* (Seattle: University of Washington Press, 1976), 113.

27. Gilligan, "The Development of Policy," 62–65.

28. Paul S. Sutter, "'A Blank Spot on the Map': Aldo Leopold, Wilderness, and U.S. Forest Service Recreation Policy, 1909–1924," *Western Historical Quarterly* 29 (Summer 1998): 187–214.

29. Donald C. Swain, *Wilderness Defender: Horace M. Albright and Conservation* (Chicago: University of Chicago Press, 1970), 98.

30. Frank A. Waugh, "Recreational Uses on the National Forests—A Report to Henry S. Graves," 1917, typescript. Quoted in Gilligan, "The Development of Policy," 75.

31. Henry Graves, "Policy Letter from the Forester, No. 5—National Parks," January 1919, Record Group 95–4, Records of the Forest Service, National Archives, Washington, DC. Summarized in Steen, *The U.S. Forest Service: A History*, 121–22.

32. For instance, it authorized a Mount Baker Recreation Area, which effectively ended a drive for a Mount Baker National Park that had reached Congress in 1916.

33. Stephen T. Mather, "The National Parks on a Business Basis," *Review of Reviews* 51 (April 1915): 429–31.

34. Stephen T. Mather, "The Ideals and Policy of the National Park Service Particularly in Relation to Yosemite National Park," in Ansel F. Hall, ed., *Handbook of Yosemite National Park* (New York: G. P. Putnam's Sons, 1921), 81.

3   WILDERNESS BECOMES AN ISSUE FOR THE PARK SERVICE

1. U.S. Department of the Interior, National Park Service, *Report of the Director of the National Park Service to the Secretary of the Interior for the Fiscal Year Ended June 30, 1920* (Washington, DC: Government Printing Office, 1921), 13.

2. Ibid.

3. For a description of conservation policy during this period, see Donald C. Swain, *Federal Conservation Policy, 1921–1933* (Berkeley: University of California Press, 1963).

4. Robert Shankland, *Steve Mather of the National Parks*, 3rd ed. (New York: Alfred A. Knopf, 1970), 219.

5. Swain, *Federal Conservation Policy*, 170.

6. Sutter, "A Blank Spot on the Map," 193–96.

7. Aldo Leopold, "The Wilderness and Its Place in Forest Recreation Policy," *Journal of Forestry* 19 (November 1921): 718–21. Reprinted in Susan L. Flader and J. Baird Callicott, eds., *The River of the Mother of God and Other Essays by Aldo Leopold* (Madison: University of Wisconsin Press, 1991), 78.

8. Ibid., 79.

9. Ibid., 80.

10. Sutter, *Driven Wild: How the Fight against Automobiles Launched the Modern Wilderness Movement*, 58.

11. Leopold, "The Wilderness and Its Place in Forest Recreation Policy," 79.

12. Aldo Leopold, "Wilderness as a Form of Land Use," *Journal of Land and Public Utility Economics* 1, no. 4 (October 1925): 398–404. Reprinted in Flader and Callicott, *The River of the Mother of God*, 135.

13. Aldo Leopold, "The River of the Mother of God," in Flader and Callicott, *The River of the Mother of God*, 125.

14. Ibid., 140.

15. Sutter, *Driven Wild: How the Fight against Automobiles Launched the Modern Wilderness Movement*, 85.

16. It should be noted that nowhere in the Park Service documents the author has reviewed from this period is Aldo Leopold even mentioned. Still, debate in the National Conferences on Outdoor Recreation reveals that Leopold's thinking was widely examined by people struggling to define roles in outdoor recreation for the Park Service and Forest Service.

17. Dilsaver, *America's National Park System: The Critical Documents*, 53.

18. National Park Service Conference, November 13–17, 1922. "Superintendents Resolution on Overdevelopment," NPS History Collection, Harpers Ferry, Box K5410 (hereafter cited as HFC).

19. Ibid.

20. Quoted in Shankland, *Steve Mather of the National Parks*, 243.

21. Swain, *Federal Conservation Policy*, 128.

22. For an overview of the growing conflict, see Steen, *The U.S. Forest Service: A History*, 152–62.

23. Quoted in James B. Trefethen, "The 1928 ORRRC," *American Forests* 68 (March 1962): 38.

24. National Conference on Outdoor Recreation, *Proceedings of the National Conference on Outdoor Recreation, 1926*. 69th Cong., 1st Sess., Senate, 1926, Document No. 117, 32.

25. Ibid., 64.

26. Ibid., 64–65.

27. Ibid., 65.

28. Joint Committee on Recreational Survey of Federal Lands of the American Forestry Association and National Parks Association, *National Conference on Outdoor Recreation: Report of the Joint Committee on Recreational Survey of Federal Lands of the American Forestry Association and the National Parks Association to the National Conference on Outdoor Recreation: Recreation Resources of Federal Lands* (Washington, DC, 1928), 90.

29. Ibid., 102.

30. Ibid., 109.

31. Ibid.

32. John C. Merriam, speech delivered to the National Parks Association, 1931. JM.

33. Horace M. Albright and Frank J. Taylor, "The Everlasting Wilderness," *Saturday Evening Post* 201 (September 29, 1928): 28, 63, 66, 68.

34. Ibid.

35. Carr, *Wilderness By Design*, 189–247.

36. O. A. Tomlinson to Director, June 11, 1928. Quoted in Catton, *Wonderland*, 238.

37. A. E. Demaray to O. A. Tomlinson, July 10, 1928. In Catton, *Wonderland*, 238.

38. O. A. Tomlinson to Director, July 17, 1928. In Catton, *Wonderland*, 239.

39. Runte, *Yosemite: The Embattled Wilderness*, 143.

40. Ibid., 157.

41. Acting Superintendent Leavitt to Director, National Park Service, October 8, 1927. Quoted in Runte, *Yosemite: The Embattled Wilderness*, 147.

42. Ibid., 148.

43. Ibid., 158.

44. Sellars, *Preserving Nature in the National Parks*, 108–12.

45. Ibid., 91–148.

46. L. F. Kneipp, "Recreational Value of National Forests," *Parks and Recreation* 8, no. 4 (March–April 1925): 300.

47. From a statement issued by Associate Forester E. A. Sherman, in an editorial, "Recreation Principles for the National Forests," *American Forests and Forest Life* 31 (July 1925): 424.

48. W. B. Greeley to District Foresters, December 30, 1926. Quoted in Gilligan, "The Development of Policy," 100.

49. Gilligan, "The Development of Policy," 108.

50. W. B. Greeley, "What Shall We Do with Our Mountains?" *Sunset* 59 (December 1927): 14.

51. Mimeographed supplement to the Forest Service Administrative Manual distributed June 29, 1929. Quoted in Craig W. Allin, *The Politics of Wilderness Preservation* (Westport, CT: Greenwood Press, 1982), 74.

52. Gilligan, "The Development of Policy," 127; Allin, *The Politics of Wilderness Preservation*, 74.

1. Robert W. Righter, *Crucible for Conservation: The Creation of Grand Teton National Park* (Boulder: Colorado Associated University Press, 1982), 39–40.

2. U.S. Congress, *Congressional Record*, 71st Cong, 3rd Sess., 6791. Quoted in John Ise, *Our National Park Policy: A Critical History* (Baltimore: Johns Hopkins University Press, 1961), 333.

3. Adolph Murie, "Report on the Qualifications and Development of Isle Royale as a National Park," June 13, 1935. Box ISRO, HFC.

4. John J. Little, "Island Wilderness: A History of Isle Royale National Park" (PhD dissertation, University of Toledo, 1978), 201.

5. Shankland, *Steve Mather of the National Parks*, 300.

6. U.S. Department of the Interior, National Park Service, *The National Parks: Shaping the System* (Washington, DC: NPS Division of Publications, 1991), 21.

7. Rothman, *America's National Monuments: The Politics of Preservation*, 202.

8. Horace M. Albright, "The National Park System and Its Future," in Harlean James, ed., *American Planning and Civic Annual* (Washington, DC: American Planning and Civic Association, 1939), 225.

9. Rosalie Edge, *Roads and More Roads in the National Parks and National Forests.* Pamphlet No. 54, Emergency Conservation Committee. In Dilsaver, *America's National Park System: The Critical Documents*, 137–41.

10. John Roberts White, "Wilderness Policies," in James, *American Planning and Civic Annual* (1936), 35.

11. Arno B. Cammerer, "Standards and Policies in National Parks," in James, *American Planning and Civic Annual* (1936), 20.

12. National Parks Association, "Losing Our Primeval System in Vast Expansion," *National Parks Bulletin* 13, no. 61 (February 1936): 2.

13. Minutes of the Board of Trustees, National Parks Association, May 14, 1936. National Parks Conservation Association Papers, Washington, DC (hereafter cited as NPCA).

14. Miles, *Guardians of the Parks*, 71–95.

15. Sellars, *Preserving Nature in the National Parks*, 93.

16. Ibid., 98.

17. Carr, *Wilderness by Design*, 194–95.

18. Ibid., 241.

19. Thomas C. Vint, "Development of National Parks for Conservation," in James, *American Planning and Civic Annual* (1938), 71.

20. Ibid., 69.

21. Carr, *Wilderness by Design*, 242.

22. Ben W. Twight, *Organizational Values and Political Power: The Forest Service ver-*

sus the *Olympic National Park* (University Park: Pennsylvania State University Press, 1983), 13.

23. Gilligan, "The Development of Policy," 144.

24. F. A. Silcox Letter to Regional Foresters, June 30, 1934. Quoted in Gilligan, "The Development of Policy," 182.

25. F. A. Silcox Memo to Mr. Kneipp and Mr. Granger, November 13, 1935. Quoted in Gilligan, "The Development of Policy," 135–36.

26. Robert Marshall to William P. Wharton, December 14, 1937, Washington Office Files. Quoted in Gilligan, "The Development of Policy," 192.

27. James P. Gilligan interview with L. F. Kneipp, November 8, 1952. In Gilligan, "The Development of Policy," 196.

28. Ibid., 199.

29. Arno B. Cammerer, "Standards and Policies in National Parks," in James, *American Planning and Civic Annual* (1936), 19.

30. Arno B. Cammerer, "Maintenance of the Primeval in National Parks," *Appalachia* 22 (December 1938): 207.

5   MORE FERMENT AND EXPANSION

1. John Ise, *Our National Park Policy: A Critical History*, 370.

2. Frederick Law Olmsted Jr. and William P. Wharton, "The Florida Everglades," *American Forests* 38 (March 1932): 143, 147. Quoted in Runte, *National Parks: The American Experience*, 134.

3. Ibid.

4. U.S. *Statutes at Large* 48 (1934): 817.

5. National Park Service Memorandum, Arno B. Cammerer, April 2, 1934. Quoted in Runte, *National Parks: The American Experience*, 135.

6. Quoted in Twight, *Organizational Values and Political Power*, 46.

7. Henry S. Graves to Herbert A. Smith, December 29, 1936. Quoted in Twight, *Organizational Values and Political Power*, 88–89.

8. Harold L. Ickes, "The Olympic National Park." In James, *American Planning and Civic Annual* (1938), 11.

9. Ibid., 16.

10. Ibid., 12.

11. Ibid., 15–16.

12. Cammerer to Moore, September 27, 1938. RG 79, National Archives (hereafter cited as NA). Quoted in *Olympic National Park: An Administrative History* (Seattle: National Park Service, Pacific Northwest Region, 1990), 91.

13. Quoted in Cammerer, "Maintenance of the Primeval in National Parks," 212.

14. Lary M. Dilsaver and William C. Tweed, *Challenge of the Big Trees: A Resource His-*

tory of Sequoia and Kings Canyon National Parks (Three Rivers, CA: Sequoia Natural History Association, 1990), 204–5.

15. For the long story of congressional struggles over the Gearhart bill, see Irving Brant, *Adventures in Conservation with Franklin D. Roosevelt* (Flagstaff, AZ: Northland Publishing, 1988), 147–218.

16. Ibid., 165–66.

17. U.S. Department of the Interior, National Park Service, *Proceedings of the First National Conference*, November 1–30, 1929. HFC.

18. See Stephen J. Pyne, *Year of the Fires: The Story of the Great Fires of 1910* (New York: Penguin Books, 2001), 9 passim.

19. Sellars, *Preserving Nature in the National Parks*, 91–148.

20. Ibid., 93.

21. Shankland, *Steve Mather of the National Parks*, 248–49.

22. John R. White, *Annual Report of the General Grant Park*, 1922, 122. HFC.

23. Rick Hydrick, "The Genesis of National Park Management: John Roberts White and Sequoia National Park, 1920–1947," *Journal of Forest History*, 28, no. 2 (April 1984): 75.

24. John R. White, "Standards and Policies Applied to Wilderness Values," January 23, 1936. Quoted in Hydrick, "The Genesis of National Park Management," 72.

25. Dilsaver and Tweed, *Challenge of the Big Trees*, 167.

26. Ibid.

27. Ibid., 184.

28. White to Farquhar, February 7, 1945. Quoted in Hydrick, "The Genesis of National Park Management," 81.

29. Dilsaver and Tweed, *Challenge of the Big Trees*, 196.

30. David Louter, *Windshield Wilderness: Cars, Roads, and Nature in Washington's National Parks* (Seattle: University of Washington Press, 2006), 50.

31. Arthur Demaray to Field Officers, November 11, 1936. Box L48, Wilderness, to 1938. HFC.

32. E. Lowell Sumner Jr., "The Wilderness Problem in the National Parks." Excerpt from *Special Report on a Wildlife Study of the High Sierra in Sequoia and Yosemite National Parks and Adjacent Territory*. Attached to memo to field officers from Acting Director Demaray, November 11, 1936. HFC.

33. E. Lowell Sumner Jr., "Losing the Wilderness Which We Set Out to Preserve." Box L48, Wilderness, to 1938. HFC.

34. Ibid., 16.

35. Arno Cammerer to Henry Baldwin Ward, June 4, 1935. File: Correspondence, Arno Cammerer, RG79. NA.

36. Horace Albright, "A National Park Platform," in James, *American Planning and Civic Annual* (1938), 32.

37. Sumner, "Losing the Wilderness," 15.

1. Olympic National Park 1940 Master Plan, Folder No. 1, Cartographic Collection. NA.

2. Ibid.

3. Ibid.

4. Report on Round Table Discussion Participated in by Conservationists, Directors of the Sierra Club, Park Superintendents, and Regional Office Officials, March 12, 1940. U.S. Department of the Interior, National Park Service, Region IV, San Francisco. RG 79, Records of Newton B. Drury, Box 23, Entry 19. NA.

5. See Dilsaver and Tweed, Challenge of the Big Trees, 227–328.

6. Donald C. Swain, "The National Park Service and the New Deal," Pacific Historical Review 41 (August 1972): 331.

7. Ise, Our National Park Policy: A Critical History, 448.

8. Report on a Master Plan Conference on Kings Canyon, July 11, 1941. U.S. Department of the Interior, National Park Service, Washington office. RG 79, Records of Newton B. Drury, Box 11, Entry 19, Kings Canyon File. NA.

9. The author examined the Kings Canyon Master Plans and others at the National Archives, Cartographic Division, College Park. The specific plan cited is Kings Canyon Master Plan, 1941.

10. Yard to John Sieker, January 12, 1942. Box 4:410, Correspondence File, Wilderness 1939–59. TWS.

11. Yard to Conrad Wirth, January 22, 1943. RG 79, Records of Newton B. Drury, Box 25, Entry 19, Wilderness Society File. NA.

12. Drury to Yard (draft), February 15, 1943. RG 79, Records of Newton B. Drury, Box 25, Entry 19, Wilderness Society File. NA.

13. Ibid.

14. Quoted in Stephen Fox, "We Want No Straddlers," The Living Wilderness 48 (Winter 1984): 12.

15. Murie to Robert F. Griggs, May 30, 1945. Box 1: 100–200. TWS.

16. Fox, John Muir and His Legacy, 12.

17. U.S. Department of the Interior, National Park Service, Annual Reports of the Director, 1945–1955.

18. Minutes, National Parks Association Executive Committee, April 18, 1946. NPCA.

19. Bernard DeVoto, "The National Parks," Fortune 35 (June 1947): 135.

20. Minutes, National Parks Association Annual Meeting, April 9, 1946. NPCA.

21. See Mark Harvey, A Symbol of Wilderness: Echo Park and the American Conservation Movement (Albuquerque: University of New Mexico Press, 1994); Elmo Richardson, Dams, Parks and Politics: Resource Development and Preservation in the Truman-Eisenhower Era (Lexington: University of Kentucky Press, 1973); and Donald Worster, Rivers of Empire: Water, Aridity, and the Growth of the American West (New York: Pantheon, 1985).

22. Sellars, *Preserving Nature in the National Parks*, 177.

23. Dennis M. Roth, *The Wilderness Movement and the National Forests* (College Station, TX: Intaglio Press, 1988), 7.

24. Drury to W. C. Gilbert, Acting Director, Legislative Reference Service, November 30, 1948. Box 4:300, File: Correspondence, USDI-NPS, 1936–49. TWS.

25. Ibid.

26. C. Frank Keyser, "The Preservation of Wilderness Areas (An Analysis of Opinion on the Problem)," Washington, DC: Legislative Reference Service, Library of Congress, August 24, 1949.

27. Roth, *The Wilderness Movement and the National Forests*, 7.

28. David Brower, *Wildlands in Our Civilization* (San Francisco: Sierra Club Books, 1964), 135.

29. Quoted by Timothy Rawson, *Changing Tracks: Predators and Politics in Mt. McKinley National Park* (Fairbanks: University of Alaska Press, 2001), 234.

30. Michael Cohen, *The History of the Sierra Club: 1892–1970* (San Francisco: Sierra Club Books, 1988), 125.

31. Newton B. Drury, "National Parks in Wartime," *American Forests* 49, no. 8 (August 1943): 375.

32. Waldo G. Leland, "Newton Bishop Drury," *National Parks Magazine* 25, no. 105 (April–June 1951): 63–64.

33. Ibid., 66.

34. Ibid., 65.

35. Packard to William Wharton, January 17, 1951. Box 4:103, File: Correspondence, Newton B. Drury, 1951–60. TWS.

36. Swain, *Wilderness Defender*, 292. See also Conrad L. Wirth, *Parks, Politics, and the People* (Norman: University of Oklahoma Press, 1980).

37. Cohen, *The History of the Sierra Club*, 120.

38. Swain, *Wilderness Defender*, 292.

39. Harvey, *A Symbol of Wilderness*, 290.

40. Ibid.

41. John Muir, *A Thousand Mile Walk to the Gulf*, William F. Bade, ed. (Boston: Houghton Mifflin Company, 1916), 354.

42. Brower, *Wildlands in Our Civilization*, 151.

43. Ibid., 158.

44. Cohen, *The History of the Sierra Club*, 133.

45. U.S. Department of the Interior, National Park Service, *Annual Report of the Director, National Park Service to the Secretary of the Interior for the Fiscal Year Ended June 30, 1954* (Washington, DC: Government Printing Office, 1955), 331.

46. Bernard DeVoto, "Let's Close the National Parks," *Harper's* 27 (October 1953): 51.

47. Ibid., 52.

48. Wirth, *Parks, Politics, and the People*, 261–62.

49. Ibid., 259.

50. Editorial, "The Park Service and Wilderness," *National Parks Magazine*, 31, no. 130 (July–September 1957): 104; David R. Brower, "Mission 65 Is Proposed by Reviewer of the Park Service's New Brochure on Wilderness," *National Parks Magazine* 32, no. 132 (January 1958): 3.

51. Lemuel A. Garrison, *The Making of a Ranger: Forty Years in the National Parks* (Salt Lake City: Howe Brothers, 1983), 259.

52. Ibid., 260.

53. Wirth, *Parks, Politics, and the People*, 290–91.

54. Minutes of the Board of Trustees, National Parks Association, May 10, 1956. NPCA.

55. Garrison, *The Making of a Ranger*, 259.

56. Ibid.

57. Ibid.

58. Sellars, *Preserving Nature in the National Parks*, 202.

59. Ibid.

7   THE DRIVE FOR A WILDERNESS ACT

1. Howard Zahniser, "The Need for Wilderness Areas." Reprinted by The Wilderness Society. Box 4:300, File: National Wilderness Preservation System, Wilderness Bill Advocacy, Correspondence, 1970s. TWS.

2. Michael McCloskey, "The Wilderness Act of 1964: Its Background and Meaning," *Oregon Law Review* 45, no. 4 (1966): 294.

3. Roth, *The Wilderness Movement and the National Forests*, 9.

4. Wirth to Howard Zahniser, March 19, 1956. Box 5:100, File: National Wilderness Preservation System, Wilderness Bill Advocacy, Council of Conservationists, 1956–59. TWS.

5. Memorandum from Director, National Park Service, to Legislative Council, Office of the Solicitor, n.d. Box L48, Wilderness, 1960–. HFC.

6. Olson to Hubert Humphrey, April 3, 1956. Box 5:100, File: National Wilderness Preservation System, Wilderness Bill Advocacy, Correspondence, 1956. TWS.

7. Fred Smith to Howard Zahniser, April 16, 1956. Box 5:100, File: National Wilderness Preservation System, Wilderness Bill Advocacy, Correspondence, Council of Conservationists, 1956–59. TWS.

8. Albright to David Brower, April 24, 1956. Box 5:100, File: National Wilderness Preservation System, Wilderness Bill Advocacy, Correspondence, Council of Conservationists, 1956–59. TWS.

9. Memorandum from Fred Smith to Albright, Brower, Gabrielson, Penfold, and Zahniser, December 17, 1956. Box 5:100, File: National Wilderness Preservation Sys-

tem, Wilderness Bill Advocacy, Correspondence, Council of Conservationists, 1956–59. TWS.

10. Zahniser to John Oakes, January 8, 1957. Box 5:100, File: National Wilderness Preservation System, Wilderness Bill Advocacy, Correspondence, Council of Conservationists, 1956–59. TWS.

11. Brower to Howard Elliott, May 24, 1957. Box 5:100, File: National Wilderness Preservation System, Wilderness Bill Advocacy, Correspondence, Council of Conservationists, 1956–59. TWS.

12. Howard Zahniser, "One-Page Statement." Box 1:100–200, File: Governing Council Correspondence, 1956–59. TWS.

13. Ibid.

14. See Nash, *Wilderness and the American Mind*; Michael Frome, *Battle for the Wilderness* (New York: Praeger, 1974); Allin, *The Politics of Wilderness Preservation*; and Roth, *The Wilderness Movement and the National Forests.*

15. Roth, *The Wilderness Movement and the National Forests*, 10.

16. An Address by Conrad L. Wirth, Director, National Park Service, Before the Fifth Biennial Conference on Wild Lands in Our Civilization, March 16, 1957. Box 5:202–300, File: National Wilderness Preservation System, Campaign Speeches, 1957–70. TWS.

17. Ibid.

18. Humphrey to Alexander Hildebrand, March 14, 1957. Box 5:500, File: National Wilderness Preservation System, Wilderness Bill Advocacy, Correspondence, January–April 1957. TWS.

19. Quoted in Brower, *Wildlands in Our Civilization*, 175.

20. Quoted by Howard Zahniser in his statement "Our Outdoor Recreation Inventory," May 14, 1957. Box 202–300, File: National Wilderness Preservation System, Legislation: Statements, Congressional Hearings, 1957–59. TWS.

21. Statement to Committee Chair Claire Engle from Undersecretary of the Interior Hatfield Chilton, June 18, 1957. Box 5:100, File: National Wilderness Preservation System, Statements before Committees, 1957. TWS.

22. Zahniser to Horace Albright, July 3, 1957. Box 5:100, File: National Wilderness Preservation System, Wilderness Bill Advocacy, Correspondence, May–July 1957. TWS.

23. Quoted in an editorial, "The Park Service and Wilderness," *National Parks Magazine* 31, no. 130 (July–September 1957): 129–10.

24. Zahniser to Howard Elliott, July 5, 1957. Box 5:100, File: National Wilderness Preservation System, Wilderness Bill Advocacy, Correspondence, May–July 1957. TWS.

25. National Park Service, *The National Park Wilderness* (Washington, DC, 1957),

25. This was explicitly not a government publication. It stated, "Publication of this Brochure was made possible through a donation by a friend of the National Park Service."

26. Brower, "Mission 65 Is Proposed by Reviewer of the Park Service's New Brochure on Wilderness," 3.

27. Scoyen to Conrad Wirth, January 15, 1958. Box 5:100, File: National Wilderness Preservation System, Wilderness Bill Advocacy, Correspondence, January–May 1958. TWS.

28. Zahniser to Harvey Broome, January 31, 1958. Box 5:100, File: National Wilderness Preservation System, Wilderness Bill Advocacy, Correspondence, January–May 1958. TWS.

29. Secretary Fred Seaton to Senator James Murray, July 22, 1958. Box 5:100, File: National Wilderness Preservation System, Wilderness Bill Advocacy, Correspondence, June–July 1958. TWS.

30. S. 4028, 85th Cong., 2nd Sess.

31. Eivind Scoyen, "The National Park Wilderness," March 19, 1959. Box L48, Wilderness. HFC.

32. Squad Meeting minutes, April 6, 1959. RG 79, Box 23, Entry 12, Office Files of Wirth. NA.

33. Squad Meeting minutes, August 18, 1959. RG 79, Box 23, Entry 12, Office Files of Wirth. NA.

34. Sellars, *Preserving Nature in the National Parks*, 193.

35. U.S. Congress, *Congressional Record* 106 (July 2, 1969): 15564.

36. Squad Meeting minutes, February 29, 1960. RG 79, Box 23, Entry 12, Office Files of Wirth. NA.

37. Devereaux Butcher, "Resorts or Wilderness?" *Atlantic* 207 (February 1961): 51.

38. Wirth to Stewart Udall, March 10, 1961. Box K5440, Policy and Philosophy, 1960–67. HFC.

39. Wirth, *Parks, Politics, and the People*, 262.

40. Udall to Conrad Wirth, March 20, 1961. Box K5440, Policy and Philosophy, 1960–67. HFC.

41. Ibid.

42. Udall to Clinton Anderson, February 24, 1961. Box 5:202–300, File: National Wilderness Preservation System, Legislation: Statements, Congressional Hearings, 1961. TWS.

43. U.S. Congress, *Congressional Record* 108 (May 1, 1962): 7482.

44. Outdoor Recreation Resources Review Commission, *Study Report 3: Wilderness and Recreation—A Report on Resources, Values, and Problems* (Washington, DC: Government Printing Office, 1962), 13.

45. Ibid., 305.

46. Allin, *The Politics of Wilderness Preservation*, 133.

47. House Subcommittee on Public Lands, Hearings on H.R. 9070, H.R. 9162, and S. 4, April 27–May 1, 1964, 1205.

1. Ronald A. Foresta, *America's National Parks and Their Keepers* (Washington, DC: Resources for the Future, Inc., 1984), 67.

2. Sellars, *Preserving Nature in the National Parks*, 204.

3. A. Starker Leopold et al., "Report of the Advisory Board on Wildlife Management," March 4, 1963. Insert in *National Parks Magazine* 37, no. 186 (April 1963).

4. E. T. Scoyen, "Conditions Surrounding Appointments as Director of the National Park Service," mimeographed memorandum, n.d. Box 4:300. TWS.

5. Memorandum from Secretary of the Interior Udall to National Park Service Director Hartzog, July 10, 1964. In Dilsaver, *America's National Park System: The Critical Documents*, 272–76.

6. Foresta, *America's National Parks and Their Keepers*, 107.

7. John McPhee, "Profiles—George Hartzog," *New Yorker* 17 (September 11, 1972): 62.

8. Dilsaver, *America's National Park System: The Critical Documents*, 273–74.

9. U.S. Public Law 88–577, 88th Cong., September 3, 1964, Wilderness Act.

10. John C. Hendee, George H. Stankey, and Robert C. Lucas, *Wilderness Management*, 2nd ed. (Golden, CO: North American Press, 1990), 108.

11. Sellars, *Preserving Nature in the National Parks*, 194.

12. Hendee, Stankey, and Lucas, *Wilderness Management*, 118–19.

13. Ibid., 120.

14. Memorandum from George Hartzog to Ted Swem, December 3, 1964. Box 18. TS.

15. Based on a memorandum from the Director to Chief, Office of Resource Planning, "Land Classification" (date unclear). Box L48, Wilderness. HFC.

16. Theodore Swem, "Master Plan—A Tool for Total Management." Paper presented at the National Park Service Superintendents Conference, Gatlinburg, Tennessee, September 12–17, 1965, 9–10. Copy provided by Ted Swem.

17. George B. Hartzog Jr., "Our Expanding Horizon of Public Service." Paper presented at the National Park Service Superintendents Conference, Gatlinburg, Tennessee, September 12–17, 1965, 9–10. Box K5410. HFC.

18. Ibid., 11.

19. Ibid., 13.

20. Wilderness Regulations of the U.S. Department of the Interior, Title 43, Part 19, Section 19.2, February 17, 1966.

21. Minutes, Director's Staff Meeting, August 18, 1966. Box L48, Wilderness. HFC.

22. Ibid., 12.

23. Stewart Brandborg, "The Future with the Wilderness Act: Setting New Patterns under a Landmark Law." Paper presented at the Sixth Biennial Northwest Wilderness Conference, Seattle, WA, April 1966. Box 14:300. TWS. See also Memo from

Brandborg to Members of State Wilderness Committees and Cooperators, September 23, 1965, Box 5:00; Rupert Cutler to Karl S. Landstrom, December 8, 1965, Box 4:30; Landstrom to Charles Stoddard, January 6, 1966, Box B:30; Brandborg to Harvey Broome et al., November 26, 1965; and Michael McCloskey to Brandborg, December 1, 1965, Box 5:00. All in TWS.

24. Quoted in Frome, *Battle for the Wilderness*, 176.

25. Minutes, Director's Staff Meeting, August 18, 1966. Box L48, Wilderness. HFC.

26. Ibid., 12.

27. George B. Hartzog Jr., "National Park Wilderness Planning Procedures," August 8, 1966. Box L48, Wilderness. HFC.

28. National Park Service Plan, Draft for NPS Conference of Challenges, Yosemite National Park, October 13–18, 1963. Box L48, Wilderness. HFC.

29. RG 79, Office Files of Wirth, Box 23, Entry 12, August 18, 1959. NA.

30. Minutes, Director's Staff Meeting, August 18, 1966, 7. Box L48, Wilderness. HFC.

31. J. Michael McCloskey, "Statement of the Sierra Club on Proposals for Wilderness Areas within Lassen Volcanic National Park, California," September 27, 1966, 1–2. Box 7:110. TWS.

32. Ibid., 5.

33. S. Herbert Evison to Laurance S. Rockefeller, October 21, 1966. Box 2. HE.

34. Evison to Hearings Officer, Isle Royale National Park Wilderness Proposal, January 29, 1967. Box 2. HE.

35. Evison to George B. Hartzog Jr., January 19, 1967. Box 2. HE.

36. Remarks of George B. Hartzog Jr., Director, NPS, USDI, at the Tenth Biennial Wilderness Conference of the Sierra Club, San Francisco, California, April 7, 1967. Box L48, Wilderness. HFC.

37. Stewart Brandborg, "The Wilderness Act in Practice: The First Three Years," April 7, 1967, 8. Box 14:300–500. TWS.

9   WILDERNESS REVIEWS RELUCTANTLY COMPLETED

1. U.S. Congress, *Congressional Record* 116 (September 21, 1970): 32749.

2. John M. Kauffmann to Chief, Division of Wilderness Studies, November 20, 1968. Box 8. JK.

3. U.S. Senate, Committee on Interior and Insular Affairs, Subcommittee on Public Lands, *Preservation of Wilderness Areas, Hearing on S. 2453 and Related Wilderness Bills.* 92nd Cong., 2nd Sess., 1972, 62.

4. Memorandum from Stanley C. Joseph, Assistant Director, to Chiefs, Office of Resource Planning, SSC, and WG, February 26, 1969. Box L48, Wilderness. HFC.

5. U.S. House of Representatives, Lava Beds Wilderness, House Report 1421 to Accompany H.R. 5838, 92nd Cong., 2nd Sess., 1972.

6. Memorandum from Walter J. Hickel to George B. Hartzog, June 18, 1969, 2. Box K5410. HFC.

7. Ibid., 5.

8. Ernest M. Dickerman, "The National Park Wilderness Reviews," *The Living Wilderness* 34, no. 109 (Spring 1970): 40–49.

9. Harthon L. Bill to Rep. Philip J. Philbin, May 22, 1970. Box 4:30. TWS.

10. Leslie Glasgow to George P. Hartzog Jr., July 6, 1970. Box L48, Wilderness. HFC.

11. Memorandum from Director to Directorate, July 28, 1970. Box L48, Wilderness. HFC.

12. Mimeographed Record of July 31, 1970, Meeting on Accelerated Wilderness Program. Recorded by James W. Stewart. Box L48, Wilderness. HFC.

13. Director's Staff Meeting Minutes, 1970–1984. Box 4019, General Collection. HFC.

14. John P. Saylor to Asst. Sec. Leslie L. Glasgow, October 14, 1970. Box 1:1. HC.

15. Leslie L. Glasgow to John P. Saylor, October 29, 1970. Box 1:1. HC.

16. Stewart M. Brandborg to William E. Kriegsman, October 21, 1970. Box 1:1. HC.

17. Rogers C. B. Morton to George B. Hartzog Jr., June 17, 1971. Box 5410, Policy and Philosophy. HFC.

18. 2 Stat. 926, Sec. 604, October 2, 1968.

19. David Louter, *Contested Terrain: North Cascades National Park Service Complex—An Administrative History* (Seattle: National Park Service, 1998), 60–61.

20. U.S. Senate, *Preservation of Wilderness Areas*, 59.

21. Ibid., 59–60.

22. Ibid., 62.

23. Ibid., 114.

24. Ibid., 119.

25. Dickerman to Stewart Brandborg et al., May 9, 1972. Box 4:410. TWS.

26. Ibid.

27. Asst. Secretary to Directors of BSFW and NPS, June 24, 1974, 2. Box 1:1. HC.

28. Ibid., 3.

29. Ibid., 4.

30. Transcript of interview of Nathaniel P. Reed with Loretta Neumann, editor, *Newsletter*, National Park Service, April 3, 1973. Box 5410, Policy and Philosophy. HFC.

31. "The Wilderness Record," *The Living Wilderness* (Autumn 1972): 5–9.

32. Frank Church, statement in U.S. Senate, *Preservation of Wilderness Areas*, 59–60.

33. Hartzog offers his explanation of what happened in George B. Hartzog Jr., *Battling for the National Parks* (Mt. Kisko, NY: Moyer Bell Limited, 1988), 237–48.

34. Ibid., 262–63.

35. Foresta, *America's National Parks and Their Keepers*, 85.

36. See Miles, *Guardians of the Parks*, 237–83.

37. See Roth, *The Wilderness Movement and the National Forests*, 37–62.

38. Briefing Book, House Oversight Hearing, March 7, 1975. Box K5410. HFC.

10 WILDERNESS IN ALASKA

1. Theodore Catton, *Inhabited Wilderness: Indians, Eskimos, and National Parks in Alaska* (Albuquerque: University of New Mexico Press, 1997), 215.

2. U.S. Census Bureau, *Alaska: Population of Counties by Decennial Census, 1900 to 1990*, compiled and edited by Richard L. Forstall, www.census.gov/population/cencounts/.

3. Catton, *Inhabited Wilderness*, 215.

4. G. Frank Williss, "Do Things Right the First Time": *The National Park Service and the Alaska National Interest Lands Conservation Act of 1980* (Washington, DC: U.S. Department of the Interior, National Park Service, 1985), 64.

5. Ibid., 35.

6. Hartzog to George L. Collins, November 13, 1964. Cited in Williss, *Do Things Right the First Time*, 35.

7. U.S. Congress, *Congressional Record*, Senate, 156 (January 1970): 24424.

8. "Statement on H.R. 3100 and Related Bills to Provide for Settlement of Certain Land Claims of Alaska Natives by Stewart M. Brandborg, House Committee on Interior and Insular Affairs, May 3, 1971," Conservationists Involvement in Alaska—The Wilderness Society through 1975, Swem Papers. TS. Cited in Williss, *Do Things Right the First Time*, 74.

9. Williss, *Do Things Right the First Time*, 93.

10. For treatments of this aspect of national park history, see Keller and Turek, *American Indians and National Parks*, and Spence, *Dispossessing the Wilderness: Indian Removal and the Making of the National Parks*.

11. John M. Kauffmann, *Alaska's Brooks Range: The Ultimate Mountains* (Seattle: Mountaineers, 1992), 135.

12. Catton, *Inhabited Wilderness*, 199–200.

13. Ibid., 210.

14. Ibid., 213.

15. Williss, *Do Things Right the First Time*, 152.

16. Kauffmann, *Alaska's Brooks Range*, 132.

17. Robert Cahn, *The Fight to Save Wild Alaska* (Washington, DC: National Audubon Society, 1982), 15.

18. Williss, *Do Things Right the First Time*, 173.

19. Ibid., 175.

20. Ibid., 219.

21. P.L. 97–487, Sec. 201, (4)(a).

22. Ibid.

23. Ibid., Section 803.

24. Quoted in T. H. Watkins, "The Perils of Expedience," *Wilderness* 54, no. 191 (Winter 1990): 29.

11 A NEW SORT OF NATIONAL PARK WILDERNESS

1. Watkins, "The Perils of Expedience," 79.

2. Williss, *Do Things Right the First Time*, 290.

3. Ibid., 281.

4. Ibid., 292.

5. Frank B. Norris, *Isolated Paradise: An Administrative History of the Katmai and Aniakchak National Park Service Units, Alaska* (Anchorage: National Park Service, 1996).

6. "Northern Alaska Environmental Center v. Hodel," 15 ELR 21048, *Environmental Law Reporter* (1985), www.elr.info/litigation/vol.15/15.21048.html (this site is no longer active).

7. Personal communication to author from John Reynolds, June 21, 2003.

8. ANILCA, Title 16, 3191(a).

9. Williss, *Do Things Right the First Time*, 270.

10. Ibid., 271.

11. Ibid., n. 277.

12. Ibid., 294.

13. P.L 96–487, Title II(4)(a).

14. Quoted in National Park Service, Draft Statement for Management, Gates of the Arctic National Park and Preserve, May 1982, 5. Box 8. JK.

15. Ibid., 15.

16. Ibid., 31–33.

17. John Adams et al., Letter to Dick Ring from the Fairbanks Environmental Center, 4. Box 8. JK.

18. Roderick Nash, "Comments on the Draft Statement for Management for Gates of the Arctic National Park and Preserve with Emphasis on the Problem of Air Access and Wilderness Values," September 10, 1982. Box 8. JK.

19. Stephen Alleman to Dick Ring, June 28, 1982. Box 8. JK.

20. T. Destry Jarvis to Dick Ring, August 30, 1982. Box 8. JK.

21. National Park Service, Draft General Management Plan/Environmental Assessment, Land Protection Plan, Wilderness Suitability Review, Gates of the Arctic National Park and Preserve, Anchorage, AK, March 1985, 116.

22. Ibid., iv.

23. Ibid., 137.

24. Ibid., 138.

25. John Kauffmann to Regional Director, June 25, 1985. Box 8. JK.

26. National Park Service, General Management Plan, Land Protection, Wilderness Suitability Review, Gates of the Arctic National Park and Preserve, Anchorage, AK, 1986, 127.

27. Ibid., 128–29.

28. Ibid., 134.

29. Kauffmann, *Alaska's Brooks Range*, 163.

30. Boyd Evison to John Kauffmann, April 1991. Box 7. JK.

31. Ibid.

32. National Park Service, General Management Plan, Gates of the Arctic National Park and Preserve, 217.

33. National Park Service, Final Environmental Impact Statement, Wilderness Recommendation, Gates of the Arctic National Park and Preserve, Anchorage, AK, 1988, 77.

34. Quoted in Randy R. Rogers, "Management Decision Process Review," *Northern Line* 8, no. 5 (October–November 1986): 3.

35. H.R. Rep. 95–1045, pt. 1, 157; emphasis in the original. Quoted in Allen E. Smith et al., *Alaska National Interest Lands Conservation Act: A Citizen's Guide* (Washington, DC: The Wilderness Society, 2001), 54.

36. Boyd Evison to John Kauffmann, June 28, 1988. Box 7. JK.

37. The Wilderness Society, *The Alaska Lands Act: A Broken Promise* (Washington, DC: The Wilderness Society, 1990), 48.

38. Smith et al., *Alaska National Interest Lands Conservation Act: A Citizen's Guide*, 54.

39. National Park Service, Final Environmental Impact Statement, Wilderness Recommendation, Gates of the Arctic National Park and Preserve, 69.

40. Quoted in Patricia Tyson Stroud, "Forerunner of American Conservation: Naturalist Thomas Say," *Journal of Forest and Conservation History* 39 (October 1995): 187.

41. George Catlin, *North American Indians: Being Letters and Notes on Their Manners, Customs, and Conditions, Written during Eight Years Travel amongst the Wildest Tribes in North America, 1832–1839*, 2 vols. (London: George Catlin, 1880), 1:295.

42. See Catton, *Inhabited Wilderness*, for an extensive treatment of this complex idea.

12 PARK WILDERNESS AFTER THE REVIEWS

1. The Wilderness Society, "The Wilderness System," *The Living Wilderness* 38, no. 128 (Winter 1974–75): 41.

2. U.S. Congress, *Congressional Record, House*, 97th Cong., 2nd Sess., 1976, 31889.

3. Little, "Island Wilderness: A History of Isle Royale National Park," 208.

4. Allin, *The Politics of Wilderness Preservation*, 196.

5. John Jacobs, *A Rage for Justice: The Passion and Politics of Phillip Burton* (Berkeley: University of California Press, 1995), 356.

6. U.S. House, Committee on Interior and Insular Affairs, Subcommittee on National Park and Insular Affairs, *Legislative History of the National Parks and Recreation Act of 1978*, 95th Cong., 2nd Sess. Committee Print 11, 495.

7. Ibid.

8. Brock Evans, "Wilderness Politics," *Sierra Club Bulletin* 61, no. 8 (September 1976): 16.

9. U.S. Congress, *Congressional Record*, Senate (March 15, 1988): S2261. Quoted in Louter, *Contested Terrain: North Cascades National Park Service Complex*, 300.

10. See Frank Wheat, *California Desert Miracle: The Fight for Desert Parks and Wilderness* (San Diego: Sunbelt Publications, 1999).

11. National Park Service, Wilderness Recommendation, 1972, Grand Canyon Complex, 20. Included in Additions to the National Wilderness System, Communication from the President to Congress, Part 5, House Document 93–357, September 21, 1972.

12. National Park Service, *Grand Canyon Management Plan, Final Environmental Impact Statement*, 1973, 16.

13. U.S. Senate, Subcommittee on Parks and Recreation Hearings on S. 1296, January 20, 1973.

14. *MSLF vs. Whalen, et al.*, U.S. District Court (Phoenix): 2:CV-80–233PHX CLH, closed July 16, 1981. Cited in R. Bryant McCulley, *Wilderness Management Plan for Grand Canyon National Park and the Colorado River: A Study in Conjunction with American Whitewater* (Master's thesis, University of Strathclyde, Glasgow, Scotland, August 1999), 21.

15. P.L. 96–514.

16. *Grand Canyon Private Boaters Association vs. Alston*, U.S. District Court (District of Arizona): CV-00–1277–PCT-RGR-TSZ.

17. National Park Service, *Annual Wilderness Report 2002–2003*, Appendix 1, Washington, DC, July 2003.

18. These areas include Arches National Park, Assateague Island National Seashore, Big Bend National Park, Bryce Canyon National Park, Canyonlands National Park, Capitol Reef National Park, Cedar Breaks National Park, Colorado National Monument, Crater Lake National Park, Craters of the Moon National Park, Cumberland Gap National Park, Dinosaur National Monument, El Malpais National Monument, Glacier National Park, Grand Tetons National Park, Great Smoky Mountains National Park, Yellowstone National Park, and Zion National Park.

19. National Park Service, *Wilderness Report 2000–2001*, prepared for the National Wilderness Steering Committee, June 2002, 13.

20. Units for which recommendations have been completed but in 2002 awaited action in the Office of the Director were Aniakchak National Monument, Bering Land Bridge National Monument, Cape Krusenstern National Monument, Denali National

Park, Gates of the Arctic National Park, Glacier Bay National Park, Katmai National Park, Kenai Fjords National Monument, Kobuk Valley National Monument, Lake Clark National Park, Noatak National Monument, Wrangell-St. Elias National Park, Yukon-Charley Rivers National Park, and Grand Canyon National Park. Some of these are additions to existing park wilderness areas. Those awaiting secretarial decision were Bighorn Canyon National Recreation Area, Cape Lookout National Seashore, Glen Canyon NRA, Sleeping Bear Dunes National Lakeshore, and Voyageurs National Park.

21. National Park Service, *Annual Wilderness Report 2002–2003*, Appendices 2 and 3.

22. Ibid., 8.

13 THE WORK CONTINUES

1. National Park Service, *Backcountry Management Plan, North Cascades National Park Complex*, March 14, 1974, Sedro-Woolley, WA, 7.

2. National Park Service, *Lassen Volcanic National Park Backcountry Management Plan*, 1975. Quoted in National Park Service, *Preserving Our Natural Heritage*, Vol. 1: *Federal Activities* (Washington, DC: Government Printing Office, 1975), 222.

3. National Park Service, *Management Policies 1978* (Washington, DC), chap. 6, sec. 2.

4. National Park Service, *Management Policies 1988* (Washington, DC), chap. 6, sec. 3.

5. Ibid., chap. 6, sec. 4.

6. Ibid., chap. 6, sec. 2.

7. National Park Service, *Management Policies 2001* (Washington, DC), vol. 6, sec. 2.1.

8. Ibid., chap. 6, sec. 2.2.

9. Ibid., chap. 6, sec. 3.7.

10. Cited in Jonathan B. Jarvis, "The Wilderness Act and the NPS Organic Act: A White Paper Discussion," unpublished internal National Park Service document, March 1994.

11. Robert Cahn, "The National Park System: The People, the Parks, the Politics," *Sierra* 68, no. 3 (May–June, 1983): 51.

12. Ibid., 49.

13. National Park Service, Ranger Activities Division, *Wilderness Task Force Report on Improving Wilderness Management in the National Park Service* (Washington, DC: National Park Service, September 3, 1994).

14. Ibid., 18.

15. Remarks by Roger G. Kennedy before the 6th National Wilderness Conference, November 14–18, 1994, Santa Fe, New Mexico, 1, www.nps.gov/partner/speechsf .html (this site is no longer active).

16. Ibid., 2.

17. Ibid.

18. Memo to Field Area Directors et al., from Chairman, National Wilderness Steering Committee, n.d. box l48, Wilderness. HFC.

19. Memo to Members and Liaison, National Wilderness Steering Committee from Deputy Wilderness Program Coordinator, March 4, 1997. Box L48, Wilderness. HFC.

20. Richard West Sellars, "The Path Not Taken: National Park Service Wilderness Management," *George Wright Forum* 17, no. 4 (2000): 4.

21. Ibid., 6.

22. Ibid., 7.

23. Ibid., 5.

24. Bob Krumenaker, "Wilderness and Natural Resource Management in the NPS: Another View," *George Wright Forum* 18, no. 1 (2001): 11–12.

25. Ibid.

SOURCES

MANUSCRIPT COLLECTIONS

HC   Harry Crandall Collection, Denver Public Library, Denver, Colorado

HE   Herbert Evison Collection, Denver Public Library, Denver, Colorado

HFC   National Park Service History Collection, Harpers Ferry, West Virginia

JK   John Kauffman Collection, Denver Public Library, Denver, Colorado

JM   John Merriam Papers, Library of Congress, Washington, DC

NA   Records of the National Park Service, National Archives and Records Administration, Washington, DC

NPCA   Records of the National Parks and Conservation Association, Washington, DC, and Denver Public Library, Denver, Colorado

TS   Theodore Swem Collection, Denver Public Library, Denver, Colorado

TWS   Wilderness Society Collection, Denver Public Library, Denver, Colorado

SELECTED BIBLIOGRAPHY

Albright, Horace M. "National Parks in Conservation and Land Use." *Journal of Forestry* 31 (March 1933): 255–62.

Albright, Horace M., and Robert Cahn. *The Birth of the National Park Service: The Founding Years, 1913–33*. Salt Lake City: Howe Brothers, 1985.

Albright, Horace M., and Marian Albright Schenck. *Creating the National Park Service: The Missing Years*. Norman: University of Oklahoma Press, 1999.

Albright, Horace M., and Frank J. Taylor. "The Everlasting Wilderness." *Saturday Evening Post* 201 (September 29, 1928): 28, 63–68.

————. *Oh, Ranger!* Stanford: Stanford University Press, 1928.

Allin, Craig W. "Hidden Agendas in Wilderness Management." *Parks and Recreation* 20, no. 5 (May 1985).

————. "Park Service v. Forest Service: Exploring the Differences in Wilderness Management." *Policy Studies Review* 7, no. 2 (Winter 1987): 385.

————. *The Politics of Wilderness Preservation.* Westport, CT: Greenwood Press, 1982.

————. "Wilderness Preservation as a Bureaucratic Tool." In *Federal Lands Policy*, edited by Philip O. Foss. Westport, CT: Greenwood Press, 1987, 127–38.

Backes, David. "Wilderness Visions: Arthur Carhart's 1922 Proposal for the Quetico-Superior Wilderness." *Forest and Conservation History* 35 (July 1991): 128–37.

Bade, William Frederic. *The Life and Letters of John Muir.* Boston: Houghton Mifflin Company, 1924.

Ballou, William Hosea. "An Adirondack National Park." *American Naturalist* 19 (1885): 579.

Belasco, Warren James. *Americans on the Road: From Autocamp to Motel, 1910–1945.* Cambridge, MA: MIT Press, 1979.

Bent, Allen H. "The Mountaineering Clubs of America." *Appalachia* 14 (December 1916): 5–18.

Brant, Irving. *Adventures in Conservation with Franklin D. Roosevelt.* Flagstaff: Northland Publishing, 1988.

Broome, Harvey. "The Last Decade, 1935–1945." *The Living Wilderness* 10 (December 1945): 13–17.

————. "Origins of The Wilderness Society." *The Living Wilderness* 5 (July 1940): 13–14.

Brower, David R. "Mission 65 Is Proposed by Reviewer of the Park Service's New Brochure on Wilderness." *National Parks Magazine* 32 (January 1958): 3–5, 45–47.

Brown, William F. *A History of the Denali-Mount McKinley Region, Alaska.* Santa Fe: National Park Service, 1991.

Bryant, Harold C. "A Nature Preserve for Yosemite." *Yosemite Nature Notes* 6 (June 1927): 46–48.

Buchholtz, C. W. *Man in Glacier.* West Glacier, MT: Glacier Natural History Association, 1976.

————. *Rocky Mountain National Park: A History.* Boulder: Colorado Associated University Press, 1983.

Butcher, Devereux. "Resorts or Wilderness?" *Atlantic* 207 (February 1961): 47–51.

Cahn, Robert. "Alaska: A Matter of 80,000,000 Acres." *Audubon* 76 (1974): 3–13, 66–81.

————. *The Fight to Save Wild Alaska.* Washington, DC: National Audubon Society, 1982.

————. "The Race to Save Wild Alaska." *The Living Wilderness* 41 (1977): 13–43.

Callicott, J. Baird., and Michael P. Nelson, eds. *The Great New Wilderness Debate.* Athens: University of Georgia Press, 1998.

Cameron, Jenks. *The National Park Service: Its History, Activities and Organization.* Service

Monographs of the United States Government, 11. New York: Brookings Institution, 1922.

Cammerer, A. B. "Maintenance of the Primeval in National Parks." *Appalachia* 22 (December 1938): 207–13.

———. "Our National Parks: Their Present Status and Service to the Public." *Parks and Recreation* 8, no. 3 (January 1925): 185–202.

Carhart, Arthur H. "Recreation in Forestry." *Journal of Forestry* 21 (January 1923): 10–14.

———. "Recreation in the Forests." *American Forestry* 26 (May 1920): 268–72.

———. "What Is Recreation's Next Step?" *American Forestry* 26 (October 1920): 593–98.

Carr, Ethan. "Park, Forest, and Wilderness." *George Wright Forum* 17, no. 2 (2000): 16–30.

———. *Wilderness By Design: Landscape Architecture and the National Park Service.* Lincoln: University of Nebraska Press, 1998.

Carter, Luther J. "Wilderness Act: Great Smoky Plan Debated." *Science,* July 1, 1966, 39–44.

Catton, Theodore. *Inhabited Wilderness: Indians, Eskimos, and National Parks in Alaska.* Albuquerque: University of New Mexico Press, 1997.

———. *Land Reborn: A History of Administration and Visitor Use in Glacier Bay National Park and Preserve.* Anchorage, AK: National Park Service, 1995.

———. *National Park, City Playground: Mount Rainier in the Twentieth Century.* Seattle: University of Washington Press, 2006.

———. *Wonderland: An Administrative History of Mount Rainier National Park.* Seattle: National Park Service, 1996.

Cermak, Robert W. "In the Beginning: The First National Forest Recreation Plan." *Parks and Recreation* 9, no. 11 (November 1974): 20–33.

Cohen, Michael. *The History of the Sierra Club: 1892–1970.* San Francisco: Sierra Club Books, 1988.

———. *The Pathless Way: John Muir and the American Wilderness.* Madison: University of Wisconsin Press, 1984.

Cole, David N. "Paradox of the Primeval: Ecological Restoration in the Wilderness." *Ecological Restoration* 18 (Summer 2000): 77–86.

Collins, George L., and Lowell Sumner. "Northeast Arctic: The Last Great Wilderness." *Sierra Club Bulletin* 38 (1953): 13–26.

Conservation Foundation. *National Parks for the Future.* Washington, DC: Conservation Foundation, 1972.

Cronon, William. "The Trouble with Wilderness: or, Getting Back to the Wrong Nature." *Environmental History* 1, no. 1 (January 1996): 7–28.

Darling, F. Fraser, and Noel D. Eichorn. *Man and Nature in the National Parks.* Washington, DC: Conservation Foundation, 1967.

Demars, Stanford E. "Romanticism and the American National Parks." *Journal of Cultural Geography* (1990): 17–21.

Dennis, John G. "National Park Service Research in Alaska 1972–76." *Arctic Bulletin* (1977): 275–84.

Diettert, Gerald A. *Grinnell's Glacier: George Bird Grinnell and Glacier National Park.* Missoula, MT: Mountain Press Publishing Company, 1992.

Dilsaver, Lary M., ed. *America's National Park System: The Critical Documents.* Lanham, MD: Rowman and Littlefield, 1994.

Dilsaver, Lary M., and William C. Tweed. *Challenge of the Big Trees: A Resource History of Sequoia and Kings Canyon National Parks.* Three Rivers, CA: Sequoia Natural History Association, Inc., 1990.

Discha, Julius. "How the Alaska Act Was Won." *The Living Wilderness* 44 (1981): 4–9.

Drummond, Alexander. *Enos Mills: Citizen of Nature.* Niwot, CO: University Press of Colorado, 1995.

Edge, Rosalie. *Roads and More Roads in the National Parks and National Forests.* New York: Emergency Conservation Committee, 1936.

Emergency Conservation Committee. *Twelve Immediately Important Problems of the National Parks and of Wildlife Conservation.* New York: Emergency Conservation Committee, 1935.

Engberg, Robert, and Donald Wesling, eds. *John Muir to Yosemite and Beyond: Writings from the Years 1863 to 1875.* Madison: University of Wisconsin Press, 1980.

Evarts, Hal G. "The Mountain Wilderness." *Saturday Evening Post* 195 (June 27, 1923): 16–17, 76, 78, 81, 84.

Fleming, Donald. "Roots of the New Conservation Movement." *Perspectives in American History* 6 (1972): 7–94.

Foresta, Ronald A. *America's National Parks and Their Keepers.* Washington, DC: Resources for the Future, Inc., 1984.

Fox, Stephen. *John Muir and His Legacy: The American Conservation Movement.* Boston: Little Brown and Company, 1981.

———. "We Want No Straddlers." *The Living Wilderness* 48 (Winter 1984): 5–19.

Frome, Michael. *Battle for the Wilderness.* New York: Praeger, 1974.

———. *Strangers in High Places: The Story of the Great Smoky Mountains,* rev. ed. Knoxville: University of Tennessee Press, 1980.

Garrison, Lemuel A. *The Making of a Ranger: Forty Years in the National Parks.* Salt Lake City: Howe Brothers, 1983.

Gates, Paul Wallace. *History of Public Land Law Development.* Washington, DC: Government Printing Office, 1968.

Gifford, Terry, ed. *John Muir: His Life and Letters and Other Writings.* Seattle: Mountaineers, 1996.

Gilligan, James P. "The Development of Policy and Administration of Forest Service Primitive and Wilderness Areas in the Western United States." PhD diss., University of Michigan, 1953.

Glover, James M. *A Wilderness Original: The Life of Bob Marshall*. Seattle: Mountaineers, 1976.

Graham, Frank, Jr. *The Adirondack Park: A Political History*. Syracuse, NY: Syracuse University Press, 1978.

Greeley, William B. "The Forest Service Is Sticking to Its Job." *Outlook* 139 (March 4, 1925): 336–39.

———. "Recreation in the National Forests." *Review of Reviews* 70 (July 1924): 65–70.

———. "What Shall We Do with Our Mountains?" *Sunset* 59 (December 1927): 14.

———. "Wilderness Recreation Areas." *Service Bulletin* 10 (October 1926): 1–3.

Haight, Kevin. "The Wilderness Act: Ten Years After." *Environmental Affairs* 3 (1974): 279.

Haines, Aubrey. *Mountain Fever: Historic Conquests of Rainier*. Portland: Oregon Historical Society, 1962.

Harmon, David. "Cultural Diversity, Human Subsistence, and the National Park Ideal." *Environmental Ethics* 9, no. 2 (1987): 147–58.

Hartzog, George B., Jr. *Battling for the National Parks*. Mt. Kisco, NY: Moyer Bell Limited, 1988.

Harvey, Mark. *A Symbol of Wilderness: Echo Park and the American Conservation Movement*. Albuquerque: University of New Mexico Press, 1994.

———. *Wilderness Forever: Howard Zahniser and the Path to the Wilderness Act*. Seattle: University of Washington Press, 2005.

Hendee, John C., and Chad P. Dawson. *Wilderness Management*, 3rd ed. Golden, CO: Fulcrum Publishing, 2002.

Hendee, John C., George H. Stankey, and Robert C. Lucas. *Wilderness Management*, 2nd ed. Golden: North American Press, 1990.

Hornaday, William T. "America's Next Great Playground: Glacier Park in Northwestern Montana." *Recreation* 31 (May 1910): 211–16.

Hyde, Anne Farrar. *An American Vision: Far Western Landscape and National Culture, 1820–1920*. New York: New York University Press, 1990.

Hydrick, Rick. "The Genesis of National Park Management: John Roberts White and Sequoia National Park, 1920–1947." *Journal of Forest History* 28, no. 2 (April 1984): 68–81.

Ickes, Harold. *The Secret Diary of Harold L. Ickes*. New York: Simon and Schuster, 1953.

———. "Secretary Ickes Speaks on National Parks." *American Forests* 39 (June 1933): 274.

Ise, John. *Our National Park Policy: A Critical History*. Baltimore: Johns Hopkins University Press, 1961.

Jones, Holway R. *John Muir and the Sierra Club: The Battle for Yosemite*. San Francisco: Sierra Club Books, 1965.

Kauffmann, John. "Noatak." *The Living Wilderness* (Winter 1975): 17–33.

Keiter, Robert B. "National Park Protection: Putting the Organic Act to Work." In *Our*

Common Lands: Defending the National Parks, edited by David J. Simon. Washington, DC: Island Press, 1988, 75–86.

Keller, Robert H., and Michael F. Turek. *American Indians and National Parks*. Tucson: University of Arizona Press, 1998.

Kingery, Hugh E. *The Colorado Mountain Club: The First Seventy-Five Years of a Highly Individual Corporation, 1912–1987*. Evergreen, CO: Cordillera Press, 1981.

Kittredge, Frank A. "The Campaign for Kings Canyon National Park." *Sierra Club Bulletin* 45, no. 9 (December 1960): 41–43.

Krumenaker, Robert. "New Wilderness Can Be Created: A Personal History of the Gaylord Nelson Wilderness at Apostle Islands National Lakeshore." *George Wright Forum* 22, no. 3 (2005): 35–49.

———. "Wilderness and Natural Resource Management in the NPS: Another View." *George Wright Forum* 18, no. 1 (2001): 11–12.

Lee, Ronald F. *Family Tree of the National Park System*. Philadelphia: Eastern National Park and Monument Association, 1974.

Leopold, Aldo. "The Last Stand of Wilderness." *American Forests and Forest Life* 31 (October 1925): 45–47.

———. "Some Thoughts on Recreational Planning." *Parks and Recreation* 18 (December 1934): 136–37.

———. "The Wilderness and Its Place in Forest Recreation Policy." *Journal of Forestry* 19, no. 7 (1921): 718–21.

———. "Wilderness as a Form of Land Use." *Journal of Land and Public Utility Economics* 1 (1925): 398–404.

———. "Wilderness Is a Land Laboratory." *The Living Wilderness* 6 (1941): 3.

———. "Wilderness Values." National Park Service Yearbook: Park and Recreation Progress. Washington, DC, 1941.

Leopold, A. Starker, Stanley A. Cain, Clarence H. Cottam, Ira N. Gabrielson, and Thomas L. Kimball. "Wildlife Management in the National Parks." *Journal of Forestry* 69, no. 4 (1963): 32–35, 61–63.

Lien, Carsten. *Olympic Battleground: The Power Politics of Timber Preservation*. San Francisco: Sierra Club Books, 1991.

Lillard, Richard G. "The Siege and Conquest of a National Park." *American West* 5, no. 1 (1968): 28–31, 67, 69–71.

Little, John J. "Island Wilderness: A History of Isle Royal National Park." PhD diss., University of Toledo, 1978.

Louter, David. *Contested Terrain: North Cascades National Park Service Complex—An Administrative History*. Seattle: National Park Service, 1998.

———. *Windshield Wilderness: Cars, Roads, and Nature in Washington's National Parks*. Seattle: University of Washington Press, 2006.

Mackintosh, Barry. "Harold L. Ickes and the National Park Service." *Journal of Forest History* 29 (April 1985): 78–84.

Magoc, Chris J. *Yellowstone: The Creation and Selling of an American Landscape, 1870–1903.* Albuquerque: University of New Mexico Press, 1999.

Marshall, Bob. "The Problem of Wilderness." *Scientific Monthly* 30 (1930): 141–98.

Mather, Stephen T. "Engineering Applied to National Parks." *Proceedings of the American Society of Civil Engineers* 4 (December 1928): 2673–84.

———. "A Glance Backward at National Park Development." *Nature Magazine* 10 (August 1927): 112–15.

———. "The Ideals and Policy of the National Park Service Particularly in Relation to Yosemite National Park." In *Handbook of Yosemite National Park*, edited by Ansel Hall. New York: G. P. Putnam's Sons, 1921, 77–86.

———. "The National Parks on a Business Basis." *Review of Reviews* 51 (April 1915): 429.

———. *Progress in the Development of National Parks.* Washington, DC: Department of the Interior, 1916.

McCloskey, Michael. "Evolving Perspectives on Wilderness Values: Putting Wilderness Values in Order." In *Preparing to Manage Wilderness in the 21st Century: Proceedings of the Conference*, edited by P. C. Reed. General Technical Report SE-66. Asheville, NC: USDA Forest Service, Southeastern Forest Experiment Station, 1990, 13–18.

———. "The Wilderness Act of 1964: Its Background and Meaning." *Oregon Law Review* 45 (1966): 288–321.

———. "Wilderness Movement at the Crossroads, 1945–1970." *Pacific Historical Review* 41 (August 1972): 346–61.

McFarland, J. Horace. "The Value of National Scenery." Speech reprinted in *American Civic Association Bulletin* 2, no. 3 (June 1908).

Miles, John C. *Guardians of the Parks: A History of the National Parks and Conservation Association.* Washington, DC: Taylor and Francis, 1995.

Mills, Enos. *Your National Parks.* Boston: Houghton Mifflin, 1917.

Muir, John. *A Thousand Mile Walk to the Gulf.* William F. Bade, ed. Boston: Houghton Mifflin Company, 1916.

———. "The Wild Parks and Forest Reservations of the West." *Atlantic Monthly* 81 (January 1898): 15–28.

Murie, Olaus J. "Wilderness on Yellowstone Lake." *National Park Magazine* 33 (December 1959): 2–5.

Musselman, Lloyd K. *Rocky Mountain National Park: Administrative History, 1915–1965.* Washington, DC: Department of the Interior, 1971.

Nash, Roderick. "John Muir, William Kent and the Conservative Schism." *Pacific Historical Review* 36 (November 1967): 423–33.

———. *Wilderness and the American Mind*, 4th ed. New Haven: Yale University Press, 2001.

National Park Service. *Administrative Policies for Natural Areas of the National Park System.* Washington, DC: U.S. Department of Interior, 1968.

———. *Administrative Policies for Natural Areas of the National Park System.* Washington, DC: U.S. Department of Interior, 1970.

———. *Olympic National Park: An Administrative History*. Seattle, Pacific Northwest Region, 1990.

———. "Report of the Director of the National Park Service to the Secretary of the Interior for the Fiscal Year Ending June 30, 1920." Washington, DC: Government Printing Office, 1920.

———. *State of the Parks 1980: A Report to Congress*. Washington, DC: U.S. Government Printing Office, 1980.

———. *Statement for Management, Wrangell-Saint Elias National Park*. Anchorage: National Park Service, 1983.

———. "Wilderness Preservation and Management." *National Park Service Management Policies*. Washington, DC: U.S. Department of the Interior, 1978.

National Parks Association. "Losing Our Primeval System in Vast Expansion." *National Parks Bulletin* 13 (February 1936): 1–4.

———. "National Primeval Park Standards: A Declaration of Policy." *National Parks Magazine* 83 (October 1945): 6–11.

National Parks Conservation Association. *Preserving Wilderness in Our National Parks*. Washington, DC: NPCA, 1971.

Norris, Frank B. *Isolated Paradise: An Administrative History of the Katmai and Aniakchak National Park Service Units, Alaska*. Anchorage: National Park Service, 1996.

Olmsted, Frederick Law. "The Distinction between National Parks and National Forests." *Landscape Architecture* 6, no. 3 (April 1916): 114–15.

Olsen, Russ. *Administrative History: Organizational Structures of the National Park Service, 1917 to 1985*. Washington, DC: National Park Service, 1985.

Olson, Sigurd F. "We Need Wilderness." *National Parks Magazine* 84 (January 1946): 18–29.

Orsi, Richard J. "'Wilderness Saint' and 'Robber Baron': The Anomalous Partnership of John Muir and the Southern Pacific Company for Preservation of Yosemite National Park." *Pacific Historian* 29 (Summer–Fall 1985): 135–52.

Outdoor Recreation Resources Review Commission (ORRRC). "Wilderness and Recreation: A Report on Resources, Values, and Problems." ORRRC Study Report 3. Washington, DC: U.S. Government Printing Office, 1962.

Paige, John C. *The Civilian Conservation Corps and the National Park Service, 1933–1942: An Administrative History*. Washington, DC: National Park Service, Department of the Interior, 1985.

Polenberg, Richard. "Conservation and Reorganization: The Forest Service Lobby." *Agricultural History* 39 (1965): 230.

———. "The Great Conservation Contest." *Journal of Forest History* 10 (January 1967): 13–23.

Pomeroy, Earl. *In Search of the Golden West: The Tourist in Western America*. New York: Alfred A. Knopf, 1957.

Proceedings of the National Parks Conference Held at Berkeley, California, March 11, 12, and 13, 1915. Washington, DC: Government Printing Office, 1915.

Proceedings of the National Parks Conference Held at Washington, DC, January 2, 3, 4, 5, and 6, 1917. Washington, DC: Government Printing Office, 1917.

Proceedings of the National Parks Conference Held at Yellowstone National Park, September 11 and 12, 1911. Washington, DC: Government Printing Office, 1912.

Proceedings of the National Parks Conference Held at Yellowstone National Park, October 14, 15, and 16, 1912. Washington, DC: Government Printing Office, 1913.

Pyne, Stephen J. *Year of the Fires: The Story of the Great Fires of 1910.* New York: Penguin Books, 2001.

Rawson, Timothy. *Changing Tracks: Predators and Politics in Mt. McKinley National Park.* Fairbanks: University of Alaska Press, 2001.

Reed, F. W. "The Wilderness Idea and the Forester." *American Forests and Forest Life* 32 (December 1926): 712–50.

Reich, Justin. "Re-creating the Wilderness: Shaping Narratives and Landscapes in Shenandoah National Park." *Environmental History* 6 (January 2001): 95–117.

Rettie, Dwight F. *Our National Park System.* Urbana: University of Illinois Press, 1995.

Richardson, Elmo R. "Olympic National Park: Twenty Years of Controversy." *Forest History* 12 (April 1968): 6–15.

Righter, Robert W. *Crucible for Conservation: The Creation of Grand Teton National Park.* Boulder: Colorado Associated University Press, 1982.

Robinson, Glen O. *The Forest Service: A Study in Public Land Management.* Washington, DC: Resources for the Future, 1975.

Roper, Laura Wood. *FLO: A Biography of Frederick Law Olmsted.* Baltimore: Johns Hopkins University Press, 1973.

Roth, Dennis M. *The Wilderness Movement and the National Forests.* College Station, TX: Intaglio Press, 1988.

Rothman, Hal. *America's National Monuments: The Politics of Preservation.* Lawrence: University Press of Kansas, 1989.

———. "Conflict on the Pajarito: Frank Pinkley, the Forest Service and the Bandelier Controversy 1925–1932." *Journal of Forest History* 29 (April 1985): 68–77.

———. *Devil's Bargains: Tourism in the Twentieth-Century American West.* Lawrence: University Press of Kansas, 1998.

———. "Shaping the Nature of Controversy: The Park Service, the Forest Service, and the Cedar Breaks National Monument." *Utah Historical Quarterly* 55 (Summer 1987): 213–35.

Runte, Alfred. "Are National Parks Forever? Historical Perspectives on the Time for Decision." In *Parks in the West and American Culture,* edited by E. R. Hart, 3–4. Sun Valley, ID: Institute of the American West, 1984.

———. "The Foundations of the National Parks: Ideals and Realities." *George Wright Forum* 15, no. 1 (1998): 25–32.

———. *National Parks: The American Experience*, 2nd ed. Lincoln: University of Nebraska Press, 1987.

———. *Yosemite: The Embattled Wilderness*. Lincoln: University of Nebraska Press, 1990.

Russell, Israel C. "Impressions of Mt. Rainier." *Scribner's Magazine* 22, no. 2 (August 1897): 176.

Sax, Joseph L. "America's National Parks: Their Principles, Purposes, and Prospects." *Natural History* 85 (October 1976).

———. *Mountains without Handrails: Reflection on the National Parks*. Ann Arbor: University of Michigan Press, 1980.

Schrepfer, Susan R. *The Fight to Save the Redwoods*. Madison: University of Wisconsin Press, 1983.

Scoyen, E. T. "Politics and Objectives of the National Park Service." *Journal of Forestry* 44 (September 1946): 641–46.

Sears, John F. *Sacred Places: American Tourist Attractions in the Nineteenth Century*. New York: Oxford University Press, 1989.

Sellars, Richard West. "Manipulating Nature's Paradise: National Parks Management under Stephen T. Mather, 1916–1929." *Montana: The Magazine of Western History* 43 (Spring 1993): 2–13.

———. "The Path Not Taken: National Park Service Wilderness Management." *George Wright Forum* 17, No. 4 (2000): 4.

———. *Preserving Nature in the National Parks: A History*. New Haven: Yale University Press, 1997.

———. "The Roots of National Park Management: Evolving Perceptions of the Park Service's Mandate." *Journal of Forestry* 90, no. 1 (1992): 16–19.

Sellars, Richard W., et al. "The National Parks: A Forum on the 'Worthless Lands' Thesis." *Journal of Forest History* 27 (July 1983): 130–45.

Shankland, Robert. *Steve Mather of the National Parks*, 3rd ed. New York: Alfred A. Knopf, 1970.

Shultis, John. "Improving the Wilderness: Common Factors in Creating National Parks and Equivalent Reserves during the Nineteenth Century." *Forest and Conservation History* 39 (July 1995): 121–29.

Smith, Allen E., et al. *Alaska National Interest Lands Conservation Act: A Citizen's Guide*. Washington, DC: The Wilderness Society, 2001.

Smith, Charles D. "The Appalachian National Park Movement, 1885–1901." *North Carolina Historical Review* 37 (January 1960): 38–65.

Spence, Mark David. *Dispossessing the Wilderness: Indian Removal and the Making of the National Parks*. New York: Oxford University Press, 1999.

Stagner, Howard R. "Comments on Wilderness." *Parks and Recreation* (January 1961): 11, 63–66.

————. "Reservation of Natural and Wilderness Values in the National Parks." *National Parks Magazine* 31 (July 1957): 105–6, 135–39.

Steen, Harold K. *The U.S. Forest Service: A History*. Seattle: University of Washington Press, 1976.

Strickland, Ronald Gibson. "Ten Years of Congressional Review under the Wilderness Act of 1964: Wilderness Classification through Affirmative Action." PhD diss., Georgetown University, 1976.

Sumner, E. Lowell, Jr. "The Biology of Wilderness Protection." *Sierra Club Bulletin* 27 (1942): 14–22.

————. "Losing the Wilderness Which We Set Out to Preserve." 1938, unpublished typescript.

————. "Your Stake in Alaska's Wildlife and Wilderness." *Sierra Club Bulletin* 41 (1956): 54–71.

Sutter, Paul S. "'A Blank Spot on the Map': Aldo Leopold, Wilderness, and U.S. Forest Service Recreation Policy, 1909–1924." *Western Historical Quarterly* 29 (Summer 1998): 187–214.

————. *Driven Wild: How the Fight against Automobiles Launched the Modern Wilderness Movement*. Seattle: University of Washington Press, 2002.

Swain, Donald C. *Federal Conservation Policy, 1921–1933*. Berkeley: University of California Press, 1963.

————. "Harold Ickes, Horace Albright, and the Hundred Days: A Study in Conservation Administration." *Pacific Historical Review* 34 (November 1965): 455–65.

————. "The National Park Service and the New Deal." *Pacific Historical Review* 41 (August 1972): 312–32.

————. "The Passage of the National Park Service Act of 1916." *Wisconsin Magazine of History* 50 (Fall 1966): 4–17.

————. *Wilderness Defender: Horace M. Albright and Conservation*. Chicago: University of Chicago Press, 1970.

Thompson, Roger C. "Politics in the Wilderness: New York's Adirondack Forest Preserve." *Forest History* 6 (1963): 14–23.

Trefethen, James B. "The 1928 ORRRC." *American Forests* 68 (March 1962): 8, 38–39.

U.S. Congress. Senate. *A National Plan for American Forestry*. Senate Doc. 12, 73rd Cong., 1st sess., March 13, 1933.

Unrau, Harlan D. *Administrative History: Crater Lake National Park, Oregon*. Denver: National Park Service, 1988.

Vale, Thomas R., ed. *Fire, Native Peoples, and the National Landscape*. Washington, DC: Island Press, 2002.

Vint, Thomas C. "Development of National Parks for Conservation." In *American Planning and Civic Annual*, edited by Harlean James. Washington, DC: American Planning and Civic Association, 1938, 69–77.

———. "National Park Service Master Plans." *Planning and Civic Comment* (April 1946): 21–24.

Watkins, T. H. "Alaska and the Weight of History." In *Celebrating Wild Alaska: Twenty Years of the Alaska Lands Act*. Natural Resources Defense Council and Alaska Wilderness League, 2000.

———. "The Perils of Expedience." *Wilderness* 54 (Winter 1990): 22.

———. *Righteous Pilgrim: The Life and Times of Harold Ickes*. New York: Henry Holt and Company, 1990.

Waugh, Frank A. *Recreational Uses on the National Forests*. Washington, DC: Government Printing Office, 1917.

Wharton, William P. "The National Primeval Parks." *National Parks Bulletin* 13 (February 1937): 3–5.

———. "Park Service Leader Abandons National Park Standards." *National Parks Bulletin* 14 (June 1938): 3–6.

Wheat, Frank. *California Desert Miracle: The Fight for Desert Parks and Wilderness*. San Diego: Sunbelt Publications, 1999.

Wilderness Society. "The Tower of Babel, New Style." *The Living Wilderness* 2, no. 2 (November 1936): 1–2.

Williss, George F. *"Do Things Right the First Time": The National Park Service and the Alaska National Interest Lands Conservation Act of 1980*. Washington, DC: U.S. Department of Interior, National Park Service, 1985.

Wirth, Conrad L. *Parks, Politics, and the People*. Norman: University of Oklahoma Press, 1980.

———. "Wilderness in the National Parks." *Planning and Civic Comment* 24 (June 1958): 7.

Wright, George M., Joseph F. Dixon, and Ben H. Thompson. *Fauna of the National Parks of the United States: A Preliminary Survey of Faunal Relations in National Parks*. Contributions of Wildlife Survey, Fauna Series no. 1. Washington, DC: Government Printing Office, 1933.

Wright, Gerald R., ed. *National Parks and Protected Areas: Their Role in Environmental Protection*. Cambridge, MA: Blackwell Science, 1996.

Yard, Robert Sterling. "Making a Business of Scenery." *The Nation's Business* 4 (June 1916): 10–11.

———. *National Parks Portfolio*, 6th ed. Washington, DC: Government Printing Office, 1931.

———. *Our Federal Lands: A Romance of American Development*. New York: Charles Scribner's Sons, 1928.

Young, Stephen T. "The Success of the Alaska Coalition." *National Parks* 55 (1981): 10–13.

Zahniser, Howard. "The Wilderness Bill and the National Parks." *National Parks* 31, no. 129 (April 1957): 70–76, 83–87.

INDEX

accelerated wilderness program, 190–91

Adirondack Park, 19–20

aircraft landings, Alaska, 228, 235, 238, 239

Alaska, park development: overview, 7; acreage statistics, 205, 208, 209–10, 213, 215–18; congressional approval, 217–21; and land grant process, 206–7, 208–9; land identification process, 207–12; legislative proposals, 212–21

Alaska, park management challenges: overview, 221–27, 234–35; aircraft landings, 228, 235, 238, 239; inhabitant hostility, 225, 226f, 230; isolation, 233; mining, 232–33; poaching problems, 227–28, 231–32; scale of, 205, 221, 233–34; staffing levels, 224–27; visitation patterns, 228–29, 234, 246; wilderness management planning, 235–43, 248–52; wilderness suitability studies, 243–49; Wrangell-St. Elias, 229–32

Alaska National Interest Lands Conservation Act (ANILCA), 217–23, 237, 243–44, 246

Alaska Native Claims Settlement Act (ANCSA), 208–9

Albright, Horace: administrative skills, 32–33, 67; in campaign for park bureau, 24, 30; on CCC advisory council, 72–73; Everglades committee, 90; with Hartzog, 164f; park system expansion, 68–69, 70–72, 82; planning advocacy, 57, 77–78; research reserve policy, 101; on road building, 35, 55, 290n11; system development emphasis, 108; wilderness assumption, 65, 76–77, 109; wilderness legislation, 141–42, 143

Allin, Craig, 156, 257

Allott, Gordon, 151, 154

American Forestry Association, 52–53

American Planning and Civic Association, 72, 73–74, 85

ANCSA (Alaska Native Claims Settlement Act), 208–9

Andersen, Clinton, 152, 154, 156

Andrus, Cecil, 215, 216

ANILCA (Alaska National Interest Lands Conservation Act), 217–23, 237, 243–44, 246

Anthony, Harold, 125

Antiquities Act, 28, 92

Walker, Ronald, 201, 263

War Department, 71

Washington Park Wilderness Act, 261–62

Washington state, Grand Coulee Dam, 122. *See also* Olympic National Park

watershed protection, 10, 15

Watkins, T. H., 224

Watt, James G., 222, 245, 264, 268

Waugh, Frank, 39

Whalen, William, 215

Wharton, William P., 83, 90

White, John Roberts, 13, 56, 73–74, 98, 102–5

White River National Forest, 45

Wilbur, Ray Lyman, 90

wilderness, definition challenges: after Kings Canyon addition, 100; Leopold's, 46, 51–52; at Naturalists Conference, 101–2; in ORRRC report, 154–55; rhetorical ambiguities, 15–17, 19–20; at Sierra Club conferences, 131–32; in Wilderness Act, 166–67, 168–69, 185–86; in zone planning, 78–81

Wilderness Act, overview, 5–7, 165–69, 204. *See also* National Wilderness Preservation System; review period, under Wilderness Act

Wilderness and the American Mind (Nash), 14–15

wilderness idea, emergence, 4–5, 46, 50–54

wilderness parks, creations/management: Everglades, 89–91, 100, 122, 251; Isle Royale, 68–70, 115, 179, 255–57; Olympics, 92–97, 100, 111–13. *See also* Kings Canyon National Park; National Wilderness Preservation System

The Wilderness Society: change in focus, 202; dam opposition, 130; formation of, 83; Great Smoky Mountains proposal, 175; leadership change, 119–20; Olympics park proposal, 94; Wilderness Act status reports, 188, 200; wil-

derness definition campaign, 117; wilderness legislation, 123, 260

Wilderness Use and Management section, in policy manual, 271–72

wildlife policy: Alaska, 224, 227–28, 248–50; in classification system directive, 165; ecological perspectives, 76–77, 78f, 105–7, 161; Everglades committee, 90; Mount McKinley National Park, 121, 125–26; Olympic Mountains, 92; Udall-initiated reports, 161–62; Wirth's hunting suggestion, 160; Yosemite's bear problem, 59–61

wildlife refuges, 166, 217, 258

Williss, G. Frank, 226–27, 236

Wilson, Pete, 260

Wilson, Woodrow (and administration), 18, 24, 29, 92

Wirth, Conrad: appointment/background, 127, 128–29; backcountry management plan, 150–51; career assessment, 160; funding requests, 132, 133; Mission 66 planning, 133–36, 153, 160; park management philosophy, 129–30, 144, 177–78; retirement, 160–61, 162–63; wilderness legislation, 139–40, 141–43, 145, 148–49

wolf-sheep controversy, 121, 125–26

Woodbury, Charles, 139

World War II period, 110–11, 115–21, 206

Wrangell-St. Elias National Park and Preserve, 230–33, 247

Wright, George M., 78f, 101

Wyoming, 63, 68, 258

Yampa River, 126–27, 131

Yard, Robert Sterling: eastern parks debate, 51; hopes for Park wilderness, 85; *National Parks* book authorship, 30; Olympics wilderness protection, 94; wilderness definition campaign, 117–19; Wilderness Society formation, 83; on Wirth's park perspective, 128

Yellowstone conference, 24

Yellowstone National Park: establishment process, 3–4, 9, 15, 31; in *National Parks* book, 30; road building debate, 35, 290n11; staffing levels, 224; wilderness proposals, 200, 258

Yosemite conference, 24–25

Yosemite National Park: bear crisis effects, 59–61; establishment process, 3, 10–16, 31; research reserve, 58, 61–62; wilderness proposals, 193, 260; wildlife policy, 59–61, 76

Young, Don, 247

Zahniser, Ed, 15

Zahniser, Howard: on Council of Conservationists, 141, 142; dam conflicts, 130; death, 156; on Drury's dismissal, 127; Mission 66 concerns, 133–34, 135; selection for Wilderness Society leadership, 119–20; at wilderness conferences, 126, 145; wilderness zoning proposal, 123. *See also* National Wilderness Preservation System

zoning approach: with classification system, 164–65; national parks, 57, 78–81, 117, 139; wilderness areas, 123, 138

LaVergne, TN USA
06 June 2010
185063LV00001B/6/P